Children's Early
Text Construction

Children's Early Text Construction

edited by

Clotilde Pontecorvo
University of Rome "La Sapienza"

Margherita Orsolini
University of Chieti

Barbara Burge
Lauren B. Resnick
University of Pittsburgh

LEA LAWRENCE ERLBAUM ASSOCIATES, PUBLISHERS
1996 Mahwah, New Jersey

Portions of this work are translated from *La Construzione del Testo
Scritto nei Bambini*, copyright © 1992, La Nuova Italia Editrice S.p.A.,
with permission.

Lawrence Erlbaum Associates, Inc., Publishers
10 Industrial Avenue
Mahwah, New Jersey 07430

Cover design by Jennifer Sterling

Library of Congress Cataloging-in-Publication Data

Costruzione del testo scritto nei bambini. English.
    Children's early text construction / edited by Clotilde Pontecorvo
. . . [et al.].
        p.   cm.
    Updated versions of papers originally presented at an
international workshop held Oct. 1988, Rome, Italy.
    Includes bibliographical references and index.
    ISBN 0-8058-1504-X (cloth : alk. paper)
    1. Language acquisition. 2. Composition (Language arts)
I. Pontecorvo, Clotilde. II. Title.
P118.C67413 1995
401'.93—dc20   95-12549
                                                                          CIP

Books published by Lawrence Erlbaum Associates are printed on acid-free paper,
and their bindings are chosen for strength and durability.

Printed in the United States of America
10 9 8 7 6 5 4 3 2 1

CONTENTS

INTRODUCTION

Clotilde Pontecorvo
Margherita Orsolini
Lauren B. Resnick

For decades, research on children's literacy has been dominated by questions of how children learn to read. Especially among Anglophone scholars, cognitive and psycholinguistic research on reading has been the only approach to studying written language education. Echoing this, debates on methods of teaching children to read have long dominated the educational scene.

This book presents an alternative view. In recent years, writing has emerged as a central aspect of becoming literate. Research in cognitive psychology has shown that writing is a highly complex activity involving a degree of planning unknown in everyday conversational uses of language. At the same time, developmental studies have revealed that, when young children are asked to "write," they show a surprisingly sophisticated understanding of the representational constraints of alphabetic writing systems. They show this understanding long before they can read conventional writing on their own.

The word *text* connotes the centrality of writing to the process of becoming literate. Text is the making of language as a reproducible and visible object that can be repeated, quoted, and reported. Text is a written message embedded in an artifact (e.g., a book or a letter, but also a T-shirt or a food container) that provides a context for interpreting the written signs. Learning to produce and comprehend texts is what it means to become literate.

The rich structure of meanings involved in the word *text* provided the glue that brought together a group of scholars from several disciplines in an international workshop held in Rome in October 1988 at the Dipartimento di Psicologia dei Processi di Sviluppo e di Socializzazione. Reflecting the state of the field at the time, the majority of the workshop participants were scholars working in languages other than English, especially the Romance languages. Their work reflects a linguistic and psychological research tradition that, until recently, was little known to Anglophone scholars. This volume makes available to English-language readers updated versions of the papers presented at the meeting. The topics discussed at the workshop are reflected in the chapters herein. They include the relationship between acquisition of language and familiarity with written texts, the reciprocal "permeability" between spoken and written language, the initial phases of text construction by children, and the educational conditions that facilitate written language acquisition and writing practice.

Several chapters in this volume address current theoretical questions that are worthy of special note. One very basic question concerns the impact of written texts on children's acquisition of oral language. Engagement with texts, even when mediated by adults' reading aloud, is a very particular condition for language learning, which is still largely unexplored. What aspects of written language are learned via repeated hearing of written texts read aloud? How does experience of written texts affect children's oral language production? What uses of language are generalized by children when they pass from recalling a familiar text to inventing a new one? This volume does not provide definitive answers to these questions, but it does discuss and exemplify ways in which the relationships between familiarity with written texts and general acquisition of language can be investigated.

A second question discussed here concerns the ways in which children work with, interpret, and eventually come to understand the system of writing with which their culture surrounds them. It is clear that children actively try to interpret the written symbols that are widely present in everyday life, including on television, in advertising, and on food containers and shop signs, as well as in newspapers and books. Pioneering work by Ferreiro and Teberosky (1979) showed that very young, preliterate children in urban cultures were seeking out regularity and pattern in the writing system. For example, children seem to assume that signs in contiguous positions have to be different from one another and that a minimum number of signs is needed in order to have a "true" word, one that can be read by other people. These assumptions, which constrain children's perception and representation of written messages, make young children relatively competent "writers" long before they are formally introduced to reading and writing in school.

Children of very different sociocultural levels have been shown to engage spontaneously in pattern seeking and to be eager to practice writing words, messages, and names. Indeed, one of the most productive activities for children's further literacy development is simply writing (and then reading) their first names. This apparently rote process is, in fact, an analytical activity through which children become acquainted with a conventional repertoire of letters that they can then use to write other words. This process, in turn, can occasion a metacognitive reflection on the correspondence between visual signs and sound patterns that is fundamental to literacy. It is interesting in this regard to remember that, as Gelb (1963) emphasized in his classical work on the history of writing, the writing of first names was a critical activity for pushing certain cultures toward phonetization in their writing systems.

A main point of discussion in the contributions to this volume concerns the role of the linguistic environment in children's literacy development. This seems to be an issue that cannot be decided in a clear-cut way. Children obviously work to interpret the information offered by the print that surrounds them. When they grow up in an alphabetic culture, they quickly develop an alphabetic way of writing. That is, they allow letters and letter strings to stand for phonemes rather than for whole words or morphemes. They also, however, respect constraints that seem to be independent of—even sometimes in conflict with—the particular written language to which they are exposed. For example, Italian children at a certain stage of development deny the validity of doubled consonants, even though doubled consonants are normal in Italian. This seems to be because they believe that contiguous marks must be different to qualify as acceptable writing. To clarify the role of exogenous and endogenous variables in the acquisition of writing systems, some of the chapters in this volume investigate and compare different writing systems and languages (e.g., Spanish and Italian) and the impact they have on children's early acquisition of writing.

In investigating different writing systems as well as different traditions of literacy education, some points of convergence have emerged. Awareness of the phoneme is acquired only through the mastery of an alphabetic system of writing. Prior to such mastery, among preliterate children the syllable appears to be a more natural unit of segmentation. The discovery that children who are asked to write words go through a stage in which they represent the syllable as a writing unit (e.g., IAEA for Italian word *primavera*, which means "spring") challenges a traditional view according to which children's phonological awareness is a prerequisite for both reading and writing. This finding suggests that there is, in fact, a complex interaction between the two processes. That is, their very first attempts at writing and reading can be for children a natural way of analyzing language and detaching the mental representation of words from the "online" constraints of spoken language production (Tolchinsky Landsmann, Teberosky, & Matas, 1993). Thus, writing activities introduce a metalinguistic practice that can have important consequences for children's phonological awareness.

Another traditional assumption challenged in this volume is that writing is only, or mostly, a system for transcribing speech. Writing systems, it is proposed here, are better thought of as conceptual models for representing speech. Even an alphabetic system has many ideographic aspects that have to be understood by children. Ideographic aspects are involved, for example, in word segmentation, blank spaces, layout of the written text, use of upper and lower case, and, last but not least, writing homophones, which have to be recognized and produced either through a sight knowledge of the words or a morphophonemic analysis of them. Thus, even in an alphabetic system, the metalinguistic activity called on in writing does not only consist of analyzing the speech "sound." Many other structural aspects of language must also become objects of reflection, planning, and analysis, as Olson (1993) showed in a manner grounded in a critical reanalysis of the history of writing.

Writing is a visual semiotic system in which there are symbols—including colons, commas, and question marks—that do not represent words but instead convey information at many different levels: semantic, syntactic, macrotextual. Punctuation has been the object of normative grammars, but it is still largely unexplored by linguistic analysis. How punctuation is acquired by children, which this volume begins to address, is crucial to our understanding of the development of literacy. Use of punctuation reflects the writer's control of the organization of text. The marking of reported speech, the signaling that a part of the text is concluded, and the separating of words in a list are examples of how writing requires reflexive symbols—mirroring particles that give information about the structure of the text itself. How much awareness and metapragmatic competence are required in learning to use punctuation? Or does the influence run in the other direction? That is, do children become aware of the structures involved in their written texts only as they attempt to reproduce and reinvent punctuation?

Several different models of the psychological processes involved in learning to write are discussed in this volume. The cognitive model of writing, which characterizes writing as a problem-solving activity, has positively affected writing instruction by shifting attention from the products to the processes of writing. The cognitive perspective, however, does not take account of other dimensions of the writing process, especially the embedding of writing within social and cultural practices (Resnick, 1990) and its dependence on specific goals and social functions (Boscolo, 1995).

Developmental research on early literacy has been more successful in integrating psychogenetic and sociocultural approaches into a coherent theoretical framework. This is shown particularly in this volume in chapters reporting studies of the interaction between children's growing competence and the instructional environment, whether of family or preschool. These studies show how adult monitoring and intervention into child speech, and group discussion on text planning and revision (to name only two examples) function to scaffold performance and extend children's language capabilities. We still need, however, more extensive ethnographic research on writing practices, research that extends to everyday functions of writing such as making notes, lists, or tables. From an educational and developmental point of view, this means that it will not be possible to treat the context of text production as a variable to be controlled experimentally; rather, it must be treated as a network of relations among writer(s), reader(s), texts, and culture (Boscolo, 1995).

INTRODUCTION TO THE SECTIONS OF THE BOOK

The first chapter of this volume is aimed at providing a theoretical introduction for the topics developed later. Pontecorvo and Orsolini start from a definition of literacy in terms of the complex knowledge and skills involved in the early phases of written language acquisition and set out the fundamental aspects of research on the construction of the writing system. The complex relationship between spoken and written language is examined, and the construction of the idea of text in children is analyzed.

In the first section of the book, devoted to written and oral forms in children's language, the relationship between orality and writing is discussed. Sulzby's chapter suggests two innovative concepts for our way of thinking about written language acquisition: the concepts of emergent literacy and repertory. The first includes all of a child's knowledge and skills that precede and lead to a mastery of conventional reading and writing forms. The concept of repertory suggests that knowledge of written language is acquired analogously to oral language: in communicative situations, specific contexts, and cultural interactions. Children enrich their own repertory of linguistic "usage" (written and oral) rather than building up cognitive objects of growing.

The novelty of Abaurre's position, which stresses the role of orality rhythms in the forms of children's writing, is to draw researchers' attention to linguistic aspects that are generally ignored: prosody, modes of pronunciation, and rhythms. Abaurre discusses the hypothesis that there are interactional contexts in which different linguistic units become more prominent: The syllable or wider sections of spoken language can be focused by particular intonation patterns and modes of pronunciation.

A text construction situation that is halfway between orality and writing is that of story production and story dictation. The last two chapters in the first section are on this topic. Orsolini and Di Giacinto describe the main changes that take place in linguistic form and cohesion procedure in 4- to 5-year-olds. Their study shows significant differences between the narrative structure of a story that is invented versus a story that is retold. Zucchermaglio and Scheuer examine a story dictation activity in which kindergarten children were helped to understand the distinction between conversation and composition. The study investigates children's ability to use a written register and to differentiate between written and oral styles.

In the second section, dedicated to writing as a system of representation, different theoretical and methodological perspectives of research on reading and writing acquisition are presented. Tolchinsky Landsmann compares three different models (behaviorist, sociocultural, and constructivist) in order to clarify the respective roles that they each assign to both the environment and the subject in written language acquisition. The author's view is that the constructivist perspective, from which her own research is carried out, lacks an explicit notion of context and its role in cognitive development. Recent contributions of connectionism to developmental research are also discussed.

Besse examines several methodological problems involved with experimental situations in which children were asked to write. The study uses a longitudinal method to observe children's written language acquisition from kindergarten to elementary school. Its most revealing result is that all subjects, independently of their initial level of written language conceptualization, reached an "alphabetic" hypothesis after 6 months of primary school.

Ferreiro, Pontecorvo, and Zucchermaglio face the question of how children interpret the doubling of letters in two different writing systems (Italian and Spanish). Their study shows that children refuse the doubling, irrespective of how much they have been exposed to this written pattern in their respective languages. It concludes that children's ideas about the structure of written words are, to a large extent, unaffected by the frequency of written patterns in the input to which children are exposed.

The last two chapters of this section deal with the structuring of text. Writing requires separation and framing devices, both in sentences and in extended text. These framing functions, which in spoken language are largely implemented through intonation and pauses, have to be visually structured in writing. Simone's chapter looks at the comma, an entity that is important but difficult to grasp. With theoretical clarity, he examines its role as interface between different structural levels: syntactic, lexical, and pragmatic. An analytical examination of the functions of the comma sheds light on the difficulties that the unskilled writer encounters in using the comma. Ferreiro and Zuchermaglio investigate the punctuation of children (Spanish- and Italian-speaking) in the second and third years of primary school who had been asked to rewrite the story of *Little Red Riding Hood*. This story is rich in reported speech: The canonic dialogue between Little Red Riding Hood and the wolf dressed as the grandmother is perhaps among the best known to children. The study shows that reported speech is the first textual space in which children use punctuation.

The third section focuses on the learning of different genres of written language. Boscolo begins the section with a study of expository text production, analyzing the ways in which children of different ages connect and integrate sentences in the composition of texts. The chapter investigates the role of structure and content by asking subjects to write a text by sequencing single information units that have already been supplied by the researcher. Results show a significant effect of age in text organization and an effect of subject matter in the use of cohesion devices.

Pontecorvo and Morani analyze the stories of children in the first and second years of primary school. A detailed syntactic and lexical analysis identifies the stylistic elements (repetition, rhythm, and parallelism) of written stories that are also the focus of children's interaction in dyadic text production. This study suggests that interaction between children is both an instrument for facilitating text production and a means for studying the process of writing.

Teberosky analyzes the news written by primary school children in an educational context in which newsletter articles were read, commented on, and used as pretext (*avant-texte*) for the writing activity. A detailed analysis of the syntactic and lexical forms used by children in their news shows that the acquisition of a new type of text is accompanied by the acquisition of new linguistic forms.

Tornatore analyzes the use of written language in codifying and data-recording activities from kindergarten onward. She identifies the cognitive operations that accompany this activity and that are, for the most part, motivated by daily organizational needs or by investigations of a scientific type. This study suggests that, in cognitive activities such as categorizing or reasoning, written language has a peculiar structure and a style that children cannot immediately derive from the more familiar activities of writing narrative texts.

The final section of the volume contains four chapters with an educational focus. Pascucci Formisano provides a picture of the early literacy educational practices observed in a sampling of the first year in some primary schools in central and southern Italy. A worrisome situation emerges: teaching focused exclusively on the alphabetic code; children could transcribe only sentences copied from the blackboard or dictated by the teacher; and no space was given to story reading, conversation, or text planning.

In a case study, Conte, Rampelli, and Volterra analyze the evolution of textual competence in a deaf girl. Their chapter shows how, in a school in which the transmission of knowledge occurs primarily by means of the vocal acoustic channel, the deaf child is excluded from this knowledge and acquires even the most basic reading and writing skills in a partial way.

Teale and Martinez' chapter describes analytically an activity that is still not very widespread in schools: reading texts aloud, which is proposed for children as a means of active text comprehension. Observations of four teachers reading children the same book showed that each teacher carried out the activity by emphasizing different aspects of the text and stimulating different processes in children. In turn, each teacher's style had an effect on the children's memory and comprehension of the text.

The last chapter in the volume is by Goodman, who shows how children's discourse about language reveals the knowledge, the attitudes, and the models that children use to build up written language. The role of the educational environment is decisive for the emergence of this discourse. It is useless to teach children metalinguistic competence; instead, these skills should be allowed to be constructed when children can talk about, comment on, and explain what they are writing.

REFERENCES

Boscolo, P. (1995). The cognitive approach to writing and writing instruction: A contribution to a critical appraisal. *Cahiers de Psychologie Cognitive, 14*(4), 343–366.

Ferreiro, E., & Teberosky, A. (1979). *Los sistemas de escritura en el de sarrollo del nino* [Literacy before schooling]. Mexico City: Siglo XXI Editores.

Gelb, I. J. (1963). *A study of writing.* Chicago: University of Chicago Press.

Olson, D. R. (1993). How writing represents speech. *Language and Communication, 13*(1), 1–17.

Resnick, L. B. (1990). Literacy in school and out. *Daedalus, 119*, 169–185.

Tolchinsky Landsmann, L., Teberosky, A., & Matas, J. (1993, October). *Phonological knowledge and writing: A developmental study in two writing systems.* Second Workshop of the Network on "Written Language and Literacy" of the European Science Foundation, Wassenaar, Netherlands.

WRITTEN AND ORAL FORMS IN CHILDREN'S LANGUAGE

1

WRITING AND WRITTEN LANGUAGE IN CHILDREN'S DEVELOPMENT

Clotilde Pontecorvo
University of Rome "La Sapienza"

Margherita Orsolini
University of Chieti

Scholars of developmental psychology usually agree that children's acquisition of spoken language is one of the most impressive intellectual feats that most people will ever perform. Learning communicative functions, acquiring new words, mastering the basic structure of a native language—these are remarkable achievements that are extremely difficult to explain. The same sense of wonder usually is not associated with children's acquisition of written language. Traditionally, literacy has been conceptualized as a process in which teaching prevails over learning and instruction enables children to transfer linguistic knowledge to a visual rather than auditory modality. An implicit tenet of this concept of literacy is that written language is not a language per se, but just a different modality for expressing meanings.

In recent years, however, research within domains as different as anthropology, sociolinguistics, cognitive psychology, and history of writing systems has introduced new ideas about written language and literacy. Anthropological and sociolinguistic studies have investigated differences between literacy and orality (Goody & Watt, 1963; Ong, 1982), between spoken and written language (Chafe, 1982), and among speech events that conform in different degrees to the requirements of written texts (Tannen, 1985). These studies suggested that in many cultures the development of writing invokes new strategies of discourse construction and new linguistic structures. These structures, in turn, tend to be used by literate speakers whenever their discourse has a high level of planning (Ochs, 1983) and formality. The reciprocal permeability of spoken and written language with respect to lexical choices, syntactic structures, and discourse organization calls into question the notion of a clear-cut separation between literacy and oral language acquisition. In some cultures, for example, children first acquire language in part by participating in various activities that use writing and written texts. Literacy can thus be construed as any process of language acquisition and transmission that occurs in contexts where people read, write, and produce discourses with linguistic forms typical of written texts.

Some studies in cognitive psychology, influenced by historical investigations of Greek culture (Havelock, 1963) and anthropological research on how literacy "domesticated" the savage mind (Goody, 1968), have explored the cognitive consequences of literacy (Olson, 1977, 1986; Olson & Torrance, 1987) and the peculiarities of a literate versus an oral world representation. That literacy per se can generate cognitive changes in its users has been questioned (Scribner & Cole, 1981). However, the Olson studies reveal that writing and written texts do challenge subjects with new linguistic and cognitive demands. In particular, the fact that a text, unlike the spoken word, does not disappear after it is read opens the way to complex interpretation of meanings and to discussions of the plausibility of interpretations. From these studies arises a concept of literacy as knowing from texts (Olson, 1985) and of literacy acquisition as mastering text-oriented activities such as quoting, rephrasing, and interpreting. According to Harris (1989), writing introduces a distinction between speech and language by creating an "autoglottic" space in which sentences (as opposed to utterances) are "unsponsored," that is, they exist independently of their authors and can be analyzed. Thus, what is meant can be more easily distinguished from what is said, and the abstract character of sentences enables the development of a grammar, a logic, and a philosophy.

Is the "literate mind" linked to the alphabetic system of writing? That claim was strongly defended by Havelock (1963, 1982), who argued that the introduction of an alphabetic system in ancient Greece set the stage for all philosophical and scientific developments until the rise of Western modern science. This position is now strongly opposed from several different points of view. Historical approaches to the origin of writing systems (Harris, 1986; Sampson, 1985) have radically questioned the view that alphabets are the point of maximum development of writing systems (Gelb, 1963). Indeed, systems as different as the logographic (e.g., Chinese, in which characters stand for morphemes), the ideographic (as the Japanese refer to their writing, in which characters represent meanings), and the syllabary (e.g., the Semitic scripts) have their own advantages and limits and involve peculiar relationships with the language that is spoken. Different writing systems bring different aspects of language into focus, and no single writing system, including the alphabetic, brings every component of spoken language into awareness (Olson, 1991). Actually, no real system of writing can be completely identified with one of the categories. Even alphabetic writing is mixed with nonalphabetic features. Halliday (1985) emphasized that any given instance of written language is mixed and intermediate, and that, because all languages are highly complex, a writing system has to be flexible to accommodate that complexity.

Because a central component of a writing system is the visual notation used to convey meanings, the visual forms produced with the intention of writing are the relevant object to analyze when studying literacy acquisition. A completely new psycholinguistic approach (Ferreiro & Teberosky, 1979) began to investigate children's production of writing. Ferreiro and Teberosky identified children's strategies of combining written marks and showed how children learn to map written marks onto specific functions. These studies revealed that children are precociously engaged in the process of becoming literate, and develop hypotheses about the relationships between written symbols and what they denote long before they are formally taught to read and write. Moreover, children try to understand and learn not only the written code but also the ways in which the whole writing system operates.

Children's acquisition of literacy is assumed to be a multifaceted process. It is the acquisition of new linguistic forms that results from being acquainted with the language used in written texts or in textlike discourses. It is also the acquisition of specific text-oriented activities, such as quoting discourses or explaining stories. Finally, it is understanding and mastering the system used in a specific culture for writing and reading a language.

ORAL AND WRITTEN FORMS IN CHILDREN'S ACQUISITION OF LANGUAGE

Spoken and written language have often been described as having dramatically different syntactic and semantic structures. Chafe (1982, 1985) pointed out that written texts have more integrated linguistic units, containing noun or verb phrases often expanded with adverbials or relative clauses. And, on the other hand, oral discourse has a rather fragmented nature, with coordinations largely prevailing over subordinations and with intonation providing a major device for linking utterances. However, other scholars have argued that the same differences can be found by comparing speech events that have little personal involvement versus those with great personal involvement (Tannen, 1985) or planned versus unplanned activities. Ochs (1983) analyzed highly planned discourses, such as lectures, and found that they have morphosyntactic structures typical of written language. Similar results emerge from other studies (Berretta, 1990), showing that in lectures speakers use cohesive devices in a rather different way than in conversations. For example, in lectures they are more likely to maintain referents with definite nouns than pronominalizations.

These findings again suggest that, when we want to identify specific features of written language, we should dismiss any concern for bare "modality" (i.e., a language that is written rather than spoken). We can find, in fact, "written uses of language" in conversation (Tannen, 1985) and story telling (Sulzby, 1985), and also "cues of oral language" in written texts. For example, when texts are constructed primarily by transcribing oral narrative episodes, as was the New Testament, what has been already written does not seem to orient or constrain subsequent writing activity. In the New Testament, the same events (Ong, 1982) are narrated in slightly different versions; this seems to happen not because different points of view are introduced but because subsequent transcribers rely on their oral memory of the discourse rather than on the previously written record. In the Middle Ages, some stylistic features of texts were very close to an oral style, because texts were often circulated by being read aloud to an audience. The preface of a manuscript could contain a formulaic presentation (Ong, 1982), such as "Here, dear reader, is a book that someone wrote about . . . ," that is suited to the particular oral situation in which the manuscript could be read.

The proportion of oral and written forms in a text is the result of multiple influencing factors: the genre of the text (e.g., scientific papers vs. newspaper articles), the author's representation of the situation in which the text will be circulated (e.g., television news vs. private reading), the physical medium in which writing is produced that makes revision more or less easy (e.g., stone vs. paper), and the strategy used to compose the text (e.g., dictating vs. writing).

Thus producing language in a written modality does not necessarily result in selecting linguistic structures and lexical forms that are typical of written texts. Both spoken and written forms can be used in speech and text, and this is particularly true of narratives. Let us illustrate this point further. It is usually taken for granted that writing allows a deep control of the semantic organization of discourse. Indeed, we know that expert writers produce texts in cycles of planning, lexicalization, and revising activities that drive, respectively, organization of semantic content, access to linguistic forms, and control of pragmatic, lexical, and morphosyntactic choices (Flower & Hayes, 1980). Thus, writing can greatly facilitate coordination among these cognitive activities: It allows what was produced previously to be modified several times. This kind of coordination seems to be much more difficult with oral discourse. However, lack of written records may not prevent speakers from producing highly accurate semantic organization with very controlled selection of linguistic forms. Studies of oral poets have shown that a great deal of semantic content can be organized in memory and associated with formulas and conventional phrases. When online discourse production draws on this repertoire of memorized information, cognitive resources can be dedicated to more local planning, such as producing single clauses and linking short units of discourse. As a result, the oral discourse can have good coherence and cohesion, because it is a highly planned activity.

This discussion suggests that in investigating the impact of literacy on children's language acquisition we cannot rely on comparing linguistic structures (e.g., syntax and cohesive devices) of oral and written texts. Oral texts can be planned speech events, whereas written texts may have been produced by children using oral rather than written strategies. Indeed, it has been observed that when elementary school children are not taught to plan large chunks of semantic content by writing down ideas and are not trained to revise what they have been writing, texts are produced using strategies resembling those that underlie conversation. Specifically, every current utterance is both the result of a semantic and a lexical choice and the input for the next utterance (Bereiter & Scardamalia, 1982). Pairs of utterances are thus linked, but overall organization is lacking. Moreover, the absence of revising activity prevents children from exploring different linguistic ways to express the same meaning and from having control of lexical choices. In sum, elementary school children may not produce texts with the cognitive strategies that maximize the advantages of having visible rather than audible linguistic forms.

In summary, when we investigate children's written and oral versions of the same task, we are comparing texts that may have been produced with similar strategies. Moreover, both types of texts may present a blend of oral and written uses of language, because of the children's overall experience with reading or listening to literate texts.

An alternative way to address the issue of the impact of writing on children's language is to investigate how familiarity with written texts can introduce written forms in children's production and comprehension of language. If we assume the reciprocal permeability of spoken and written modalities with respect to lexical choices, syntactic structures, and organization of the discourse, then familiarity with books and texts introduces an important source of variation in language acquisition. Children who frequently have adults reading books to them or telling stories that conform to a literate style (Heath, 1982; Michaels & Collins, 1984) may receive—at least for a subset of linguistic forms—a special kind of input that is more likely to occur with written texts.

Michaels and Collins (1984) analyzed spoken narratives produced by both children familiar with a literate style and children more likely to use oral-based strategies. They found that the two groups of children differed with respect to how to introduce a new character. The first group used an indefinite noun with a relative clause describing the action in which the character was involved (e.g., "There was a man who was picking some pears"). The oral-based strategies group used a definite noun phrase, with a deictic expression (e.g., "It was about this man"). Thus, familiarity with written style seems to greatly affect the children's use of cohesive devices in narratives, even when narratives are spoken rather than written.

This result is partly confirmed by a study in which use of referential devices to introduce, maintain, and reintroduce references to characters was analyzed (Orsolini & Di Giacinto, chap. 4, this volume). Four-year-old children's narratives were elicited in two different contexts. In the first, children invented stories that were subsequently enacted with model toys; in the second, a story was read by an adult, audio recorded, and listened to by the children, who then were requested to retell it. In this second context, children were far more likely to introduce a new animate referent with an indefinite noun, whereas in the spontaneous narratives of the first context the children used mostly definite nouns. Children's use of a more conventional way to introduce new referents into the context where they were retelling a story confirms that familiarity with texts can remarkably affect children's acquisition and use of language. Texts probably highlight some linguistic structures, making them somehow ritualistic and predictable. This can be the case for the indefinite referential expressions that very often co-occur with a formulaic opening (Bamberg, 1987).

In summary, the impact of writing on children's language should be addressed by taking into account that activities with texts are very particular "ecological niches" for language acquisition. Indeed, some features of texts may create relevant learning conditions for language acquisition.

Written texts have a unique mixture of variety and conventionalization in lexical choices related to a specific genre. Narratives, for example, are very specialized contexts for words denoting people's feelings and thoughts (Olson & Astington, 1990), or for adverbial phrases and past participle forms used to temporally structure events. The occurrence of this specialized lexicon in texts that are read and that children enjoy memorizing probably introduces some peculiar language learning condition. That is, when a child hears a word for the first time in a text being read by an adult and then hears the same word again when the text is reread, the reoccurrence of the word within the same linguistic context may greatly help the child to grasp the word meaning. Text, with its stable message, introduces a great deal of lexical and semantic predictability (but also the danger of a semantic overrestriction).

Again, some complex syntactic structures (e.g., the relative clauses) that adults use in conversation in co-occurrence with various speech acts are found in written narratives in co-occurrence with conventional and predictable acts such as the introduction or reintroduction of a character.

In summary, written texts are bound by conventions and rules that make complex linguistic forms somehow predictable in their function within the text.

Finally, when children and adults talk about the situation narrated by the text, a unique experience with reformulation is offered to the child: The same events that are described in the text with certain words are then referred to by the adult with different words. Texts open semantic content to reinterpretation and make linguistic forms available for quotations, rephrasings, and metacommunication.

CHILDREN'S EARLY ACTIVITIES WITH TEXTS

Texts in the Latin tradition are woven things (from the past participle of *texere*, meaning "to weave"). In the Middle Ages, *text* meant "literaryness of what is written" (Segre, 1985, p. 29), and the term denoted both the signs and the physical medium in which the texts were written. In the Western tradition, texts become objects, artifacts that convey information through both linguistic forms and graphic conventions. The spatial location of the message, the peculiar links between pictures and writing, the blank space separating different parts—all introduce autonomous information beyond that conveyed by the words themselves. Texts are stable and transportable objects, and, because of this property, they can partially free language from its actual producer.

When referring to oral discourse as texts, we should not forget that in this case there is no physical object, but only a semantic content or a set of linguistic forms made relatively stable by speakers' memory. With this in mind, we can explore how children deal with oral texts and how a discourse can be transformed into a stable entity that can be reproduced, transmitted to different people, or embedded in a wider discourse. These issues can be addressed by investigating how children learn to quote discourses. The idea underlying quotations is that a linguistic entity can be reproduced and separated by the wider discourse unit in which it is embedded.

Quotations should first be differentiated from "textual deixis" (Lyons, 1977) and "metalanguage." When a deictic expression, such as a demonstrative pronoun, refers to an antecedent speech unit (e.g., "Can you repeat *that*?"), linguistic forms are transferred into referential objects. That is, reference is made to the linguistic forms (i.e., a phoneme, a word, or a whole sentence) rather than to extralinguistic entities. However, when reference is made by using a metalinguistic expression, linguistic entities are designated with lexical devices that provide some descriptive information on them. Thus, in "Could you repeat that *word*?") metalanguage is involved, and *word* is used to differentiate a specific kind of entity from many that could be selected.

Quotations in narratives may deploy deictic devices to introduce a particular type of speech event (e.g., dialogue between characters) in the discourse context. A variety of prosodic and lexical indices, such as intonation or verb tense shift, can be used to frame a discourse as a reported speech. In contrast, when metalanguage is used, quotations are made with explicit lexical devices (e.g., verbs such as *say* or *tell*) that frame the quoted message and somehow describe the kind of speech event being produced. In other words, the framing lexical device introduces the upcoming speech event (Hickmann, 1985) by providing some descriptive information about it. On the other hand, the quoted message may be framed only with indices that, in one particular discourse context, help to signal the type of speech event being performed and to separate the current speech event from the previous one. This happens in a narrative, for example, when there is a shift from third-person verbs to first- or second-person verbs (e.g., "And he met a cat and a fox. Where are you going, little boy?"), or from declarative to interrogative sentences. In this case, the shift of person in the verb and the pragmatic link between the verb and the narrative both signal that a character is speaking.

Some studies have investigated the developmental changes in children's quotations of discourse. Hickmann (1985) addressed the issue of when children use a metalanguage to frame a quoted message and overtly refer to speech events. She analyzed narratives by presenting films consisting mostly of dialogue between two characters and found that children 7 and 10 years old were very likely to use some lexical device (e.g., a verb such as *say*) to frame quoted discourse. Conversely, 4-year-olds were more likely to report speech with no lexical device to frame the quotation. This suggests that children's use of metalanguage increases with schooling. It is not clear, however, whether preschool children have means other than lexical devices to frame different kinds of speech events and to signal to the addressee the type of speech being performed.

Other studies have shown that preschool children do use other kinds of linguistic devices. Wolf and Hicks (1989) analyzed replica play narratives in which children invented a story as they played out sequences of events using small toys as actors. Narratives were analyzed by coding each clause as a stage-managing function (when children interacted with the observer to organize the play), a narrative function (when children moved the story line ahead by inventing new events), or a dialogue function (when focus was on characters' speech). According to Wolf and Hicks, even 3-year-old children can signal characters' speech by framing it with a shift in the verb form (e.g., a shift from declaratives to imperatives). However, 4- and 5-year-olds use a richer variety of indices to frame quoted discourse. In particular, they use the shift from past tense forms to present tense forms to signal that the speech event being performed is dialogue between characters.

Studies investigating children's social pretend play have found that 4-year-olds can frame the type of speech event in which they are engaged by overtly marking the transition from a planning discourse, in which a pretend scenario is invented and negotiated, to a role-playing discourse, in which the participants enact a pretend role and produce speech as characters (Auwarter, 1986; Garvey & Kramer, 1989; Giffin, 1984; Musatti & Orsolini, 1993). In this play context, the verb shift from third to first or second person is exploited less than in the narrative context, because the planning of the plot usually occurs in the dialogue between the participants and involves the participants themselves as possible characters. For example, a child saying "Why don't you give me some medicine?" could either contribute to the plot (discussing a scenario in which someone is sick) or enact a role (the sick person speaking to the doctor). Thus, first- and second-person verbs are not very effective devices for signaling a shift from planning the play to enacting the play itself. In many languages, including French and Italian, children use a shift from imperfect to present tense forms to signal a transition from planning to enactment (Musatti & Orsolini, 1993; Van Gessel-Hotcker, 1989). In this case, past tense forms are not used to narrate events but rather to signal either that discourse is about planning the scenario or that it is a negotiatory phase of the play, different from enacting a role and speaking as a character.

Berthoud-Papandropoulou and Kilcher (1987) investigated preschool children's ability to transmit messages. Children were asked by the experimenter to report a message to a second adult (e.g., "Go and tell her to build four houses"). The messages that children had to report varied in pragmatic function (e.g., directives vs. assertions) and in syntactic structure. A remarkable developmental change was found in this study: The 3-year-olds effectively transmitted messages consisting only of directives, whereas the 5-year-olds also conveyed assertions and questions when they were elicited by an overt framing mark signaling that there was a message to be repeated (e.g., "Go and ask this—who has to live close to the cows?"). Thus, young children's understanding of discourse as a message to be disembedded from a wider speech event and reported seems to be facilitated when messages consist of directives. Actions that the interlocutor is requested to do are probably more easily understood as autonomous units. Also, Wolf and Hicks (1989) found that the 3-year-olds were more likely to produce characters' speech consisting of imperatives.

In summary, children as young as 3 years old can frame the type of speech event being performed and can mark a shift from a narrative discourse to a dialogue-between-characters discourse. In the preschool years, children seem to develop a greater variety of linguistic devices to serve the framing function and a growing capability to organize different kinds of speech acts as units that can be chunked and reported. These findings on preschoolers' ability to embed a text in a wider discourse and to signal the type of speech being performed suggest that we should be more cautious in interpreting the changes observed in primary school children. Because 7- to 9-year-old children are more likely to use lexical devices (e.g., *say*) to refer to an incoming speech event, have they acquired a new linguistic and cognitive function or just a more conventional and refined way of quoting discourse? An increased experience with written texts, involving more familiarity with a lexicon describing linguistic entities and mental states (Olson & Torrance, 1987), may, in fact, make children use more conventional ways of reporting and quoting discourses. Research on preschoolers' skills in quoting discourse suggests that primary school children may have learned just to map onto a lexical device the very same function that younger children begin to perform through deictic devices.

The preceding overview suggests that preschool children have a notion of text in terms of a unit that can be reported, transmitted, and separated by a wider discourse. We may wonder whether children have a similar notion for the semantic content of texts, in terms of a stable message whose truth can be claimed or questioned. It has been argued that preschool children are not able to judge the content autonomously conveyed by what is said, as distinguished from what can be inferred or imagined (Torrance & Olson, 1987). In particular, Torrance and Olson (1987) found that 4- and 5-year-olds were very likely to confuse what a speaker said and what the listener could reasonably infer from the speaker's message. On the other hand, primary school children were more aware of the actual content of texts as autonomous from possible interpretations and inferences.

However, investigations of children's arguments show that preschoolers have quite sophisticated abilities in judging the content of what has been said and in signaling whether it was true or just hypothetical. Again, children do not use metalinguistic verbs such as *hypothesize* or *assert* but instead use linguistic indices. For example, an analysis (Orsolini, 1993) of 4-year-olds' disputes shows that, in children's causal explanations, both *because* and *if* can be used to describe a dependence link between an event and a condition (e.g., "If you put it on the fire, it melts"). However, the two connectives are used by children to convey different pragmatic meanings. *Because* conveys a very strong speaker's commitment to the truth of what has been said, whereas *if*, from the point of view of the speaker, involves a false or only partially true assertion. Thus, preschool children assume the content of a previous claim as a true or partially true message and signal their stance about the message by using different causal connectives (Orsolini, 1993). This observation suggests that preschool children can separate the actual semantic content of their own speech from its truth value. They can speak of events referred to by another speaker and, at the same time, signal that they do not believe those events to be true.

In some instructional contexts, preschool children have also been observed making explicit the distinction between what was said in a text and what could be inferred. Pontecorvo and Orsolini (1990) analyzed discussions between three groups of 5-year-old children and their teacher. These discussions concerned a story previously read to the children by the teacher; at crucial points, the reading was interrupted, and the children were asked to predict how the story would continue. During the discussions, the teacher asked the groups of children to explain some of the characters' motives and plans, and to evaluate the cleverness of the characters. In two groups, disagreement on evaluations of the characters' cleverness was spontaneously resolved by children (none of whom could read or write) who mentioned what was said in the text. For example, a child arguing about the age of the main character of the story challenged a participant's claim in this way: "How do you know how old she is? It's not written down: If it was written down the teacher would have told us."

These observations suggest that children's notion of text has been underestimated. Children's familiarity with texts can be well advanced even at preschool age, enabling them to understand that what is written is different from what can be imagined or hypothesized. Moreover, familiarity with textlike discourses enables children to use a complex repertoire of indices (i.e., tense forms, modality, person marks on the verb, connectives) to either separate the actual message from its truth value or frame a reported discourse.

CHILDREN'S ACQUISITION OF A WRITING SYSTEM

The industrial revolution and the development of democracy placed greater pressure on all workers and male citizens to become literate. The social need was mostly for reading skills, whereas the standard requirement for writing was only to be able to trace one's own signature. At the same time, in some European countries, writing was considered not only unnecessary but also morally danger-ous for women, because they could use it to write letters to lovers (Petrucci, 1978).

Has the greater social relevance of reading over writing affected research attitudes? Scholars have investigated reading much more than writing, particu-larly after psychologists found that, as a cognitive process, reading allows us to understand how second-order symbols are processed by the human mind. The focus on reading brought about a conception of learning a written language in terms of a cognitive process in which graphemic forms are mapped onto pho-nemic units and vice versa. However, the basic question of how a writing system can be understood and mastered as a semiotic system was not addressed until researchers investigated early writing development.

The seminal study of Ferreiro and Teberosky (1979), based on extensive observations, identified the major trends in understanding a writing system for Spanish-speaking children. Those trends were confirmed for languages as differ-ent as Catalan (Teberosky, 1982), Italian (Pontecorvo & Zucchermaglio, 1990; Zucchermaglio, 1991), French (see Besse, chap. 7, this volume), Hebrew (Tol-chinsky Landsmann, 1988), Portuguese, and English (Bissex, 1980).

These studies showed that children actively engage in writing and in reading, first in nonconventional ways, with no ontogenetic priority given to one or to the other activity. Young children elaborate personal hypotheses about the meaning of what is written not only in books and newspapers but also on food boxes, beverage containers, posters, advertisements, shop signs, calendars, street signs, bus numbers, and so on (Sinclair, 1988). Written messages are not only symbols to be interpreted but also objects that are somehow used by people and variously embedded in everyday cultural practices (Heath, 1983). As for any other sociocul-tural object, children's learning unfolds in the context of the social practices of reading and writing in which adults and older siblings are engaged.

Through involvement in a variety of reading and writing practices, written messages somehow start to be analyzed by the child, and written symbols begin to be understood as "substitute objects" (Ferreiro, 1988a), that is, as elements in a semiotic system. Some children eventually understand these objects as representing sounds and then subunits of spoken linguistic forms. Although this is not a general requirement of every writing system, it is necessary to alphabetic ones.

The point can be further illustrated by distinguishing between two layers in a writing system (Harris, 1992): a notation system, consisting of graphic marks constructed and differentiated according to visual rules; and a sign system, consisting of graphic marks mapped onto well-established functions by the relationships with a specific language. Early writing acquisition is focused on both layers: Children learn the graphic forms typical of a specific notation system, attempt to differentiate them from other graphic displays, and reconstruct the prototypical patterns of sequences of written marks. At the same time, children map sequences of written marks onto functions, first by assigning a meaning to their writing and then by establishing some correspondence between graphic and phonological forms. The basic puzzle to be solved by children is how to coordinate patterns of the notation system with functional units of the sign system.

Studies on early writing acquisition share a method of tapping children's representations: Children who have not yet received any systematic teaching and cannot be considered conventionally literate are asked to write and to read and interpret their own writing. This method raises the problem of how children interpret the adult's request for writing, being, as they are, aware that they have not been taught to write. Besse (chap. 7, this volume) expresses his concerns about preschool children being conscious of their own incompetence in writing and reading. Indeed, the risk of extorting answers from children (Perret-Clermont, Schubauer-Leoni, & Trognon, 1992) and having peculiar experimental artifacts is reduced when children are acquainted with writing activities in their preschool setting. In fact, other studies have shown that when an experimenter asks children to perform activities (e.g., writing, interpreting sequences of written marks) very similar to those typical of their preschool setting, major findings of previous studies are replicated (Pontecorvo, 1991; Zucchermaglio, 1991).

The remainder of this chapter provides an overview of the main phases of children's writing acquisition; details can be read elsewhere (Ferreiro, 1988b; Ferreiro & Teberosky, 1979; Pontecorvo, 1991).

The initial phase of writing development begins with the differentiation of writing from drawing. The differentiation takes place together with the first production of drawings that convey an autonomous meaning (Lurçat, 1965). This happens when children begin to represent classes of objects (Sinclair, 1982) by using a kind of "drawing stenography" that looks rather simple and even stereotyped. Children draw prototypes (an object representative of a whole category) and begin to write objects' names that have nothing to do with spoken words. For example, they may use single different marks for the name of each depicted object. In other words, children seem to consider the name as a kind of conceptual information about the object. This is the beginning of a development that takes the child from writing marks that are only graphical objects to marks that mean something because they represent concepts and names. Probably for this reason, some children at this phase adopt an iconic hypothesis: the bigger the object, the longer the name.

In the second phase, children explore the graphic and syntactical regularities of the notation system. How long should a sequence of written marks be to be considered a meaningful unit? And how internally differentiated should this sequence be? Children have been observed to develop constructive hypotheses that follow an internal logic of development. In order to have a set of interpretable marks (even if the meaning still needs to be drawn from the context), children follow some *quantitative* conditions (e.g., a minimum number of written marks, usually three) and some *qualitative* ones (e.g., presence of graphical variety). This variety is considered external when children use marks to write the names of different objects (Ferreiro, 1988a) and internal when children use different marks within the same writing, particularly avoiding having the same marks in a contiguous position. At this point, children are mainly interested in understanding the formal principles of the writing system of their culture, which is not only a set of notational elements that are rather easily acquired by the children, but also a system that follows particular constraints in combining and ordering marks. A first step in children's orthographic development appears in the use of the preceding general rules in letter sequences and word formation.

Beyond these formal ways of differentiating writings, children often use modes of differentiation (Pontecorvo & Zuccermaglio, 1988) that suggest a sensitivity to meaning. For example, how should the names of objects be written that differ only because of their size or quantity? Children have been asked to write the diminutive and the plural of a base word that had previously been written (Pontecorvo & Zuccermaglio, 1988). For example, after children were asked to write *PALLA* ("ball"), they were asked to write *PALLINA* ("little ball"). In Italian, because the diminutive suffix always makes the word longer, this request might introduce a cognitive conflict: representing a smaller object with a longer word. Conversely, plural forms (which in Italian are produced with a vowel substitution) keep the word the same length while representing a greater quantity of objects compared with the singular form. About half of the children attempted to keep an isomorphism between writing the base and the inflected forms, introducing changes of size (for the diminutive) and repetition of symbols (for the plural). Thus, similarities and differences in meaning tend to be projected onto similarities and differences in writing before children understand that graphic marks have to do with spoken rather than conceptual forms.

In the third phase of writing development, children seem to grasp that what is written has something to do with what is said: Utterances that sound longer have to be written with more marks. Children attempt to coordinate phonological and written representations even before any conventional learning occurs. After some attempts at coordination, children usually adopt a syllabic hypothesis, linking each mark to a syllable, at first in unconventional ways. A very early strategy is to keep the right rhythmic match between number of marks and number of uttered syllables. This strategy very often poses conflicts for children when they try to read, because what they have written may be longer than what they are saying. For instance, they can use three marks for writing the bisyllabic word *casa*, and they "read" aloud only the first two marks, referring to the two syllables of the uttered word.

A conflict appears frequently in children reading their own writing (see Besse, chap. 7, this volume) when they delete letters they have previously written or attribute a particular role to them because there are "too many" for a syllabic reading. This cognitive conflict is most likely to occur when the child writes words that he or she has been taught to write (e.g., his or her own name). When these words are read syllabically, the child realizes that there are too many marks. The same thing happens when children write a monosyllabic word with at least three marks (following the condition of the minimum quantity), which then presents too many marks for a syllabic reading. Some children explicitly say that more letters are needed for writing than for reading!

When children following a syllabic hypothesis start to use a conventional repertoire of vowels and consonants, variations may appear due to the particular system of writing in their language. In Italian and Spanish, vowels are more frequently used to represent the corresponding syllable than in French or English.

The ontogenetical priority of syllabic recognition has been confirmed in a study with Italian children (Devescovi, Orsolini, & Pace, 1989). In an experimental situation, 4-, 5-, and 6-year-old children were asked to identify phonemes, syllables, and morphemes in sets of words in which these units could be in either the initial or the final position. The results clearly showed that correct syllable recognition was a function only of age, whereas correct phoneme and morpheme recognition depended on school grade instead of age. The two variables were controlled by interviewing 6-year-olds enrolled in either kindergarten or first grade.

Empirical evidence of children's syllabic hypothesis has also been provided through observations of spontaneous writing, that is, writing produced by children without an adult's direct request (Zucchermaglio, 1991). These observations have confirmed that children use syllabic-based representations to write words and have ruled out any doubt (as raised by Abaurre, chap. 3, this volume) about children's syllabic interpretations being generated by the experimental situation and particularly by the experimenter's word pronunciation.

Children's writing is regarded as alphabetic when it contains regular correspondences between phonemes and graphemes. Children's understanding of the system is not an all-or-nothing phenomenon but a long journey toward the mastery of a particular sign system. Thus, children do not immediately use all the phonemes of the language in their writings. The initial parts of words (and then the final parts) are more easily represented alphabetically, whereas the rest may still be represented syllabically.

At this point, children begin to develop a phonological analysis linked to their writing and reading activities. This is strongly dependent on the requirements of the specific writing system they are learning. A systematic study by Teberosky, Tolchinsky Landsmann, Zelcer, Gomes de Morais, and Rincon (1993) compared how two different writing systems (the Catalan and the Hebrew) were phonologically analyzed by young children. This research aimed to study the role of phonological segmentation skills in children's writing development. Most studies that have explored the issue of whether phonological segmentation is a necessary condition or a consequence of learning to read have given little or no attention to its possible links to writing. This study, however, started from the research data that syllables have a phonic substratum that phonemes lack. Thus, children become aware of phonematic differences only when they can refer to writing. By comparing two different alphabetic systems, the research shows that writing offers an external representative support that facilitates the separation and identification of phonemic units, with differences in unit selection due to the two systems.

Although syllabic segmentation can be developed in children independently of their writing development, access to phonic structure is possible only through writing activity or systematic teaching. Indeed, although segmentation into syllables precedes the capability to produce an alphabetic written product, knowing to write alphabetically does not necessarily lead to an exhaustive phonetic segmentation. The use of the phonological analysis is a rather late resource in writing acquisition and depends on the spelling options offered by the particular writing system. A syllabary system involves a representation of language different from an alphabetic system, and confronts the child with specific cognitive problems that should be examined in a cross-cultural perspective. Levin and Korat (in press) showed that for Hebrew, in which the words derive from a consonantal core through morphological transformations and affixes, it is possible for both the listener and the beginning reader to identify semantic content, syntactic category, and spelling by recognizing root and morphological structure.

The alphabetic phase, however, does not mark the end of the literacy process. As a subjective accomplishment, literacy has a long developmental process that begins before school instruction and continues long after the first years of formal instruction. It involves learning the word segmentation typical of a certain writing system (Ferreiro & Pontecorvo, 1993), as well as quotative structures (Blanche-Benveniste, 1991) and use of punctuation and textual layouts. These are all nonalphabetic aspects of our writing systems—which are all mixed as Halliday (1985) reminded us—and children must face them to become fully literate. Punctuation is discussed in some of the chapters in this volume (Simone, chap. 9; Ferreiro & Zucchermaglio, chap. 10). A current comparative study with Mexican, Italian, and Brazilian children is examining the use of punctuation in primary school children who are requested to write down a well-known story.

With regard to text layout, a recent study (Pontecorvo, 1994) examined how children represent different types of text: namely, words requested by an adult, names referring to the children's preferred toys, a well-known nursery rhyme, an interrogative sentence uttered by the experimenter, and a well-known story. Results showed that children changed their writing strategies and textual layouts according to the type of text. The nursery rhyme was much less segmented than the story, whereas the writing about the toys was always segmented and often written in listlike form. Some older children divided the rhyme into lines corresponding to the verse, whereas the sentence uttered by the adult tended to be written in a more continuous way. The story was segmented into words, even by the younger children, and also segmented into paragraphs corresponding to a structural articulation. Thus, children seem to have a rather detailed knowledge of how different types of text can be organized in micrographic and macrographic units.

In conclusion, it is worth repeating that studies of early writing acquisition rely on a method requiring children to produce something that they have not been trained to produce. From the children's errors in those studies, we can infer representations and learning trends. For many scholars, it is not surprising that children's errors can be an important source of evidence for analyses of language acquisition. It is common to assume that, because spoken language is spontaneously produced rather than taught, spoken language acquisition can be investigated by observing children from their very first communicative attempts and by analyzing children's errors in terms of rules or underlying representations. Unfortunately, it is also rather common to assume that, because written language is taught, children's errors are evidence only of lack of learning. When children's literacy activities are investigated in terms of underlying knowledge, their acquisition of written sign systems can be as striking as that of spoken language.

This discovery should emigrate from laboratory settings to educational contexts that could take advantage of children's hypotheses by allowing them to write and read autonomously in interactional settings and to produce texts without a central concern for avoiding mistakes. Children's autonomous writing can be an important anchor point both for researchers and for teacher-led activities.

LEARNING TO WRITE IN SCHOOL

If writing is primarily an activity of text construction carried out within conventionalized structures and discourse genres, with the means offered by a writing system, learning to write in school, even in the early phases, is much more than mastering an alphabetic code.

However, in considering young children's developing competence in writing within the real context of school practice, one cannot separate in a clear-cut way learning the writing system from learning the written language. Children practice and explore a writing system by producing types of text that they differentiate from the start by using the linguistic and pragmatic knowledge they have already developed through oral interaction, and gradually using the new means offered by any writing system: not only symbols for representing letters and words but also layout, punctuation, diacritical marks, and division in lines and paragraphs. Thus, there is no ground in teaching to assume an ideological opposition between learning the writing system versus learning the written language, as well as between learning to communicate through writing versus learning the proper written forms of the different writing genres. Obviously, these are different aspects of writing acquisition that have to be separated for research purposes, as has been done in this chapter.

Written text construction is a cognitive and linguistic activity in which children engage from the very beginning when trying to understand the writing system and produce texts. Until recently, primary schools in all countries had been mostly engaged in "teaching the code" rather mechanically by regarding the process of learning to write as a passage through a hierarchy of skills that have to be exercised in isolation. It is now considered inappropriate for teachers to first teach the code (or the writing system) and only afterward allow children to write meaningful texts. However, notwithstanding the established competences of young children about the concept of a text, first-grade children (Pascucci Formisano, chap. 15, this volume) frequently have no opportunity to practice meaningful writing and reading activities. School practices in writing can range from the attitude that children should write spontaneously (which ignores the conventionalized aspect of the different types of text that literate people engage when writing) to the attitude that children should compose texts, beginning with molecular pieces such as words, phrases, and sentences (which ignores the very textual or structured feature of any text). The latter practice has often been proposed for handicapped children (e.g., the deaf) who have had no exposure to spoken texts and who have the maximum need of developing a representation of a text (see Conte, Pagliari Rampelli, & Volterra, chap. 16, this volume).

Research on children's early writing development has suggested changing educational practices concerning text construction. First, the discovery of young children's autonomous activity about notational and writing systems does not mean that school has nothing to do with this. School can contribute systematically to helping children break the code by organizing learning activities that support the analytical work of children about the system: linguistic plays on words (e.g., crossword puzzles, rhymes, anagrams), use of typewriters or word processors, or production of school newspapers. Children can be motivated to engage in instructional proposals devoted to completing the mastery of the writing system, even independent of the communicative aims of the written product.

Second, a much larger range of text genres could be presented to children. Although the narrative genre has priority because it is strictly linked to early social and cognitive development (as shown by Bruner, 1990, and Nelson, 1989), children can also engage in expository, informative, and argumentative text construction. A variety of literacy practices (D. Resnick & L. B. Resnick, 1990) should be proposed to them from the beginning.

Third, new methodologies that have proved useful in research on children's literacy development could be transferred to preschool and primary school settings (Teberosky, 1988). For instance, children can invent a story as they play out sequences of events, using small toys or puppets as actors. Alternatively, they can play at transmitting and executing messages from an adult. Moreover, small groups of children can interact in order to elaborate a story, starting from a verbal or figurative stimulus: For example, a story dictated to an adult serving as a scribe quickly provides a text for examination without burdening the children with transcribing (Pontecorvo & Zucchermaglio, 1989). Children can also interact in dyads, without adult support, and produce a text (e.g., a story, an informative text) by alternating in the role of writer.

One relevant educational implication of current research on children's early text construction has been the creation of various teaching–learning activities in which all the functions of writing (and reading) are explored, including the informational, the interpersonal, the persuasive, and the poetic. Although the last function requires more attention to form than to function, it can be very attractive, even for young children who already enjoy playing with words (see Pontecorvo & Morani, chap. 12, this volume) and can be engaged in the world of poetry and rhyme in which the form overrides the content.

Writing is a multifaceted practice that can be activated within different social settings that vary as a function of motives, topics, and addressees. Thus, in school contexts, learning to write can be practiced through the progressive appropriation of a set of cultural practices in written text production supported by socially shared activity. Introducing new writing practices also involves a change of the whole educational context in which children should be allowed to think, and writing is not reserved to school aims. Research examples (such as those proposed in this book), which in many cases have been introduced into real school settings, show that this change is possible and desirable.

ACKNOWLEDGMENT

The writing of this chapter was supported by a 1993–1994 grant from the Italian National Council of Research to the first author for a research project on the acquisition of written language in children. This chapter was planned and discussed jointly by both authors. Parts 1, 4, and 5 were written by Clotilde Pontecorvo, and Parts 2 and 3 were written by Margherita Orsolini.

REFERENCES

Auwarter, M. (1986). Development of communicative skills: The construction of fictional reality in children's play. In J. Cook-Gumperz, W. Corsaro, & J. Streeck (Eds.), *Children's world and children's language* (pp. 205–230). Berlin: Mouton de Gruyter.

Bamberg, M. (1987). *The acquisition of narratives.* Berlin: Mouton de Gruyter.

Bereiter, C., & Scardamalia, M. (1982). From conversation to composition: The role of instruction in a developmental process. In R. Glaser (Ed.), *Advances in instructional psychology* (Vol. 2, pp. 1–64). Hillsdale, NJ: Lawrence Erlbaum Associates.

Berretta, M. (1990). Catene anaforiche in prospettiva funzionale: Antecedenti difficili [Anaphorical chains in functional perspective: Difficult antecedents]. *Rivista di Linguistica, 1–2,* 91–120.

Berthoud-Papandropoulou, I., & Kilcher, H. (1987). "Que faire quand on me dit de dire?" L'enfant messager des paroles d'autrui dans une situation de communication: Recherche exploratoire ["What to do when I am told to tell?" An exploratory investigation on children's reports on others' messages]. *Archives de Psychologie, 55,* 219–239.

Bissex, G. (1980). *GNYS at WRK.* Cambridge, MA: Harvard University Press.

Blanche-Benveniste, C. (1991). Le citazioni nell'orale e nello scritto [Quotations in spoken and written language]. In M. Orsolini & C. Pontecorvo (Eds.), *La costruzione del testo scritto nei bambini* (pp. 259–273). Firenze, Italy: La Nuova Italia Editrice.

Bruner J. (1990). *Acts of meaning.* Cambridge, MA: Harvard University Press.

Chafe, W. L. (1982). Integration and involvement in speaking, writing, and oral literature. In D. Tannen (Ed.), *Spoken and written language* (pp. 35–53). Norwood, NJ: Ablex.

Chafe, W. L. (1985). Linguistic differences produced by differences between speaking and writing. In D. R. Olson, N. Torrance, & A. Hildyard (Eds.), *Literacy, language and learning* (pp. 105–123). Cambridge, England: Cambridge University Press.

Devescovi, A., Orsolini, M., & Pace, C. (1989). Consapevolezza linguistica nei bambini di età prescolare [Linguistic awareness in preschool children]. *Rassegna Italiana di Linguistica Applicata, 21*(1–2), 153–178.

Ferreiro, E. (1988a). Introduction to early literacy, Special issue of *European Journal of Psychology of Education, 3*(4), 365–370.

Ferreiro, E. (1988b). L'ecriture avant la lettre [Writing before literacy]. In H. Sinclair (Ed.), *La notation grafique chez le jeune enfant: Language, nombre, rythmes et melodies* (pp. 17–70). Paris: Presses Universitaires de France.

Ferreiro, E., & Pontecorvo, C. (1993). Le découpage graphique dans des récits d'enfants entre 7 et 8 ans. Etude comparative espagnol-italien [Graphic segmentation in stories of 7- to 8-year-old Italian and Spanish children]. *Etudes de Linguistique Appliquée, 3,* 21–36.

Ferreiro, E., & Teberosky, A. (1979). *Los sistemas de escritura en el desarollo del niño* [Literacy before schooling]. Mexico: Siglo XXI Editores.

Flower, L. S., & Hayes, J. R. (1980). The dynamics of composing: Making plans, juggling constraints. In L. W. Gregg & E. R. Steinberg (Eds.), *Cognitive processes in writing* (pp. 31–50). Hillsdale, NJ: Lawrence Erlbaum Associates.

Garvey, C., & Kramer, T. L. (1989). The language of social pretend play. *Developmental Review, 9,* 364–382.

Gelb, I. J. (1963). *A study of writing.* Chicago: University of Chicago Press.

Giffin, H. (1984). The coordination of meaning in the creation of a shared make-believe reality. In I. Bretherton (Eds.), *Symbolic play: The development of social understanding* (pp. 73–101). New York: Academic Press.

Goody, J. (1968). *Literacy in traditional societies.* Cambridge, England: Cambridge University Press.

Goody, J., & Watt, I. (1963). The consequences of literacy. *Contemporary Studies in Society and History, 5,* 304–345.

Halliday, M. A. K. (1985). *Spoken and written language.* Oxford: Oxford University Press.

Harris, R. (1986). *The origin of writing.* London: Duckworth.

Harris, R. (1989). How does writing restructure thought? *Language & Communication, 9*(2–3), 99–106.

Harris, R. (1992, September). *Ecriture et notation* [Writing and notation]. Paper presented at Workshop on Orality and Literacy, ESF Network on "Written Language and Literacy," Siena, Italy.

Havelock, E. A. (1963). *Preface to Plato.* Cambridge, MA: Harvard University Press.

Havelock, E. A. (1982). *Greece and its cultural consequences.* Princeton, NJ: Princeton University Press.

Heath, S. B. (1982). What no bedtime story means: Narrative skills at home and school. *Language in Society, 11,* 49–76.

Heath, S. B. (1983). *Ways with words: Language, life and work in communities and classrooms.* Cambridge, England: Cambridge University Press.

Hickmann, M. (1985). Metapragmatics in child language. In E. Mertz & R. J. Parmentier (Eds.), *Semiotic mediation: Psychological and sociological perspectives* (pp. 177–201). New York: Academic Press.

Levin, I., & Korat, O. (in press). Sensitivity to phonological, morphological, and semantic cues. Early reading and writing in Hebrew. *Merrill-Palmer Quarterly.*

Lurçat, L. (1965). Evolution du graphisme entre trois et quatre ans. La differenciation entre le dessin et l'écriture [Graphic development between 3 and 4 years. Differentiation between drawing and writing]. *Revue de Neuropsychiatrie Enfantine, 13*(1–2), 33–44.

Lyons, J. (1977). *Semantics* (Vol. II). Cambridge, England: Cambridge University Press.

Michaels, S., & Collins, I. (1984). Oral discourse styles: Classroom interaction and the acquisition of literacy. In D. Tannen (Ed.), *Spoken and written language* (pp. 219–244). Norwood, NJ: Ablex.

Musatti, T., & Orsolini, M. (1993). Uses of past forms in the social pretend play of Italian children. *Journal of Child Language, 20,* 619–639.

Nelson, K. (1989). *Narratives from the crib.* Cambridge, MA: Harvard University Press.

Ochs, E. (1983). Planned and unplanned discourse. In E. Ochs & B. B. Schieffelin, *Acquiring conversational competence* (pp. 129–157). London: Routledge & Kegan Paul.

Olson, D. (1985). Introduction. In D. R. Olson, N. Torrance, & A. Hildyard (Eds.), *Literacy, language and learning. The nature and consequences of reading and writing* (pp. 1–15). Cambridge, England: Cambridge University Press.

Olson, D. R. (1977). The language of instruction: On the literate bias of schooling. In R. C. Anderson, R. J. Spiro, & W. E. Montague (Eds.), *Schooling and the acquisition of knowledge* (pp. 65–91). Hillsdale, NJ: Lawrence Erlbaum Associates.

Olson, D. R. (1986). The cognitive consequences of literacy. *Canadian Psychology, 27*(2), 109–121.

Olson, D. (1991, October). *What writing does to the mind.* Paper presented at the conference on Functional Literacy, Tilburg, The Netherlands.

Olson, D. R., & Astington, J. (1990). Talking about text: How literacy contributes to thought. *Journal of Pragmatics, 14*(5), 557–573.

Olson, D. R., & Torrance, N. (1987). Language, literacy, and mental states. *Discourse Processes, 10*(2), 157–167.

Ong, W. J. (1982). *Orality and literacy: The technologizing of the word.* London: Methuen.

Orsolini, M. (1993). "Because" in children's discourse. *Applied Psycholinguistics, 14,* 89–120.

Perret-Clermont, A.-N., Schubauer-Leoni, M. L., & Trognon, A. (1992). L'extorsion des responses en situation asymmetrique [Extorting answers in asymmetric situation]. *Verbum, 1/2,* 3–33.

Petrucci, A. (1978). Per la storia dell'alfabetismo e della cultura scritta [For a history of literacy and written culture]. *Quaderni Storici, 38,* 451–465.

Pontecorvo, C. (1994). Iconicity in children's first written texts. In R. Simone (Ed.), *Iconicity in language* (pp. 277–307). Amsterdam: John Benjamins.

Pontecorvo, C., & Orsolini, M. (1990, May). *Literacy as a discourse practice.* Paper presented at the 2nd International Congress for Research on Activity Theory, Lahti, Finland.

Pontecorvo, C., & Zucchermaglio, C. (1988). Modes of differentiation in children's writing construction. *European Journal of Psychology of Education, 3*(4), 371–384.

Pontecorvo, C., & Zucchermaglio, C. (1989). From oral to written language: Preschool children dictating stories. *Journal of Reading Behavior, 21*(2), 109–126.

Pontecorvo, C., & Zucchermaglio, C. (1990). A passage to literacy: Learning in a social context. In Y. Goodman (Ed.), *How children construct literacy: Piagetian perspectives* (pp. 59–93). Exeter, NH: Heinemann.

Resnick, D. P., & Resnick, L. B. (1990). Varieties of literacy. In A. E. Barnes & P. N. Stearns (Eds.), *Social history and issues in human consciousness: Some interdisciplinary connections.* New York: New York University Press.

Sampson, G. (1985). *Writing systems.* Stanford, CA: Stanford University Press.

Scribner, S., & Cole, M. (1981). *The psychology of literacy.* Cambridge, MA: Harvard University Press.

Segre, C. (1985). *Avviamento all'analisi del testo letterario* [Introduction to the analysis of literary text]. Torino, Italy: Einaudi.

Sinclair, H. (1982). El desarollo de la escritura: Avances, problemas y perspectivas [The development of writing: Advances, problems and perspectives]. In E. Ferreiro & M. Gomez Palacio (Eds.), *Nuevas perspectivas sobre los procesos de lectura y escritura* (pp. 93–106). Mexico: Siglo XXI Editores.

Sinclair, H. (Ed.). (1988). *La notation grafique chez le jeune enfant: Language, nombre, rythmes et melodies* [Graphic notation in children: Language, number, rhythms and melodies]. Paris: Presses Universitaires de France.

Sulzby, E. (1985). Children's emergent reading of favorite storybooks: A developmental study. *Reading Research Quarterly, 20,* 458–481.

Tannen, D. (1985). Relative focus on involvement in oral and written discourse. In D. R. Olson, N. Torrance, & A. Hildyard (Eds.), *Literacy, language and learning* (pp. 124–147). Cambridge, England: Cambridge University Press.

Teberosky, A. (1982). Construccion de escrituras a través de la interaccion grupal [Construction of writing through group interaction]. In E. Ferreiro & M. Gomez Palacio (Eds.), *Nuevas perspectivas sobre los procesos de lectura y escritura* (pp. 155–178). Mexico: Siglo XXI Editores.

Teberosky, A. (1988). La dictée et la rédaction de contes entre enfants du même âge [The reciprocal dictation and composing of tales by children of the same age]. *European Journal of Psychology of Education, 3*(4), 399–414.

Teberosky, A., Tolchinsky Landsmann, L., Zelcer, J., Gomes de Morais, A., & Rincon, G. (1993). Segmentation phonologique et acquisition de l'écriture: Une étude dans deux systèmes orthographiques [Phonological segmentation and writing acquisition: A study in two writing systems]. *Etudes de Linguistique Appliquée, 3,* 41–56.

Tolchinsky Landsmann, L. (1988). Form and meaning in the development of writing. *European Journal of Psychology of Education, 3*(4), 385–398.

Torrance, N., & Olson, D. R. (1987). Development of the metalanguage and the acquisition of literacy. *Interchange, 18*(1–2), 136–146.

Van Gessel-Hotcker, R. (1989). *Communication épiludique verbale dans le jeu de fiction chez les enfants entre 3 et 5 ans en interaction spontanée dans la crèche* [Verbal communication in the pretend play of children aged 3 and 5]. Unpublished doctoral dissertation, Université de Genève, Switzerland.

Wolf, D., & Hicks, D. (1989). The voices within narratives: The development of intertextuality in young children's stories. *Discourse Processes, 12,* 329–351.

Zucchermaglio, C. (1991). *Gli apprendisti della lingua scritta* [The apprentices of written language]. Bologna, Italy: Il Mulino.

2

ROLES OF ORAL AND WRITTEN LANGUAGE AS CHILDREN APPROACH CONVENTIONAL LITERACY

Elizabeth Sulzby
The University of Michigan

This chapter presents theoretical ideas about the nature of the transition that children make from emergent to conventional literacy and about how they use oral and written language in literacy episodes during this period. The chapter is written from the perspective of emergent literacy. Research has shown convincingly that young children know much about reading and writing long before they become conventional readers and writers (Bus & van IJzendoorn, 1988a, in press; Clay, 1966; Ferreiro & Teberosky, 1982; Mason & Allen, 1986; Sulzby, 1983, 1994; Sulzby & Teale, 1991; Teale, 1987). What they know, however, is qualitatively different from the knowledge of a literate adult. Some researchers (Barnhart, 1988; Ferreiro & Teberosky, 1982) have shown that school instruction that assumes an adult, conventional set of understandings about print begins for many children long before they in fact hold such understandings. Such instruction ignores children's emergent literacy development and the nature of their transitions into conventional literacy.

Emergent literacy research has tended to end at the point where research in early literacy or beginning reading used to begin: with the child's first transition into conventional literacy. Emergent literacy replaces the earlier notion of reading readiness as a period preceding reading by treating the emergent development as legitimate parts of reading and writing development rather than as a totally new development. Research in emergent literacy, such as that by many authors in this volume, represents an important step forward in recognizing the continuity of emergent literacy development with what comes afterward. As Teale and Sulzby (1986) stressed, however, the term *emergent* connotes both continuity and discontinuity in development. It is time once again to reexamine some of the discontinuity in development and to follow children's development into becoming conventional readers and writers.

My definition of emergent literacy (see Sulzby, 1989), "the reading and writing behaviors and concepts of young children that precede and develop into conventional literacy" (p. 88), focuses rather specifically on discontinuity within another previously ill-defined arena of study: conventional literacy. In this chapter, I address what I mean by emergent and conventional literacy, offer a set of working definitions of conventional literacy, and discuss some ways that young children use oral and written language in their reading and writing behaviors in two specific kinds of tasks (i.e., storybook reading and story writing) as they approach conventional literacy.

My discussion addresses the nature of the transition for English-speaking children primarily, because the English alphabetic system has features not necessarily shared by all alphabetic systems (cf. the work of Ferreiro & Teberosky, 1982, on Spanish-speaking children). English requires a step beyond the phonetic level, to what Chomsky and Halle (1968) called *morphophonemic* (although I am not sure that it is an adequate term). Although other alphabetic systems also include degrees of morphophonemic knowledge, English does so to a degree that it has often been described by casual observers as nonphonetic. In English, many cues to etymological relatedness are available across form cases and are revealed in different stress patterns within the word, shifting phonetic patterns. (And, of course, as in all languages, speakers from different regions tend to have different pronunciation patterns.) The result is that children need much flexibility with the phonemic system and also attentiveness to graphemic patterns, elements that they show in the process of becoming conventional readers and writers.

A word of warning should be given here. At first, this introduction may sound as if I am proposing a stage theory. I am not doing that, except in the broadest sense; instead, as I discuss emergent storybook reading and writing, I return to this issue and propose what I call a *repertoire theory of language development*, with a sociocultural as well as psycholinguistic base.

CONVENTIONAL LITERACY

Having opened the door to considering emergent literacy behaviors (e.g., scribbling and reading from pictures) to be legitimate parts of literacy, we must now reconsider what behaviors and understandings would be necessary for the child to move from emergent to conventional literacy. I consider a child to be reading conventionally when he or she is able to understand a written text, attend to and use the print cues provided by the author, and move in a flexible and coordinated fashion across various aspects or strategies in order to obtain understanding satisfactory to the reader (Sulzby, 1985).[1] Operationally, I have suggested that children do not need to have mastered all preceding knowledge in order to read in this manner, building on the theory that reading is a coordinated set of knowledges organized to be accessed interactively (Rumelhart, 1977). This will become clearer when I discuss the developmental patterns of storybook reading, a subset of reading that has attained a cultural position of honor with attendant well-known routinized speech behaviors in many literate societies, including those in the United States.

Conventional writing is more elusive. First, parents and the child's literacy environments appear to have many variable ways of scaffolding children's writing interactions. Second, the onset does not appear to be as dramatic as does that of reading, although in both cases the onset actually is gradual. For now, I define *conventional writing* as being written connected discourse that another conventionally literate person can read without too much difficulty and that the child can read conventionally (see Sulzby, 1989). To write in this manner, the child needs to have coordinated the same aspects that were coordinated in conventional reading.

To read conventionally, I have argued (Sulzby, 1983), the child needs to have some but not total understanding of the following three aspects, defined developmentally: knowledge of letter–sound relationships; realization that the word is a stable, memorable unit; and a sense of text comprehension, including the idea that text also is a stable, memorable object. Each of these aspects has its own developmental path for the emergent readers and writer, and these paths may not yet be fully developed; they are not necessarily the same for each child.

From this definition, new text becomes a predictable entity for a reader, and old text, including one's own writing, becomes a stable entity in memory that can be retrieved from memory as well as through using prediction. Comprehension monitoring becomes a checking of the child's text rendering with the conception held in memory, whether that conception is derived predictively or memorially. There is also a key affective component in conventional reading and writing; a child's conception of his or her own knowledge has become confirmed in action so that the child believes that he or she can read or write and can persevere across problematic areas by using strategies flexibly. Reaching this period of knowledge and belief is a long developmental process, highly affected by the social environment.

---

[1]There are three sets of "standards" operating here: the author's seeming intention for the text, the reader's sense of satisfaction, and the judgment that the child is strategically gaining information from the three sources or aspects (letter–sound, word, and comprehension of text, each discussed later). But we must ask which of these judgments counts or matters in particular instances. This definition is tendered for use by a literate adult knowledgeable about literacy development. We do not know definitively what standards children use to judge that they are reading conventionally. We do know that they fluctuate in their judgments and the bases for them. The knowledgeable, literate adult would be dependent on the child's demonstrated behavior, including the expression of satisfaction in understanding.

I focus first on differing ideas about the relationships of oral and written language within language acquisition during the preschool years. Then I describe patterns of children's use of oral and written language features in emergent storybook reading and story writing tasks. Both of these tasks have been used in lines of research that I have pursued for a number of years. The aspects of reading are reviewed in relation to children's emergent storybook reading behaviors; then they are compared with some characteristics in children's emergent writing and rereading from writing. Finally, I comment on key features of oral language in literacy episodes as the child approaches conventional literacy.

ORAL LANGUAGE, WRITTEN LANGUAGE, AND THE YOUNG CHILD

Previously, children were thought to acquire oral language in their homes, and then, at school age (the equivalent of kindergarten or first grade or whenever formal reading instruction starts), to begin to learn written language. *Language* was equated with oral language, and *literacy* was something related to but quite different from oral language. More recent research has shown that, during infancy and the preschool years, children acquire written language alongside oral language and that the two are intertwined and interrelated, changing their relationships during the process of the child's development (Harste, Woodward, & Burke, 1984; Sulzby, 1983; Sulzby & Teale, 1987; Teale, 1987). The theoretical framework guiding my work assumes that each child acquires the abilities to read and to write within a culture in which both oral and written language are being acquired simultaneously, and that the two together comprise "language." An important part of the child's language task is to work out the interrelationships between oral and written language that are sanctioned in different social situations within his or her culture.

This position differs considerably from earlier views in which the child was assumed to acquire oral language readily, rapidly, and painlessly, with little direct tuition, and, later, to acquire reading and writing as somewhat artificial second-level coding systems (Bloomfield, 1933; Chomsky, 1985; Jesperson, 1938/1968; Pyles, 1971; see Sulzby, 1987), requiring much instruction. Many other researchers (Chafe, 1982; Hyon & Sulzby, 1994; Michaels, 1991; Michaels & Cazden, 1986; Scollon & Scollon, 1981; Snow, 1983; Sulzby & Teale, 1987; Tannen, 1982) have begun to investigate the relationships between oral and written language usage across cultures and social/cultural situations, showing that our earlier ideas of language have been limited and that the relationships between oral and written language, although complex and somewhat fluid, are important to our understanding of how children and adults use language.

Thus, one way to examine emergent literacy is to observe how children sort out the relationships between oral and written language that exist in their culture. My work has stressed the necessity for separating the nature of oral and written language, as systematic linguistic patterns used in particular kinds of situations, from their physiological delivery forms (Sulzby, 1986a). Thus, a child can be observed to "speak written language" or to "write oral language." To signal this distinction as well as the constructive nature of children's development, I often use the terms *writtenlike language* and *orallike language*. I use the term *language* to encompass both oral language and written language and also the communicative competence needed to select appropriate linguistic devices for oral and written situations.

In this regard, children provide a wonderful challenge to our assumptions about oral and written language during the period in which they become conventionally literate. My interest in this topic has led me to use particular research designs to study emergent literacy. I have designed situations in which children are asked to read and write before they are conventionally literate. The major tasks I have used are asking a child to read a favorite storybook that has been read to him or her repeatedly or asking a child to write and reread a story of his or her own composition. Both are acts involving connected discourse that traditionally call on certain linguistic devices to meet the constraints of the situations. They also call on the cultural standards that have been sanctioned and shared in such situations as reading formally published books or negotiating and discussing family letters, bills, or application forms. The language used in the book or composed text should be "decontextualized" sufficiently for a nonpresent audience to comprehend it without the context surrounding the writer at the time of composition (Olson, 1977; Ong, 1982; Scollon & Scollon, 1981). By watching the compositional and comprehension behaviors of young children, we can see how a young language user sorts out these constraints in a given operational situation of communicating.

My studies of emergent storybook reading (Sulzby, 1985, 1994) have demonstrated that younger children use characteristics of conversational language and of the oral monologue in storybook reading attempts and that, as they gain experience, they gradually adjust their speech toward the form of a written monologue—that sounds like an uninterrupted speech composed for a written format. Teale and I (Sulzby & Teale, 1987) found that parents of both low- and middle-income Anglo and Hispanic children who are in the habit of reading storybooks to their children gradually scaffold a given child's language from dialogic exchanges into that of the storybook, adjusting their language to the needs of the child. Pellegrini and his colleagues (Pellegrini, Brody, & Sigel, 1985; Pellegrini, Perlmutter, Galda, & Brody, 1990) found similar adjustments to the child's level of development with some parents of African-American Head Start children, whereas others (Edwards, 1989; Heath with Thomas, 1984) have found that other parents of such children seem to lack strategies for scaffolding sufficiently for children but are able to respond to intervention.

In my research, colleagues and I have studied acts of reading and writing and the language and nonverbal responses that surround it. We have listened to children's speech samples to determine if they contain features of written language, and we have analyzed children's written products or transcripts to determine if they contain features of oral language and vice versa. We have looked for the communicative competence of the child in switching appropriately from oral to written usage in oral and written situations and in giving clear signals of the switches being made. With the kind of distinctions summarized here, the transition into conventional literacy can only be considered part of a lifelong developmental path into highly developed literacy. Nonetheless, the remainder of this chapter focuses on the period just preceding the child's first becoming conventionally literate.

EMERGENT STORYBOOK READING AND ASPECTS OF READING

My research in storybook reading began in 1979, when about half of the children in a suburban kindergarten class outside Chicago, Illinois, began "reading" when asked to "tell me about your book" in a metacognitive interview about reading and writing. Their behavior was remarkable in that, although displayed over a wide range, each child's intonation and wording shifted when entering this new situation. Some children shifted to less complex language than they had just used in conversational exchanges; others shifted to more complex syntactic and lexical choices and to a reading intonation.

After that time, I asked children to "read" from favorite storybooks, either those that they selected themselves or that their teachers or parents had read to them repeatedly. The behaviors that the children displayed seem to fall into a classification scheme with developmental properties, known as the Sulzby (1985, 1994) Classification Scheme for Emergent Reading of Favorite Storybooks.[2] That is, younger children show a predominance of the behaviors that lie high in the tree structure shown in Fig. 2.1, whereas older children cluster around the lower branches. The major categories of emergent storybook reading are picture-governed reading, stories not formed; picture-governed reading, oral languagelike stories formed; picture-governed reading, written languagelike stories formed; and print-governed reading.

---

[2]*Children* in this context refers to children who have been read to and who engage in emergent reading attempts. We have found these behaviors in the United States across ethnic and income levels but with some predictable cultural differences across speakers from different groups. Independent reading attempts have also been elicited from children from low and middle socioeconomic groups who have been read to repeatedly in research studies in the Netherlands (Bus & van IJzendoorn, 1988a, in press; Bus, van IJzendoorn, & Sulzby, 1994–1995 unpublished videotaped raw data).

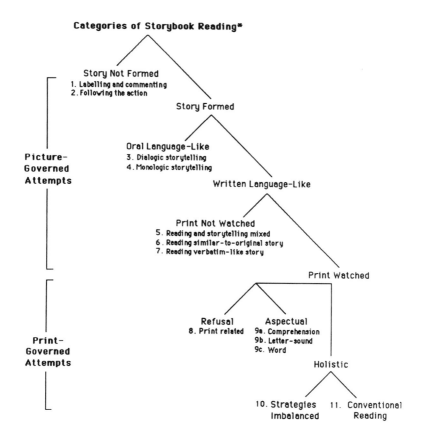

Categories of Storybook Reading*

Story Not Formed
1. Labelling and commenting
2. Following the action

Story Formed

Oral Language-Like
3. Dialogic storytelling
4. Monologic storytelling

Picture-
Governed
Attempts

Written Language-Like

Print Not Watched
5. Reading and storytelling mixed
6. Reading similar-to-original story
7. Reading verbatim-like story

Print Watched

Refusal   Aspectual
8. Print related   9a. Comprehension
                    9b. Letter-sound
                    9c. Word

Print-
Governed
Attempts

Holistic

10. Strategies   11. Conventional
    Imbalanced   Reading

---

* This figure includes independent reading attempts only: the child is making the reading attempts without dependence upon turn-taking reading or interrogation by the adult.

FIG. 2.1. Sulzby Classification Scheme for Emergent Reading of Favorite Storybooks. From E. Sulzby (1985). Children's emergent reading of favorite storybooks: A developmental study. *Reading Research Quarterly, 20,* 458–481. Copyright 1985 by the International Reading Association. Reprinted by permission.

From age 2 or so until the point at which they begin to read primarily attending to print (print-governed reading), children display a number of abilities pertinent to examining their transitions into conventional literacy. Children engage in scaffolded conversation; they construct oral monologues that have the features of oral storytelling for a present audience; they create written monologues (delivered orally) that have intonation, syntactic structure, and lexical choices appropriate to a written situation. Early on, a listener would have some difficulty distinguishing between children's speech used for reading and their speech addressed to a listener. Gradually, children's speech and paralinguistic behaviors begin to contain clear signals of switches between "reading" and "talking" to a listener. Example 1 contains a transcript from a 4-year-old girl who makes clear switches between reading and talking; her "reading" speech has been italicized.

Example 1

Text	Child's Storybook Reading
(Page 16)	*He fell out of the tree.* (looking at right
DOWN, OUT OF THE TREE HE WENT.	page) *It was a l-ong, way down.*
	(pauses, looks across room then
	makes a comment, an aside, to adult)
	Some, sometimes I—get water from
	that drinking fountain (points) and I
	take it into the /water/.
	(referring to fountain outside door)
	Adult: Uh-hmm.
	Child: (laughs, seeming to catch her
	mistake) I mean into the room.
	(turns to pp. 17–18, props up book)
(Page 17)	
DOWN, DOWN, DOWN! IT WAS A	
LONG WAY DOWN.	
(Page 18)	Child: *He looked around. He did not*
THE BABY BIRD COULD NOT FLY.	*see her.* (glances from page to page
	without lingering long on either;
	turns to p. 20)

This child pointed to print most of the time throughout the book, usually with a bottom-to-top, right-to-left sweep; she was classified as "reading aspectually" with a focus on comprehension. After her aside about the drinking fountain, she returned to the reading attempt, marking the shifts from and back to reading clearly with the direction of her gaze, intonation, choice of lexical items, and syntactic structures.

Oral and Written Monologues
(Reading Attempts With Pictures)

The Sulzby Classification Scheme sorts children's reading attempts (sometimes called *reading reenactments*) according to several criteria, but the primary distinction is made at the level of the total structure. Various features, including intonation, syntax, and lexical choice, are described elsewhere (Sulzby, 1985; Sulzby & Zecker, 1991), but all are subordinated to the judgment about the text as a whole. The contrast between an oral monologue (monologic storytelling) and written monologue (reading similar-to-original story and reading verbatim-like story) provides very clear contrastive contexts for examining children's concepts for oral and written discourse. In both of these types of emergent readings, pictures are the focus of children's attention. An *oral monologue* is a storybook reading attempt that sounds as if it is "a story told face-to-face" (Sulzby, 1985, p. 468). Although the story forms a whole, it is contextualized to the pictures that both the reader and listener can see, using referential devices that extend outside the text words, exophorically, using intonational features to construct shared meaning. The intonation sounds like storytelling rather than reading. In contrast, written monologues consist of language so decontextualized (or recontextualized) that they can be understood, largely without reference to the present context between reader and listener, including the text's pictures. The child's intonation is like that of a reader.

Oral and written monologues are interesting because they can be formed as equally complex structures and yet use many quite different linguistic devices. In recent years, my colleagues and I have begun examining whether some of these features can be perceived independently of the judgments on the structural whole. When independent raters have attempted to use the classification scheme by checking off the presence or absence of the separate features, this procedure has typically led them to erroneous classifications. Hence, we approached the question from another perspective: We examined whether, once the broad structural classifications were made, the separate features were nevertheless perceptible in some fashion.

First, we (Reuning, 1986; Sulzby & Reuning-Hegland, in preparation) tested whether judges who were blind to conditions could distinguish between storytelling and reading intonation independent of syntax and lexical choice. Comparable sections of reading attempts were selected that we had judged to be oral languagelike and written languagelike. When a filter was placed over children's speech, blocking out the understanding of words and leaving the intonational curves, judges were able to distinguish reliably between storytelling and reading intonation.

Sulzby and Zecker (1991) examined linguistic features of children's story reading attempts independently of intonation. We examined transcripts of Spanish-speaking children's reading attempts that had previously been classified at the structural level by using the Sulzby scheme as being either oral or written monologues, using verbatimlike stories as the extreme version of the written monologue.[3] We drew heavily on the work of Chafe (1982) for relevant contrasts. As expected, written monologues had more instances of dialogue carriers placed after quoted speech. In contrast with oral monologues, the children's written

---

[3]This is a further analysis of Sulzby data reported in Sulzby and Teale (1987). The children were kindergartners, newly immigrated to the United States from Mexico. The transcripts were in Spanish and translated into English. Analyses reported here were done on the original Spanish versions.

monologues more frequently introduced characters explicitly, used appropriate determiners, and used explicit subjects (S-P clauses rather than the acceptable P clause structure for Spanish). Contrary to descriptions by Chafe (1982) and Olson (1977), children used introductory coordinating conjunctions equally frequently in both oral and written monologues (i.e., they began sentences with *and* or *and then* [*y, y despues*]). It is our impression (untested as yet) that intonational information was used to override information from simple coordinating conjunctions in the initial position. That is, these Spanish–English bilingual children use clearer sentence-final intonation and sentence-initial intake of breath in written monologues than in oral monologues.

While children are mastering these features of written language, they are also mastering two other strategies that are important in the transition to conventional literacy: prediction and comprehension monitoring. Both are critical to text comprehension.

Prediction of expected text in emergent storybook reading is often seen in overgeneralizations of written language patterns. Some children insert "sets of threes" or other literary devices in a text that does not contain them. Some make excessive use of patterns that are present, such as specifying speakers in dialogue carriers, as shown in Example 2. The original text (Eastman's *Are you my mother?*) read, "Then he came to a dog. 'Are you my mother?' he said to the dog." The reference to "he" for "the baby bird" was clear from the preceding text. In the example, the child overspecified both the placement of dialogue carriers and lexicalization of the participants.

Example 2

Child: The baby bird said to the dog: "Are you my mother?" said the baby bird to the dog.

Second, and critically tied to prediction, is comprehension monitoring as seen in self-corrections. In oral monologues and dialogic storytelling forms of emergent storybook reading and in face-to-face conversational speech, children typically use online monitoring and corrections such as, "The mo—baby bird was walking." In written monologues, repairs tend to be made more deliberately, with clearer signaling, such as, "The mo—, no, I mean, the *baby* bird was walking." This is often seen when a child stops reciting a favorite storybook on a particular page and asks the adult to "read that one, 'cause I forgot it." Some children then recite the page again, making changes more consistent with their ongoing text construction rather than taking the adult's reading as sufficient and just going on to the next section.

The preceding discussion has focused on children's reading attempts before they use print as a primary source of what is read. From studying children's emergent storybook reading just before they attend consistently to print, we can see that they are developing a number of key reading behaviors. They use "reading intonation," a staccato, deliberative, word-by-word rendering of speech.[4] This involves segmentation of the speech flow into individual words. This segmentation can also be seen in self-corrections such as those described earlier and particularly those in which a child slowly repeats or quotes his or her own speech, highlighting the problematic word or phrase: "I mean, the *baby bird*." Children use syntax and word choices appropriate to written language, especially that of the book itself. Children actively construct a given text in light of a mental representation, evidence of which is reflected in prediction and self-correction. The ability to predict what a text is expected to be like and to monitor the production against the expected model is particularly important as children begin to use print cues more deliberately.

In the preceding examples of prediction and comprehension monitoring, each child was actually creating a text quite a bit different from the printed text. Yet, each such child showed the growth of internal expectations that a text will be stable, memorable, retrievable, and correctable; the child can depend on the text and correct his or her reading behaviors and strategies in reacting to the text. However, we should also note that, overall during this period of development, children's speech in emergent reading becomes more verbatimlike, so that predictions from memory and construction are more likely to match the printed text, particularly because children are also constructing other reading behaviors and understandings during this time.

During the period in which children are reading storybooks emergently while looking at pictures, many other things have been going on in their literacy development, involving other tasks and situations. They have been learning to recognize some conventional words, in Ferreiro's (1986) sense of a *stable string*. They have probably also been learning some letter–sound relationships and may be beginning to use invented spelling or sounding out for some isolated words. Children often show signs of this growing ability by interrupting a written monologue to identify salient print, perhaps in an illustration. It appears that, even before acting as if print is what gets read in storybooks, children are actively constructing all three aspects of reading: comprehension, letter–sound relationships, and word knowledge. The next section examines the three aspects in more detail.

Print-Governed Reading: An Overview

As shown in Fig. 2.1, much development occurs after the child begins to treat the printed text as the source of what gets read in reading. As we see, the child does not treat the printed text simply as an object of deciphering (in Ferreiro

---

[4]They may also use another form of reading intonation, which Reuning (1986) described as sounding like an expressive oral reader.

& Teberosky's sense, 1982; cf. Juel, 1988) but as a source of comprehension, a source from which the child constructs meaning.

There are four subcategories of print-governed reading attempts. The first is "refusing to read based on print awareness." In this, children state specifically or indicate behaviorally that they cannot read the print. Many children mention one or more of the three aspects of reading, stated negatively: I cannot read because I don't know those words; because I can't sound those [words] out; because I don't know it [the text]. The latter point is often made along with a request for the adult to read a page or more to the child.

When a child refuses to read, we typically initiate supported or interactive reading, hoping to shift the child to an independent reading attempt as soon as possible. In supported or interactive reading at this level, the child may point to parts of the print and ask the adult to read it.

The second subcategory of reading with attention to print is "reading aspectually." This subcategory has three functionally equivalent parts, because the child now breaks the act of reading apart to focus, separately, on three aspects. These aspects are explained in detail later in the chapter.

Third is the subcategory just prior to reading independently from print: "reading with strategies imbalanced." In this, the child has put the aspects of reading back together sufficiently to construct a whole text while attending to print but, when faced with difficulty, overdepends on one or more of the separate aspects.

The final subcategory, "reading independently," marks either a sudden or gradually growing awareness by the child that he or she can go back and forth across the aspects of reading in order to make sense of the text. As the child reads, often an observer gets the impression of automaticity, as if the aspects are skillfully internalized, but when the child miscues, an observer can note the coordinated use of the separable aspects.

Katy (age 5) was reading a storybook section in which an owl character hoots as well as speaks. The book author had played around with the relationship between the hooting sound and what the owl "says." (The dialogue carriers were also shifted away from the typical format.) Katy wrestled with the actual print, its possible interpretation, and responded with annoyance, after checking letter–sound, word, and comprehension aspects.

Example 3

Text	Child
"NOW IS THE TIME FOR FUN," HE SAID. "WHO," SAID SAM, "WHO! WHO WANTS TO PLAY?"	*Now is the time for fun. He asked who* . . . —asked *who?* /a/ - /s/, Said *who?*! *That* doesn't make sense! Said *who?* Said *what?* This is *stupid!*

Often, children's requests for such aid reveal the use of all aspects of reading, followed by an appeal for assistance or a rejection of the text as being evidently miswritten, or, as Katy put it, "Stupid!"

The independent or conventional reader can be described as being both less textbound and yet more accurate in reproducing both the wording and the author's intended meaning; there is, in other words, clear evidence of predicting and confirming strategies (Sulzby, 1985).

I have described the classification scheme (Fig. 2.1) as providing a developmental ordering that should vary according to how deeply embedded literacy is within cultural practices that involve children. Thus, it is far from a stage theory of the universal sort; rather, the behaviors may seem stagelike only because the storybook routine is very deeply embedded in so-called mainstream culture. With those U.S. children from groups with storybook reading quite firmly embedded in family practice, the subcategory of the oral monologue is not found frequently. These children move back and forth between "reading dialogically" and "reading and storytelling mixed." In families in which oral storytelling is more honored and reading to children less important, one would expect a higher frequency of oral monologues. Indeed, oral monologues were found somewhat more frequently in U.S. classrooms with children of lower socioeconomic status (LSES) and Appalachian heritage and much more frequently in the Spanish emergent readings of LSES children of recent Mexican immigration (Sulzby & Teale, 1987; Sulzby & Zecker, 1981).

As our research has progressed, we have found more evidence that the categories and subcategories of storybook reading (Sulzby, 1985, 1994) have psychological reality within the constraints of this social situation: storybooks have been read to the child frequently and repeatedly; an adult requests or listens to a reading in an expectant, confident manner; and this occurs in a nonthreatening instructional environment (at home or school). One subcategory, "reading aspectually," was advanced with caution earlier (Sulzby, 1985). This subcategory appears now to be fairly well established and to have important implications in the transition to conventional literacy. Because it seems to be a period in which children pull together and analyze their growing knowledges from other areas such as phonological awareness, letter exploration, invented spelling, memorized words, and comprehension strategies, reading aspectually deserves careful consideration.

An Examination of Reading Aspectually

As described in the overview, reading aspectually is a three-part subcategory in which the child focuses on one aspect of reading at a time, although he or she may shift across aspects within one reading attempt. Reading aspectually follows the print-based refusal subcategory—a refusal to read based on specifically stated or demonstrated awareness that the print is read and that the child believes he or she lacks specific knowledge. As mentioned earlier, these refusals are often tied to one or more of the three aspects seen in reading aspectually. It immediately precedes the subcategory of reading with strategies imbalanced in which the strategies are used to track visually and read from connected text but children use an overemphasis on one or more aspects, in contrast with reading conventionally, when they call on all aspects in a flexible and coordinated manner in order to construct meaning.

When reading aspectually, the child tries to read and focuses attention on one or more aspects, while neglecting the rest. The child may seem to regress from the high level of comprehension seen in the subcategories of reading similar to original story or reading verbatimlike. Although the aspects are described as if they are separate, a number of children (Sulzby, 1985; Teale, 1985) move back and forth across aspects within a given text.

A child may begin to read a text that he or she has previously read monologically but now may focus on letter–sound knowledge, sounding out words endlessly, phoneme by phoneme, and often blending the sounds into nonsense words. Or the child may focus on the aspect of known words, going through a familiar text, just picking out a list of words he or she recognizes. This usually comprises an odd, sometimes repetitive list, such as "Grandma, the, and, the, a, and." The comprehension aspectual focus appears on the surface to be most like the "reading monologically" behavior, except that now children are attending to print fairly consistently. There is some evidence that there may be a memory decrement for the same child reading aspectually with a comprehension focus, in contrast with reading monologically.

The three aspects are presumed to be functionally equivalent, and there is some evidence that this is the case. It appears that children are more specifically aware of the aspects of reading and of their ability to focus attention on and practice the aspects. Here, in letter–sound and word aspects, children are coordinating explorations in reading from other contexts such as copying environmental print, writing stable strings (Ferreiro, 1986), sounding out words in invented spelling, or focusing on phonemic awareness or word writing, often from instructional activities. Certainly, the impact of *Sesame Street* and other informal lessons via games or television should not be ignored.

I call attention to the aspects of reading for several reasons, one of which is the reviving visibility of research focusing on linguistic awareness, including phonemic awareness (see Adams, 1990; Juel, 1988; Juel, Griffith, & Gough, 1986; Stanovich, 1986; Sulzby & Teale, 1991). Linguistic awareness research as a broad area focuses on all the aspects of reading just described. Research in which the question is whether or not phonemic awareness precedes and/or predicts reading appears to need reframing in light of the evidence that all aspects are developing prior to the transition into conventional reading and that all appear to be involved in the transition itself. The degree to which children must have conscious, metacognitive awareness of all of these aspects of literacy has not yet been sufficiently addressed.

EMERGENT WRITING AND REREADING

Most of my research on emergent writing (Sulzby, 1983, 1986a, 1989; Sulzby, Barnhart, & Hieshima, 1989) has focused on story writing and rereading. In these studies, children are asked to "write a story" and then "read me your story," with a rationale, such as "to see if it is just the way you want it to be." Children typically write in response to these elicitations using forms such as scribble, drawing, nonphonetic letter strings, invented spelling, and conventional-appearing orthography. The forms that children use to write with are only relative indicators of the children's underlying concepts about literacy; these forms of writing need to be compared with children's composing language and rereading language. Rather than progressing from scribbling and drawing through nonphonetic letter strings into invented and conventional orthography, children appear to move back and forth across forms, often using nonletter-based forms even after they seem to have good control of invented spelling.

There is some evidence that they begin to make judgments that indicate a hierarchy of sorts across the forms that do not include drawing (Shatz, Kamberelis, Halle, & Sulzby, 1991). In production, however, forms do not seem to be abandoned. Rather, the transitions appear to be the addition of new forms to a repertoire of forms, at least until the child becomes fluent in producing and has a good understanding of conventional orthography. The forms of rereading are similar to those of emergent storybook reading, but are often more difficult to judge because of the variation in length across children's stories and the relative brevity of children's written compositions in contrast with their storybook readings.

As the child nears conventional writing, two sets of behaviors are important. First, the child shows evidence of treating reading as a stable activity. The child may recite a text stably across attempts to read, even from unreadable texts such as those in scribble, drawing, nonphonetic letter strings, and pseudoletters. A text is operationally defined as stable if it contains the same semantic content in the same order (Sulzby, 1983, 1985; Sulzby, Barnhart, & Hieshima, 1989). As he or she nears conventional writing, however, the child may show additional signs of stability, such as running his or her finger along the text while reciting the words and making finger, voice, and print end simultaneously. Or, the child may match rereading speech to compositional speech. Other children achieve a match by elongating their speech, recycling speech, or recursively adding graphic text until their speech is done.

Second, the child begins to write texts that are readable to other conventionally literate people, particularly if they observed the child encoding phonetically (i.e., using invented spelling). At first, the texts may degenerate in length from the child's typical spoken speech for writing, often being only one clause or partial clause in length. Then the child increases in fluency and writes longer texts.

When children first write in invented spelling, a large percentage do not at first use the print as if it were decodable. Some children, when probed, do not locate specific words in the texts that they just sounded out to encode them (Kamberelis & Sulzby, 1988). In samples taken every 3 months from kindergarten through first grade, we saw this in 35% of the children (16 out of 46 children). An additional eight children used the text aspectually, for a total of 52% (24 of 46). In other words, they do not decode phonetically from texts that they just encoded phonetically. After they become more fluent with invented spelling, they do use the text for decoding.

As children become conventionally literate in writing, they often play around with linguistic patterns found in published books to which they have been exposed. In *The Three Bugs* (Fig. 2.2), the child begins her story with "Once there was . . ." and names the two characters Harry and Marry. She uses dialogue carriers specifying at least one participant placed in front of the quoted speech but in past tense, a fairly advanced set of devices. It is possible that the dialogue carrier in the first quotation includes both participants, but the missing punctuation creates ambiguity ("One day Harry asked Marry" or "One day Harry asked, 'Marry . . .' "). When she switches to having the characters interchange unmarked dialogue, the context is short enough to allow the reader to understand who the speakers are in the exchanges. Later, she uses punctuation, a colon, to introduce Marry's declaration that she's going to have a baby. This text appears to consist of quite an elaborate pun, including both the letter-based text and the picture.

Quoted speech is an interesting part of writing development, because in it we find oral speech that the child is attempting to reproduce in a transformed way. From the work on storybook reading and the literature on oral and written language relationships (Chafe, 1982; Ochs, 1979; Sulzby, 1986b; Tannen, 1982), I have constructed the following somewhat hierarchical scheme for the use of quoted speech in written text, as shown in emergent reading and writing. Children do not use them in all instances of writing or emergent reading; hence, their presence may not be detected easily. In handwritten composition, we are looking for the first appearance of a given usage as at least one indicator of new development. As with the forms of writing, these usages for showing quoted speech do not seem to disappear but instead to be transformed and used in a repertoire of linguistic devices. This exploratory version of the Sulzby scheme for classifying quoted speech is shown in the following summary:

- Voices—using, for example, different intonation, pitch, mannerisms for different speakers.
- Dialogue without dialogue carriers (which may be unclear).

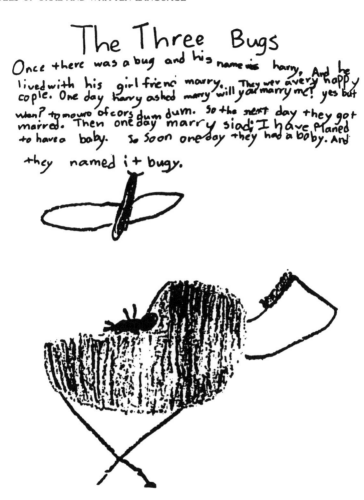

The Three Bugs

Once there was a bug and his name is harry. And he lived with his girl frienc marry. They wer a very happy cople. One day harry asked marry will you marry me? yes but when? to mowro of cors dum dum. So the next day they got marred. Then one day marry siad, I have planed to have a baby. So soon one day they had a boby. And they named it bugy.

FIG. 2.2. *The Three Bugs*: Story written in invented spelling and conventional orthography.

- Oral languagelike dialogue carriers (He says "I want my mother.").
- Dialogue carriers, past tense, first position (He said, "I want my mother.").
- Dialogue carriers, past tense, last position ("I want my mother," he said.).
- Dialogue with inserted dialogue carriers ("How can I be your mother?" *he said*, "I am a cow!" or "How," *he said*, "could I be your mother?").
- Indirect quotation in exposition (Then the baby bird went up to him and asked was he his mother.).
- Direct and indirect quotations used in narrative with clear signals to aid the reader or with adequate assumptions about readers' expectations.

Over the years, we have followed the writing development of a number of children from kindergarten through first grade. We are currently reexamining the transcripts of children composing and rereading stories to trace the evolution of children's increasingly sophisticated means of dealing with quoted speech and their metalinguistic comments about this activity.

This chapter focuses on only a small part of writing development. As discussed earlier, writing presents many puzzles, because it appears in so many variations across children's development. Nonetheless, there are understandable patterns within this development. In particular, the broad transition to becoming a conventional writer, as operationalized in the research discussed here, can be observed in children's story compositions and readings of these stories.

KEY FEATURES OF ORAL LANGUAGE DURING THE TRANSITION

From infancy through the transition to conventional literacy, children's oral language grows in various ways (Sulzby, 1986a), many of which seem to have little to do with written language situations. Some key features that can be seen in emergent literacy interactions during the transitions to conventional reading and writing include: children use oral language to interact with others about texts or to self-correct a reading attempt, they use oral language in interacting with others about ideas removed from the reading activity (e.g., asides), and they use oral speech with written languagelike patterns that show overgeneralizations from reading (i.e., "talking like a book"). As seen earlier, such interactions occur within the child's storybook reading as well as during composition and rereading.

In Example 3, Katy sounded angry when she denounced the stupidity of the text as she read it with her mother; she thus gave evidence of monitoring her own reading process. Later in the session, she interrupted the text reading to talk about another, related topic. In both instances, she (as well as most children at these advanced levels) gave clear intonational and wording signals that certain speech was reading and other speech was talking to the listener.

Most startling, however, are instances in which children overgeneralize written language patterns to oral situations. In an example from our unpublished data, George Kamberelis asked a child how she had learned to read. She began to "tell" him how in reading intonation, using literary devices in her speech. In another example (Sulzby, 1986b), a boy who had been asked to tell about a story he had written recited the story as if he were reading it. Then, when asked to read the story, he replied, in an indignant tone, that he had read it already. Similarly, Martinez, Cheyney, and Teale (1991) reported witnessing kindergartners using book language in their creation of spontaneous classroom plays.

Such exchanges suggest that children may be adding to their linguistic repertoires at least two quite complex new embryonic elements that literate adults possess. One is the ability to "speak like a book," a technique used in formal speech making or improvised formal presentations such as television interviews. Second, the child may be developing the ability to construct written language that sounds as if it were designed to be read as if it were spoken orally, often by many different speakers. This ability is seen in well-crafted novels such as Marquez' *One Hundred Years of Solitude* (1970), Olive Ann Burns' *Cold Sassy Tree* (1984), Lee Smith's *Fair and Tender Ladies* (1988), or Dostoyevsky's *The Brothers Karamazov* (1950).

THEORETICAL SUMMARY

In exploring the period during which children are just approaching conventional literacy, I have used the framework of emergent storybook reading and, in particular, aspectual reading to show ways in which oral and written linguistic strategies are intertwined during this period. In aspectual reading, which is composed of three functionally equivalent aspects (focus on letter–sound relationships, "known words," and comprehension), the children temporarily treat certain privileged kinds of speech (sounding out real words to nonsense words, reciting a list of known words, reciting text words while pointing to text without deciphering) as being reading. Other speech surrounding the reading may be and usually is clearly differentiated through intonational and wording cues. Then I briefly explored another means of dealing with oral and written language relationships: how the writer effectively embeds oral speech in a narrative or exposition. Based on a taxonomy constructed from storybook reading situations, I explored how child writers gradually incorporate quoted speech into their written texts.

The sources of children's knowledge seem to be multiple. Some seem random, such as which letters appear in a child's name; others, such as storybook reading, seem richly organized to furnish a culturally shared scaffolding; still others seem to vary across social groups and situations. For this latter point, writing in different genres comes to mind. Some children are taught the alphabet and letter sounds quite specifically; others are encouraged to scribble and pretend to write grocery lists; others receive help in copying from model texts to create thank-you notes; and others are encouraged to dictate messages. Some write by copying model behavior of adults writing around them. Whether or not a particular part of literacy development looks stagelike may be due primarily to how deeply embedded that practice is in the child's culture; hence, for most middle-income mainstream U.S. children, storybook reading looks stagelike and writing does not.

No matter how deeply embedded the practice is, however, I do not see children making many transitions in which they totally leave behind their previous understandings; rather, they seem to add to a growing repertoire of linguistic behaviors and understandings. An exception to this claim may be the transition into conventional literacy that is the closest to being a stagelike shift that I currently perceive, although that is a matter for further investigation (see Sulzby, 1994). The period just preceding and leading into conventional reading and writing is an incredibly rich one, bearing great import for the child's ability to develop into a highly proficient reader and writer throughout life. The transition into conventional literacy appears to be highly important, from both theoretical and practical perspectives.

ACKNOWLEDGMENTS

The writing of this chapter was supported in part by a grant, "Emergent Writing, With and Without the Computer," from the Spencer Foundation to Elizabeth Sulzby and Marilyn Shatz, and by a grant, "The Computer as an Evolving Literacy Tool," to Elizabeth Sulzby from the Center for Research in Learning and Schooling (CRLS) of the School of Education, University of Michigan, Ann Arbor.

REFERENCES

Adams, M. J. (1990). *Beginning to read: Thinking and learning about print.* Cambridge, MA: MIT Press.

Barnhart, J. E. (1988). The relationship between graphic forms and the child's underlying conceptualization of writing. *National Reading Conference Yearbook, 37,* 297–306.

Bloomfield, L. (1933). *Language.* New York: Holt, Rinehart & Winston.

Burns, O. A. (1984). *Cold sassy tree.* New York: Ticknor & Fields.

Bus, A. G., & van IJzendoorn, M. H. (1988a). Mother–child interactions, attachment, and emergent literacy: A cross-sectional study. *Child Development, 59*(5), 1262–1272.

Bus, A. G., & van IJzendoorn, M. H. (1988b). Patterns of attachment in frequently and infrequently reading mother–child dyads. *Journal of Genetic Psychology, 149,* 199–210.

Bus, A. G., & van IJzendoorn, M. H. (in press). Mothers reading to their three-year-olds: The role of mother–child attachment security in becoming literate. *Reading Research Quarterly.*

Bus, A. G., van IJzendoorn, M. H., & Sulzby, E. (1994–1995). Unpublished videotaped raw data.

Chafe, W. L. (1982). Integration and involvement in speaking, writing, and oral literature. In D. Tannen (Ed.), *Spoken and written language: Exploring orality and literacy* (pp. 35–54). Norwood, NJ: Ablex.

Chomsky, N. (1985). *Aspects of the theory of syntax.* Cambridge, MA: MIT Press.

Chomsky, N., & Halle, M. (1968). *The sound pattern of English.* New York: Harper & Row.

Clay, M. M. (1966). *Emergent reading behaviour.* Unpublished doctoral dissertation, University of Auckland, New Zealand.

Dostoyevsky, F. (1950). *The brothers Karamazov* (C. Garnett, Trans.). New York: Vintage Books.

Edwards, P. A. (1989). Supporting lower SES mothers' attempts to provide scaffolding for bookreading. In J. B. Allen & J. Mason (Eds.), *Risk makers, risk takers, risk breakers: Reducing the risks for young literacy learners* (pp. 225–250). Portsmouth, NH: Heinemann.

Ferreiro, E. (1986). The interplay between information and assimilation in beginning literacy. In W. H. Teale & E. Sulzby (Eds.), *Emergent literacy: Writing and reading* (pp. 15–49). Norwood, NJ: Ablex.

Ferreiro, E., & Teberosky, A. (1982). *Literacy before schooling.* Exeter, NH: Heinemann.

Harste, J. C., Woodward, V. A., & Burke, C. L. (1984). *Language stories and literacy lessons.* Portsmouth, NH: Heinemann.

Heath, S. B., with Thomas, C. (1984). The achievement of preschool literacy for mother and child. In H. Goelman, A. Oberg, & F. Smith (Eds.), *Awakening to literacy* (pp. 51–72). Exeter, NH: Heinemann.

Hyon, S., & Sulzby, E. (1994). African-American kindergartners' spoken narratives: Topic associating and topic centered styles. *Linguistics and Education, 6,* 121–152.

Jesperson, O. (1968). *Growth and the structure of the English language.* New York: The Green Press. (Original work published 1938)

Juel, C. (1988). Learning to read and write: A longitudinal study of 54 children from first through fourth grades. *Journal of Educational Psychology, 80,* 437–447.

Juel, C., Griffith, P. L., & Gough, P. B. (1986). Acquisition of literacy: A longitudinal study of children in first and second grade. *Journal of Educational Psychology, 78,* 243–255.

Kamberelis, G., & Sulzby, E. (1988). Transitional knowledge in emergent literacy. *Thirty-seventh Yearbook of the National Reading Conference, 37,* 95–106.

Marquez, G. G. (1970). *A thousand years of solitude* (G. Rabassa, Trans.). New York: Avon Books.

Martinez, M., Cheyney, M., & Teale, W. H. (1991). Classroom contexts and kindergartners' dramatic story reenactments. In J. F. Christie (Ed.), *Play and early literacy development* (pp. 119–140). Albany: State University of New York Press.

Mason, J., & Allen, J. B. (1986). A review of emergent literacy with implications for research and practice in reading. In E. Z. Rothkopf (Ed.), *Review of research in education 13* (pp. 3–47). Washington, DC: American Educational Research Association.

Michaels, S. (1991). The dismantling of narrative. In A. McCabe & C. Peterson (Eds.), *Developing narrative structures* (pp. 303–351). Hillsdale, NJ: Lawrence Erlbaum Associates.

Michaels, S., & Cazden, C. (1986). Teacher/child collaboration as oral preparation for literacy. In B. B. Schieffelin & P. Gilmore (Eds.), *The acquisition of literacy: Ethnographic perspectives* (pp. 132–154). Norwood, NJ: Ablex.

Ochs, E. (1979). Planned and unplanned discourse. In T. Given (Ed.), *Discourse and syntax* (pp. 51–80). New York: Academic Press.

Olson, D. (1977). From utterance to text: The bias of language in speech and writing. *Harvard Educational Review, 47,* 257–281.

Ong, W. J. (1982). *Orality and literacy: The technologizing of the word.* London: Methuen.

Pellegrini, A. D., Brody, G. H., & Sigel, I. E. (1985). Parents' book-reading habits with their children. *Journal of Educational Psychology, 77*(3), 332–340.

Pellegrini, A. D., Perlmutter, J. C., Galda, L., & Brody, G. H. (1990). Joint book reading between black Head Start children and their mothers. *Child Development, 61,* 443–453.

Pyles, T. (1971). *The origins and development of the English language.* New York: Harcourt Brace Jovanovich.

Reuning, C. (1986). *Prosodic features of reading intonation: An exploratory study.* Unpublished master's thesis, Northwestern University, Evanston, IL.

Rumelhart, D. E. (1977). Toward an interactive model of reading. In S. Dornic (Ed.), *Attention and performance VI* (pp. 573–603). London: Academic Press.

Scollon, R., & Scollon, S. B. K. (1981). *Narrative, literacy, and face in interethnic communication.* Norwood, NJ: Ablex.

Shatz, M., Kamberelis, G., Halle, T., & Sulzby, E. (1991, April). *Kindergartners' judgments of writing varying in conventionality.* Paper presented at the annual meeting of the Society for Research in Child Development, Seattle.

Smith, L. (1988). *Fair and tender ladies.* New York: Ballantine Books.

Snow, C. E. (1983). Literacy and language: Relationships during the preschool years. *Harvard Educational Review, 53*(2), 165–187.

Stanovich, K. (1986). Matthew effects in reading: Some consequences of individual differences in the acquisition of literacy. *Reading Research Quarterly, 21*, 360–407.

Sulzby, E. (1983). *Beginning readers' developing knowledges about written language.* Final report to the National Institute of Education (NIE-G-80-0176). Evanston, IL: Northwestern University.

Sulzby, E. (1985). Children's emergent reading of favorite storybooks: A developmental study. *Reading Research Quarterly, 20*, 458–481.

Sulzby, E. (1986a). Writing and reading as signs of oral and written language organization in the young child. In W. H. Teale & E. Sulzby (Eds.), *Emergent literacy: Writing and reading* (pp. 50–89). Norwood, NJ: Ablex.

Sulzby, E. (1986b). Young children's concepts for oral and written texts. In K. Durkin (Ed.), *Language development during the school years* (pp. 95–116). London: Croom Helm.

Sulzby, E. (1987). Children's development of prosodic distinctions in telling and dictating modes. In A. Matsuhashi (Ed.), *Writing in real time: Modelling production processes* (pp. 133–160). New York: Longman.

Sulzby, E. (1989). Assessment of emergent writing and children's language while writing. In L. Morrow & J. Smith (Eds.), *The role of assessment in early literacy instruction* (pp. 83–109). Englewood Cliffs, NJ: Prentice-Hall.

Sulzby, E. (1994). Children's emergent reading of favorite storybooks with postscript. In R. B. Ruddell, M. R. Ruddell, & H. Singer (Eds.), *Theoretical models and processes of reading* (4th ed., pp. 244–280). Newark, DE: International Reading Association.

Sulzby, E., Barnhart, J., & Hieshima, J. (1989). *Forms of writing and rereading from writing: A preliminary report.* In J. Mason (Ed.), *Reading/writing connections* (pp. 31–63). Needham Heights, MA: Allyn & Bacon.

Sulzby, E., & Reuning-Hegland, C. (in preparation). *Reading and storytelling intonation: An exploratory study.*

Sulzby, E., & Teale, W. H. (1987, November). *Young children's storybook reading: Longitudinal study of parent–child interaction and children's independent functioning* (Final report to The Spencer Foundation). Ann Arbor: The University of Michigan.

Sulzby, E., & Teale, W. H. (1991). Emergent literacy. In R. Barr, M. L. Kamil, P. Mosenthal, & P. D. Pearson (Eds.), *Handbook of reading research* (Vol. 1, pp. 727–757). New York: Longman.

Sulzby, E., & Zecker, L. B. (1991). The oral monologue as a form of emergent reading. In A. McCabe & C. Peterson (Eds.), *Developing narrative structures* (pp. 175–213). Hillsdale, NJ: Lawrence Erlbaum Associates.

Tannen, E. (1982). *Spoken and written language: Exploring orality and literacy.* Norwood, NJ: Ablex.

Teale, W. H. (1985). Unpublished videotaped raw data.

Teale, W. H. (1987). Emergent literacy: Reading and writing development in early childhood. *National Reading Conference Yearbook, 36*, 45–74.

Teale, W. H., & Sulzby, E. (Eds.). (1986). *Emergent literacy: Writing and reading.* Norwood, NJ: Ablex.

3

THE RHYTHMS OF SPEECH AND WRITING

Marie Bernadete Marques Abaurre
State University of Campinas, São Paulo

The rhythm of a sentence is reflected in the child's graphic activity, and we quite frequently encounter further rudiments of such rhythmically depictive writing of complex speech clusters. It was not invention, but the primary effect of the rhythm of the cue or stimulus that was at the source of the first meaningful use of a graphic sign.

—Luria (1929/1978, p. 86)

Linguists interested in understanding the nature of the relationship between oral and written texts might be tempted to simply compare samples of spoken and written language on the basis of their structural properties, choice of specific lexical items, degree of formalism, and other (socio)linguistic parameters.

Such parameters, however, although apparently adequate to characterize phenomena that refer to final linguistic products, do not help us understand the processes underlying oral and written discourse elaboration. The straightforward application to products of purely descriptive and comparative procedures is problematic. Theoretically speaking, it is more interesting to identify the general processes of linguistic performance that might explain not only the specific aspects of spoken and written discourse organization but also the autonomous status that writing, as a semiotic system, has acquired with respect to the spoken language.

47

TEMPORAL RHYTHM OF SPEECH, SPATIAL
RHYTHM OF WRITING

One of the fundamental characteristics of spoken language is its rhythm, which results from a regular alternation, in real time, of stress patterns defined by the principles of metrical organization (Halle & Vergnaud, 1987; Hayes, 1991). Thus, a regular alternation of prominences is ultimately responsible for what is usually perceived as the natural cadence of particular speech events.

The rhythm of speech is functionally related to another kind of rhythm, the rhythm of writing, which—from the point of view of the silent reader—is determined predominantly by syntactic/spatial/graphic elements. The temporal dimension is absent from the final written product, being manifest, in real-time terms, during the process of writing only. The rhythm of writing, determined by specific formal requirements of prose (and its genres), verse, and style, defines the way a particular piece of writing breathes after the rhythmic gesture of the hand that led to its production becomes frozen under the form of graphic markings on a blank page (see, in this respect, Brooks & Warren, 1938/1960; Eco, 1984; Meschonic, 1982). Direct comparison of oral and written language samples can, therefore, be misleading, because the two systems, although related (and mutually translatable), are relatively autonomous from a semiotic point of view, each being organized according to specific rules and principles.

One important aspect of the general process of writing acquisition is children's elaboration of the differences between the natural, prosodically determined rhythm of spoken language (differently manifested in specific discourse frames) and the elaborate and multiform "rhythm of writing." This chapter discusses the hypothesis according to which children, early in the process of writing acquisition, might sometimes, albeit unconsciously, use their perception of the rhythmic and intonational prominences of speech when analyzing and segmenting language in specific reading and writing contexts. This hypothesis is based on the observation that relevant aspects of spoken Portuguese rhythmic patterns are frequently registered in children's first written texts.

Ferreiro and Teberosky (1979) and Ferreiro (1988) showed that children, even before exposure to formal instruction about writing, are able to segment oral language in terms of syllables and to associate such segmented units to letters in writing. Such interesting research findings pose a particularly interesting question: What are the specific stylistic contexts of speech production that favor syllable scansion? My hypothesis in this chapter is that the syllable is a prosodic (rhythmic/intonational) unit spontaneously recognized by the speakers under specific utterance conditions. One such condition involves a particular mode of pronunciation characterized by explicit scansion and by a *staccato* (disconnected) mode of syllable articulation in discourse.

Two examples of initial writing produced by Brazilian children illustrate my hypothesis. The first example is from an experiment in which an adult tried to elicit written production from a group of preschool children, with the purpose of identifying their hypotheses and levels of conceptualization about the basis of alphabetical writing. Data from the chosen experimental episode show that work centered on words and sentences (on the part of both the experimenter and the children), as well as the negotiation about their written form, naturally leads to moments of *staccato*, emphatic pronunciation, with salience attributed to syllables. The example also shows that prosodic units larger than the syllable might influence language segmentation.

The second example comes from a text spontaneously written by a boy who already understood the alphabetic basis of Portuguese writing. Analysis of the chosen text suggests that, in order to master the rhythm of written discourse, children must learn that the structures of written language are not isomorphic with the prosodic and syntactic units of the spoken language.

THE STRESS-TIMED RHYTHM
OF BRAZILIAN PORTUGUESE

From a phonetic point of view, languages have traditionally been grouped in two main types, *stress-timed* or *syllable-timed*, according to their rhythm (Dauer, 1983; Gibbon & Richter, 1984; Hoequist, 1983a, 1983b; Lehiste, 1970; Pike, 1946). In a stress-timed language such as Portuguese (Abaurre, 1981; Abaurre & Cagliari, 1986; Abaurre-Gnerre, 1979; Cagliari, 1982; Major, 1981, 1985; Simões, 1987) or English, spoken discourse consists of rhythmic units (or *feet*), starting with a strong, stressed beat that is followed in its turn by a variable number of weak beats. Each rhythmic beat is filled with phonological segments that may correspond to one or more phonetic syllables. Time intervals between stressed beats are perceived as isochronous.

In particular discourse contexts, regular stress-timing can be interrupted, usually for clarifying or emphasizing purposes. This does not mean that stress-timed rhythm in such situations will be replaced by syllable-timed rhythm. It only means that fluent discourse rhythm (based on the recurrent succession of strong and weak beats) is suspended. Scansion, then, takes place, producing a staccato effect. Whole utterances (or parts of utterances) can thus be pronounced in what I refer to as the *staccato* mode of pronunciation.

In stress-timed languages, segmenting procedures leading to the staccato effect define a particular rhythmic patterning characterized by a marked cadence resulting from the frequent occurrence of strong beats and pauses at short, isochronous intervals. In staccato, the frequent pauses facilitate analysis of the segmental material into units smaller than those perceived in an *andante* cadence (see Abaurre-Gnerre, 1976) when segmentation is determined by a stress-timed patterning and the occurrence of larger phonological portions of utterances compressed in weak beats is frequent. The succession of strong beats usually

followed by pauses in the staccato mode of pronunciation is, therefore, responsible for the typical staccato cadence, markedly different from that of stress-
timed rhythm, characterized primarily by the strong and weak beat alternation.

The choice of a staccato cadence frequently results in the segmentation of
the utterance in a sequence of the smallest possible rhythmic units, the syllables.
It need not always be so, however, and, even in staccato, strong beats may
sometimes be filled with more than one phonetic syllable. For example, the
Portuguese sentence, *O menino caiu da mesa* (The boy fell from the table), can
be segmented in seven strong beats in staccato:[1]

$$[\; \upsilon \; \wedge \; m\iota \; \wedge \; ni\tilde{n}\omega \; \wedge \; ka \; \wedge \; i\underset{\smile}{\upsilon} \; \wedge \; da \; \wedge \; meza \;]^2 \qquad (1)$$
$$ 1 \qquad 2 \qquad 3 \qquad 4 \qquad 5 \qquad 6 \qquad 7$$

Notice that only five of the seven beats correspond here to phonetic syllables.

It is also possible, even in stress-timed languages, to *syllabify* any utterance;
that is, to analyze it in all of its constituent syllables, for purposes of pronunciation. However, although speakers of any language are capable of performing
such a fine analysis of the segmental chain, this is not what they tend to do in
their spontaneous use of language. In their linguistic activity, speakers tend to
analyze the phonic material, when necessary, by also taking into account aspects
of the prosodic continuum and not only the segmental sequence (see, in this
respect, Gebara, 1984; Scarpa, 1985). Systematic syllabification, exceptional in
everyday linguistic behavior, may occur, however, under particular circumstances that are probably related to moments when spontaneous linguistic
activity is suspended and language becomes an object of analysis. The utterance
in Example 1, if syllabified, would be:

$$[\; \upsilon.m\tilde{\imath}.n\tilde{\imath}.n\upsilon.ka.i\upsilon.da.me.za \;]^3 \qquad (2)$$

In a stress-timed language, the distribution of strong beats in utterances is
based on the position of the so-called *main stress* of words (fixed, or determined
in the lexicon or by rule) and on results of the application of an algorithm of
secondary stress placement (see, e.g., Halle & Vergnaud, 1987), which does not
concern us here. It suffices to say that this algorithm cannot change the position
of the main stresses of words but simply attributes alternating prominences to
originally stressless syllables according to language-specific parameters.

Speakers have some options as to the actualization of the virtual strong beats
of utterances, and once these options are chosen, the resulting weak portions

---

[1]Phonetic symbols are from IPA (International Phonetic Association).

[2]The symbol ∧ indicates pauses.

[3]Dots indicate syllable boundaries.

of utterances can be subject to all sorts of phonological reduction under specific rhythmic conditions (Abaurre & Cagliari, 1986). Examples of such reductions are evident when comparing two occurrences of the Portuguese sentence, *Pedro está estudando na Universidade de Campinas* (Peter is studying at Campinas State University), when pronounced fluently with a stress-timed rhythm (at a normal, andante speed) and when syllabified:

Fluent:[4] [//pe: dstatst :/dɜ̃n:aʊn:veɾs:/da:dʒkɜ̃/pi͂ nas//] (3)

Syllabified:[5] [pe.dɾʊ.is.ta.is.tu.dɜ̃.dʊ.na.u.ni.veɾ.si.da.dʒi.dʒi.kɜ̃.pi͂.nas]

In a syllable-timed language such as Japanese, on the other hand, information about the duration of each syllable is given in the lexicon (Beckman, 1982). Different patterns result from the combination of short and long syllables and are transposed as such to utterances (in the context of which they may be further subjected to the rules of "rhythm morphophonemics").

The more syllable-timed a language is, the easier it is for its speakers to perceive syllables, because the rhythm of these languages is based on their duration. On the other hand, the more stress-timed a language is, the more difficult it becomes for speakers to perceive portions of fluently spoken utterances as constituted of phonetically autonomous syllables.

What is the real importance, then, of the notion of syllable in a stress-timed language such as Portuguese? Although it could be said (based on the preceding considerations) that relying on the syllable in a stress-timed language is a way of denying the characteristic rhythmic organization of such languages, there are specific discourse contexts in all languages that favor scansion procedures. Thus, under particular dialogical conditions, the staccato mode of pronunciation is assumed, and salience is given to particular words or utterances. New rhythmic patterns are then created, favoring analysis of shorter sequences of segments and, consequently, perception of phonetic syllables in any language, even in stress-timed ones. This is a frequent procedure in teaching situations, for example, or when we assume the staccato pronunciation for emphatic purposes or as a clarifying strategy.

---

[4]The continuous line below the phonetic transcription iconically indicates normal (unmarked) intonational contours; double bars (//) indicate tonal groups, usually corresponding to informational units; single bars (/) indicate borders of rhythmic groups (i.e., feet or stress groups); underlined portions of transcription indicate strong beats.

[5]Intonation and stress differences are neutralized under syllabification, which creates undifferentiated units in terms of strength. Notice the drastic reduction of phonetic material resulting from stress-timing in fluent pronunciation. Syllabification, on the other hand, provides the highest possible degree of phonetic explicitness that can be attained without artificiality.

HYPOTHESES UNDERLYING THE ANALYSIS
OF EXAMPLES

Data presented in the next two sections have led to the following hypotheses:

  • Children who are speakers of a stress-timed language perceive stress-timed rhythm and its basic prosodic units (strong and weak) more promptly than they do syllables.

  • Even speakers of a stress-timed language can use a staccato pronunciation in specific discourse contexts. They can, therefore, also perceive smaller phonetic units (which often, but not always, correspond to syllables), provided that they are contextually exposed to a mode of pronunciation based on scansion of utterances, where such units are given prominence.

  • Children can start segmenting utterances (particularly words in a list) into portions that eventually correspond to phonetic syllables. This does not mean, however, that they will always segment utterances into syllables. They may sometimes segment units that correspond to larger portions of the utterance, based on their perception of contextually defined rhythmic and intonational units.

SEGMENTING ORAL UTTERANCES:
ANALYSIS OF A PARTICULAR EPISODE

The influence of prosodic aspects on children's behavior during experiments has not gone unnoticed. Holden and MacGinitie (1972) investigated children's conceptions of word boundaries in speech and print. They interviewed 84 pre-school children and concluded that their subjects' "awareness of small function words as free forms appeared to depend at least on the context in which the word was used" (p. 554). In a sentence such as "Is Bill drinking soda?" where 65% of the subjects interpreted the auxiliary and the proper noun as one unit, the authors suggested that children's "sensitivity to the rhythmic aspects of an utterance" may influence the way they segment it. After commenting on similar examples, they concluded: "Whether some responses are in fact, based on rhythm, and what characteristics of the sentence, the child, and the experimental situation increase the likelihood of such responses are questions that remain to be investigated" (p. 554). The observations of Holden and MacGinitie hold true not only for English but probably for other stress-timed languages as well.

In this section I discuss, from a linguistic point of view, how phonetic differences (segmental and prosodic) manifested in the pronunciations of an experimenter and a preschool girl (speaking Brazilian Portuguese) during a clinical

(Piagetian) experiment may determine some segmenting procedures used by the child. Data come from a videotaped interview and represent only part of the registered dialogue. During the interview, the child was asked to write certain words and, subsequently, sentences. The experimenter aimed to create a situation that might elicit the child's hypotheses about the basis of alphabetical writing. The videotape, which includes interviews with other children, was prepared as instructional material for teachers, to illustrate how preschool children construct theories about the written language.

The following transcribed episode beautifully shows the little girl's sensitivity to the prosodic patterns of the experimenter's pronunciation.

(The experimenter calls the child's attention to particular words, and   (4)
asks her to write them down.)

1. E: Do you know what a *lapiseira* ("pencil case") is?[6]

2. S: Yes.

3. E: Write, then: [' l a p ɪ   ' z e ɾ a]

4. S: (writes on the sheet of paper) A I Z A A L U

5. E: Now read, pointing with your finger!

6. S: (reads aloud, pronouncing the utterance as if composed of two portions, each with a particular intonational contour, and making each portion correspond to a group of letters while pointing with the finger)

A I Z A   A L U

[' l a p ɪ ʌ ' z e ɾ a]

7. Oh, very good! Now I want you to write: *diretora* ("school principal")
   [' d i ɾ e   ' t o ɾ a]

8. S: (writes) I U Z M U
   Here it is!

9. E: Now read!

---

[6]Portuguese is used only in those parts of the dialogical turns where phonetic aspects (segmental and prosodic) of the experimenter's or subject's pronunciation are crucial for data interpretation.

10. S: (proceeding exactly as in Turn 6)

      I U Z   M U

      ['diɾe ∧ 'toɾa]

11. E: Uhn . . . Now write *aluno* ("pupil") ['a: 'luno]

12. S: A U O N O
13. E: Read!
14. S: ['a: 'lu n o]

(The camera is close on the child's face at this point of the interview, making it impossible to follow her segmentation of the written material.)

15. E: Read slowly so that I can see how you're reading.
16. S: A U O N O

      ['a: ∧ 'lu: ∧ 'no:]

(At this point, the experimenter asks the child to indicate what part of the utterance is represented by each written letter. She proceeds, covering with a card all letters to the right of the one she expects to be matched with a specific part of the spoken utterance. The child names the letters but does not match them with spoken syllables. The experimenter then asks the child to read the word again.)

17. E: Right! Now you're going to read to me again, slowly showing where each of the parts you read ends.
18. S: A   U O   N O

    [a: ∧ lu: ∧ no]

19. E: And here? (pointing to last *O*)
20. S: This one here? It reads . . .

    A   U O   N O

    [a: lu: n:o]

(holding the pronunciation of a long [n] until the finger reaches the O, and the [o] is finally pronounced)

21. E: Oh, then, the [n o], where is the [n o]?
22. S: It's here. (pointing to O)
23. E: Only this last one?
24. S: (nods in agreement)
25. E: Here, only?
26. S: Only here.
27. E: OK (...)
   (. . . . .)
28. Now write, *a menina ganhou uma lapiseira* ("the girl got a pencil case")
   [ʌa mɪ/n i n a ʌ g ʒ̃ / ɲ oʊ u m a l a p ɪ/z eɪ ɾ a]

29. S: (writing, while pronouncing the utterance in a whispered voice):

A I U A O   A O I A A I   U O A
| | | | | | | | |
[ḁ me̥   nḁ   g̃ʒ ɲoʊ u̥   pɪ̥   ze̥ ɾḁ]

Here it is!

30. E: Now read slowly, so that I can follow what you're reading:
31. S:

A I U   A   O A   O   I   A AI   U O A
| | | | | | | | |
[a: mɪ/nĩna g̃ʒ̃/ɲo   uma/la / pi/zeɾa]

32. E: Read again!
33. S:

A I U   A   O A   O I   A AI   U O A
| | | | | | | |
[a: mɪ/nĩna /g̃ʒ̃ɲo   uma/la / pi/zeɾa]

34. E: Up to here? (experimenter points to letter *l*)
35. S: Yes!
36. E: And these? (experimenter points to the remaining letters)
37. S: These you can also write.
38. E: Oh, yes? Can you also read them?

39. S: Read them? If you go like this . . . you get more here (moves fingers from left to right up to letter *I*, and then points to the remaining letters). . . . If you go like this . . . (running fingers very fast from left to right up to the end, and then from right to left) . . . you manage to . . . write some more.

40. E: Oh, then read like that, so that I can see.

41. S: (reads in normal, andante rate of speech, running the little finger without stopping, up to the end)

A   I   U   A   O   A   O   I   A   A   I   U   O   A

[a: m e/n ĩ n a g ʒ̃ / ɲoʊ m a/l a p e/z e ɾ a]

42. E: Oh, very good!

The first thing to notice about this experimental design is that the child is asked to write isolated words, which are necessarily given prominence in a scanned pronunciation. As the phonetic transcription indicates, the word *lapiseira* ("pencil case," Turn 3) was pronounced by the experimenter as divided into two portions or rhythmic groups, each one with a particular intonational contour. The resulting configuration corresponded to a combination of two sequences of strong/weak beats, the first one pronounced with a rising intonation, the second with a falling intonation. The child not only perceives and reproduces such a configuration when trying to read the proposed sequence of letters, but also uses it as a hint for segmenting the written material. This procedure is evident in Turn 6 when the child, while reproducing the experimenter's stress/intonation configuration, stops running the finger first at letter *A* and then at letter *U*. The same analysis holds for the experimenter's pronunciation of *diretora* ("school principal," Turn 7) and for the child's segmentation of the written sequence in Turn 10.

Note what happens to the word *aluno* ("pupil," Turns 11–27): Phonetic syllables emerge when the child assumes a staccato pronunciation, thus complying with the experimenter's expectation of a slow reading (explicit in Turn 15). Probably as a consequence of assuming a slow cadence, the child segments the utterance into four portions, each corresponding to a phonetic syllable, at the same time that she makes the local hypothesis (see Abaurre, 1988) that the written sequence of letters also must be segmented into an equal number of parts. The girl's hypothesis thus emerges in a particular prosodic and dialogical context.

When, on the other hand, children are asked to write sentences pronounced in a natural andante speed, they tend to segment them on the basis of larger rhythmic or intonational units characteristic of higher prosodic domains. This is illustrated by the subsequent turns, as shown in the following paragraph.

In Turn 28, the girl is asked to write a sentence for the first time. The sentence is pronounced in andante, and the stress-timed rhythm of Portuguese is maintained. The child's segmenting behavior becomes different with respect to writing and reading. In Turn 29, she whispers syllables while writing the sentence. It is possible that the slow rhythm of her hand gestures, typical of writing that is not yet fluent, favors such scanning. In Turn 31, however, when the girl tries to read, the natural rhythmic grouping of speech is used twice as a reference for segmentation: The letter *U* is related to [nĩna], and the letter *A* is related to [zeɾa]. In Turn 33, when asked to read again, the child segments another rhythmic group, [gɔ̃ɲo], which she relates to letter *A* after reanalyzing the sentence in terms of rhythmic feet.

Consider another suprasegmental parameter that contributes significantly to the shape of holistic configurations that envelop the segmental material and also to the perception of segmental chunks by the child. At Turn 3, we observe that the experimenter divides the pronunciation of *lapiseira* ("pencil case") into two intonational moments: a rising contour, followed by a falling one. The child, when "reading" and trying to segment the written sequence of letters in Turn 6, repeats the experimenter's intonational movement and, while so doing, segments the written material into two parts. Note how the child reproduces the rising/falling movement when reading the sequence of letters in Turn 31, where she regularly alternates rising and falling intonation contours, until she arrives at the penultimate analyzed portion. There she is forced to repeat the rising intonation of the antepenultimate chunk, because, in Portuguese, the intonation of the last part of assertive utterances must be falling. Such striking regularity seems to indicate that in this case the child is using rising/falling intonation movements in reading as guides for segmentation, making segmental phonological material fit into the prosodical frames thus defined.

The analysis of this episode shows that the relevant shifting points in intonational contours, in terms of either words or sentences, can be very salient to children. Virtual segmentation points are defined by the limits of intonational movements, and segmentation of oral or written material can be conditioned by perception of such transition points.

These observations seem to indicate, therefore, that a "syllabic" behavior on the part of the child naturally emerges in those contexts that favor the staccato pronunciation (typical, e.g., of teaching or of interviews such as the experiment just discussed). It should also be noted that children, even when segmenting speech with a staccato pronunciation, very often identify rhythmic units larger than the syllable.

Based on the preceding considerations, we can conclude that the syllable is the basic rhythmic unit of a staccato mode of pronunciation, whereas an andante speed favors identification of larger prosodic units (strength groups or tonal groups), particularly by illiterate speakers.

CONFRONTING TWO EXPERIMENTAL
SITUATIONS

Two experimental situations designed to investigate the prehistory of writing in the child should be mentioned here. They are experiments conducted by Luria (1929/1978) and Ferreiro and Teberosky (1979). These studies, although of a very different nature, are mentioned here to illustrate the effect of pronunciation used in the experimental context on children's segmentation procedures.

Luria based his experimental design on the hypothesis that even very young children (as young as 4 years of age) might understand that making scribbles on a sheet of paper can have an instrumental, mnemonic function. To test his hypothesis, he asked children to try to recall a number of sentences presented to them that usually exceeded their mechanical capacity to remember. The idea was to make children realize that they were unable to memorize all the linguistic material presented to them orally. Once they became aware of this memory limitation, they were asked to write down the material to be remembered. The children, of course, said that they did not know how to write. The experimenter then pointed out that adults who have to remember something write it on paper. Children were stimulated to invent a way of writing down what was then dictated to them. "Our experiment usually began after this," wrote Luria (1929/1978), "and we would present the child with several (four or five) series of six or eight *sentences* that were quite simple, short, and unrelated to one another" (italics added, pp. 69–70).

Words, when presented, usually followed sentences. It is not relevant here to discuss Luria's findings concerning his basic questions. It is very relevant, however, to point out that, because these children heard sentences (or even words) pronounced spontaneously, they were exposed to the fluent rhythm of Russian in the context of the experiment. One of Luria's conclusions is, therefore, not surprising: When children perceive that speech is somehow represented in writing, they try to encapsulate what they feel is the rhythm of the utterance into their writing gestures, which produces graphic markings on the blank page. Luria noted that "By the third or fourth session, a child of 4 or 5 years would begin to link the word (or phrase) given him and the nature of the mark with which he distinguished the word." He also noticed that the first differentiation made by the child "involved reflection of the rhythm of the phrase uttered in the rhythm of the graphic sign" (p. 84). The following is one of Luria's most interesting and relevant passages:

> The process of writing, which began with an indifferentiated, purely imitative, graphic accompaniment to the presented words, after a period of time was transformed into a process that on the surface indicated that a connection had been made between the graphic production and the cue presented. The child's graphic production ceased being a simple accompaniment to a cue and became its reflection—albeit in very primitive form. It began to reflect merely the rhythm of the

presented phrase: single words began to be written as single lines, and sentences as long, complicated scribbles, sometimes reflecting the rhythm of the presented sentence.

The variable nature of this writing suggests, however, that perhaps this is no more than a simple rhythmic reflection of the cue presented to the subject. Psychologically, it is quite comprehensible that every stimulus perceived by a subject has its own rhythm and through it exerts a certain effect on the activity of the subject, especially if the aim of that activity is linked to the presented stimulus and must reflect and record it. The primary effect of this rhythm also produces that first rhythmic differentiation in the child's writing that we were able to note in our experiments. (pp. 85–86)

Ferreiro and Teberosky, on the other hand, designed experimental situations to test directly the different hypotheses children are capable of making about the basis of the writing system before they have formal instruction. In Ferreiro and Teberosky's typical experimental situation, children were first asked to write isolated words that presented particular problems with respect to extension in relation to semantic content, nature of vowel nuclei, and the like. Children, by hypothesis, will show sensitivity to such variables in their choice of "written forms." In these experiments, sentences were presented later to the child, and the hypothesis underlying this order of presentation seems to be that at a particular moment the child would more naturally operate with words than with sentences, for writing purposes. It is also not surprising that, in the context of such experiments, the experimenter frequently chooses the staccato mode of pronunciation (because words are pronounced in isolation), or that children frequently respond to such a mode of pronunciation by segmenting units that correspond to phonetic syllables. However, even in these experiments, as I pointed out earlier, both the experimenter and the child are sensitive to preferential prosodic patterning of particular discourse contexts. They segment the words or utterances in terms of complex phonological units of a different nature, basically defined in terms of rhythm and intonation. Thus, even when children seem to be segmenting phonetic syllables, what they are, in fact, doing is operating in staccato, characterized by a peculiar cadence that results from pronouncing short stressed units followed by pauses.

Data of the type presented and analyzed here seem to indicate that children frequently analyze spoken utterances in terms of rhythmic and intonational units and make local hypotheses based on their perception of units that sometimes correspond to what can be analyzed, from a phonological point of view, as phonetic syllables. As I have tried to demonstrate, such units frequently acquire salience in discourse contexts that favor a staccato mode of pronunciation. Such data provide evidence for my hypothesis (Abaurre, 1988) that the microhistory of writing events must be taken into account if we want to gain knowledge about the nature of the processes of language acquisition in general and of writing acquisition in particular. Such data also show how an accurate analysis of particular dialogues—in terms of their occurrence in particular discourse frames, as well as in terms of the phonetics of the turns that take place in such contexts—might contribute significantly to a better understanding of the procedures employed by children when analyzing and segmenting oral and written linguistic material.

THE RHYTHM OF INITIAL SPONTANEOUS WRITTEN TEXTS

In this section, particular emphasis is given to the influence of the rhythm of oral language in relation to children's first written texts and to their choice of linguistic structures.

This general topic would normally require a much more detailed discussion than this chapter permits. Therefore, I outline the more important aspects of such a discussion, starting with the following consideration: Children's initial written texts are not real specimens of written language, although they already incorporate, to a varying degree, some lexical and/or syntactic elements typical of written language.[7] In many cases, the general structure of these texts closely resembles that of the spoken language. Viewed in the more general framework of a theory of language acquisition, this can perhaps be explained in terms of dominance. At a moment when writing has not yet acquired autonomy with respect to orality, dominance of the language acquisition process is still placed on the spoken language. Perception of such autonomy is closely related to the child's elaboration of the constitutive differences between spoken and written language.

It is natural that children, in their first spontaneous texts, frequently and unconsciously transpose into writing many linguistic structures typical of oral language, particularly if these children have had little or no contact with written language (e.g., through adults' reading of storybooks). Such structures reflect, in many instances, preferential choices for rhythmic organization in speech. As we know, choice of particular syntactic structures—and sometimes even the choice of particular lexical items—may be determined in oral language by rhythmic constraints. The mean length of utterances, as well as particular stress and intonational configurations, can be determined by some sort of previously programmed, discourse-specific preferential rhythmic patterning. Choice of written structures, on the other hand, is—in a certain sense and within certain limits—not bound by the same sort of constraints, being predominantly governed by the needs and requirements of a system of representation that relies strongly on lexical and syntactic elaboration, given that it cannot, by definition, rely so much

---

[7]The degree to which such elements are incorporated in initial writing is obviously related to the degree of exposure to written texts. The more children have been exposed to reading, the greater the probability is that they will incorporate written structures into their initial texts.

on the immediate context (as does oral language) as a continuous source of information for discourse interpretation (Olson, 1977). The specific rhythm of writing must, therefore, be learned and should be viewed as a particular aspect of the process of writing acquisition.

In what follows, I present an example of a spontaneous narrative that, although "written" on a sheet of paper, can still be viewed as a sample of oral language, because the chosen linguistic structures suggest a rhythmic configuration typical of spontaneous, unelaborate spoken narratives.

This narrative was produced at school by J.P.R. (an 8-year-old male first grader from a poor family), when asked by the teacher to "draw and write" a story. (Single bars are used in the transcription to signal the beginning of possible rhythmic feet in reading, with the strong beat on the first syllable. Scansion is, thus, virtual—the boy did not read his story—and represents a fluent, natural rhythm of narrative reading.)

(5)

/ ∧ *Era uma ves o jo/ão foi cassa na flo/resta eo guarda correu atrais do jo/ão o joão ca/iu eo guarda pegou /ele pediu par o /guardae o guarda soutou /ele e ele foi chamar o irmão /dele eo irmão dele foi com /ele eo guarda viu /ele e os dois co/rrerom e o guarda coreu atrais /deles e eles subiram na /árvore e a árvore caiu na casa do vi/zinho o vizinho co/rreu e os muleque darom ri/sadas e o guarda correu atrais /dele ele foi para casa /dele e ele voutou no outro dia catar o esti/lingue eo guarda correu até a ele camssa e dezisti de co/rre mais ele numca ele di/zisti o guarda dezistiu de co/rrer ∧ /fim ∧ /*

[Once upon a time John went hunting in the forest and the guard ran after John John fell and the guard caught (him) he asked the guard and the guard released him and he went to call his brother and his brother went with him and the guard saw him and the two ran and the guard ran after them and they climbed the tree and the tree fell over the neighbor's house and the neighbor ran and the urchins laughed and the guard ran after him he went home and he came back the other day (to) pick the slingshot and the guard ran until he (would get) tired and give up running but he never he gives up the guard gave up running the end.]

Notice that there are not many alternative scansions for fluent reading of this text, given the syntactic choices and cohesive devices used. (I am obviously referring to a fluent reader's performance, because the child who produced this particular written linguistic object still could not read it fluently.) Perhaps the opening lines of the text could be scanned differently, as could one or two other segments, where, by introducing pauses at the end of rhythmic feet, we might get subsequent feet starting with rhythmically relevant pauses at the place of the strong beat. Apart from that, we can easily notice the amazing regularity in terms of the mean length of rhythmic feet. Stress-timing is evidenced by interfeet isochronism (relatively disturbed only toward the end, where two longer feet are created in the proposed scansion). The personal pronoun *ele* ("he"), frequently used in different syntactic positions, is a natural candidate for feet introducer, its initial stressed phonetic syllable filling the place of the initial strong beat. Cohesion is granted almost exclusively by coordination (parataxis) of simple syntactic structures (one of the characteristics of colloquial, unelaborate narratives of this type), which contributes to (or even determines, in a certain sense) a very regular rhythmic patterning. Incidentally, the two longer feet that may disturb the regular rhythm of the text (either by disturbing expected interfeet isochronism or by forcing an increase in the normal speed of pronunciation so that isochronism can be maintained) are exactly those two cases where syntactic subordination (hypotaxis) is present.

The form and structure of the text transcribed in Example 5 are common in initial written narratives and reports produced by young Brazilian children from public schools who have had little or no contact with writing through adults' reading. Preliminary analysis of a corpus of hundreds of natural, spontaneous texts written by these children suggests some tentative conclusions that should be the object of further discussion:[8]

• Some young children produce "written" texts that are very close to oral language, in terms of syntactic structuring and rhythm, because they have not yet elaborated written syntax and its derived written "rhythm."

• Rhythm and syntax are closely associated. In the process of writing acquisition, children must progressively learn that a particular rhythm of writing is predominantly determined by coordination and subordination of elaborate syntactic structures and is not bound by temporal constraints.

THE ACQUISITION OF THE RHYTHM OF WRITING

We can now formulate some hypotheses regarding the process of writing acquisition and its relation to the more general process of language acquisition. Explaining writing acquisition means, among other things, specifying the processes that account for the differentiation of oral and written structures and the transition from the temporally bound rhythm of speech to the syntactically and graphically elaborated rhythm of writing.

The rhythm of speech has a strong iconic component, and it is frequently difficult to detach it from the meanings it carries at discourse level. In many cases, it is possible to say that particular choices of rhythmic patterning are closely related to the expressive function of language (Bühler, 1934). Rhythm, in this sense, can be viewed as a sign of the subject's emotions and attitudes.

---

[8]The corpus mentioned resulted from the Acquisition of Oral Language and Its Written Representation Project, presently conducted at the Institute of Language Studies, State University of Campinas (UNICAMP), São Paulo.

In its habitual role of supporter of segmental phonological material, however, rhythm can be viewed as merely instrumental, a necessary frame on which phonological "syntax" is organized. We could say, perhaps, that rhythm is iconic in its expressive function, whereas it is part of the symbolic function of language in its predominantly "linguistic" role as organizer of segmental material (Abaurre, 1981; Abaurre & Cagliari, 1986; Abaurre-Gnerre, 1979).

These considerations hold true not only for rhythm but also for sounds actualized in adults' use of a linguistic system in live episodes of interaction. Iconicity of sounds has not gone unnoticed in the literature concerning poetry and phonostylistics (cf. Fónagy, 1971, 1977; Jakobson, 1960). The same is true about the way gestures are used in semiotic systems in general, and we should bear in mind that sounds used with a linguistic function are also the product of articulatory gestures. Together with rhythm, which undoubtedly has a biological counterpart, sounds produced by the articulatory gestures of the vocal organs can be considered as material, phonic extensions of our own body, along a temporal dimension. Because, in their linguistic usage, rhythmic and sound patterning become conventionalized (as do gestures in their own semiotic function), we tend not to pay attention to many instances when rhythm, phonetic segments, and gestures display, in their materiality, an iconic relationship with the subject's attitudes and emotions, thus interacting with other instances when they are mere instruments or supports of symbolic language. However, the predominantly conventional, symbolic value of a linguistic system must be constructed in the process of language acquisition. Recent studies in the field suggest that, in this process, children must learn to view language as detached from themselves, as an object that can be conventionally employed to symbolize a reality that is external to the individual.

Contact with the written representation of language contributes significantly to the process of objectifying language for children who start contemplating graphically displayed linguistic objects as frozen written products. Contact with writing also contributes significantly to children's understanding of the symbolic value of a linguistic system. We must distinguish two situations, however: Children can either contemplate writing produced by somebody else (and as such it can be regarded as a frozen product), or they themselves can produce tentative written objects (and thus participate actively in a process and experience its development along a temporal axis). The latter situation defines a favorable context for a still prevalently iconic manifestation of a combination of gestures (articulatory or otherwise) and complex prosodic frames that include rhythm, intonation, and other nonsegmental features.

Children's typical behavior during initial attempts at spoken or written language segmentation suggests that they do, in fact, take gestures and prosodic frames as constitutive expansions of a "holistic" activity of discourse elaboration that can also incorporate a graphic dimension in particular circumstances. Data discussed in this chapter corroborate this assumption and support Vygotsky's interpretation of a general gesture development from iconic to instrumental (symbolic) in drawing and writing (Vygotsky, 1978). The processes of differentiating the activities of speaking, reading, and writing, of constructing the role of subject of discourse, and of constructing the symbolic dimension of language depend on a more general process of detachment from elements of experience that can be viewed as being outside the self. Such a detachment (among other things) can, therefore, be considered a condition for objectifying and analyzing language.

In conclusion, what paths should children follow in order to construct the rhythm of writing? From initial attempts at writing interpretation, strongly marked by efforts to inscribe the prosody of spoken language into graphic signs displayed on paper, children must proceed to a differentiation of the activities themselves, thus recognizing autonomy of spoken and written language as semiotic systems. Along this path, children will learn that each system has its own linguistic structuring, provides different options concerning the way meaning is formally organized, resorts differently to lexical and/or prosodic elements as category and class markers, and so on. They will learn, consequently, that written choices and possibilities define a different kind of rhythm, predominantly bound by linguistic and spatial constraints that are, in a sense, extremely different from the temporal constraints that bind spoken rhythm. By following this same path, children will finally learn that it is possible to get detached from language and to use it not merely as a predominantly iconic system but also as a formal symbolic system (in Granger's sense, 1971). As pointed out by Calvet (1984), *ce passage de l'icône au symbole semble être dans la nature des choses* [This transition movement from icon to symbol seems to be natural] (p. 109).

ACKNOWLEDGMENTS

I want to thank Claudia de Lemos for her helpful and insightful comments on earlier versions of this chapter. I also want to thank Telma Weisz and Beatriz Cardoso from FDE (Fundação para o Desenvolvimento da Educação/São Paulo), who showed me the videotapes of their experiments and kindly authorized analysis of part of their data for this chapter.

REFERENCES

Abaurre, M. B. M. (1981). Processos fonológicos segmentais como índices de padrões prosódicos diversos nos estilos formal e casual do português do Brasil [Segmental phonological processes as indicators of different prosodic patterns in formal and casual Brazilian Portuguese]. *Cadernos de Estudos Lingüísticos, 2*, 23–43.

Abaurre, M. B. M. (1988). The interplay between spontaneous writing and underlying linguistic representations. *European Journal of Psychology of Education, 3*(4), 415–430.

Abaurre, M. B. M., & Cagliari, L. C. (1986). Investigação instrumental das relações entre padrões rítmicos e processos fonológicos no português brasileiro [An instrumental investigation of the relationship between rhythmic patterns and phonological processes in Brazilian Portuguese]. *Cadernos de Estudos Lingüísticos, 10*, 39–57.

Abaurre-Gnerre, M. B. M. (1976). O status teórico dos tempos (velocidade) de pronúncia na Fonologia Gerativa Natural [The theoretical status of the speed of pronunciation in Natural Generative Phonology]. *Anais do I Encontro Nacional de Lingüística [Proceedings of the First National Linguistics Meeting]* (pp. 248–269). Rio de Janeiro: Departamento de Letras, PUC.

Abaurre-Gnerre, M. B. M. (1979). *Phonostylistic aspects of a Brazilian Portuguese dialect: Implications for syllable structure constraints.* Unpublished doctoral dissertation, State University of New York at Buffalo.

Beckman, M. (1982). Segmental duration and the "mora" in Japanese. *Phonetica, 39*, 113–135.

Brooks, C., & Warren, R. P. (1960). *Understanding poetry.* New York: Holt, Rinehart & Winston. (Original work published 1938)

Bühler, K. (1934). *Sprachteorie* [Theory of language]. Jena, Germany: Gustav Fischer Verlag.

Cagliari, L. C. (1982). A entoação e o ritmo do português brasileiro: Algumas análises espectrográficas [Brazilian Portuguese intonation and rhythm: Some spectrographic analyses]. *Revista IBM, 4*(13), 24–33.

Calvet, J. L. (1984). Au pied de la lettre [Literally]. *Langages, 75*, 103–110.

Dauer, R. M. (1983). Stress-timing and syllable-timing reanalysed. *Journal of Phonetics, 11*, 52–56.

Eco, U. (1984). *Postille a "Il nome della rosa"* [Postscript to "The name of the rose"]. Milan: Fabri, Bompiani, Sonzogno, Etas.

Ferreiro, E. (1988). L'écriture avant la lettre [Writing before literacy]. In H. Sinclair (Ed.), *La production de Notations chez le jeune enfant: Langage, nombre, rythmes et mélodies* (pp. 17–70). Paris: Presses Universitaires de France.

Ferreiro, E., & Teberosky, A. (1979). *Los sistemas de escritura en el desarrollo del niño* [Literacy before schooling]. Mexico City: Siglo Veintiuno Editores.

Fónagy, I. (1971). Bases pulsionnelles de la phonation II [Instinctual bases of phonation II]. *Revue Française de Psychanalyse, 35*(4), 543–591.

Fónagy, I. (1977). Le statut de la phonostylistique [The status of phonolinguistics]. *Phonetica, 34*, 1–18.

Gebara, E. M. S. (1984). *The development of intonation and dialogue processes in two Brazilian children.* Unpublished doctoral dissertation, University of London.

Gibbon, D., & Richter, H. (Eds.). (1984). *Intonation, accent and rhythm.* Berlin: de Gruyter.

Granger, G. G. (1971). Langue et systèmes formels [Language and formal systems]. *Langages. 21*, 71–87.

Halle, M., & Vergnaud, J.-R. (1987). *An essay on stress.* Cambridge, MA: MIT Press.

Hayes, B. (1991). *Metrical theory: Principles and case studies.* Unpublished report, University of California, Los Angeles.

Hoequist, C., Jr. (1983a). Durational correlates of linguistic rhythm categories. *Phonetica, 40*, 19–31.

Hoequist, C., Jr. (1983b). Syllable duration in stress-, syllable- and mora-timed languages. *Phonetica, 40*, 203–237.

Holden, M. H., & MacGinitie, W. (1972). Children's conceptions of word boundaries in speech and print. *Journal of Educational Psychology, 63*(6), 551–557.

Jakobson, R. (1960). Linguistics and poetics. In T. A. Sebeok (Ed.), *Style in language* (pp. 350–377). Cambridge, MA: MIT Press.

Lehiste, I. (1970). *Suprasegmentals.* Cambridge, MA: MIT Press.

Luria, A. R. (1978). The development of writing in the child. *Soviet Psychology, 16*(2), 65–114. (Original work published 1929)

Major, R. C. (1981). Stress-timing in Brazilian Portuguese. *Journal of Phonetics, 9*, 343–351.

Major, R. C. (1985). Stress and rhythm in Brazilian Portuguese. *Language, 61*, 259–282.

Meschonic, H. (1982). *Critique du rythme* [Critique of rhythm]. Paris: Verdier.

Olson, D. (1977). From utterance to text: The bias of language in speech and writing. *Harvard Educational Review, 47*(3), 257–281.

Pike, K. L. (1946). *The intonation of American English.* Ann Arbor: University of Michigan Press.

Scarpa, E. M. (1985). A emergência da coesão intoacional [The emergence of intonational cohesion]. *Cadernos de Estudos Lingüísticos, 8,* 31–41.

Simões, A. R. M. (1987). *Temporal organization of Brazilian Portuguese vowels in connected speech.* Unpublished doctoral dissertation, University of Texas, Austin.

Vygotsky, L. S. (1978). *Mind in society: The development of higher psychological processes.* Cambridge, MA: Harvard University Press.

4

USE OF REFERENTIAL EXPRESSIONS IN 4-YEAR-OLD CHILDREN'S NARRATIVES: INVENTED VERSUS RECALLED STORIES

Margherita Orsolini
Paola Di Giacinto
Institute of Education and Psychology
University of Chieti

Children's use of linguistic expressions to introduce, maintain, or shift reference in narratives has been investigated in several studies (Bamberg, 1987; Hickmann, 1980, 1991; Karmiloff-Smith, 1981, 1985). But the problem of what children have actually learned when they use linguistic forms with referential functions similar to those used by the adults is still open to study. Do children learn to map linguistic forms onto more specific and differentiated functions, in much the same way as in other domains of language acquisition (Bamberg, Budwig, & Kaplan, 1991)? Or do children learn new strategies of discourse processing that enable them to select linguistic forms according to the demands of both the "macro" and "micro" construction of discourse (Karmiloff-Smith, 1985, 1986)?

The first part of this chapter reviews the results of previous studies on children's introduction, maintenance, and shift of reference.

CHILDREN'S INTRODUCTION OF REFERENCE

The reader should be aware of some problems involved in analyses of linguistic forms used to introduce reference. We commonly assume that forms such as full nouns with indefinite articles are used by the speaker to signal that a new entity is being introduced to the discourse context. This assumption often conceals the fact that selection of forms to introduce reference is deeply constrained by the discourse genre. In Italian fairy tales, for example, the main character is often introduced with indefinite expressions in a presentative formula, such as *C'era una volta* ("Once upon a time"), which places the subject of the sentence in a postverbal position. In real-life narratives, however, reference to individuals is introduced in a less conventionalized way, being expressed with definite forms when the speaker assumes that the listener has easy access to the intended referent.

Telling a story with pictures visually available to both the child and the adult—the procedure most frequently used to elicit narratives from children—can be communicatively ambiguous. On the one hand, requesting the child to tell a story should elicit from the child the referential procedures typical of fictional storytelling, particularly the use of presentative formulas and indefinite expressions to introduce characters. On the other hand, the pictures themselves introduce the characters and make them easily accessible.

An awareness of these problems will help in the evaluation of evidence emerging from various studies. Bamberg (1987) investigated narratives elicited with the picture booklet *Frog, where are you?* and found that the proportion of full nouns used with a definite article decreased with age but was relatively high even for the adults: 50% of the adults' reference introductions were with definite forms. Kail and Hickmann (1992) elicited the frog stories using either Bamberg's procedure (pictures visually available to the child and the adult) or a procedure in which a blindfolded adult listened to a child's narrative. Kail and Hickmann's study showed that 6-year-olds were likely to introduce referents with a definite or indefinite article, irrespective of the listener's visual access to the referents. Children 9 years of age were more likely to use indefinite articles when the listener did not have visual access to the referents. Only 11-year-olds invariably used indefinite expressions to introduce referents, irrespective of the communicative situation.

Thus, children do not seem to be affected by the listener's visual access to reference until 9 years of age. This suggests that when younger children use indefinite expressions in their narratives, they may attempt to reproduce a conventionalized narrative procedure, rather than monitoring the listener access to the story's character.

REFERENCE MAINTENANCE
AND REINTRODUCTION

When a character has been introduced in discourse, subsequent references to it are carried out with forms that vary according to phonological salience and richness in semantic content. Thus, forms that are weak in both phonological and semantic content (e.g., zero anaphoras) tend to be used to maintain reference, whereas more salient and semantically explicit forms (e.g., full nouns) are used to reintroduce the referent after previous discourse has been temporarily focused on a different entity. The strongest forms seem to be used when referents are not easily accessible in the discourse context, whereas the weakest forms are used when referents are highly accessible. Although different forms can serve the function of reference reintroduction, in many languages these forms tend to be full nouns. Several studies of adults' use of referential devices in narratives found that, when reference is reintroduced, full nouns are used more often than are any other linguistic forms (Bamberg, 1987; Givon, 1979; Marslen-Wilson, Levy, & Tyler, 1982).

Bamberg (1987) found that children as young as 4 years old can use different linguistic forms for reference maintenance versus reintroduction. Specifically, they use various pronominal forms to maintain reference but select full nouns to reintroduce reference. Bamberg found developmental differences on the influence of characters' topicality in reference reintroduction. Children 3 to 4 years of age seemed to be very much affected by referents' topicality rank in their selection of linguistic forms, because they used personal pronouns to reintroduce reference to the main character and full nouns for other referents. Children 9 to 10 years of age were more likely to use full nouns to reintroduce reference, irrespective of the character about whom they were speaking. Bamberg (1987) interpreted these results as evidence of a developmental shift from macro- to microdiscourse functions. Young children would use pronouns to signal that the story line was continuing, and for this reason they would use pronouns when reference was maintained and/or the main character was involved in some action. Conversely, older children would be more sensitive to "local" discourse constraints and would select full nouns versus pronouns when there was a need for shifting and/or disambiguating reference.

Karmiloff-Smith (1981, 1985) described a different developmental profile. She found that 3- to 4-year-old children have a deictic use of referential expressions, whereas 6-year-olds select referential expressions according to the different topical status of a story's characters, irrespective of whether reference is maintained or shifted. Specifically, they select pronoun forms when referring to the character who is highest in topicality and adopt a "subject thematic strategy," constructing each utterance by reserving the subject position to the main character. Karmiloff-Smith argued that the strategy used by the 6-year-olds reflects a constraint from a discourse level of processing, whereas older children's selection of pronominal and nominal forms reflects a greater control on the interplay between a discourse and an intersentential level of processing.

To recapitulate, both Bamberg (1987) and Karmiloff-Smith (1981, 1985) found that referents' topicality, particularly the status of main versus secondary character, constrains children's use of linguistic forms in narratives. In both studies, this influence from a global level of discourse is conceived as a basic step toward acquisition of narrative and discourse skills. However, two major points of controversy emerge from these studies. The first concerns the age at which children's selection of linguistic forms is somehow driven by the different functions of maintaining versus reintroducing reference. Bamberg (1987) found that this happens when children are 3 or 4 years old, whereas Karmiloff-Smith (1981, 1985) and Hickmann (1980, 1991) found that this occurs later, in the elementary school years. The second point of controversy involves the age (4 years old in Bamberg's study; 6 years old in Karmiloff-Smith's study) at which children are affected by the referents' topicality rank in their use of pronouns versus full nouns.

In this study, we analyzed the linguistic forms used in Italian children's narratives to express different referential functions. We attempted to provide further evidence that 4-year-olds' selection of linguistic forms is constrained by the different functions of introducing, maintaining, and reintroducing reference.

AN OVERVIEW OF ITALIAN LINGUISTIC FORMS USED TO MAINTAIN VERSUS INTRODUCE AND REINTRODUCE REFERENCE

In Italian, reference maintenance is usually achieved in two ways: with clitic pronouns and with person/number inflection on the verb (Berretta, 1985, 1990; Simone, 1983). Italian clitic pronouns cannot serve as the subject and are inflected for gender, number, and case. They are unstressed forms that often undergo a contraction process. Reference maintenance in the subject role is expressed by the person/number inflection on the verb. The possibility of dropping grammatical subjects, a basic feature of the Italian language, is constrained in narratives by pragmatic properties: Only when reference is continued and occupies the subject role, as in the previous clause, can reference be expressed only with person/number inflection on the verb.

Reference introduction in Italian is served by full nouns that tend to be located in a marked position such as the postverbal one (Berretta, 1990). Reference reintroduction is served by full nouns located either in a standard position (preverbal for nouns occupying the subject role, postverbal for nouns in the direct and indirect object role) or in a marked one. For example, in left dislocated sentences, the full noun in the object role is in a preverbal position, whereas the subject occupies the postverbal position. Marked positions of full nouns in the sentence are used when reference reintroduction demands a particularly strong shift of focus.

Personal pronouns tend to be used for local shifts of reference. For example, when a first clause introduces two referents in the agent role and the subsequent clause has only one of the two referents in the agent role, reference cannot be expressed only by person/number inflection on the verb but instead is expressed with either a personal pronoun or a full noun (Simone, 1990). Italian personal pronouns in the agent role are stressed forms, often used with a contrastive function (Berretta, 1990) to shift the focus of the previous utterance to a new one in the current utterance.

In summary, if we conceive a system of referential expressions organized in terms of referential strength (Simone, 1990), in which the phonologically and semantically weak forms are used for reference maintenance and some of the strong forms are used for reference reintroduction, Italian has clitic pronouns and person/number inflection on the verb at the lowest level of referential strength. Tonic personal pronouns, along with other stressed pronoun forms such as demonstratives, occupy an intermediate level, and full nouns (in a standard or marked position in the sentence) occupy the top levels.

Aims of the Study

This study addresses the issue of whether 4-year-olds' selection of linguistic forms is driven by the different functions of introducing, maintaining, and reintroducing reference. Our study also aims to explore the effect of children's familiarity with a specific "text" on their selection of linguistic forms to express reference. In particular, when children familiar with the text of a story are requested to recall it, do they use referential expressions in a more conventionalized way compared with their invented narratives?

METHOD

Subjects

We observed thirty 4-year-olds from low-income families. The education level of their parents was rather low, with 80% of their mothers having attended only elementary and intermediate grades in school. These children were not well acquainted with books: 60% of the mothers reported that their child had no books or no more than three books. The children were all enrolled in a preschool in a Rome neighborhood.

Procedure

The children were interviewed individually in a room at their school where they were alone with the experimenter, who was well known to them. Narratives were elicited in two different conditions. In the invented narratives condition, children were shown some toy models and asked to invent three stories about them. The first narrative was elicited with puppets who represented a family. In the other two narratives, each child was asked to select the characters and then invent the story. After each storytelling, the child was encouraged to dramatize the story plot with the toy models.

In the recalled narrative condition, the child was first asked to look carefully at pictures depicting the main events of the story that was going to be told.

Then the child was asked to listen twice to an audiorecorded story and to retell "the same story just heard," using the picture booklet that was still available.

Three invented stories and one recalled narrative by each child were audiorecorded and transcribed by using the "Chat" format (MacWhinney, 1991).

Coding Categories

The children's stories were first segmented into clauses (i.e., units consisting of one predicate and its arguments). Infinitives and participles that are complements of modal verbs were included with the matrix verb, as were aspectual verbs such as *mettersi a* ("set about").

Only clauses with an animate referent were coded. Clauses consisting of quotations and reported speech were not coded. We used the coding categories identified in another study (Orsolini, Rossi, & Pontecorvo, in press). Each referential expression was coded along four dimensions: the type of linguistic form, the syntactic role occupied by this form, its preverbal or postverbal position, and the referential function served in the narrative. For example, we first coded a reference if it was expressed with a full noun (definite vs. indefinite), a pronoun form (stressed pronoun forms vs. clitic pronouns), or a null form (person/number inflection on the verb). We then coded the form in terms of syntactic role (subject vs. direct, indirect, or oblique object) and position (before or after the verb). Finally, we coded the referential function in the narrative by distinguishing whether the referent was introduced for the first time (NEW), was maintained in the same (CUG) or in a different syntactic role (CDI) as compared with the previous clause, or was reintroduced (CNO).

The following example shows the categories used in our study.

1. *C'era il lupo*
   'there was the wolf'
   $1:NOM:DRE:SOG:POV:NEW

2. *che voleva mangia' il bambino*
   'who wanted to eat the child'
   $1:NUL:REL:_:_:CUG $2:NOM:DET:OGD:POV:NEW

3. *loro due, mamma e figlio, andavano nel bosco*
   'both of them, the mamma and the child, were walking in the woods'
   $3:NOM:PRO:SOG:PRV:NEW

4. *e poi incontrano il lupo*
   'and then meet the wolf'
   $3:NUL:REL:_:_:CUG $1:NOM:DET:OGD:POV:CNO

5. *il lupo mangio' loro due e il nonno*
   'the wolf ate both of them and the grandfather'
   $1:NOM:DET:SOG:PRV:CDI $3:PRO:TON:OGD:POV:CDI
   $4:NOM:DET:OGD:POV:NEW

In Clause 1, reference to the wolf ($1) occupies the subject role (SOG). It is expressed with a definite noun form that is the head of a relative clause (NOM:DRE) and is a first introduction (NEW). In Clause 2, the same referent ($1) occupies the subject role in a relative clause (NUL:REL:CUG). In the same clause, a new referent ($2) is introduced with a definite noun form (NOM:DET) in the direct object role (OGD) in postverbal position (POV). In Clause 4, the same referents ($3) introduced in Clause 3 are maintained (CUG) in the subject role and are only expressed with the person/number inflection on the verb (NUL). In Clause 4, reference to the wolf ($1) is reintroduced (CNO) in the object role and maintained in a different syntactic role (CDI) in Clause 5.

For a referent to be coded as reintroduced in the current clause, it must pass a two-step test: (a) it was introduced for the first time in some previous part of the narrative, and (b) it was not mentioned in the preceding clause. This coding decision does not apply when the preceding clause consists completely of direct speech (without a verb such as *say*), or when it is a descriptive clause with an inanimate referent, or an aside (i.e., questions addressed to the experimenter). In these target cases, we do not consider reference as interrupted, and, therefore, we look at the clause preceding the target one to decide if reference is maintained or reintroduced.

Special coding decisions are required when there are shifts from singular to plural agents and vice versa. When the previous clause has two referents in the agent role and the current clause has only one of them in the agent role, or vice versa, we conside ·ed this restriction (Simone, 1990) or widening of reference as reference re· ·o·· ·on.

RESULTS

Forms Used to Introduce, Maintain, and Shift Reference in Invented Narratives

The analysis reported here addresses the issue of whether children's selection of linguistic forms is constrained by the functions of introducing, maintaining, and shifting reference. Our analysis examines only the invented narratives, because children's linguistic production is richest there.

The linguistic forms used by children have been collapsed into three categories: full nouns (with either definite or indefinite articles), stressed pronouns (tonic personal pronouns and demonstratives), and null forms (person/number inflection on the verb and clitic pronouns). For each subject, we reported the frequency of these categories with the function of reference introduction, maintenance, or reintroduction and computed their proportions over the total number of referents expressed by the subject. In other words, for each subject we determined how many full nouns, stressed pronouns, or null forms had the function of reference introduction, maintenance, or reintroduction and then computed the proportion of each category over the total number of referents expressed by the subject. For this and our other analyses, proportions were subjected to arcsine transformations to stabilize variances.

An analysis of variance was run on these data, with function and linguistic form as within-subject factors. The main effect of function was significant, $F(3, 87) = 42.40$; $p < .0001$, showing that introduction and maintenance of reference in the same syntactic role of the antecedent clause are the most frequent functions. There was a strong effect of linguistic form, $F(2, 58) = 49.34$; $p < .0001$, with full nouns and null forms having the highest frequency. A very strong interaction of function and linguistic form, $F(6, 174) = 102.07$; $p < .0001$, was also found. Figure 4.1 shows that full nouns were the most frequent form used to introduce and, to a lesser extent, to reintroduce referents. Null forms were the most frequent form used to maintain reference.

These results show that 4-year-old children are sensitive to the different constraints exerted by the function of reference maintenance versus reference introduction or reintroduction. Null forms were selected when reference is highly accessible in the discourse context, because the antecedent clause was focused on the same entity in the same syntactic role. Full nouns were selected when a new entity had to be introduced in the discourse or reintroduced after previous discourse was focused on a different entity. This confirms Bamberg's (1987) findings that preschool children's use of linguistic forms in narratives—although

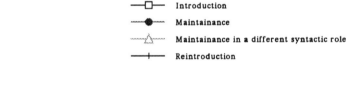

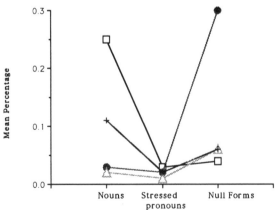

FIG. 4.1. Mean proportions of linguistic forms in different referential functions.

influenced by the nonverbal context—is also constrained by discourse functions. Despite referents always being visible in the physical context, children select specific forms according to the functions of introducing versus maintaining reference to them.

Indefinite and Definite Full Nouns in Reference Introduction

The analysis reported here addresses the issue of whether children's introduction of reference is affected by the different conditions in which narratives have been produced. Namely, are children more likely to use indefinite expressions in recalled stories where they are attempting to reproduce a text than when inventing a plot?

The linguistic forms used by the children in our study were collapsed into four categories: full nouns with definite articles, full nouns with indefinite articles, stressed pronouns (tonic personal pronouns and demonstratives), and null forms (person/number inflection on the verb and clitic pronouns). For each child, the frequency of these categories was computed over the total of reference introductions in both the invented and recalled narratives. An analysis of variance was run on these data, with forms (full nouns with either definite or indefinite articles, stressed pronouns, null forms) and task (invented vs. recalled narratives) as within-subject factors.

The main effect of form was significant, $F(3, 87) = 47.93$; $p < .0001$, with full nouns as the most frequent form. A Duncan test showed that definite full nouns were more frequent than indefinite full nouns ($p < .01$). There was a significant interaction between form and task, $F(3, 87) = 14.45$; $p < .0001$. Figure 4.2 shows that indefinite full nouns were far more frequent in recalled stories compared with the invented narratives. An analysis of simple effects confirmed that task

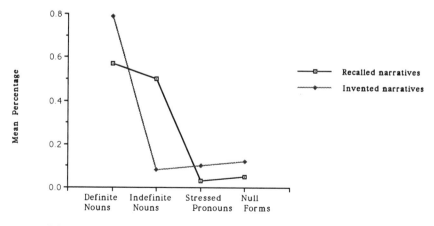

FIG. 4.2. Introduction of new referents in recalled and invented narratives.

had the strongest influence on children's production of indefinite full noun forms, $F(1, 29) = 25.86$; $p < .001$.

Our results confirm what has been found in some other studies (Bamberg, 1987; Orsolini, 1990): Children as young as 4 years old can introduce new referents with full nouns (rather than pronoun forms, as found by Karmiloff-Smith, 1981). Our results also suggest that 4-year-olds do not use indefinite expressions to signal that the referent is "new" in the discourse context. In fact, only when children recall a story previously listened to do they use indefinite expressions with relatively high frequency. In the invented narratives, they tend to use only definite expressions. This difference between the two task conditions suggests, as Bamberg (1987) argued, that children select indefinite expressions as an attempt to reproduce a narrative formula or, as we prefer to argue, a textual convention.

Textual Constraints in Children's Selection of Null Forms to Reintroduce Referents

This section addresses the issue of whether children are sensitive to the constraints exerted by a specific textual structure, consisting of adjacent clauses with a referent in the subject role expressed only by person/number expression of the verb. Remember that in Italian, when a sequence of utterances has the subject expressed only by person/number inflection on the verb, the listener expects the same entity to occupy the subject role. Conversely, when reference in the subject role is shifted, person/number inflection on the verb is not used to encode reference. This suggests the need to analyze further children's use of null forms to reintroduce referents by distinguishing selection of clitic pronouns (where referents are in the direct or indirect object role) and use of person/number inflection on the verb (where referents are in the subject role). The following examples illustrate the difference between these types of null forms.

Example 1 shows the reintroduction of reference in the direct object role in a recalled narrative (see original text of the story in the Appendix).

(Al-Dp)

1. *poi gli diceva*
   'then told him'
   (the cat told the dog)

2. *posso mangiare la tua pappa?*
   '—may I eat your supper?'

3. *basta che tu, dopo che mangiavi la pappa,*
   '—yes if you after eating the supper'
   (the dog answers the cat)

4. *mi levi da qui*
   'let me out from here'
   (the dog answers the cat)

5. *e poi lui mangiava tutta la pappa*
   'and then he ate the supper'
   (the cat eats the supper)
6. *e lo leva da li'*
   'and takes him away from there'

In Clause 6, the clitic pronoun *lo* ("him") refers to the dog. The listener has some trouble accessing the pronoun's referent, because the dog has not been overtly mentioned in the preceding antecedent clauses, although its reference has been kept active in the dialogue between the two characters (Clauses 2, 3, 4). However, when the listener hears the verb phrase "and takes him away from there," the pragmatic linkage with previous discourse enables reference resolution.

Example 2 shows the reintroduction of reference in the subject role in a recalled narrative.

(An-Cp)
7. *arriva un gatto*
   'a cat comes by'
8. *posso mangiare la tua pappa?*
   '—may I eat your supper?'
   (the cat asks the dog)
9. *e lui dice di si*
   'and he says—yes'
   (the dog says—yes)
10. *e gli scioglie la corda*
    'and unties its lace'
    (the cat unties the lace)
11. *e scappa*
    'and escapes'
    (the dog escapes)

In Clauses 10 and 11, there is a shift of reference in the subject role expressed only with person/number inflection on the verb. When adjacent clauses have the grammatical subject expressed only with person/number inflection on the verb, the Italian listener infers that the same referent occupies the subject role. Thus, the child's selection of a null form in Clauses 10 and 11 runs against strong textual expectations. In this case, from the speaker's point of view, strong pragmatic expectations also arise from the linkage between the discourse context and the predicate of the clause. For example, it is well known that the dog wants the cat to untie its leash so that it can escape. Thus, what happens in Example 2 is that pragmatic expectations and textual expectations run against each other, whereas in Example 1, no textual expectations arose from the way in which the clitic pronoun was used. This suggests that null forms used to reintroduce reference in the subject or object roles have to be distinguished.

In the analysis presented here, only children's reintroductions of referents were examined. For each child, the proportions of full nouns and null forms in the subject or in the object role (collapsing across direct and indirect object) were computed over the total of reintroductions. Two analyses of variance were run on the data of the invented and recalled narratives, with syntactic role and linguistic form as within-subject factors. Because the two analyses gave the same results, only those of the invented narratives are reported here.

The main effect of syntactic role was significant, $F(1, 29) = 58.09$; $p < .0001$, with referents in the subject role more frequent than referents in the object role. There was no main effect of linguistic form or interaction effect. Thus, when a referent was reintroduced in the subject role, the shift of reference had the same probability of being expressed with a null form or a full noun. The same result was found in the recalled narratives.

This suggests that children are not particularly sensitive to the expectations that arise from the textual structure of the immediately preceding discourse. In particular, even if the antecedent sequence of clauses has a referent in the subject role expressed only with person/number inflection on the verb, they can shift reference in the current clause, using the same referential device. This also happens in the recalled narratives, although the text of the story always reintroduces reference with a full noun. Thus, children have difficulty controlling the local construction of short sequences of utterances, irrespective of whether the narrative has to be constructed *ex-novo* or can rely on a previously heard text.

CONCLUSIONS

This study examined the relationship between linguistic forms and referential functions in 4-year-old children's narratives. Our results confirmed what was found in other studies (Bamberg, 1987). Children as young as 4 years old can select different linguistic forms according to the main functions of introducing, maintaining, and reintroducing reference. Forms with a weak phonological and semantic content, such as clitic pronouns and person/number inflection on the verb, are selected to maintain reference, and forms with a more explicit semantic content and a salient phonological content, such as full nouns, are selected to introduce reference and, to a lesser extent, shift reference.

The comparison between invented and recalled narratives suggests that children's selection of indefinite and definite forms to introduce referents is not constrained by the function of signaling the listener that the information introduced in the discourse is new. In fact, children produce indefinite expressions with a relatively high frequency only when they are attempting to reproduce the text of a previously heard story. This suggests that children select indefinite expressions in an attempt to adopt a textual convention.

The analysis of the linguistic forms used to reintroduce referents in the subject or the object role in a current clause suggests that children are not particularly sensitive to the expectations that arise from the textual structure of the immediately preceding discourse. Remember that, when a sequence of clauses has the subject expressed only by person/number inflection on the verb, the Italian listener expects that the same entity occupies the subject role. Children are not constrained by this expectation: When reference is reintroduced in the subject role, the shift of reference has the same probability of being expressed with a null form or a full noun. We explain this result by arguing that children have difficulty controlling the local construction of short sequences of utterances, irrespective of whether the child has to construct the narrative *ex-novo* or can rely on a previously heard text. In summary, our study confirms what has been found in previous studies (Bamberg, 1987; Karmiloff-Smith, 1985): that preschool children do not yet have a deep control of the content and structure of the immediately preceding discourse.

This study also shows that familiarity with text has a different impact on children's selection of referential expressions. Fictional narratives have very conventionalized ways of presenting and introducing characters. Children can understand that indefinite articles are a relevant part of these conventional procedures and can use these expressions when they attempt to reproduce the text of the story they have heard. Unlike reference introduction, reference reintroduction does not have any conventionalized procedure in narrative texts, except perhaps when reintroductions coincide with the beginning of a new episode. Thus, for reference reintroduction, children cannot simply learn a textual convention, and their selection of linguistic forms should be constrained by the content and structure of the immediately preceding discourse, in both recalled and invented narratives.

Although our findings here are consistent with the results of other studies showing that preschool children have difficulty controlling the immediately precedent discourse, several questions remain to be answered. For example, elementary school children seem to have a deeper control of antecedent spoken discourse, but they still have considerable difficulty controlling the interplay between macro- and microdiscourse construction in written text. This may suggest that controlling discourse construction is not a general discourse processing skill that can be easily transferred from spoken to written language or from a narrative to an expository genre. If there is no such general discourse skill, the role of children's pragmatic and grammatical learning must be more carefully explored. In fact, on the one hand, a deeper control of discourse construction may result from a deeper capability of pragmatically linking the current utterance with the discourse context. On the other hand, use of grammatical structures (e.g., relative and subordinate clauses) may help children to group together longer stretches of discourse, enabling them to have control of them. Thus, the general question concerning what children have learned that helps them to properly use referential expressions in narratives and, particularly, linguistic forms to reintroduce reference is still open.

APPENDIX

The following text was given to the children in our study.

> Once upon a time there was a dog named Pippo who lived tied with a rope in the garage of a house. One day his master decided to go out with the car. Pippo wanted to go out with him, but the master went out by himself and left Pippo tied by the rope. Pippo became sad and angry because he did not like to stay tied there all the time. After a while a cat came into the garage. He was dirty and hungry and wanted to eat Pippo's supper. Pippo said to him: "I'll let you eat my supper if you will untie my rope so I can get out of here." The cat ate all of Pippo's supper and then untied his rope so that Pippo could escape. Pippo ran for a long time on a trail leading into the woods. Then it was night, and Pippo realized that nobody was in the woods. He felt very lonesome. After a while a hunter came along, saying: "I was just looking for a dog who can help me catch birds." Hearing those words, Pippo answered: "I will hunt with you, but you must never tie me up." Then Pippo went with the hunter and from that day on he was happy and content.

REFERENCES

Bamberg, M. (1987). *The acquisition of narratives.* Berlin: Mouton de Gruyter.

Bamberg, M., Budwig, N., & Kaplan, B. (1991). A developmental approach to language acquisition: Two case studies. *First Language, 11,* 121–141.

Berretta, M. (1985). I pronomi clitici nell'italiano parlato [Clitic pronouns in spoken Italian]. In G. Holtus & E. Radtke (Eds.), *Gesprochenes Italienisch in geschichte und gegenwart* (pp. 185–224). Tubingen: Gunter Narr Verlag.

Berretta, M. (1990). Catene anaforiche in prospettiva funzionale: Antecedenti difficili [A functional approach to anaphoric chains: Difficult antecedents]. *Rivista di Linguistica, 2,* 91–120.

Givon, T. (1979). *Syntax and semantics 12. Discourse and syntax.* New York: Academic Press.

Hickmann, M. (1980). Creating referents in discourse: A developmental analysis of linguistic cohesion. In J. Kreiman & A. E. Ojeda (Eds.), *Papers from the parasession on pronouns and anaphora* (pp. 192–203). Chicago: Chicago Linguistic Society.

Hickmann, M. (1991). The development of discourse cohesion: Some functional and cross-linguistic issues. In G. Piéraut-Le-Bonniec & M. Dolitsky (Eds.), *Language bases . . . Discourse bases* (pp. 165–184). Amsterdam: John Benjamins.

Kail, M., & Hickmann, M. (1992). French children's ability to introduce referents in narratives as a function of mutual knowledge. *First Language, 12,* 73–94.

Karmiloff-Smith, A. (1981). The grammatical marking of thematic structure in the development of language production. In W. Deutsch (Ed.), *The child's construction of language* (pp. 121–147). London: Academic Press.

Karmiloff-Smith, A. (1985). Language and cognitive processes from a developmental perspective. *Language and Cognitive Processes, 1*, 61–85.

Karmiloff-Smith, A. (1986). From meta-processes to conscious access: Evidence from children's metalinguistic and repair data. *Cognition, 23*, 95–147.

MacWhinney, B. (1991). *CHILDES: Tools for analyzing language.* Hillsdale, NJ: Lawrence Erlbaum Associates.

Marslen-Wilson, W., Levy, E., & Tyler, L. (1982). Producing interpretable discourse: The establishment and maintenance of reference. In R. J. Jarvella & W. Klein (Eds.), *Speech, place and action: Studies in deixis and related topics* (pp. 339–378). New York: Wiley.

Orsolini, M. (1990). Episodic structure in children's fantasy narratives: "Breakthrough" to decontextualised discourse. *Language and Cognitive Processes, 5*(1), 53–79.

Orsolini, M., Rossi, F., & Pontecorvo, C. (in press). Reintroduction of referents in Italian children's narratives. *Journal of Child Language.*

Simone, R. (1983). Punti di attacco dei clitici in Italiano [Reference anchorage of clitic pronouns in Italian]. In F. A. Leoni (Ed.), *Italia linguistica* (pp. 285–307). Bologna: Il Mulino.

Simone, R. (1990). *Fondamenti di linguistica* [Foundations of linguistics]. Bari: Laterza.

5

CHILDREN DICTATING A STORY: IS TOGETHER BETTER?

Cristina Zucchermaglio
Nora Scheuer
University of Rome "La Sapienza"

The work reported here is part of an effort to understand literacy acquisition through peer interaction in educational contexts. Our interest lies in children's verbal interaction in constructive social situations in which children compose a story and dictate it to a scribe (Bereiter & Scardamalia, 1982). This method provides a way to study children's capacity to use a written form of discourse when they do not yet write autonomously. We designed an educational intervention focused on this aspect of the literacy acquisition process with a group of 5-year-old children (Zucchermaglio, 1991).

Elsewhere (Scheuer & Zucchermaglio, 1988), we analyzed the effects of the educational intervention in terms of children's ability to take into account in their productions both the requirements of written texts (meaning must be conveyed autonomously by the syntactical and lexical constraints of the text) and the possibilities they offer (written texts, being stable entities, can be reread and modified) (Sulzby, 1985; Tannen, 1985).

Here, we focus instead on the social interaction among group members during a composition task. The purpose of this study is to identify the features of verbal peer interaction when pursuing a common constructive task and to observe whether and in what ways such features change in the course of consecutive group sessions.

METHOD

Subjects

The subjects were five Italian children (three girls, two boys) who were 5-year-olds (mean age 5 years, 3 months and age range from 4;9 to 5;7) and attended a public kindergarten in Trieste. They were drawn from a larger group consisting of the twenty 5-year-olds attending the school. They were selected on the basis of their performance in an individual interview in which they composed a story and dictated it to a scribe. Five children were selected in order to create a nonhomogeneous group with respect to their levels of competence assessed by the system developed by Pontecorvo and Zucchermaglio (1989) for analyzing children's dictated stories.

Procedure

The group, coordinated by one of the researchers (N.S.), worked once per week, over a period of 2 months (for six 30-minute sessions), in a quiet room outside the classroom. During the sessions, children were asked to compose stories and to dictate them to the adult. Each child composed and dictated one piece of the story, but all five children were involved constructing the story as a whole.

The design of the intervention was based on the child's actively building his or her knowledge by interacting with objects of knowledge within the social context. We give a summary here of the methodological features of the study.

First, peer interaction, stressed as facilitating transformation and acquisition of knowledge, provided a means of sharing the cognitive burden involved in text composition (Graves, 1983) and a favorable context for working in the zone of proximal development (Vygotsky, 1966) and for the emergence of sociocognitive conflicts (Pontecorvo & Zucchermaglio, 1990). Second, the role of the adult was, on the one hand, to support and regulate peer interaction and, on the other hand, to be a conversational partner and scribe. All six sessions were recorded and fully transcribed.

Analysis

The purpose of this chapter is to explore the features characterizing peer verbal interaction in the context just described and to identify changes in interaction processes throughout the six-session intervention.

The unit used in analyzing discussion sequences was the *exchange* between children, defined as "the link between two not necessarily contiguous conversational contributions" (Orsolini, Pontecorvo, & Amoni, 1989, p. 177). A conversational contribution consists of all the utterances contained in a single turn. The link between two contributions is ensured by continuity of topic and/or pragmatic relation. Because we were interested in studying peer interaction, we took into account only children's exchanges; we did not code adult–child exchanges, isolated conversational contributions, or exchanges regulating interaction.

Example 1 illustrates how conversational contributions (CC) and exchanges (E) were counted. It contains three child CC but two child E (36–37 and 37–38):[1]

Example 1

35 Experimenter: [transcribing aloud] *Allora . . . c'era una volta . . .* (So . . . once upon a time . . .)

36 Lorenzo: *Il cane* (The dog)

37 Myriam: *No! Il gatto e il cane/* (No! The cat and the dog)

38 Lorenzo: *E i era fratellini.* (They were brothers)

A quantitative analysis of the distribution of conversational contributions and of exchanges was carried out. We assessed how CC were distributed between the children (taken as a single category) and the adult throughout the sessions and then among the five subjects. A ratio of child exchanges to child CC was also calculated for each session.

We now describe the system of analysis used. Two different aspects of interaction were distinguished and further analyzed: modes of interaction and content of the interaction.

Modes of Interaction: How Do Children Discuss?

In order to analyze modes of interaction between partners, we have adapted an exchange typology developed by Orsolini, Pontecorvo, and Amoni (1989). This typology distinguishes between exchanges involving agreement and exchanges involving opposition. Furthermore, within each type of exchange, it makes it possible to analyze whether the speaker takes the partner into account.

Simple exchanges (either consensual or conflictual) are those that merely express a point of view, neither justifying it nor integrating or elaborating on aspects of another person's discourse. An exchange is considered integrated when the partner is present in the speaker's discourse: On the one hand, the presence of arguments, clarifications, or requests for information indicates that the speaker is attempting to involve the partner; on the other hand, elaborating elements of the partner's discourse indicates that what the partner says has been taken into account.

Our adapted version of the typology, used for calculating frequency distribution, enabled us to distinguish the following exchange types:

---

[1]When a single CC participated in more than one E, it was coded as contributing to two exchanges.

Consensus

Simple exchanges:
- Agreement with a preceding statement, with no justification for that agreement offered.
- Unvaried repetitions of a previous statement or variations in only the form of the statement.

Integrated exchanges:
- Justification for agreeing with a previous statement.
- Elaboration of a previous statement with which the speaker agrees; it is explained, clarified, completed, restructured, or new related aspects are introduced.
- Requests for explanations, clarifications, or additional information about a preceding statement with which the speaker agrees.
- Taking into account the partner's requested explanation, clarification, or request for additional information.

Conflict

Simple exchanges:
- Disagreement with a previous statement, without justification.
- Unjustified counteroppositions (reaffirmation or repetition of a point of view that has been objected to).
- Assertions that contradict a previous statement, without justification.
- Proposal of excluding alternatives to a preceding statement, with no justification or explanation for such choice.

Integrated exchanges:
- Disagreement with a justification in terms of causes, effects, reasons, motives, laws, or proofs.
- Justified counteropposition—a point of view that has been rejected is sustained but reformulated to make it clearer, stronger, or more sensible to the partner through clarification or presentation of causes, effects, reasons, motives, laws, or proofs.

Consensual and conflictual exchanges of both simple and integrated levels are illustrated in Example 2. At the beginning of this sequence, Martina (119) provides a justification for objecting to Donatella's proposal; in terms of the effects of such choice, Donatella (124) accepts Martina's objection and then proposes an alternative. Martina (125) agrees with it and develops it. Nazareno (128) supports his disagreement with that possibility by presenting a weak proof: He never saw any robots who watch TV. Lorenzo (129) first explains to him that it is possible and then develops Martina's proposal.

Example 2

117 Experimenter: [reads the story as dictated to that point, responding to Donatella's request. The main character in the story is a robot.]

118 Donatella: *E adesso si spacca!* (And now it splits!)

119 Martina: *Ma no! Che se il robot si spacca, si spacca anche il panino! Che schifo!* (No! If the robot splits, the sandwich will also split! It's disgusting!) [in the story, the robot had just eaten a sandwich] [related to 118; confl; int.] [Lorenzo laughs]

120 Myriam: *Mangia il panino di vetro* . . . (It eats the glass sandwich) [related to a much earlier CC]

121 Experimenter: *Donatella diceva che il robot si spacca* . . . (Donatella says that the robot will split)

122 Lorenzo: *Noo!* (Noo!)

123 Nazareno: *Sii!* (Yes) [related to 122; confl; simple]

124 Donatella: *Beh, mettiamo invece che va a casa a guardare la TV.* (It would be better to say that the robot will go to the house to watch TV) [related to 119; cons; int]

125 Experimenter: [writing it down] *Va a casa a guardare* . . . (Will go to the house to watch . . .)

126 Martina: */la TV di vetro/* (The glass TV) [related to 124; cons; int.]

127 Myriam: *Si!* (Yes!) [related to 126; cons; simple]

128 Nazareno: *Oh, Dio! Non ho mai visto un robot che guardi la TV.* (Oh my God! I never saw a robot watching TV.) [related to 127; confl; int.]

129 Lorenzo: *Ma può darsi* . . . (It could be . . .) [related to 128; confl; int.] *Mettiamo che guarda la TV con la sua bambina.* (Let's say that the robot watches the TV with his child.) [related to 126; cons; int.]

130 Experimenter: *Scriviamo quello?* (Do we write this down?)

131 Children: *Si.* (Yes)

Content of the Interaction: What Aspects of the Story Composition Process Do the Children Discuss?

The categories used to analyze the content of exchanges are related to the different dimensions implied by the task of "composing a written story" (Pontecorvo & Zucchermaglio, 1989).[2] We have distinguished four content areas: story structure, story planning, decontextualization, and composition process.

---

[2]Because CC in our corpus were usually short and to the point, no problems arose from double classifications in content categories.

Story Structure. This consists of episode, characters, setting, and conventional expressions typical of the story genre (Stein & Glenn, 1979). In the following example, children have the problem of deciding the story's genre (fiction or reality):

Example 3

[The children are composing a story about a boy and a snowman. They are now in the middle of the story.]

139 Donatella: *E dopo andavano a sciare* . . . (And then they go skiing)

140 Lorenzo: [laughing] *Un pupazzo sciando!* (A puppet that skis)

141 Myriam: *Bene, si, eh?* (Well, yes?)

142 Donatella: *Io sono andata a sciare e ho visto* (I went skiing and I saw.)

143 Lorenzo: *Mica sciano i pupazzi!* (The puppets didn't go skiing!)

144 Martina: [addressing Lorenzo] *E' una fantasia!* (It's a fantasy!)

Story Planning. In the following sequence, which occurred before the story was composed and transcribed, the children are involved in choosing the topic around which the story would be constructed:

Example 4

[The children have just been requested to compose a story "in which something happens."]

48 Lorenzo: *It bambino tornò a casa e poi arrivarono i fantasmi.* [as a proposal] (The child came back home and then the ghosts are coming)

49 Nazareno: *Sì! I fantasmi, i fantasmi!* (Yes, the ghosts, the ghosts!)

50 Martina: *No, facciamo di macchine* (No, make it cars!)

51 Myriam: *Di macchine!* (Yes, cars!)

52 Donatella: *Anch'io! Sì! Sì!* (Yes, me too!)

53 Martina: *Sì, sì!* (Yes, yes!)

54 Lorenzo: *No! No!* (No! No!)

55 Nazareno: *No!* (No!)

56 Martina: *Sì, sì!* (Yes, yes!)

57 Experimenter: *Forse invece di dirvi "sì, sì" o "no, no" potete dire perché sì o perché no.* (It would be better, instead of saying "yes" or "no," to say why yes or no.)

58 Martina: *Ma io voglio fare una storia di ma-cchi-ne!* (I prefer a car story!)

59 Donatella: *Anch'io!* (Yes, me too)

60 Martina: *Oppure di robot* . . . (Maybe robots . . .)

61 Lorenzo: [pleased, laughing] *Di robot!* (Robots!)

62 Nazareno: *Sì!!* (Yes!!)

63 Experimenter: *Facciamo una storia di robot, allora?* (We plan to compose a robot story?)

64 Children: *Sì!* (Yes!)

Decontextualization. The content of an exchange is also concerned with creating contextual comprehension for the story. Discussion refers to the use of linguistic options (e.g., how to express the interdependence between parts of the text and how to convey reference) so that meaning is autonomously conveyed by the constraints set by a written text (Smith, 1984). The content of an exchange is placed in this category not merely because connectives are expressed by adequate linguistic devices or because a reference is conveyed clearly, but also because the discussion is focused on connectives or on an expression of reference.

In the following sequence, exchanges refer to the way to convey reference, which is reformulated every time in a clearer way:

Example 5

167 Donatella: [dictating] *Metti il cane e il gatto.* (Write down the dog and the cat.)

168 Lorenzo: [dictating] *Fanno baruffa.* (Are quarreling.)

169 Experimenter: *Con chi?* (With whom?)

170 Lorenzo: *Da soli!* (Alone!)

171 Myriam: *Fra di loro!* (With each other!)

172 Donatella: *Il cane col gatto.* (The dog with the cat.)

Composition Process. Includes text segmentation, dictation (of something on which the group has already agreed), editing (signaling title and author/s of the story), looking back at the written text, and modifications of the text during or after composition (exchanges about modifications of aspects or parts of the story that have already been decided; Michaels & Collins, 1984).

During the sequence immediately preceding Example 5, modifications to the text were discussed:

Example 6

164 Experimenter: [while transcribing a passage on which the children had already decided] *Bene . . ./dopo fanno baruffa e dopo piangono/* (OK . . ./then they quarrel and then they cry)

165 Myriam: *Non si capisce!* (Doesn't work!)

166 Lorenzo: *No!* (No!) [agrees with Myriam]

167 Donatella: *Metti /il cane e il gatto/* (OK, write down/the dog and the cat/) [she proposes to insert the agents of the action before presenting the action itself]

In order to explore whether different types (consensus/conflict) and levels (simple/integrated exchanges) of interacting correspond to different contents of discussion, we mapped the two previous analyses (the mode and the content of interaction).

Results

Based on the results of our previous work on these data (Scheuer & Zuccher-maglio, 1988), we decided to group the six sessions in two sets of three sessions each. The sessions grouped together were similar in terms of the distribution and type of adult and child CC. The first set of sessions (S1) refers to Sessions 1, 2, and 3, whereas the second set (S2) refers to Sessions 4, 5, and 6.

Talking: Who and How Much? Examining the distribution of conversational contributions and of exchanges (see Tables 5.1 and 5.2), we see that, as adult CC diminish, both child participation (CC) and child interaction (exchanges) increase.

At first the ratio between child exchanges and child CC is 1 to 3, whereas in the second set of sessions it is about 1 to 2. Although we are not analyzing the modality of the adult's intervention here, it is interesting to note that, in particular, her CC favoring child interaction diminish considerably; during S2, children participate and interact more without any adult's support.

Participation is distributed equally among children throughout all six sessions. Nazareno's, Myriam's, and Lorenzo's contributions to conversation were always around 20%; but Donatella, who at the beginning almost did not participate, became a more active member of the group, achieving levels of participation even higher than those of her companions. On the other hand, Martina, who at first was the most talkative group member, had a decrease in participation.

TABLE 5.1
Number and Percentage of Child (CH) and Adult (A)
Conversational Contributions (CC) for the First (S1)
and Second (S2) Sets of Sessions

	CH CC	A CC	Total
S1	426	241	667
	(64%)	(36%)	
S2	500	158	658
	(76%)	(24%)	

TABLE 5.2
Number and Percentage (Over Total Amount of Child CC)
of Child Exchanges for the First (S1) and Second (S2) Sets of Sessions

	Exchanges	CH CC
S1	127	426
	(30%)	
S2	273	500
	(55%)	

Inventing a Story: Smooth or Clashing Interaction? Table 5.3 shows that, for our corpus, the most important type of exchange is consensus and that this trend becomes stronger (56% for S1 and 76% for S2).

Agreement with partners' proposals or opinions is expressed; partners' ideas are developed or are requested to be developed. In fact, integrated exchanges are the most frequent smooth interaction; they constitute almost two thirds of the consensual exchanges throughout sessions. The proportion of integrated consensual exchanges remains constant, although the amount of consensual interaction is three times more frequent from S1 to S2. Conflictual interaction is greatly diminished from the first to the second set of sessions (44% for S1, 24% for S2).

If we consider absolute numbers instead of percentages, the number of conflictual exchanges is constant throughout the sessions; as children interact more (the ratio of exchanges to total CC rises), more consensual interaction occurs, whereas a minimal level of opposition is maintained.

When co-constructing a story, children presenting an opposite position seldom (approximately 20%) tried to convince partners by providing justifications for their objections. They usually expressed a point of view without presenting any support for such a position (approximately 80% of simple exchanges); they merely stated disagreement or presented an alternative proposal.

TABLE 5.3
Number and Percentage of Exchanges by Type (Consensus–Conflict)
and by Level (Simple–Integrated) for the First (S1)
and Second (S2) Sets of Sessions

	Consensus			Conflict			
	Simple	Integrated	Total	Simple	Integrated	Total	Total
S1	27	44	71	46	10	56	127
	(38%)	(62%)	(56%)	(82%)	(18%)	(44%)	
S2	77	130	207	51	14	65	272
	(37%)	(63%)	(76%)	(78%)	(22%)	(24%)	

Example 7

[When the story was almost finished, Lorenzo proposed to modify it by introducing two characters. Nobody acknowledged his proposal.]

187 Experimenter: *E cosa vi pare? Sarebbe più bella così?* (What's your opinion? Would it be better?)

188 Myriam: *No!* (No!)

189 Donatella: *No!* (No!)

190 Martina: *Sììì!* (Yes!)

191 Donatella: *No!* (No!)

192 Martina: *Sììì!* (Yes!)

193 Myriam: *Nooo!* (No!)

194 Martina: *Sì!* (Yes!)

195 Myriam: *Nooo!* (No!)

196 Experimenter: *Ma perché "no" o perché "sì"? Occorre dire perché, altrimenti non ci capiamo . . .* (But why are you saying "no" or "yes"? You must say why; otherwise we don't understand anything . . .)

It is interesting to note that, for both consensus and conflict, the pattern of distribution of exchanges between levels is almost constant throughout the sessions.

Let's Talk About . . .   An analysis of the content of exchanges shows that children's discussions are as involved with aspects related to the structure of the story (51% for S1, 43% for S2) as with the process of composition (41% for S1, 42% for S2). As Table 5.4 shows, most exchanges referred to these two topics throughout the sessions, whereas children almost never discussed ways of conveying meaning within the constraints of a written text (2% for S1 and for S2). Planning the story—an operation to be exercised in advance on a nonexistent future text—was one aspect that was discussed with increasing frequency (6% for S1, 13% for S2). The distribution of exchanges among content categories was constant throughout sessions, with the only relevant variation concerning plan-

TABLE 5.4
Number and Percentage of Exchanges by Content Area—Story
Structure (S), Planning (P), Decontextualization (D), and Process
of Composition (PR)—for the First (S1) and Second (S2) Sets of Sessions

	S	P	D	PR	Total
S1	64	8	3	52	127
	(51%)	(6%)	(2%)	(41%)	
S2	117	34	6	116	273
	(43%)	(13%)	(2%)	(42%)	

ning. As planning became a significant topic for discussion, the importance of story structure slightly decreased. The decline in this last category may be due precisely to the fact that aspects related to it (e.g., characters, episode, setting) in S2 are decided beforehand.

Example 8

21 Experimenter: *Di che cosa può essere questa storia?* (What could be the topic of this story?)

22 Lorenzo: *La storia . . . di una borsetta.* (The story . . . of a handbag.) [He laughs and everybody laughs.]

23 Lorenzo: *La storia borsetta, sì!* (Yes, the handbag story!)

24 Donatella: *Ma no!* (No!)

25 Myriam: *Nooo!* (Nooo!)

26 Lorenzo: *Sì, sì, sì!* (Yes, yes, yes!)

27 Experimenter: *Vediamo . . . facciamo una storia di . . . ?* (OK . . . we will write a story about . . . ?)

28 Myriam: *Un gattino.* (A small cat.)

29 Experimenter: *Un gattino?* (A small cat?)

30 Lorenzo: *Sì, anche di un cane! Tutti e due erano fratellini.* (Yes, also about a dog! They are brothers.)

31 Experimenter: *E come cominciamo a scriverla?* (And how do we begin to write?)

32 Lorenzo: *Dal cane. No, dal gatto.* (From the dog. No, from the cat.)

33 Myriam: *C'era una volta un gatto.* (Once upon a time there was a cat.) [They continue by composing a story about two brothers, a cat and a dog.]

Around 40% of the exchanges refer to the composition process. Activities such as segmenting the text and editing or modifying it (actions resulting from the previous action of constructing the story) are discussed. It is interesting to observe that children who are not used to composing written texts are able, from the beginning, to handle the text being composed as an object on which various activities may be exercised.

A careful analysis of the exchanges in this category reveals intracategory changes. At first, most exchanges related to editing; after the text was constructed, however, the end and authors were signaled or a title was introduced. During the second set of sessions, exchanges in this category were much more varied. For instance, dictation became a moment in itself: A piece was dictated only after it had been decided by the group. Besides, the burden of dictation was shared among group members:

Example 9

[later on during the same session as Example 7]

66 Lorenzo: *Andavano a fare una passeggiata.* (They are going to walk.)

67 Donatella: *Sì!* (Yes!)

[The adult begins to transcribe.]

68 Donatella: [dictating] /*a fare*/ (/they are going/)

69 Lorenzo: *Una passeggiata e dopo andavano.* (A walk and then they went.)

70 Experimenter: [as a request to adapt speed] *una pa-sse-ggiata. Punto?* (a walk. Period?)

71 Lorenzo: *No* (No)

72 Donatella: [dictating] *e dopo andavano a casa* (and then they went home.)

73 Exp [transcribing] *e dopo . . .* (and then . . .)

74 Donatella: *andavano* (they went)

75 Myriam: *a casa!* (home!)

It was also mainly during the second set of sessions that children returned to the written text during and after composition, and proposed and discussed corrections and revisions.[3]

Mapping Modes and Content of Interaction. First, we analyze the relation between type and content of exchanges (see Table 5.5). In the first set of sessions, consensual interaction occurred most often when the children talked about aspects linked to the story structure (57%) and when they referred to the composition process (35%). The remaining consensual exchanges concerned planning (7%).

Conflict occurred almost as often when the children were discussing story structure (43%) as when they were discussing aspects concerning process (48%). The other cases of conflictual exchanges occurred when planning or decontextualization was discussed (5% and 4%, respectively).

During the second set of sessions, somewhat different features emerged. Story structure was no longer the topic on which most consensus was reached; the children reached consensus at least as often on composition process as on story structure (47% and 43%, respectively). No changes occurred in the frequency of the children's discourse about planning and decontextualization.

The relation of conflict to planning changed, however, between the first and the second sessions. Although the relative amount of conflictual exchanges that occurred while the story structure was being discussed remained constant (42%), a large proportion occurred during planning (29%), and the frequency of conflict

---

[3]Examining the content of isolated CC (i.e., those that do not present a continuing topic or have a pragmatic relation with any other CC) and of CC related to an adult question or answer, the same distribution and the same trend are found! Not only are these CC initially concentrated mainly on story structure and process but, in the second set of sessions, planning emerges as an area for discussion, corresponding to a proportional decrease in the amount of CC referring to story structure.

TABLE 5.5
Number and Percentage of Consensual and Conflictual Exchanges
by Content Area for the First (S1) and Second (S2) Sets of Sessions

Content of Exchange	S1		S2	
	Consensus	Conflict	Consensus	Conflict
S	40	24	89	28
	(57%)	(43%)	(43%)	(42%)
P	5	3	15	19
	(7%)	(5%)	(7%)	(29%)
D	1	2	6	0
	(1%)	(4%)	(3%)	
PR	25	27	97	19
	(35%)	(48%)	(47%)	(29%)
Total	71	56	207	66

during discussions on the composition process declined (29%). No conflictual exchange was associated with decontextualization.

We now reconsider the results of the distribution of exchanges taken as a whole, by area of content (see Table 5.4). By mapping type and content, we can see that, on the one hand, the consolidation of planning as an area for discussion during S2 is not related to all exchanges but rather to conflictual interaction in particular. On the other hand, the proportion of exchanges referring to process remains constant throughout sessions, because the increase of consensual interaction compensates the drop in the amount of conflict within process discussions. Thus, although the total number of exchanges about process is constant, the participation of consensual and conflictual exchanges varies.

Mapping interaction levels and content also shows that higher levels of interaction are achieved in different areas of content for each of the exchange types (see Table 5.6). In S1, the highest proportion of integrated exchanges occurred in story structure (75%). When process was being discussed, simple and integrated exchanges were equally likely (52% and 48%, respectively). No trend in planning and decontextualization was apparent for so few cases. A different pattern emerges from the analysis of S2, because the area of content for which the higher proportion of integrated exchanges occurred turns out to be process (70%). Integrated exchanges continued to be the most frequent (although not as frequent as during S1) during discussions regarding story structure (60%). In the case of interaction about planning, simple exchanges were the most frequent (73%). Finally, for the two categories that together include almost all consensual exchanges, the proportion of integrated exchanges is above one half throughout the sessions.

With regard to conflict (see Table 5.7), the highest levels of interaction were achieved during discussion about process in both the first and second sets of

TABLE 5.6
Number and Percentage of Simple and Integrated Consensual Exchanges
by Content Area for the First (S1) and Second (S2) Sets of Sessions

Content of Exchange	S1			S2		
	Simple	Integrated	Total	Simple	Integrated	Total
S	10	30	40	36	53	89
	(25%)	(75%)		(40%)	(60%)	
P	3	2	5	11	4	15
	(60%)	(40%)		(73%)	(27%)	
D	1	0	1	1	5	6
	(100%)			(17%)	(83%)	
PR	13	12	25	29	68	97
	(52%)	(48%)		(30%)	(70%)	

TABLE 5.7
Number and Percentage of Simple and Integrated Conflictual Exchanges
by Content Area for the First (S1) and Second (S2) Sets of Sessions

Content of Exchange	S1			S2		
	Simple	Integrated	Total	Simple	Integrated	Total
S	22	2	24	23	5	28
	(92%)	(8%)		(82%)	(18%)	
P	3	0	3	16	3	19
	(100%)			(84%)	(16%)	
D	1	1	2	0	0	0
	(50%)	(50%)				
PR	20	7	27	13	6	19
	(74%)	(26%)		(68%)	(32%)	

sessions (26% and 32% of integrated exchanges, respectively). Within the remaining content areas (story structure during S1 and S2, and planning during S2), the proportion of integrated exchanges was under 20%. The proportion of integrated exchanges was much lower in conflict than in consensus.

DISCUSSION

An analysis of the distribution of both the children's and the adult's participation clearly shows that, as the adult's intervention diminished, the children's participation increased. It is important to note that what is really increasing in the children's contributions is the exchanges between children: That is, not only do children become more able to participate in the discussion but they also become more able to interact with each other. To interact productively, a learning phase is necessary in which the adults learn to speak less and the children learn to speak about the same thing and to manage their interactions autonomously (Formisano & Zucchermaglio, 1987). This is reciprocal learning: The adult learns to leave the children cognitive and social space, and the children learn to benefit from this in the social process of knowledge construction.

Another measure of the productivity of peer interaction, from the point of view of the content of interaction, is the "well-formed" structure of the stories composed by the children, as well as the more planned process of their composition. With regard to the latter, we found that, just from the first session of work, more consensual exchanges than conflict exchanges occurred, and this difference increased by the end of the work. We think that this result depends strictly on the interactive task. The task of composing a story is open without a fixed and correct ending, as there would be, for example, in scientific or mathematical tasks (Pontecorvo, Castiglia, & Zucchermaglio, 1983). At the same time, the task requires that children compose only one story, thus obliging them to choose among many possible solutions to the task. The only way to solve this type of task is to exploit constructive synergies among children and, therefore, to prefer the consensual exchanges.

Moreover, it is important to note that the majority of the consensual exchanges were of a high level; that is, there was active and constructive consensus (e.g., integrate, expand, ask for clarification, complete, restructure). This means that the children—as a group—did not allow only one single child to construct a well-formed story, but that all the children actively contributed to the collective construction of the best story that the group—as a group—could compose at a given moment.

Among the conflictual exchanges (less frequently present than the consensual ones), the high levels of interaction are less present: In this type of task (and with children of this age), it seems to be very difficult to justify explicitly one's own position and at the same time produce arguments against another's position. It is impossible to appeal to common evidence, but it is necessary to make a claim based on metacognitive and metalinguistic strategies (e.g., "If we write it down what you are suggesting, the reader could not understand . . .").

In the task we used, the learning goal was not the restructuring of a phenomenon representation or the appropriation of new information; instead, the goal was to allow children to learn strategies and processes to utilize in a new communicative context. For children of the age and competence of those in our study, this makes it much more difficult to use "opposing skills" in an open task that allows more than one good solution (why is one story better than another one). It seems necessary, therefore, to consider more carefully the cognitive features of a task on which children will be interacting and to avoid interpreting as general processes what are rather specific ones, because they are directly connected at the different interaction contexts and tasks.

REFERENCES

Bereiter, C., & Scardamalia, M. (1982). From conversation to composition: The role of instruction in developmental process. In R. Glaser (Ed.), *Advances in instructional psychology* (Vol. II, pp. 132–165). Hillsdale, NJ: Lawrence Erlbaum Associates.

Formisano, M., & Zucchermaglio, C. (1987). La costruzione sociale della lingua scritta [The social construction of written language]. *Scuola e Città, 4,* 155–164.

Graves, D. H. (1983). *Writing: Teachers and children at work.* Exeter, NH: Heinemann.

Michaels, S., & Collins, J. (1984). Oral discourse styles: Classroom interaction and the acquisition of literacy. In D. Tannen (Ed.), *Spoken and written language: Exploring orality and literacy* (pp. 86–102). Norwood, NJ: Ablex.

Orsolini, M., Pontecorvo, C., & Amoni, M. (1989). Discutere a scuola: Interazione sociale e attività cognitiva [Discussing at school: Social interaction and cognitive activity]. *Giornale Italiano di Psicologia, 16,* 3.

Pontecorvo, C., Castiglia, D., & Zucchermaglio, C. (1983). Discorso e ragionamento scientifico nelle discussioni in classe [Discourse and scientific reasoning in class discussions]. *Scuola e Città, 10,* 447–461.

Pontecorvo, C., & Zucchermaglio, C. (1989). From oral to written language: Preschool children dictating stories. *Journal of Reading Behavior, 21*(2), 109–125.

Pontecorvo, C., & Zucchermaglio, C. (1990). A passage to literacy: Learning in a social context. In Y. Goodman (Ed.), *How children construct literacy* (pp. 55–78). New York: International Reading Association.

Scheuer, N., & Zucchermaglio, C. (1988). Costruire una storia scritta . . . sempre più scritta! [Constructing a written story . . . more and more written]. *Scuola e Città, 8,* 344–355.

Smith, F. (1984). The creative achievement of literacy. In H. Goelman, A. Oberg, & F. Smith (Eds.), *Awakening to literacy* (pp. 169–188). London: Heinemann.

Stein, N. L., & Glenn, C. G. (1979). An analysis of story comprehension in elementary school children. In R. Freedle (Ed.), *New directions in discourse processing* (Vol. II, pp. 53–120). Norwood, NJ: Ablex.

Sulzby, E. (1985). Kindergartners as writers and readers. In M. Farr (Ed.), *Children's early writing development* (pp. 112–137). Norwood, NJ: Ablex.

Tannen, D. (1985). Spoken and written narrative in English and Greek. In D. Tannen (Ed.), *Coherence in spoken and written discourse* (pp. 33–57). Norwood, NJ: Ablex.

Vygotsky, L. S. (1966). *Pensiero e linguaggio* [Thought and language]. Firenze, Italy: Giunti e Barbera.

Zucchermaglio, C. (1991). *Gli apprendisti della lingua scritta* [The apprentices of written language]. Bologna, Italy: Il Mulino.

WRITING AS A SYSTEM
OF REPRESENTATION

6

THREE ACCOUNTS OF LITERACY AND THE ROLE OF THE ENVIRONMENT

Liliana Tolchinsky Landsmann
Institute of Educational Sciences
University of Barcelona

During the last decade, increasing interest has developed about the description and explanation of children's knowledge about writing prior to being formally taught to read and write. Researchers have studied children from a variety of racial and ethnic backgrounds as well as from a range of economic levels. There seems to be no doubt that children in all of these conditions are sensitive to the formal features of writing and to the different functions that written language fulfills (Ferreiro & Teberosky, 1979/1982; Gibson & Levin, 1975; Harste, Woodward, & Burke, 1984). It also seems that the hypotheses children build about the writing system "are not idiosyncratic but developmentally ordered" (Ferreiro, 1986, p. 16). Moreover, empirical studies in different languages (e.g., Spanish, English, French, Portuguese, Italian, Hebrew, and Catalan) have proved that some of these hypotheses[1] reappear in different linguistic environments and in Semitic as well as Latin orthographies (Tolchinsky Landsmann, 1991a). The fact that some of the children's ideas about writing are developmentally ordered and recurrent in different environments has led some researchers to characterize the acquisition of writing as a "psychogenetic process, in the Piagetian sense" (Ferreiro, 1986, p. 16) or to speak about the "ontogenesis of written language" (Scinto, 1986, p. 30). They hint at a sort of self-propelled, natural process of acquisition.

---

[1]I have used the term *hypotheses* very loosely here to keep in line with the literature I quote. I do not regard this term as appropriate, however, in describing the kind of knowledge children of the age range discussed here have about writing.

The object of knowledge, that is, the writing system, is a cultural artifact. The process of becoming literate occurs in a web of social interactions (Scribner, 1984) and is mediated by different cultural representations of literacy (Sperber, 1984; Street, 1984). On this basis, another account emphasizes the need to distinguish between natural and cultural phases in the acquisition of written language (Luria, 1929/1978). Still other perspectives stand in sharp contrast with the previous one by postulating that reading and writing must be carefully and laboriously taught.

My aim in this chapter is to characterize some of these perspectives about reading and writing.[2] Specifically, I look at the way diverse perspectives have dealt with the spontaneity and universality implied in the notions of ontogenesis and with the cultural and social determination implied in the notion of literacy. In the first part of this chapter, I present three of these perspectives: the reductionist, the sociocultural, and the constructivist. In the second part, I argue that the reductionist and the sociocultural accounts have a definite view of the role of the environment in the process of becoming literate, whereas the constructivist account does not yet. I further suggest a number of questions that should be formulated concerning different kinds of contexts if we aim to spell out a constructivist theory of the role of the environment in literacy.

THREE CONCEPTUALIZATIONS OF THE PROCESS OF BECOMING LITERATE

"More profound in its own way than the discovery of fire or the wheel"—this is how Diringer (1961, p. 19) described the impact of writing on the course of human history. The writing revolution was the first of the great communication revolutions in the history of mankind. The next came several thousand years later with the advent of printing. It is not a trivial matter to remain outside of these revolutions. On one hand, it is certain that, both at an individual and at a social level, illiteracy and poverty nearly coincide. On the other hand, however, similar social conditions do not provoke similar ease in learning to read and to write. It is not surprising then that the study of these processes has been a constant theme in psychology.

The psychological description of the way individuals become literate has been approached from different perspectives. I focus here on the reductionist,

---

[2]A previous version of this chapter was written about 5 years ago and published in Italian (Tolchinsky Landsmann, 1991b). Since then I have explored three related themes: the relationship between the acquisition of writing and the acquisition of other notational systems, specifically the numerical system; the psychological reality of literary genres; and the relationship between phonological awareness and the acquisition of writing in different orthographies. This work led me to revise some of the psychological principles explaining literacy acquisition and to consider anew the contribution of connectionism to constructivist accounts. That is the reason I have included these issues in this version.

the sociocultural, and the constructivist. Each of them has provided alternative explanations of the language component that ultimately explains the process of learning to read, the mechanisms involved in this process, and the relative role of the subject and the environment in this process. In spite of these differences, many researchers within the three frameworks seem to coincide in their conception of the relationship between spoken language and writing. They share the "Greek tradition,"[3] a tradition for which the spoken is the real, the natural language, whereas the written is a derivative, an imperfect representation of speech. Although these researchers recognize the existence of other writing systems, they judge them under the "tyranny of the alphabet" (Harris, 1986, p. 30). Accordingly, they interpret the history of writing (and the ontogenesis) as teleologically oriented to attain the best form, alphabetic writing. This conception of writing is so widespread and rooted in modern linguistics that it is not surprising that it stands as the basis of almost every psychological explanation of the ways individuals become literate. Some developmentalists (Scinto, 1986; Tolchinsky Landsmann & Teberosky, 1992) have only recently departed from this conception. Based on some of the ideas of Prague functionalists (e.g., Vachek, 1966, 1973); we look at the spoken and the written forms as two equipollent systems of language. Because they are equipollent, although functionally distinct, they affect each other.

The Reductionist Account

I include under the rubric of reductionist several diverse lines of thought that share the conviction that the ability to read and the ability to write can be decomposed into a number of simpler components. These all view the simplest component, the ability to manipulate phonemic segments, as ultimately responsible for learning to read. These lines of thought differ, however, in whether they think this ability is very specific or the result of a general learning mechanism. This difference has led to contrasting positions regarding the role of the environment in the learning process.

A clear illustration of a reductionist account is the *simple view* proposed by Gough (Gough & Tunmer, 1986; Juel, Griffith, & Gough, 1986). In the simple view, reading ability is composed of two factors: decoding and comprehension. Decoding is the process that leads to word recognition: "Learning to *break the code* of written text is partly dependent on knowing that words are sequences of meaningless sounds (i.e., phonemes) which can be independently manipulated. . . . Comprehension is the process by which the meanings of words are integrated into sentences and text structures" (Juel, 1988, pp. 2–3).

---

[3]Aristotle wrote the following in *De Interpretatione* (1.4-6): "Words spoken are symbols or signs of affections or impressions of the soul; written words are the signs of words spoken." The Aristotelian view was echoed in the 18th century by Rousseau and in the 20th century is no longer considered a possible view but an accepted fact.

The phonological component is viewed as the component ultimately responsible for learning how to read. Similarly, the ability to write can be decomposed into two basic components: spelling and ideation. Spelling, which also requires a "certain degree of phonemic awareness" (Juel, 1988, p. 4), is viewed as the inverse of decoding: It enables composition of words. Ideation is "the ability to generate and organize ideas into sentence and text structures" (p. 6). Both the basic abilities and the learning process are defined by reducing complex composites to simpler components: Knowledge of texts is explained in terms of knowledge of words, knowledge of words in terms of knowledge of sounds. Not only the normal learning process but also difficulties in the learning process or in performance are explained by the same reductionist principle.

> Poor lower order processes may impede the development of higher order processes. Until the lower order process of spelling is somewhat automatic . . . the attention of the writer may be diverted from higher order composing processes. . . . The development of automatic lower level processing of words may also be required for attention to be fully focused on comprehension when reading. (Juel, 1988, p. 6)

As long as lower level processes are not automatized, higher level processes cannot be attended to. Differences between written and spoken language are minimized because a single underlying process is seen as producing both reading and listening comprehension. The view of a single general mechanism underlying every learning process and across-the-board difficulties has exerted a strong influence on remediation and teaching practices up to now.

The reductionist outlook is a clear outcome of the "Morgan canon" by which, whenever possible, higher mental processes have to be interpreted "as an outcome of the exercise of one which stands lower in the psychological scale" (Lloyd Morgan, 1894). British empiricism provided the basis for this reductionism, because on this account universal ideas result from a comparison of complex ideas, whereas complex ideas are an outcome of *simple ideas* and simple ideas are produced by the impression of the *qualities of the objects*. Higher forms of knowledge can be reduced to a series of associative habits that explain the laws of attraction of the ideas that are produced by exposure to the object. The same series of habits holds for any linguistic or cognitive domain. Most studies of behaviorist inspiration believe that the same general mechanism explains every learning process. Those studies have linked, for example, reading difficulties to spatial orientation or to holistic perception capacities (Bender, 1957).

When pedagogical alternatives are elaborated on this basis, they tend to manipulate the learning environment following a similar reductionist canon. Accordingly, basal texts are prepared to provide children with reading materials of graded difficulty. Texts are organized from simple words to longer paragraphs, and their vocabulary is purposely simplified. The criterion for *simple* is determined by the component supposed to be responsible for learning how to read; that is, the phonological structure of the word. The words and sentences included in the basal texts are selected according to their phonological structure or their sound combination, rather than for meaning or narrative coherence. The outcome of this simplified and graded organization is a special *literary genre*, a genre serving not for reading but for learning how to read.

Another line of research evolved during the 1970s from the studies on skilled readers and the neuropsychology of acquired reading disorders. These researchers adopted a different conceptual framework, that of the information processing approach; that is, the view of the cognitive apparatus as a network of partially autonomous functional units, sometimes called *modules*, which can be analyzed both through experimental manipulation and through the effects of brain damage. Reading disorders are assumed to be derived from affected specific components of the language/reading module (Shankweiler & Crain, 1986).

With respect to the role of the environment, as with respect to the specificity of the mechanism involved in the learning process, the two lines of thinking have contrasting positions. For the studies of behavioristic inspiration, the environment is the key; for those studies that have grown out of a biological perspective on language and cognition, the environment has only a triggering effect, that is, exposure to alphabetic writing.

When no complex principled knowledge is assumed on the part of the beginning reader that could mediate or interfere with the controlled presentation of the reading materials, all the burden of success or failure is put on the environment. Initial individual differences are interpreted either as failure or as a success of the child's learning environment to enhance these purported lower level factors. For instance, lack of phonemic awareness is attributed to "certain dialects and second languages which are spoken at home" and high level of phonemic awareness to the "time spent at home with word play, pig Latin" (Juel, 1988). Later individual differences are also explained in similar environmental terms such as "reading experiences in school rather aversive" (Juel, 1988, p. 17). Either by failing to provoke the emergence of the required lower level abilities or by wasting the opportunity to correct the initial failure, the environment appears to be responsible for everything children know or do not know about written language.

The direction of progress in learning posited by reductionists, that is, from letter–sound correspondences to text organization, as well as the basic role they attribute to the phonological component, is controversial. Studies on text production in early childhood have shown that children know about the language to be written before they know how to draw letters or how to correspond letters to sounds. They are able to differentiate between narratives and descriptions before they are able to write a story conventionally (Tolchinsky Landsmann, 1990). They produce texts that are constrained by the journalistic style even though they can hardly decode a newspaper (Teberosky, 1990; see also chap.

13, this volume). These studies have shown that higher level notions are already present from the initial moments of acquisition and may interact with lower level notions during the whole acquisition process.

Furthermore, empirical work on the development of literacy before schooling has shown that children's concern with letter–sound correspondences is a relatively late notion. Young preschoolers are sensitive to the formal constraints of written words long before recognizing any correspondence between letters and sounds. For example, being asked to separate cards that are "good for reading" or "good for writing" from those that are not, they reject cards displaying strings of identical letters or strings containing a mixture of letters, geometric signs, and ciphers. This rejection is based on strictly formal grounds and has nothing to do with the decoding ability of these children. Moreover, some 4- to 5-year-olds have been found to select the number and variety of letters used in their writing to represent characteristics of the referent rather than the sound pattern of the words they were attempting to write. Thus, when asked to write *hen* and then *chick*, they may use a few of the letters from the first word to form the second, as if trying to represent both the semantic overlap and the difference in size (Ferreiro & Teberosky, 1982). Similarly, preschoolers tend to represent in writing semantic relationships between sentences (Tolchinsky Landsmann, 1988). Only later on in development do children resort to letter–sound correspondences as the main guideline to interpret and to produce written words.

Regarding the fundamental role attributed to phonological awareness, empirical work has already shown that this capacity is more a result than a precursor of learning how to read in an alphabetic system (cf. Ehri, 1985; Ehri & Wilce, 1980; Hohn & Ehri, 1983; Morais, Cary, Jeans, & Bertelson, 1979; Read, Yun-Fei, Hong-Yin, & Bao-Qing, 1986). In line with Content (1984) and Stanovich (1986), I think it is more accurate to speak at least of reciprocal influence between phonological awareness and learning to read.

Ongoing research in collaboration with Ana Teberosky provides further support for the hypothesis of reciprocal influence. We are looking at the relationship between phonological segmentation and the acquisition of writing in three languages and two orthographic systems: the Latin system used to write Spanish and Catalan and the Hebrew system. Preschoolers, first graders, and second graders, in Spain and Israel, respectively, were asked to participate in a variety of oral segmentation and writing tasks. The words selected for those tasks were the same in all three languages, except for variations in pronunciation (e.g., *pizza*). I discuss here only one task and some of the results that are relevant to my argument.

Children were asked to repeat a word said by the experimenter "in little bits, as little as possible" (Tolchinsky Landsmann & Teberosky, 1993, p. 95). The children provide a variety of ways of segmenting the words. However, the preferred unit of segmentation was the syllable. This tendency did not show significant differences by language or by orthographic system. In second grade, after one year of formal teaching, all the children were reading and writing conventionally but only some could segment the words into consonants and vowels, pronounced separately. This finding, that despite knowing to read and write children did not segment into consonants and vowels, is interesting although not very original. The most important finding for our argument, however, is that quite a few Hebrew-speaking children segmented in a way that no Spanish-speaking children or Catalan-speaking children did: They pronounced only the word consonants, omitting the vowels. This segmentation procedure can only be explained as a result of exposure to the Hebrew writing system that includes only letters for consonants, because the graphic signs for vowels are contained in an optional system of diacritics.

In contrast to the reductionist account, the picture provided by these studies is of a complex reorganization of knowledge at different levels rather than of a linear movement from lower to higher level ability components. Furthermore, the last study just mentioned suggests a stronger influence of writing on phonological analysis rather than the other way around.

The Sociocultural Account

An alternative description of the process of becoming literate comes from the Vygotskian *sociocultural* approach to the study of mind (Vygotsky, 1978). Vygotsky was among the first psychologists to consider that written language should be an object of psychological interest. According to Vygotsky, the aim of any scientific psychology is to study "higher order psychological functions," that is, uniquely human ones. Because writing is uniquely human, it constitutes an object of inquiry for scientific psychology. Moreover, because one of Vygotsky's basic tenets was his reliance on the genetic method (Wertsch, 1985, 1991), he thought the acquisition of written language should be studied from its very beginning.

Both Vygotsky and Luria accepted the principle that all psychological processes have a basis in reflexes. However, they resisted the American position that complex psychological processes can be reduced to chains of reflexes. Humans are able to make indirect connections between incoming stimulation and their own responses through various mediating links, especially language (Cole, in Luria, 1976). Vygotsky (1928) claimed that there are two main lines in the development of the child's behavior: the natural or organic and the cultural. Although both are subject to similar influences, they are qualitatively different. Natural development provides the conditions and the energy for cultural development. Social interaction provides the organizational principles for cultural development. Mediation turns natural development into cultural development. According to Vygotsky, cultural development:

> is subject to the influence of the same two main factors which take part in the organic development of the child, namely the biological and the social. . . . Only at a certain level of the internal development of the organism does it become

possible to master any of the cultural methods. Also an organism internally prepared absolutely requires the determining influence of the environment in order
to enable it to accomplish that development. However, the relation of the two
factors in the development of this kind (cultural) is materially changed. The active
part is played by the organism which masters the means of cultural behavior
supplied by the environment. But the organic maturation plays the part of a *condition* rather than a motive power of the process of cultural development, since
the structure of that process is defined by outward influences. . . . It can be defined
as outer rather than as inner-growth. (1928, pp. 423–424)

Following this distinction between natural and cultural development, Vygotsky contrasted written speech to oral speech in terms of their origin. He wrote,
"Oral speech evolves naturally in the process of social interaction between
children and adults" whereas "Written speech emerges as the result of special
learning" (Luria, 1982, p. 165). Loyal to the Aristotelian tradition, he affirmed that
"A feature of this system is that it is a second-order symbolism . . . a system of
signs that designate the sounds and words of spoken language, which in turn
are signs of real entities and relationships" (Vygotsky, 1978, p. 106). Despite this,
the phonological component is considered transitional. The mediation of speech
must be overcome so that writing "becomes direct symbolism."

Early stages of development of any psychological function would be natural,
whereas from a certain point on, internalized forms of social interaction with
expert adults would structure the development of this function to higher levels.
Internalization is the internal reconstruction of an external operation. The basic
notion is that we observe those in the social environment around us as acting
in certain ways, and we internalize their actions (and their speech as a form of
action) so that they become part of ourselves. Consistent with this view, Vygotsky sketches the four main stages of "the *education* of the psychogenesis of
cultural forms of behavior" (1928, p. 424). The first is described as the stage of
primitive behavior or natural psychology. The other three are characterized by
the child's increasing internalization of tools and cultural methods and an increasing consciousness of his own psychological operations. Within this framework, it was Luria who directly studied the development of writing. In his study,
Luria asked preschoolers to recall a number of sentences that "exceeded the
child's mechanical capacity to remember" (Luria, 1929/1978, p. 149). Based on
this procedure, he identified four stages similar to the ones that Vygotsky had
found in the development of other functions: (a) undifferentiated-noninstrumen-
tal, (b) undifferentiated ostensive sign use, (c) undifferentiated to differentiated
transformation of sign-stimulus to sign-symbol, and (d) pictographic use of signs.
From the third stage on, the natural development of writing turns into cultural
development (Luria, 1929/1978; Scinto, 1986). The third stage is crucial because
the child grasps the fundamental relationship of *standing for*. In Luria's view, the
essential point is that the symbolic relation was established, although it was not
established in relation to the sound patterns of words.

I see two main limitations regarding the specific analysis of the "prehistory of written language" in Luria's work. First, only the instrumental function of writing is stressed. In conceiving of writing as an auxiliary technique, used mainly for recording, he failed to see what children already know about writing as a domain of knowledge. It is clear from Luria's examples that his subjects were already producing linear, discontinuous, writinglike productions; he only emphasized, however, that they were not using letters. Even the children's attempts to represent the rhythm of the phrases was disregarded. Only their struggling to represent the content of the phrases was taken into account, and this despite the fact that those attempts may have contributed to the eventual phonetization of children's written representations.

The second limitation concerns Luria's conclusion that once children learn the alphabet, the whole developmental process starts again. Luria wrote that "in the first stage of symbolic alphabetic writing the child begins with a stage of undifferentiated writing he had already passed through long before" (1929/1978, p. 187). Because the studies were not longitudinal, this statement is indeed problematic, but the epistemological implication is the most interesting. This interpretation is very illustrative of the author's belief in the strength of cultural information: in this case, the information of conventional letter's shape. It was easier for Luria to consider that children who know how to draw conventional letters but still produce undifferentiated writings are starting the whole developmental cycle again, rather than to accept that children who are familiar with the conventional letters and children who are not may still be at the same level of writing development. That is, they could still be at a stage where they produce similar writing patterns for different utterances, despite knowing some conventional letters.

Besides these limitations, the merits of the Vygotskian approach are beyond question. It brought the study of writing within the scope of psychological research. It highlighted the possibility of a natural source for written language development and revealed the crucial role of mediation in psychological development. Nevertheless, it still advocates a dualistic conception of development. Natural development is the condition, the energetic principle, but the laws of organization are provided from outside by the structure of social interaction and cultural institutions.[4] This is clear from the following statement: "A child mastering Russian or English and a child mastering the language of some primitive tribe, masters, in connection with the environment in which he is developed,

---

[4]This is true in spite of the inner transformations that must occur as the functions are internalized. The process of internalization consists of a series of transformations: (a) An operation that initially represents an external activity is reconstructed and begins to occur internally; (b) an interpersonal process is transformed into an intrapersonal one; and (c) the transformation of an interpersonal process into an intrapersonal one is the result of a long series of developmental events. (For a discussion of this issue, see Glick, 1983; Tolchinsky Landsmann, 1991a.)

two totally different systems of thinking" [italics added] (Vygotsky, 1928, p. 424). As one of the main representatives of what Sternberg (1990) called "the sociological metaphor of mind," Vygotsky was convinced that by similar socialization processes the effects on the development of intelligence are qualitatively different.

The natural/cultural distinction and the adult's role in early literacy development are far from being clear cut. Humans have a "print-out facility" (Wilks, 1982) for creating notations in every culture and environment. In some communities, this natural tendency led to the invention of writing, whereas in some others it did not (and we are far from knowing why this was so; see Harris, 1986, for a discussion).

It is also evident that children growing up in literate communities show a natural sensitivity to the notational environment. The superordinate features of writing become part of children's graphic expression very early on, independent of race, socioeconomic status, or microcultural milieu (Gibson & Levin, 1975; Harste, Woodward, & Burke, 1984). Latin letters are incorporated into Mexican, Spanish, and Italian children's repertoire and Hebrew letters into Israeli children's repertoire. Children usually do not invent or create writing; instead, they discover the features of the writing system in their environment. However, the processes of discovery seem to be self-directed and not an outcome of the sort of instructional influences of expert adults. Such interactions are the ones supposed by Vygotsky to promote development. We can hardly think about parents teaching or explaining to their children that "in order to write you have to use a certain number and variety of letters," yet these are precisely the sorts of constraints children apply to their writing. Some studies have shown, for instance, that, after a period in which children produce long strings of undifferentiated marks to represent any utterance, they tend to write strings of about three nonrepeated marks. A similar progression from undifferentiated to constrained writing was found among Russian, Spanish, and Hebrew speakers. The same principles of minimal quantity and variety appear to regulate preschoolers' productions in Latin as well as in Semitic orthographies. It is true that the constraints of number and intrastring variety are part of the notational constraints of the writing system, but have you noticed that? Have you noticed that most of the meaningful words you read usually consist of between four and six letters? Have you realized that you will not find a word containing the same letter more than three times? This is precisely the point. What seems to be a relevant input for the child is not a relevant input for the ex-child. And the most complex aspect of this development is that certain principles reappear in different orthographies.

If we object to the reductionist as well as the sociocultural explanation of the role of the environment, shall we then define the ontogenesis of writing as independent of it? Let us look at what Piagetians have to say on this issue.

The Constructivist Account

The distinction between natural and cultural lines of development or between everyday and scientific concepts is not relevant in Piagetian accounts. The same categories of knowledge are assumed to organize any content. Like the reductionists, Piagetians propose a continuity from reflexes to axioms. This continuity, however, is not proposed in terms of the outputs of evolution over time, which are considered to be qualitatively different, but in terms of the functional mechanisms responsible for these outputs. The famous trilogy—*assimilation, accommodation,* and *equilibration* (cf. Piaget, 1975)—is proposed as the explanatory functional factor for developmental change and change in performance in any domain. Piaget's account is the most closely detailed attempt anywhere to attribute the development of mental life to a continuous process of self-generation, or construction, whereby one form builds on the ones before it (Sugarman, 1993).

Subjects are expected to construct their knowledge in any domain. On this basis, a group of Piagetian scholars undertook the study of writing ontogenetically (Ferreiro & Teberosky, 1979). Remember that, during the hegemony of the Piagetian paradigm and until the late 1970s, writing was considered a school subject and not an object of psychological inquiry. Writing was not even considered an object of study for linguistics, which was absolutely dominated by the Aristotelian conception of writing. In this context, approaching the study of writing as a domain of development was a courageous endeavor. The idea was that, instead of determining the sequences of learning from the adult's point of view, psychologists and educators must explore the child's point of view about reading and writing. After more than 10 years of empirical research, it is clear to scholars that young children construct knowledge about writing as a notational system, about the language component writing represents, and about the content and the syntactic structure of written language.

Initial Piagetian research focused on describing the development of writing before children master the alphabetic principle (for a more detailed description, see Ferreiro, 1986). According to this description, children's consideration of the phonological component is one of the necessary steps in development, although not the earliest one. The learning process cannot be reduced to "breaking a code," but rather it should be seen as the construction of a complex system of the representation of writing as a domain of knowledge and as a referential tool. In line with the basic tenets of Piagetian theory, the invoked learning mechanism is a general one: "In order to acquire knowledge about the writing system, children proceed the same way as in other domains of knowledge: They try to assimilate the information provided by the environment" (Ferreiro, 1990, p. 14). Learning, it is explained, proceeds by hypothesis testing: "They experiment with the object (the writing system) to test their 'hypothesis' " (Ferreiro, 1990, p. 14). And the environment's main role is to provide information, but always interacting with the subject's assimilatory schema.

The consequences of this initial research were very important: Writing was recovered as an object of study both for developmental psychology and for kindergartners and preschoolers; it has also led to a general revision of many teaching principles that were current during the 1980s. Subsequent research within the constructivist paradigm explored children's knowledge beyond the alphabetic principle, analyzing text production and genre differentiation in early childhood. Children aged 4 to 7 years of age were asked to rewrite, to reconstruct, to dictate to friends, and to write narratives, news, poetry, descriptions, and so on. This line of work demonstrates that, before children know how to write, they know about the language to be written (Teberosky, 1987, chap. 13, this volume; Tolchinsky Landsmann, 1990). To understand this statement, one must recall the distinction between *writing* as a notational system or as a modality and *language to be written* as a register or a discursive organization (Ludwig, 1983; Tannen, 1985). As a notational system, writing is a collection of graphic marks that function according to certain rules. The use of writing in different communication situations has generated a variety of discursive organizations that, after so many years of writing use, have become part of the cultural representation of literate communities. These discourse organizations appear typically but not exclusively, in writing. The distinction of writing/language to be written aims to capture the differentiation between the material written aspect and the linguistic expression. This line of research shows that the canonical organization of narratives, the "pyramidal" organization of news, and the static linear organization of descriptions are all part of the linguistic competence of children growing up in a literate community.

Another line of research being developed is trying to embrace the new developments of the constructivist account in cognitive developmental psychology, after Piaget. Before discussing it, I provide a summary of some of the new developments in constructivism.

The similarities and differences between the reductionists with a behavioristic flavor and reductionists with a "modular" flavor, and between Vygotskians and Piagetians, are intricate. Piagetians coincide with behaviorist-reductionists in their attribution of a single mechanism to account for development. They differ from modular-reductionists in their defense of across-the-board development. Vygotskians, instead, postulate different mechanisms for different types of knowledge, but the types of knowledge they consider (e.g., everyday vs. scientific) are not relevant for Piagetians or for modularists. Vygotskians, on the other hand, come much closer to behaviorist-reductionists than to Piagetians in the role they attribute to the environment. Exogenous agents, such as objects that produce sensations or expert adults who promote learning, are leading factors both for reductionists and Vygotskians. On the other hand, endogenous factors (i.e., the subject's assimilation schema) are the central actors in Piaget's scenarios.

After Piaget, however, many researchers thought that if infants relied only on what Piaget attributed to the initial state (i.e., reflexes, the functional invariant, and an inchoate view of reality) they could not, by means of assimilatory processes, develop the behavioral coordinations they display, much less the subsequent advances in language and logic (Meltzoff, 1982; Sugarman, 1993). This belief was supported by the empirical findings obtained in hundreds of laboratories throughout the world about the cognitive and representational capacities of the newborn child. Research on infancy has demonstrated how well equipped humans come into the world. Infants respond to sets of objects in numerically relevant ways (Starkey, Spelke, & Gelman, 1983); 72 hours after birth, they are able not only to recognize their mother's voice but also to learn how to change their pattern of sucking in order to hear the voice of their own mother more frequently than other voices (DeCasper & Fifer, 1980). Rather than being involved in a "blooming, buzzing confusion," infants enter the world with preferences for certain types of stimulation.

It was not only the Piagetian account of the infant's mind that began to be contradicted, but also the unity and generality of Piaget's stages that came under attack, specifically his view that language is "all of a piece with acquisitions made at the level of sensorimotor intelligence" (Piaget, 1979, p. 148). From this stance you might predict that linguistic retardation would necessarily accompany severe cognitive retardation. However, such a prediction would turn out to be wrong, as was shown by several studies of children with internal hydrocephaly and spina bifida and those with William Syndrome. All these studies coincided in showing that complex syntax and lexicomorphology may coexist with very severe general cognitive impairments (Bellugi, Marks, Bihrle, & Sabo, 1988; Cromer, 1994).

With this evidence, a strong domain-specific nativism started to gain the favor of many developmental psychologists, a nativism that assumed that a number of prewired modules constrain the processing of specific classes of stimuli and leave for the environment only a releasing effect. For such nativism, development is "logically impossible" (Fodor, 1979, p. 148); "It is never possible to learn a richer logic on the basis of a weaker logic, if what you mean by learning is hypothesis formation and confirmation."

What alternative is there for those who become convinced that infants are born much better equipped than Piaget supposed but are also convinced of the possibility for change and the emergence of novelty in human development? What if one wants to avoid the "constructivist fallacy" (Flanagan, 1987, p. 137)? Is there any way to reconcile nativism and constructivism? Is there any other explanation of learning, not in terms of hypothesis testing but still preserving the active role of the subject?

Some developmentalists are convinced that in order "to fully understand human development one must invoke an epistemology that embraces both innately specified predispositions and an epigenetic-constructivist view of learning. Only in this way can one understand how development gets off to a head start and yet ends up with the flexibility and creativity of human cognition"

(Karmiloff-Smith, 1992b, p. 19). The constructivist fallacy can be avoided by accepting some degree of preformation of the representational system, because "preformation does not preordain the environmental sensitivity of the system" (Flanagan, 1987, p. 142). Furthermore, other models of learning processes have been developed showing that hypothesis testing is not the only possible way of active learning, especially not in the initial phases of acquisition of any new knowledge. A continually growing number of developmentalists have started to consider connectionist models of learning as a suitable explanation in line with the more general tenets of Piaget's epistemology (Bates & Elman, 1992).

It is impossible to provide here even a short explanation of the way connectionist models function, but I cannot avoid mentioning the growing influence of these models in developmental psychology,[5] although I used to agree with many developmental psychologists who saw in them "a return to Associationism in high tech clothing" (Jusczyk & Bertoncini, 1988, p. 218). The connectionist revolution aims to overthrow a notion that has been with us since ancient times: the notion that cognition is governed by rules (Dreyfus, 1988), that active learning is a process of hypothesis testing. We used to explain children's mistakes and creations in terms of application of other than adult's rules, of a different "logic." Connectionist models attempt, among other things, to show how approximations to rule-based behavior can be achieved through processes that do not involve rules as agents in the process. They have overcome the limitation of the digital computer in which states are processed as symbols specifying a set of sequential operations. They envisage knowledge as a vast network of interconnected elements, which—like the neurons on which they are modeled—do not individually signify anything. Instead, as Rumelhart (1989) put it, "All the knowledge is in the connections" (p. 135).[6]

This network involves extensive parallel distributed processing (PDP), which has important effects on learning and representation. Representations[7] can be continuous and graded. It is possible to speak about degrees of knowledge, and anyone who has worked with children will agree that that is the best way to describe the kind of knowledge children show about a particular domain. And most important, this system does change as a function of learning, displaying forms of organization that were not placed there by a programmer. The final product is codetermined by the initial setting of the system and the data to which it is exposed. Each state is a product of the environment and of the previous history of the system. It is a self-organizing sensitive system. Another

---

[5]To gain a sense of how connectionist models actually work, see Rumelhart and McClelland (1986), and for a very didactic and simple (nonmathematical) explanation, see Bereiter (1991).

[6]Connectionists initially avoided the term *representation*; they prided themselves on having systems dynamics with "no representations." More recently, however, connectionists have begun to refer to this level as *the layer of internal representations*.

[7]For an excellent explanation of the possibilities and limitations of connectionist models for developmental psychology, see Karmiloff-Smith (1992a).

consequence "goes right to the heart of the Piagetian view of the process of development" (Karmiloff-Smith, 1992a): The same continuous process of assimilation and accommodation operates. Qualitative differences, stagelike transitions, are not a result of discrete changes in structure or learning algorithms, but instead a result of slow incremental learning until, at some point, a cumulation of small changes produces an important modification in output.[8]

My guess is that in the domain of literacy we will be able to explain some of the "wonders" we could not explain before. For example, the wonder of a 4-year-old realizing that intrastring variety is a relevant constraint for writing. In connectionist terms, such children were not "realizing" and were not inventing a rule. Rather, they were reacting sensitively to the notational constraints of the environment. In the meantime, until it is possible to test my speculation, I have undertaken a series of experiments to determine whether children are really sensitive to the constraints of the notational environment and to what extent the development of writing is domain specific (Tolchinsky Landsmann & Karmiloff-Smith, 1992, 1993).

Children's environment is pervaded with notations: writing, written numerals, diagrams, maps, and pictures. However, are young children sensitive to the formal aspects of the differences between these notational domains? Unlike Luria and Vygotsky, who focused only on the instrumental function of writing, in this work we draw a distinction between notations as domains of knowledge in which each notational domain is a formal problem space for the child and notations as referential communicative tools. Do young children impose different constraints on writing and number notation when these are focused on as domains of knowledge? In one experiment, we presented children with a series of cards to be sorted into those that are "good for writing" and those that are not. Another set was used for a similar task concerning number notation. The set of cards contained real words, strings of either identical or different letters, single numbers, mixtures of letters and numbers, and mixtures of letters, drawings, and geometric shapes. We found that well before they are able to read and write, young children are sensitive to the formal constraints that differentiate between writing and number notation. Mixtures of systems are rejected for both writing and number notation. Single elements are accepted for writing but not for number. Repetition of elements is more accepted for numbers than for writing. By contrast, linkage between elements is accepted for writing but rejected for numbers. Children as young as 4 years of age do not confuse writing with number notation; they impose different constraints on each system.

Findings such as these, showing children's input sensitivity and specificity, together with what is currently known about infants' initial knowledge, pose a

---

[8]I am aware that I have not included in this review the work on word recognition and reading developed within the connectionist framework (e.g., Content, 1991). I am also aware that consideration of this line of work will lead to a full revision of what I have called the "reductionist" paradigm. I leave this topic for another time, however.

serious challenge for people seeking to determine which features of the environment influence development.

ROLE OF CONTEXTS

The difficulties in specifying the features of the environment that may affect ontogenesis, as well as the best environment to enhance development, are well expressed by Gelman (1994):

> Once we grant that children construct representations, that they take an active part in the building up of their own knowledge, we must likewise grant that they have much to say about the definition of what counts as relevant inputs. Therefore, to have a constructivistic theory of learning and development, we have to do more than map the nature of the implicit knowledge base a child or an adult constructs. We must develop a constructivist theory of the environment and its use. (p. 55)

The difficulty in determining what counts as a "relevant input" was well illustrated by our own examples in early literacy development. Four- and 5-year-olds were found to select number of elements and intrastring variety as important features of writing, two features of written strings of which adults are hardly aware.

The problem becomes even more difficult when we consider that any constructivist approach must be interactionist. The conceptual object of a constructivist theory of environment cannot be the environment per se. From a constructivist point of view, environments have to be defined *for* and *by* subjects. Environments change as a function of the previous history of the subject. Hence, the conceptual object of this theory has to be the "territory" of interaction between subject and environment. I call these territories *contexts* to distinguish them from *environments*. The latter are defined from outside, whereas the former are conceived in interaction with the subject. I suggest that the relevant questions to be answered by a sound theory of environment would emerge in exploring two main contexts: the acquisition context and the linguistic context.

The Acquisition Context

Following Berry and Irvine (1986), I distinguish four levels at which the acquisition context can be explored: the *ecological*, the *experiential*, the *performance*, and the *experimental*. Although Berry and Irvine defined these four levels in order to study how they affect intelligence and the way it is evaluated, I found them very useful in formulating some of the questions concerning the acquisition of literacy. At the highest level is the *ecological environment*. This kind of environment comprises all of the permanent or almost permanent characteristics that provide the backdrop for human action. It is the natural cultural environment in which a person lives. The second level is the experiential, or the pattern of recurrent experiences within the ecological environment that provides a basis for learning and development. The third level is the performance context, which is itself nested under the first two kinds. This level comprises the limited set of environmental circumstances that account for particular behaviors at specific points in space and time. Finally, under these three levels is the experimental level of context. This level comprises environmental characteristics manipulated by psychologists and others to elicit particular responses.

Written language is both a cultural representation and a cultural artifact with which the individual enters into direct personal relationship. In this sense, written language is part of both the ecological environment of a literate community and the experiential environment, in the case of a literate person. As part of the ecological environment, it is a point of view affecting our perception of language, of cognitive functions, and of social relationships (Illich & Sanders, 1988) and constantly molding the personal appropriation. Cultural representations are *epidemic* (Sperber, 1984); they are transmitted even without the formal interventions of adults or institutions whose social purpose is to teach. When the individual starts his or her own literacy process, he or she is already a transmitter as well as a receiver of a cultural representation of literacy. Some representations are common to every literate society, whereas others are unique to a particular society. Common to every literate society, for instance, is the notion that there are texts, that is, a particular kind of object distinguished from physical objects. For children born in a literate society, this notion is part of their initial state.

Therefore, two levels of environment must be explored in analyzing the context of acquisition: the experiential, reflecting the social, material, or pedagogical circumstances of the subjects when dealing directly with the cultural artifact in their own personal situations; and the ecological, reflecting the cultural representations of literacy that necessarily mediate any direct and personal experience with written language. The puzzle to be solved is that of the relative effect of each of these contexts on becoming literate.

The same personal experiences with written language may have very different meaning and impact on learning, depending on the mediating role of the existing cultural representations. For instance, the process of memorizing a text and repeating it ad infinitum may have a different impact on development mediated by the cultural representation of literacy in Morocco, with its particular cultural representation of Islamic literacy (Spratt & Wagner, 1986), than in a middle-class neighborhood of Barcelona.

The initial research within the Piagetian framework was carried out through more or less structured individual interviews (cf. Ferreiro, 1985; Tolchinsky Landsmann & Levin, 1985, 1987) or in school contexts (Teberosky, 1987). In the interviews, only general characteristics of the subjects' experiential environment were taken into account. In the research in school contexts, only the written products were analyzed. Neither contextual variations nor the characterization of the ecological environment mediating children's performance was taken into account.

Other lines of research have analyzed the experiential environment, characterized in terms of the home background of subjects, to determine its effect on literacy development (Wells, 1985). One of the shortcomings of this type of research is that literacy development is equated with success at school. Another is its correlational design. Children are tested in various aspects of literacy development, and their achievement levels are then correlated with particular home background characteristics. Because psychologists agree that establishing a correlational link is a long way from providing an explanation value, some of them have replaced the correlational design by a naturalistic paradigm. This paradigm "at least enables one to document what is actually occurring in the home and to observe links between these practices and effects on the child developing reading and writing activities" (Teale, 1986, p. 174).

Links, however, are never observed but rather created. To create these links, we need a conception of what is developing, not in terms of school success, but in terms of the particular aspects of written language that are being acquired in the literacy process. Otherwise, one may accept that everything affects acquisition, as reflected in the following conclusion by Teale: "Children's progress in reading and writing is the product of (a) adult–child (or sibling–child) interactions, which involve literacy, (b) the child's independent explorations with written language and (c) observations of others using written language" (1986, p. 174). The crucial issue is to distinguish the relevant features of context affecting literacy development as well as to distinguish between common basic competencies and those that are developed by specific experiential environments.

With this goal in mind, I have designed a series of studies to explore the influence of diversity of the performance environment on text production and differentiation. Children share the same ecological environment but differ in their performance environment. In these studies, the final state was not determined by school achievement but rather by the evolution of specific aspects of literate knowledge: the capacity to differentiate between narratives and descriptive texts and the syntactic organization of the texts. First, I traced the developmental path of text differentiation from kindergarten to first grade, and then I examined how these aspects were affected by contrasting learning environments in second grade. One learning environment was characterized by the use of multiple types of texts as part of the obligatory curriculum, whereas the other used one textbook for teaching reading. The contrasts were not created for research purposes; rather we took advantage of the fact that in Israel it is possible to find two classes working in the same school with different curricula.

Based on a methodology of analysis developed by Blanche-Benveniste and her colleagues (Blanche-Benveniste et al., 1979; Blanche-Benveniste & Jeanjean,

1980), it was possible, inter alia, to make an inventory of the syntactic constructions and discursive features characterizing the different texts children produced (Tolchinsky Landsmann & Sandbank, in press). Results showed that neither text differentiation nor syntactic organization of texts was affected by the performance environment. We did not find more children differentiating between narratives and descriptions or children using more complex constructions in one environment than in the other. Pedagogical influences were evident, however, in the variety of paradigms and in the multiplicity of stylistic resources. The idea that syntactic organization is unaffected by pedagogical environments finds additional support, at least for the same sociocultural level of the studied groups, in an earlier study by Teberosky (1987) in which the same methodology of analysis was used for different types of texts. Although the texts analyzed by Teberosky were gathered in the context of a pedagogical intervention, similar syntactic constructions were found in the narrative texts of 7- to 8-year-olds.

It is not enough, however, to point at basic competence and eventual effects of learning environments. One of the convergent conclusions in the studies on emergent literacy is that most children in a literate society have numerous experiences with written language before they even get to school (Harste, Woodward, & Burke, 1984; Heath, 1983; Teale, 1986). Despite this, their engagement in literacy activities is crucially different thereafter (Heath, 1983). Some of them will remain active readers and writers, whereas some of them will only occasionally open a newspaper. Furthermore, because not enough time has passed to verify the influence of pedagogical innovations based on the constructivist line of research, we do not know whether children who are educated in environments working with different types of texts and registers from the very beginning will become more creative and active readers and writers as adults. A sound theory of context should distinguish the relative weight of ecological, experiential, and performance environments of acquisition in determining definite aspects of writing and long-term development.

Linguistic Context

The second type of context that has to be explored is *linguistic context*. The four levels that were distinguished for analyzing the context of acquisition are also valid for exploring the role of the linguistic context in literacy. The ecological level relates to the language and the orthographic system to which the developing subject is exposed. The experiential level is concerned with the constant pattern of linguistic experience directly related to the child, specifically constant patterns of linguistic interaction at home and at school. At a performance level, one must locate the immediate and limited linguistic experience children may have in specific time and space, for example, intervention programs. Finally, the experimental level relates to the local linguistic context in which individual responses are produced and gathered for research.

We have to clarify the role of particular languages and orthographic systems—the ecological level—in the developmental order and eventual emergence of certain notions. As I mentioned before, some work on this line is currently being undertaken together with Teberosky. We are looking for the relationship between phonological segmentation and writing development in different orthographic systems. Previous research on Spanish-speaking children has shown that when children start looking for correspondences between graphic and linguistic units they resort to the syllabic hypothesis. As they grow older and go through a series of cognitive conflicts, they grasp the alphabetic principle, that is, that letters represent vocalic and consonantal segments. It may be the case that these hypotheses are well supported only for certain languages and orthographic systems.

The emergence of the syllabic hypothesis, for instance, may depend on the syllabic structure of the language. All languages have vowels and consonants, and all can be described in terms of syllables. However, whereas some languages have a very uniform syllable structure (e.g., only CV or CVC sequences), others tolerate great variations. French speakers listening to French words resort to syllabification, whereas syllabic segmentation is very rare in English speakers listening to English words (Cutler, Mehler, & Segui, 1986). Segmentation strategies seem to be language specific (Mehler, Dommergues, Frauenfelder, & Segui, 1984) and may inhibit the emergence of spontaneous syllabic correspondences. This may explain why there is no mention of a syllabic period in early literacy research that was carried on with an English-speaking child (Bissex, 1980), but Kamii seems to have found it (Ferreiro, 1990). We find a similar situation with the alphabetic hypothesis. Hebrew-speaking children do not arrive at an exhaustive alphabetic hypothesis. They may produce some syllabic-alphabetic representation, but only for those cases for which the orthographic system provides an orthographic graphic representation.

On the experimental level, we have to clarify the role of local linguistic contexts in individual responses. When children are required to read a series of sentences they have written, they tend to segment them into words rather than into syllables. These same children, however, tend to use a syllabic segmentation when reading back a list of words they have written. At this level of development, the syllable is not an absolute unit of correspondence but rather is relative to the local linguistic context, in this case to the linguistic unit the child is aiming to segment (Tolchinsky Landsmann, 1991a). Therefore, it is reasonable to assume that the emergence of a syllabic hypothesis in development will be relative to both the ecological and experimental level of context.

Literacy Development in Context

The domain of literacy is undergoing a process of change similar to the one that occurred in the domain of spoken language acquisition. The facts leading to these changes are similar: the recognition that infants come to the world better equipped than was supposed by Piaget and the need to accept a certain amount of innate equipment, the evidence that certain developmental facts reappear in different environments, and an increasing belief in the domain specificity of language (and writing). In short, this means the acceptance of certain degrees of innatism, universality, and domain specificity.

One might agree with the nativist position in that children bring from birth a number of principles and parameters, in that the linguistic capacity is an autonomous cognitive system and the constraints determining acquisition are language specific; in other words, that language acquisition *happens* to the child, that the language organ grows in the child with only minimal environmental triggering. However, language seems to grow very differently in different children and in different social groups. The differences may not be relevant if they are evaluated according to the list of universal parameters, but they may have tremendous social consequences. They may determine success or failure at any level of social interaction. Realizing this, researchers started to explore the features of interactive situations that may influence the acquisition process. Studies have shown that semantic contingency, shared topics of conversation, and child-centered speech correlate positively with rate of development, whereas directiveness (e.g., commands, requests, directions, and instructions) correlates negatively (Lieven, 1982; Snow & Goldfield, 1983). It has also been shown, however, that preverbal mother–child interaction is not generally predictive of children's later vocabulary progress (Bates, Bretherton, & Snyder, 1988). It is important to discern which interactional routines form contrasting contexts for the emergence of significant differences at any linguistic level.

The same holds true for literacy. One may agree that humans have an inborn printout capacity, that writing is domain specific, and that the development of writing goes through a number of obligatory steps prior to mastering the alphabetic principle or the principle on which the writing system they are exposed to is based. One might even demonstrate that before the age of 6 children differentiate the basic literary genres. However, for some of these writers and readers, this knowledge is only the initial phase of their life-long journey through literacy. For others, this knowledge is almost the final phase. They will hardly touch a book or a pencil during the rest of their lives. Or, even avoiding such extremes, some of them will be able to read, to criticize, and to invent different types of texts, whereas others will laboriously manage with basic textbooks. Again, it is important to discern the contextual variables that will account for the emergence of significant differences. I agree with Chomsky (1988) that, without a system of formal constraints, there are no creative acts. The purpose is not to replace the internal self-organized framework for development with an external modeling mechanism. However, the internal system and the acquisition process will be better understood by analyzing the effect of context in development, in both spoken language and literacy.

REFERENCES

Aristotle. (1938). *De interpretatione* (H. P. Cook, Trans.). London: Loeb Classical Library.

Bates, E., Bretherton, I., & Snyder, L. (1988). *From first words to grammar: Individual differences and dissociable mechanisms.* Cambridge, England: Cambridge University Press.

Bates, E., & Elman, J. (1992). *Connectionism and the study of change* (Tech. Rep. No. 9202). La Jolla: University of California, San Diego, Center for Research in Language.

Bellugi, U., Marks, S., Bihrle, A. M., & Sabo, H. (1988). Dissociation between language and linguistic functions in William Syndrome. In D. Bishop & K. Mogford (Eds.), *Language development in exceptional circumstances* (pp. 38–57). London: Churchill Livingstone.

Bender, L. (1957). Specific reading disability as a maturational lag. *Bulletin of The Orton Society, 7,* 9–18.

Bereiter, C. (1991). Implications of connectionism for thinking about rules. *Educational Researcher, 20,* 10–16.

Berry, J. W., & Irvine, S. H. (1986). Bricolage: Savages do it daily. In R. J. Sternberg & R. K. Wagner (Eds.), *Practical intelligence: Nature and origins of competence in the everyday world* (pp. 271–306). Cambridge, England: Cambridge University Press.

Bissex, G. (1980). *GNYS AT WRK. A child learns to write and read.* Cambridge, MA: Harvard University Press.

Blanche-Benveniste, C., Borel, C., Deulofeu, J., Durand, J., Giacomini, A., Loufrani, C., Meziane, T., & Pazeri, R. (1979). Des grilles pour le francais parle [Grilles for spoken French]. *Recherches sur le Francais Parle, 2,* 136–206.

Blanche-Benveniste, C., & Jeanjean, C. (1980). *Evaluation comparee des moyens d'expression linguistique d'enfants francophones et non-francophones d'origine dans les memes classe* [Evaluation of means of linguistic expression in French speaking and non-French speaking children attending the same classes] (Recherche No. 2.14.01). Universite de Provence, Aix-en-Provence.

Chomsky, N. (1988). *Language and problems of knowledge.* Cambridge, MA: MIT Press.

Content, A. (1984). L'analyse phonetique explicite de la parole et l'acquisition de la lecture [Explicit phonetic analysis of spoken words and reading acquisition]. *L'Anne Psychologique, 84,* 555–572.

Content, A. (1991). Les mots ecrits: Approche connexioniste [Written words: A connectionist approach]. In R. Kolinsky, J. Morais, & J. Segui (Eds.), *La reconnaiscance des mots dans les differents modalities sensorielles: Etudes de psicolinguistique cognitive* [Word recognition in different sensorial modalities: Psycholinguistic studies] (pp. 237–276). Paris: Presses Universitaire de France.

Cromer, R. F. (1994). A case study of dissociation between language and cognition. In H. Tager-Flusberg (Ed.), *Constraints on language acquisition: Studies of atypical children* (pp. 141–153). Hillsdale, NJ: Lawrence Erlbaum Associates.

Cutler, A., Mehler, J., & Segui, J. (1986). The syllable's differing role in the segmentation of French and English. *Journal of Memory and Language, 25,* 385–400.

DeCasper, A. J., & Fifer, W. P. (1980). On human bonding: Newborns prefer their mother's voice. *Science, 208,* 1174–1176.

Diringer, D. (1961). *Writing.* London: Duckworth.

Dreyfus, H. L. (1988). The Socratic and Platonic basis for cognitivism. *AI and Society, 2,* 99–112.

Ehri, L. C. (1985). Effects of printed language acquisition on speech. In D. R. Olson, N. Torrance, & A. Hildyard (Eds.), *Literacy, language, and learning: The nature and consequences of reading and writing* (pp. 333–367). New York: Cambridge University Press.

Ehri, L. C., & Wilce, L. S. (1980). The influence of orthography on readers' conceptualization of the phonemic structure of words. *Applied Psycholinguistics, 1,* 371–385.

Ferreiro, E. (1985). Literacy development: A psychogenetic perspective. In D. R. Olson, N. Torrance, & A. Hildyard (Eds.), *Literacy, language, and learning: The nature and consequences of reading and writing* (pp. 217–228). New York: Cambridge University Press.

Ferreiro, E. (1986). The interplay between information and assimilation in beginning literacy. In W. Teale & E. Sulzby (Eds.), *Emergent literacy: Writing and reading* (pp. 15–49). Norwood, NJ: Ablex.

Ferreiro, E. (1990). Literacy development: Psychogenesis. In Y. Goodman (Ed.), *How children construct literacy: Piagetian perspectives* (pp. 12–25). Newark, DE: International Reading Association.

Ferreiro, E., & Teberosky, A. (1982). *Literacy before schooling*. New York: Heinemann.

Flanagan, O. J. (1987). *The science of the mind*. Cambridge, MA: MIT Press.

Fodor, J. (1979). Fixation de croyances et acquisition de concepts. In M. Piattelli-Palmarini (Ed.), *Theories du langage, theories de l'apprentissage* (pp. 219–225). Paris: Seuil.

Gelman, R. (1994). Constructivism and supporting environments. In D. Tirosh (Ed.), *Implicit and explicit knowledge: An educational approach* (pp. 45–60). Norwood, NJ: Ablex.

Gibson, E., & Levin, H. (1975). *The psychology of reading*. Cambridge, MA: MIT Press.

Glick, J. (1983). Piaget, Vygotsky, and Werner. In S. Wapner & B. Kaplan (Eds.), *Toward a holistic developmental psychology* (pp. 35–52). Hillsdale, NJ: Lawrence Erlbaum Associates.

Gough, P. B., & Tunmer, W. E. (1986). Decoding, reading and reading disability. *Remedial and Special Education, 7*, 6–10.

Harris, R. (1986). *The origin of writing*. Oxford, England: Duckworth.

Harste, J., Woodward, V. A., & Burke, C. (1984). *Language stories and literacy lessons*. New York: Heinemann.

Heath, S. B. (1983). *Ways with words*. Cambridge, England: Cambridge University Press.

Hohn, W. E., & Ehri, L. C. (1983). Do alphabet letters help prereaders acquire phonemic segmentation skill? *Journal of Educational Psychology, 75*, 752–762.

Illich, I., & Sanders, B. (1988). *The alphabetization of the popular mind*. San Francisco: North Point Press.

Juel, C. (1988, April). *Learning to read and write: A longitudinal study of fifty four children from first through fourth grade*. Paper presented at the meeting of the American Educational Research Association, New Orleans.

Juel, C., Griffith, P. L., & Gough, P. B. (1986). Acquisition of literacy: A longitudinal study of children in first and second grade. *Journal of Educational Psychology, 78*, 243–255.

Jusczyk, P., & Bertoncini, J. (1988). Viewing the development of speech perception as an innately guided learning process. *Language and Speech, 31*, 217–238.

Karmiloff-Smith, A. (1992a). *Beyond modularity: A developmental perspective on cognitive science*. Cambridge, MA: MIT Press.

Karmiloff-Smith, A. (1992b). Self-organization and cognitive change. *Substratum, 1*, 19–44.

Lieven, E. V. M. (1982). Context, process and progress in young children's speech. In M. Beveridge (Ed.), *Children thinking through language* (pp. 124–135). London: Edward Arnold.

Lloyd Morgan, C. (1894). *Introduction to comparative psychology*. London: Scott.

Ludwig, D. (1983). Writing system and written language. In F. Coulmas & K. Ehlich (Eds.), *Writing in focus* (pp. 31–43). Berlin: Mouton.

Luria, A. R. (1976). *Cognitive development: Its cultural and social foundations*. Cambridge, MA: Harvard University Press.

Luria, A. R. (1978). The development of writing in the child. In M. Cole (Ed.), *The selected writings of A. R. Luria* (pp. 145–194). New York: M. E. Sharpe. (Original work published 1929)

Luria, A. R. (1982). *Language and cognition*. New York: Wiley.

Mehler, J., Dommergues, J., Frauenfelder, V., & Segui, J. (1984). The syllable's role in speech segmentation. *Journal of Verbal Learning and Verbal Behavior, 20*, 298–305.

Meltzoff, A. (1982). Imitation, intermodal coordination and representation in early infancy. In G. Butterworth (Ed.), *Infancy and epistemology: An evaluation of Piaget's theory* (pp. 85–111). New York: St. Martin's.

Morais, J., Cary, L., Jeans, A., & Bertelson, P. (1979). Does awareness of speech as a sequence of sounds arise spontaneously? *Cognition, 5*, 323–331.

Piaget, J. (1975). *L'equilibration des structures cognitives: Probleme central du developpement* [Equilibration of cognitive structures] (Etudes d'Epitemologie genetique, XXXIII). Paris: Presses Universitaires de France.

Piaget, J. (1979). La psychogenese des connaissances et sa signification epistemologique [Psychogenesis of knowledge and its epistemological meaning]. In M. Piatelli-Palmarini (Ed.), *Theories du langage, theories de l'apprentissage* (pp. 12–18). Paris: Seuil.

Read, C., Yun-Fei, Z., Hong-Yin, N., & Bao-Qing, D. (1986). The ability to manipulate speech sounds depends on knowing alphabetic writing. *Cognition, 24*, 31–44.

Rumelhart, D. E. (1989). The architecture of mind: A connectionist approach. In M. I. Posner (Ed.), *Foundations of cognitive science* (pp. 133–159). Cambridge, MA: MIT Press.

Rumelhart, D. E., & McClelland, J. L. (1986). *Parallel distributed processing.* Cambridge, MA: MIT Press.

Scinto, L. (1986). *Written language and psychological development.* London: Academic Press.

Scribner, S. (1984). Literacy in three metaphors. *American Journal of Education, 93*, 7–21.

Shankweiler, D., & Crain, S. (1986). Language mechanisms and reading disorder: A modular approach. *Cognition, 24*, 139–168.

Snow, C., & Goldfield, B. A. (1983). Turn the page please. Situation-specific language learning. *Journal of Child Language, 10*, 551–570.

Sperber, D. (1984). Anthropology and psychology: Towards an epidemology of representation. *Man, 20*, 1–17.

Spratt, J. E., & Wagner, D. A. (1986). The making of a FQIH: The transformation of traditional Islamic teachers in modern time. In M. I. White & S. Pollak (Eds.), *The cultural transition: Human experience and social transformation in the third world and Japan* (pp. 89–112). Boston: Routledge & Kegan Paul.

Stanovich, K. E. (1986). Matthew effects in reading. Some consequences of individual differences in the acquisition of literacy. *Reading Research Quarterly, 21*, 360–406.

Starkey, P., Spelke, E., & Gelman, R. (1983). Detection of 1–1 correspondences in human infants. *Science, 222*, 79–81.

Sternberg, R. (1990). *Metaphors of mind: Conceptions of the nature of intelligence.* Cambridge, England: Cambridge University Press.

Street, P. (1984). *Literacy theory and practice.* Cambridge, England: Cambridge University Press.

Sugarman, S. (1993). Piaget on the origins of mind: A problem in accounting for the development of mental capacities. In E. Dromi (Ed.), *Language and cognition: A developmental perspective* (pp. 67–74). Norwood, NJ: Ablex.

Tannen, D. (1985). Relative focus on involvement in oral and written discourse. In D. Olson, N. Torrance, & A. Hildyard (Eds.), *Literacy, language, and learning: The nature and consequences of reading and writing* (pp. 124–147). Cambridge, England: Cambridge University Press.

Teale, W. H. (1986). Home background and young children's literacy development. In W. Teale & E. Sulzby (Eds.), *Emergent literacy: Writing and reading* (pp. 173–206). Norwood, NJ: Ablex.

Teberosky, A. (1987). *La comprension de la escritura en el nino* [Children's understanding of writing]. Unpublished doctoral dissertation, University of Barcelona, Spain.

Teberosky, A. (1990). Reescribiendo noticias: Una aproximacion a los textos de ninos y adultos en proceso de alfabetizacion [Rewriting news: An approach to texts produced by adults and children in the process of becoming literate]. *Anuario de Psicologia, 47*, 11–28.

Tolchinsky Landsmann, L. (1988). Form and meaning in the development of written representation. *European Journal of Educational Psychology, 3*, 385–398.

Tolchinsky Landsmann, L. (1990). La produccion de relatos en ninos entre cinco y siete anos: Organizacion sintactica y funciones narrativas [Five- to seven-year-olds' production of narratives: Syntactic structures and narrative functions]. *Anuario de Psicologia, 47*, 64–87.

Tolchinsky Landsmann, L. (1991a). The conceptualization of writing in the confluence of interactive models of development. In L. Tolchinsky Landsmann (Ed.), *Culture, schooling, and psychological development* (pp. 87–111). Norwood, NJ: Ablex.

Tolchinsky Landsmann, L. (1991b). Genesi della lingua scritta e ruolo dell'ambiente: Tre paradigmi teorici a confronto [Three accounts of literacy development and the role of the environment]. In M. Orsolini & C. Pontecorvo (Eds.), *La costruzione del testo scritto nei bambini* (pp. 149–172). Rome: La Nuova Italia.

Tolchinsky Landsmann, L., & Karmiloff-Smith, A. (1992). Children's understanding of notations as domains of knowledge versus referential-communicative tools. *Cognitive Development, 7*, 287–300.

Tolchinsky Landsmann, L., & Karmiloff-Smith, A. (1993). Las restricciones del conocimiento notacional [Constraints on notational knowledge]. *Infancia y Aprendizaje, 59–60*, 19–51.

Tolchinsky Landsmann, L., & Levin, I. (1985). Writing in preschoolers: An age-related analysis. *Journal of Applied Psycholinguistics, 6*, 319–339.

Tolchinsky Landsmann, L., & Levin, I. (1987). Writing in four to six year olds: Representation of semantic and phonetic similarities and differences. *Journal of Child Language, 14*, 127–144.

Tolchinsky Landsmann, L., & Sandbank, A. (in press). Text production and text differentiation: Developmental changes and educational influences. In S. Strauss (Ed.), *Learning environments and psychological development*. Norwood, NJ: Ablex.

Vachek, J. (1966). *The linguistic school of Prague*. Bloomington: Indiana University Press.

Vachek, J. (1973). *Written language*. The Hague: Mouton.

Vygotsky, L. (1928). The problem of the cultural development of the child. *Journal of Genetic Psychology, 2*, 415–434.

Vygotsky, L. (1978). *Mind in society*. Cambridge, MA: Harvard University Press.

Wells, G. (1985). Preschool literacy-related activities and success in school. In D. Olson, N. Torrance, & A. Hildyard (Eds.), *Literacy, language, and learning: The nature and consequences of reading and writing* (pp. 229–255). Cambridge, England: Cambridge University Press.

Wertsch, J. (1985). *Vygotsky and the social formation of mind*. Cambridge, MA: Harvard University Press.

Wertsch, J. (1991). Sociocultural setting and the zone of proximal development: The problem of text-based realities. In L. Tolchinsky Landsmann (Ed.), *Culture, schooling, and psychological development* (pp. 71–86). Norwood, NJ: Ablex.

Wilks, Y. (1982). *Machines and consciousness* (Rep. No. CSCM-8). University of Sussex, England: Cognitive Studies Center.

7

AN APPROACH TO WRITING
IN KINDERGARTEN

Jean-Marie Besse
Laboratory of Psychology
of Education, Lyon

In France, kindergarten does not provide a systematic approach to teaching the relationship between reading and writing, although children have an initiation into writing during the last year of preschool.[1] How do children enter into the first steps of writing, and, in particular, how do they understand the characteristics of the writing system? What conceptualizations do these children form of written text?

Ferreiro's research (Ferreiro, 1978, 1984; Ferreiro & Gomez Palacio, 1982a, 1982b; Ferreiro & Teberosky, 1979) on the psychogenesis of literacy provides a new theoretical base for answering such questions. Her study has emphasized children's progressive reconstruction of writing system principles, indicating the stages through which young Hispanic children pass when learning the structure of written language. Ferreiro also has broken new ground in advocating new methodological approaches, showing how researchers can request a written production of a young child who is not yet capable of reading and writing.

The research presented in this chapter aims to describe the processes that young French-speaking children reveal within the context of written production. By inviting the children to produce a written form (words and sentences) that had not yet been presented in class and had not yet been the basis of learning and reproduction, we expected answers to several questions. What do the children show, through these written productions and the reactions within the situation, that relates established hypotheses to the system of French as a written language? What ideas do the children construct concerning the structure and the functions

---

[1] In the French system, 3 years of preschool education are offered before elementary school.

of the written form? What cognitive steps are adopted by the children attempting to write something that has been learned neither at school nor in the family context?

GOALS AND EXPERIMENTAL POPULATION

The main objective of this research project, which was primarily concerned with analyzing certain processes that come into play when kindergarten children take up writing, was to determine if the results of Ferreiro's work can be extended to a French-speaking population.

We first had to determine if Ferreiro's research methodology could be replicated and, if so, integrated into our research procedures and techniques. Second, we intended to produce detailed analyses of the strategies adopted by children faced with producing the written form. Third, we wanted to study how written production might give rise to cognitive conflict for the children, leading to a resolution of a problem that they had not seen before. In order to understand the significance of what the children produced, we had to take into account the dynamics of the session itself. For this, we studied specific interactions between the children and the observer who was involved in this experimental relationship. Each child had a specific way of engaging in these interactions, and each manifested original cognitive dynamics.

Our research on these issues was based on our observations of children at three different times. Each subject was observed twice during the kindergarten year (first in December 1986 through January 1987, and then in May through June 1987). During the first year of elementary school, 14 of these children were again observed. A comparison of the three observations of each child shows the evolution of their conceptualizations over a period of more than a year.

The beginning sample contained 27 children, all attending the same kindergarten class in suburban Lyon, ranging in age from 5 years, 0 months to 6 years, 4 months. The socioeconomic background of the children was middle class.

This analysis is followed by details on the different stages identified, placing them in relation to cognitive problems posed by the very structure of the three experimental situations.

METHODOLOGY

The experimental design for this research[2] was directly inspired by Ferreiro's research, especially that done in Mexico in 1980–1981 and first published in Mexico City (Ferreiro & Gomez Palacio, 1982a).

---

[2]Research protocols were established and observations were compiled by a team of the PsyEF (Laboratoire de Psychologie de l'Education et de la Formation), Université Lumière LYON 2, consisting of J.-M. Besse, M.-M. de Gaulmyn, D. Ginet, S. Colella, M.-H. Luis, F. Mazuir-Gaete, and O. Rolland-Comte.

Our experimental writing production situation is based on the results of previous research (Besse, 1988). Kindergarten children in these earlier studies revealed many of the types of conceptualization regarding written text that had been described by Ferreiro. Although all subjects produced differentiated writing samples for each utterance requested, only some of them were able to establish a correspondence between the phonic and graphic aspects of written text. By the end of the year, several had arrived at an alphabetic hypothesis.

Our first studies had allowed us to uncover a number of attitudes that apparently are specific to these French-speaking children. Several children refused to produce any written form other than their first name, although their teacher regarded several of them as being subjects already "ripe" for reading. Such behavior on the part of the children led us to see the need to modify the administration of the research protocol as defined by Ferreiro. Our modifications mainly concerned the type of utterances produced by the interviewer, but we also specified and adapted the conditions of dialogue with the child.

The Choice of Utterances

The situations are presented through three separate observation sessions consisting of a request to write words and then sentences during the course of an interview in which the child was alone with two adults (the experimenter/interviewer and the observer/cameraman).

Protocol of the First Observation

During the first observation, we tested material consisting of 10 utterances produced by the experimenter: six words and four sentences. To account for possible difficulties linked to the order of presentation, one half of the group was presented first with words, whereas the other half began with the sentences. Likewise, the request that the children write their names came at the beginning for half of the group and at the end for the other half.

The experimenter asked the children to mark the following words: *ballon* (ball), *dormir* (sleep), *télévision* (television), *vacances* (vacation/holiday), *difficile* (difficult), and *bille* (marble). Each word was dictated once the preceding word had become the object of written production. Then the following sentences were given: *On joue pas au ballon, ici* (We don't play ball here); *Moi, j'aime regarder la télé* (I like to watch T.V.); *Mon copain, y [il] m'a pris toutes mes billes* (My friend took all my marbles); and *C'est quand les vacances?* (When is vacation?).

Three criteria helped to determine the choice of sentences used:

- The sentences we selected were taken from among expressions frequently used by such children; the standard school register and that of standard written French were not the only ones considered and presented.

- Our sentences reused words that the children had previously been asked to write in isolation.
- Our sentences included an interrogative sentence as well as a sentence with a negation.

The experimenter aimed at an intonation typical for the region, with no emphasis on syllabification, unlike what is done in certain dictation exercises in French teaching methods.

Protocol of the Second Observation

We asked the children to mark five words and three sentences. One sentence included each child's first name: we wanted to see how the children treated this known written form in the context of a sentence in which unknown words (i.e., their written form) were also to be produced. The children were not requested to write their names until the end of the session, as a type of signature for their written work. One half of the group began with the words; the other half began with the sentences.

The words requested were the following: *automobile* (car), *voyageur* (traveler), *maintenant* (now), *chercher* (get/fetch), and *mer* (sea). The sentences were: *J'attends qu'on vienne me chercher* (I'm waiting for someone to come get me); *Moi, je sais pas nager dans la mer* (I don't know how to swim in the sea); and *Dis-moi, [prénom de l'enfant], tu trouves pas que les autos font trop de bruit?* (Tell me, [child's name], don't you think cars make too much noise?).

Protocol of the Third Observation

In the third session, we used six words and four sentences. The children were requested to write their names after the interview. All the children began with the words and ended with the sentences. The words requested were: *ami* (friend), *courir* (run), *récréation* (recess/playtime), *chocolat* (chocolate), *rigolo* (funny), and *pain* (bread). The sentences were: *Tu aimes la récré?* (Do you like recess?); *Ici, [prénom de l'enfant], on peut pas goûter* (Here, [child's name], we can't have a snack); *Moi, j'ai du pain et du chocolat* (I have bread and chocolate); and *Mes amis, y jouent au loup* (My friends are playing tag).[3]

Instructions for the Interview

Other than asking for this creation of original utterances, we utilized several arrangements in terms of the technical aspects described later under which the interview was undertaken, particularly for the second and third observations.

---

[3]In this third observation, the experimenters were S. Colella and F. Mazuir-Gaete, with S. Larderet and C. Thollet videotaping the session.

The First Observation

Before constructing the contents of the first session, we tried to understand what could account for the children's refusal to comply with a request, as had been observed in our previous research. We asked ourselves how kindergarten children would interpret our request. In a French-speaking community, such a request would be unusual; therefore, we reasoned, certain children would be very surprised to be asked to produce writing without a model.

In our earlier research, the children often responded that they did not know how or that they had not learned it at school. Their motor behavior and facial expressions (e.g., physically recoiling or fidgeting) indicated that they were uncomfortable with the situation. Although many of the children seemed to agree to take part in the requested activity, they apparently did so to avoid disappointing the adult. Some children finally consented to produce some writing, yet easily changed their first interpretation of the written production to conform with the utterance when repeated by the experimenter.

Such considerations led us to present our requests for written production in the course of conversation by slowly revealing the element that would be requested in writing; we wanted to place these "forms of writing" in a context of reassurance for the young child.

The interview with each child begun by the interviewer introducing everyone present and explaining the presence of the taping equipment, with a statement such as: *"Bonjour, on va travailler ensemble, avec ce monsieur [cette dame] qui est là pour m'aider. On est là pour comprendre comment les enfants travaillent, mais on n'est pas des maîtres d'école"* (Today you and I are going to work together, and this man [this woman] is here to help me. We are here to see how children work, but we are not schoolteachers).

Once the conversation had begun, the experimenter proposed: *"Je voudrais savoir comment tu le marques, ça [mot ou phrase à demander], sur cette feuille de papier, avec le stylo"* (I would like to know how you would write this [word or sentence requested] with the pen on this piece of paper). Once the child wrote a response, the next question was: *"Maintenant, tu peux dire ce que tu as marqué là, en montrant avec ton doigt?"* (Now, can you say out loud what you wrote there, pointing to it at the same time with your finger?).

The Last Two Observations

The first session was videotaped and aimed to provide a basis for an analysis concerning the interactional situations between adult and child. We attempted to understand the dynamics of each child's mental activity, to discover strategies used, while also determining speech acts with the experimenter that were relied on in the conversation. This last point in particular led us to modify the interview used in the second and the third sessions in order to minimize the influence of the adult's discourse in the experiment.

By this time, we were more familiar to the children, and they understood the general framework of the situation. The interview with the child began as follows:

Nous allons continuer de travailler avec toi pour mieux comprendre comment vous faites pour marquer des choses sur le papier. Tu te souviens que ce qui nous intéresse, nous, c'est ce que toi, tu sais faire, tout seul, avec ce que tu as appris et aussi ce que tu n'as pas encore appris, mais que tu peux essayer de faire. Parce que tu sais déjà beaucoup de choses. Nous ne mettons pas de "juste" ou de "faux" quand vous travaillez (We are going to work together with you again to see how all of you as children in school write things on paper. Remember that we are interested in what you, just you, can write because you have already learned it. Even if you haven't learned it, go ahead and try because you already know lots of things. For us, there is no right or wrong answer when you work).

Before the child wrote anything, the experimenter asked the child to repeat the utterance aloud before writing it. During the oral interpretation of the written production, the adult was careful not to give clues concerning how to divide the sentence into letters, syllables, or other groupings. When there was a difference between what the child pronounced and what had been requested, the experimenter would ask the child, "How do you know?" without immediately repeating the forgotten or deformed utterance.

After requesting the "reading" of the sentences the child had written, the experimenter used the "request to point and verbalize" technique described by Ferreiro and Gomez Palacio (1982a). The questions corresponding to this technique were, respectively: *"Où as-tu marqué [tel ou tel mot]?"* (Where did you write [the given word]?) and *"Qu'as-tu marqué là?"* (What did you write there?). At the end of the interview, the child was invited to reread the written production corresponding to both the first word requested and the first sentence.

FINDINGS

As noted earlier, the data collected during these three observation sessions were produced in situations adapted from those of Ferreiro's research. Our interviews had the following general characteristics.

First, the children were confronted with unusual requests coming from adults:

- In a setting that was different from the school, the children were asked individually to write things that had not yet been taught. They worked in a one-to-one situation, under the supervision of an observer and in front of a videocamera.
- The request for words solicited such responses as the writing of nouns without articles and verbs without subjects or adverbs. The sentences that

were requested could include a negation, could be in the form of a question, and could be expressed in a familiar register.

- After the writing production, the children had to point to the word they had just written and say it aloud.
- As early as the second observation, the children had to point to and verbalize parts of the sentences immediately after writing them and then had to verbalize a word and a sentence at the end of the interview.
- As early as the second observation, the children had to write a sentence containing elements not necessarily learned previously, along with their name, which was already a familiar written form.

Second, in these interviews, the children manifested various sorts of behavior, among them surprise at the instructions, silence, and apparent acceptance of the request. The experimenter assisted the child's activity by restating the instructions and appearing to be more or less satisfied with the child's work: *voilà* (there), *bien* (good), *"Tu vois que tu y arrives"* (You see, you can do it), *très bien* (very good). When the children expressed an inability to answer and persistently refused to write what was requested, the experimenter invited them to draw one of the words [*ballon* (ball), during the first session] and would then ask, *"On ne peut pas le marquer encore autrement?"* (Isn't there another way it can be marked?).

Through these exchanges, the children were able to understand the experimenter's expectations and to try, for the most part, to respond to them. Often, however, the children considered their responses adequate, even when they were erroneous: When possible, the experimenter tried to create conditions for cognitive conflicts during the activities, using various means, particularly requests to point and verbalize in the second session.

Observed Conduct

A detailed analysis of each child's conduct in the three sessions revealed several types of behavior when the child was presented with the requested task. From the first session, we observed a significant diversity of approaches taken by the children in the given situation. Some exhibited a marked sense of astonishment, others showed an attitude of inhibition, others immediately attempted to make the written production, and still others commented on the request.

With regard to the production of written text, we noted that certain children would not write anything before first trying to draw what was to be written. Some children varied the number of graphemes, from one word to another; some used this quantitative variation of graphemes to distinguish between words and sentences; and others isolated the "words" in the sentences. We also noticed significant differences in the children's repertoire of graphemes, their reaction at producing a monosyllabic word, and their use of conventional phonic values.

In the "reading" of the written text, we noticed that several children could not reconstruct the utterance, because some were attached to the naming of graphemes and others to clues inferred from their written text. During the "reading," the children's finger movements varied from continuously underlining throughout to grapheme-by-grapheme progression to advancement by groups of graphemes to making efforts to find a correspondence between the utterance and the written text. Variations in some children's finger movements at each reading (two readings were generally requested for each production) were observed.

Categories Established During the First Session

We regrouped the behavior types adopted by the children into the following categories in order to clarify the conceptualizations revealed in the children's conduct.

Group A. No written production. These children produced no written form apart from their first name and last name. They refused to go on to the other requested productions, contenting themselves with drawing. Four children comprised this group (see Fig. 7.1).

Group B. Written production without oral retention. The children in this group agreed, sometimes after going through a drawing stage, to produce the requested written texts. The meaning they attributed to their writing, when they read it, was directly linked to their recollection of what had been requested by the experimenter. Because they sometimes made mistakes in this reconstruction, the experimenter then asked them, by repeating the utterance, if that was really what they had been requested to write. These children then "reread" the adult's utterance into their production, without seeming to attach any importance to the fact that the same written text could have two different meanings.

Exper. : "Je m'appelle Dominique, et toi ?" [My name is Dominique, what's yours?]
Nicolas : ....(se triture la bouche) [contorts his mouth]
Exp. : "Tu peux le marquer ?" [Can you write it?]
Nicolas : (opine de la tête) [Nods yes]

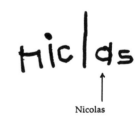

Movement of the finger :

"Reading" :   Nicolas

FIG. 7.1. Nicolas A. Session 1 (5;3), Group A.

We identified two subsets within this group. The first subset, Group Ba, was composed of 11 children. In their written productions, they generally used the same number of graphemes to write the words and the sentences (see Fig. 7.2).

The second subset, Bb, contained four children who showed a quantitative difference between their productions corresponding to the words and those corresponding to the sentences. Some of them even placed one or several separations between "words" in one or more sentences (see Fig. 7.3).

Group C. Written/oral adjustments. These children tried in various ways to adapt the written text they were producing to the utterance requested by the experimenter, which they verbalized afterward.

We found three subsets within this group. The first, Ca, was composed of three children who read the written production by syllabifying vocalization, which was at times linked to a parallel movement of the finger. Furthermore, the utterance was "read" to correspond with the space of the written text (see Fig. 7.4).

The second subgroup, Cb, consisted of two children who, over and above the behavior manifested by Ca, significantly increased the number of graphemes to write a monosyllabic word.

Containing only one child of our sample, the third subgroup, Cc, was characterized by a syllabic analysis: Hugo (see Fig. 7.5) began by producing a correct written example of his name. When asked by the experimenter to show what

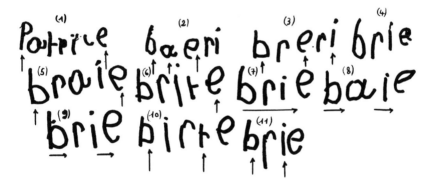

1. Patrice
2. C'est quand, les vacances ?
3. On joue pas au ballon, ici
4. Moi, j'aime regarder la télé
5. Mon copain, y m'a pris toutes mes billes
6. Ballon
7. Dormir
8. Télévision
9. Vacances
10. Difficile
11. Bille

1. Patrice
2. When is vacation?
3. We don't play ball here
4. I like to watch T.V.
5. My friend took all my marbles
7. Sleep
8. Television
9. Vacation
10. Difficult
11. Marble

FIG. 7.2. Patrice. Session 1 (5;2), Group Ba.

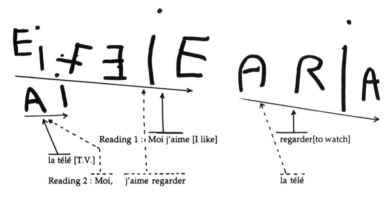

"Reading" : ?....(ne se souvient plus) [doesn't remember]
Exp. : "Difficile" [Difficult]
Lamine : "Di-ffi-ci-le"

FIG. 7.3. Lamine. Session 1 (5;9), Group Bb.

had been written, Hugo, in a first reading, attributed the first syllable of his name to the first grapheme (h), then the second to the second grapheme (u). Unsatisfied with this interpretation, Hugo continued with a second reading, ignoring the first grapheme and correctly naming the second letter. The child's third attempt attributed the second syllable of the name to a single grapheme (g); finally, he correctly named the last letter (o).

Hugo then adopted this syllabic interpretation for the interpretation of the request of words, so this hypothesis seems to have guided his written produc-

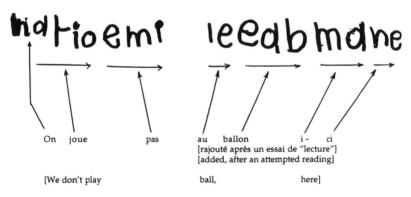

FIG. 7.4. Sandra. Session 1 (5;8), Group Ca.

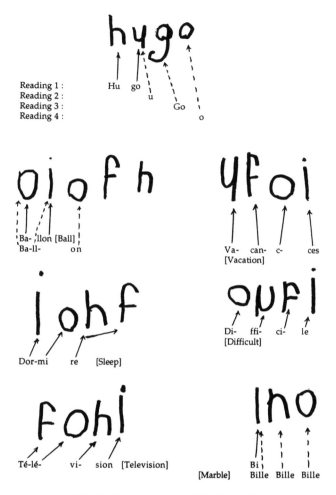

FIG. 7.5. Hugo. Session 1 (5;11), Group Cc.

tion. The conflict described by Ferreiro (Ferreiro & Gomez Palacio, 1982a) concerning the monosyllabic word was exhibited here: Hugo hesitated between the syllabic hypothesis and that of minimal quantity of graphemes for the creation of a written word when requested to write *bille* (pronounced as a monosyllabic word in French). After a first, unsatisfying attempt, Hugo managed to deal with the problem by attributing the word *bille* to each grapheme.

Group D. Phonetic analysis. The two children in this group attempted a phonetic analysis of the utterance, managing to produce conventional phonic values for the first letter of some written texts, but subsequently abandoned their work and commented on their lack of knowledge. For them, the written text

Samy : "Oui, mais je sais pas écrire....C'est comment "quand" ? J'écris
comme je veux ? Je sais écrire "Samy" en plus. [Yes, but I don't know how to
write "quand" (when)? I write how I want to? I know how to write Samy,
too]
Exp. : "Peut-être qu'on peut marquer autrement ?" [Can you write it another
way?]
Samy : "Un "a", c'est comme çà, comme Samy... C'est qua-a-a-and... Un E.
["A" is like this, like Samy...It's qua-a-a-and...an E]

Reading : "un [s], un [a], un E. [a [s], an a and an E]

FIG. 7.6.   Samy. Session 1 (6;1), Group D.

contained signs that only someone who was a proficient reader could read (see Fig. 7.6).

Categories Established During the Second Session

To the criteria established in the first session, we added elements of behavior shown in the request to point (pointing that was coherent or not in terms of the position of the requested word in the uttered sentence and in the written text; adequate pointing), to verbalize, reactions to writing one's name within a sentence, and the behavior shown in response to the request for the final verbalization (written form corresponding to the first word and to the first sentence).

After the second session, we regrouped the categories as follows.

Group A. These children did not succeed in producing written text other than their names. There were three subjects in this group.

Group B. Children in this group produced differentiated written texts, but "read" them only by their recollection of the utterance. These subjects showed little coherence when pointing and failed in their verbalizations. Subgroup Ba, who wrote no more graphemes for the sentences than for the words, contained three subjects. Subgroup Bb, who indicated a quantitative difference between words and sentences, was made up of three children.

Group C. The criteria for this group, which contained 12 children who adapted their written text to the utterance, were modified with an additional criterion concerning the children's behavior when confronted with the request to point: Verbalization was not relevant for this category because the children were naming the letters. The three children in Subgroup Ca did not produce coherent pointing and did not progress, from this point of view, throughout the session. One child, Subgroup Cb, significantly increased the number of graphemes when writing the monosyllabic word and did some coherent pointing. One subject, Subgroup Cc, made a syllabic analysis of his written texts (using two or three graphemes for one syllable) and managed some coherent pointing. The four children in Subgroup Cd engaged in pointing that was often coherent. In Subgroup Ce, the pointing of the two children was always coherent. One child, Subgroup Cf, always pointed successfully at the exact spot that the "reading" of the sentence called for (coherent pointing within the space of the written text and pointing adapted to the dividing up of the text; see Fig. 7.7).

Group D. This group of children attempted a phonetic analysis of the utterance. There were no subjects in Group D in this second session.

Group E. The three children in this new group managed a type of alphabetical writing (cf. Ferreiro & Gomez Palacio, 1982a; see Fig. 7.8).

Categories Established for the Third Session

By the third session, all the children observed had arrived at the alphabetical hypothesis. The following criteria were used to analyze their productions: Their breaking up of the spoken utterance into phonemes was always effective—even the complex forms were reconstructed as, for example, in *récréation* [RekReas3] (recess), *j'aime* [ʒɛm] (I like)—or failed with some elements; the analysis of the words in the sentences led or did not lead to their separation; or the order of

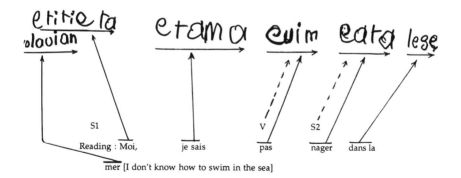

Pointing to 1 : mer (S1) [sea]
Pointing to 2 : nager (S2) [swim]
Verbalization : pas (V) [not]

FIG. 7.7. Laetitia. Session 2 (6;0), Group Cf.

Reading : "moi, je sais pas nager dans la mer"

[I don't know how to swim in the sea]

FIG. 7.8. Samy. Session 2 (6;4), Group E.

the words in the sentences was or was not respected. Correctness of spelling was not taken into consideration in this analysis.

The results of the third session led us to refine the internal breakdown of Group E that had been formed after the second session. Subgroup Ea contained a single subject who did not always manage correct phonetic analyses, did not always separate words, and arranged some words in random order. Subgroup Eb was made up of five children who respected the order of the words in the sentence but were not successful in their word separations or in all of the phonetic analyses. Subgroup Ec was composed of two children who succeeded in their phonetic analyses and respected the word order of the sentence but did not take all of the separations into account. Six subjects, Subgroup Ed, met all three criteria used (cf. Fig. 7.9).

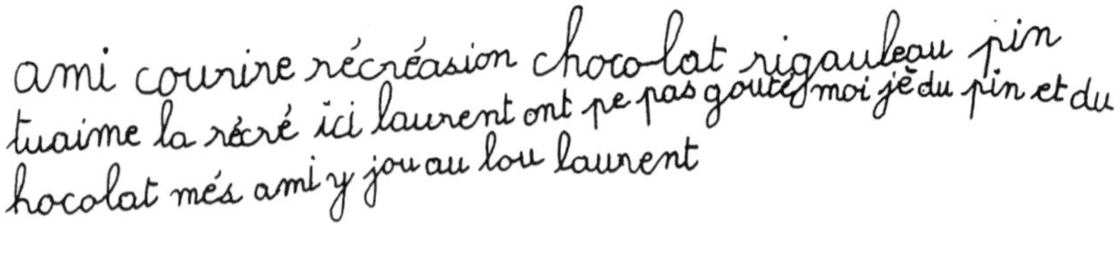

ami courire récréasion chocolat rigauleau pin tuaime la récré ici laurent ont ne pas gouté moi je du pin et du hocolat més ami y jou au lou laurent

Utterances : Ami. Courir. Récréation. Chocolat. Rigolo. Pain. Tu aimes la récré ? Ici, Laurent, on ne peut pas goûter. Moi, j'ai du pain et du chocolat. Mes amis, y jouent au loup.

[Friend. Run. Recess. Chocolate. Funny. Bread. Do you like recess? Here, Laurent, we can't have a snack. I have bread and chocolate. My friends are playing tag.]

FIG. 7.9. Laurent. Session 3 (6;6), Group Ed.

Results of the Three Sessions

Table 7.1 indicates the age and the categories used for each child at each session and shows the great variety of responses brought to our writing production situation by the kindergarten children. We distinguished four main types of categories in Session 1. Of the 24 children present for Session 2, three were placed in Category E, thus broadening the range of conceptualizations. At the third session, following 6 months of regular instruction in reading, all subjects in the sample were able to reproduce the utterances by adopting an alphabetical-type hypothesis. The transitions from one category to another occurred in the same direction, from B to E, and seemed, therefore, to fit an ordered sequence. Table 7.2 indicates the progress of the 14 subjects who were observed in all three sessions. Table 7.2 also reveals the diversity in progression rates up to Level E of the 14 subjects who were observed in all three sessions.

TABLE 7.1
Results From the Three Sessions

Name	Session 1: Age		Session 2: Age		Session 3: Age	
Cédric	Ba	5;0	Cd	5;5	Ed	6;2
Julien A	Cb	5;1	Ce	5;8	Eb	6;5
Patrice	Ba	5;2	Ba	5;9	Ea	6;6
Aurore	Ba	5;2	Ce	5;9		
Frédéric	Bb	5;3	Cb	5;8		
Nicolas A	A	5;3	E	6;1	Ed	6;5
Caroline	Ba	5;3	Ca	5;8		
Séverine	A	5;5	A	5;9	Eb	6;6
Julien B	Cb	5;5	Ca	5;9	Eb	6;6
Laurent	Ba	5;5	Cd	5;9	Ed	6;6
Marjorie	Ba	5;5	Bb	5;10	Ec	6;8
Gabriel	Ba	5;6	Bb	5;10		
Karine	Ba	5;7	Ba	6;1		
Laetitia	Ca	5;7	Cf	6;0	Ed	6;11
Marc-Antoine	Ba	5;7	Ca	5;11		
Axelle	Ba	5;7	Ba	5;11		
Sandra	Ca	5;8	Cd	6;1	Ec	6;11
Leslie	Ba	5;9				
Lamine	Bb	5;9				
Halima	A	5;10				
Benoît	D	5;10	E	6;2	Ed	7;0
Stéphane	Ca	5;10				
Nicolas B	Bb	5;11	Bb	6;4		
Christophe	A	5;11	A	6;3	Eb	7;1
Hugo	Cc	5;11	Cc	6;3		
Marianne	Bb	6;0	Cd	6;4	Eb	7;2
Samy	D	6;1	E	6;4	Ed	7;2

TABLE 7.2
Types Of Progression Over the Three Sessions

Name	Session 1	Session 2	Session 3
Séverine	A	A	Eb
Christophe	A	A	Eb
Nicolas A	A	E	Ed
Patrice	Ba	Ba	Ea
Marjorie	Ba	Bb	Ec
Laurent	Ba	Cd	Ed
Cédric	Ba	Cd	Ed
Marianne	Bb	Cd	Eb
Sandra	Ca	Cd	Ec
Laetitia	Ca	Cf	Ed
Julien A	Cb	Ce	Eb
Julien B	Cb	Ca	Eb
Samy	D	E	Ed
Benoît	D	E	Ed

Our analysis, based on Tables 7.1 and 7.2, suggests several conclusions:

• Although Session 2 allowed us to observe a range of responses at least as broad as those in Session 1, the demands of this situation continued to impede three children (i.e., one ninth of the sample), except for their names.

• By requesting that the child point and verbalize, as well as by inserting the child's name into the sentence, the experimenter obliged the child to produce an original cognitive endeavor.

• Our organization of categories enabled us to situate the children rather effectively throughout these writing production sessions with respect to their cognitive activity. The subject's evolution followed the order of the categories, which, therefore, reflected different levels of conceptualization of written text. The subgroups provided an early indication of developmental stages within the categories.

• The paths taken by the children indicate that there was more than just one way to arrive at Subcategory Ed by the first grade if we consider that satisfying the three criteria of the third session constitutes a relevant point on which one can interpret the work produced by the children in our situations.

DISCUSSION

Our study, undertaken in the context of French-speakers, confirms the importance of the psychogenetic approach developed by Ferreiro to understand children's construction of writing. This study of the conceptualizations of young

French children with respect to their written language required some modifications compared with data collected among the Hispanic groups, without questioning the general model. The data procured in France contained most elements of the Hispanic model while following an adapted methodology. Further studies should take into consideration the following points.

Methodology

A number of improvements should be integrated into future research on French children. For example, the utterances used during Sessions 1 and 2 could be better adapted to kindergarten children by avoiding verbs and adverbs for the words given in isolation and by looking for nouns with a clear syllable-graphemic correspondence; thus, for example, choosing *chocolat* (chocolate) "cho-co-lat" over *courir* (run): "cou-ri-re" or "cou-rir," and having the referent well identified.

Instructions for the children should be clarified to minimize the paradoxical character of the requests (e.g., "You don't know how, but do it like people who know how to write" could become "Try to do it like big people who already know how to write"). The other modifications introduced seem to have shown their utility (e.g., pointing, verbalization, insertion of the child's name into the sentence).

Psychogenesis of Literacy and Social Interactions

In addition to making these methodological changes, future research could focus on the activity of writing production of two children who are asked to perform the same writing production task together. In the transactions required to reach a joint decision, an observer could scrutinize the arguments used to produce writing to be read by a third party.

Psychogenesis of Literacy and Preschool

On several occasions during this study, we examined the material that the subjects of our sample had received with regard to literacy, information that had been conveyed by the French preschool to prepare the children for reading. Because this initial material involved various methods, depending on the teachers, our remarks cannot have a general application.

In several children who knew the names of the letters, we observed an ability to "sound out" the letters. However, if three children were able to make a phonetic analysis of the utterance in May or June of the kindergarten year, was this due to school or to their own cognitive ability? The information conveyed at school, identical for all of them, was far from being integrated in the same way by all the subjects of our study. If some of these elements of knowledge can be prepared and taught, is it true that others must be constructed by each subject? How are they linked to the types of conceptualization that children form of written text?

Although the levels of conceptualization of literacy that appeared in Ferreiro's study seemed less clear and turned off their course in some way by this initiation to writing in a French kindergarten class, the psychogenetic progression observed in our sample reveals the role of cognitive activity of the young child through literacy. These results also indicate the need to study languages with different systems underlying the correspondence between graphemes and phonics.

REFERENCES

Besse, J.-M. (1988). L'enfant et la construction de la langue écrite: Une approche génétique [Children's construction of literacy: A psychogenetic approach]. *Voies Livres, 9,* 1–27.

Ferreiro, E. (1978). What is written in a written sentence? A developmental answer. *Journal of Education, 160*(4), 25–39.

Ferreiro, E. (1984). The underlying logic of literacy development. In H. Goelman, A. Oberg, & F. Smith (Eds.), *Awakening to literacy* (pp. 154–173). London: Heinemann.

Ferreiro, E., & Gomez Palacio, M. (1982a). *Analisis de las perturbaciones en el proceso de aprendizaje escolar de la lectura y la escritura (5 fasciculos)* [Analysis of difficulties in the learning of literacy]. Mexico: Direccion General de Educacion Especial.

Ferreiro, E., & Gomez Palacio, M. (Eds.). (1982b). *Nuevas perspectivas sobre les procesos de lectura y escritura* [New perspectives on processes of literacy]. Mexico City: Siglo XXI Editores.

Ferreiro, E., & Teberosky, A. (1979). *Los sistemas de escritura en el desarrollo del nino* [Literacy before schooling]. Mexico City: Siglo XXI Editores.

8

PIZZA OR PIZA?
HOW CHILDREN INTERPRET THE
DOUBLING OF LETTERS IN WRITING

Emilia Ferreiro
Die-Cinvestav, Mexico D.F., Mexico

Clotilde Pontecorvo
Cristina Zucchermaglio
University of Rome "La Sapienza"

INTRODUCTION

In studies of the development of literacy competence in children speaking different languages, two basic organizational principles are emerging: the minimum quantity principle and the internal variety principle (Ferreiro & Teberosky, 1982; Pontecorvo & Zucchermaglio, 1988, 1990). These two principles mark an important step in the process of written language construction: They allow the child to judge whether or not writing is readable (and understandable). According to the minimum quantity principle, a written word is a set of ordinal parts (letters) that must equal a certain number (normally this number is three). According to the internal variety principle, a written word is a set of different parts (letters) and cannot include the same letter more than once. This latter principle can be understood in two different ways:

• Strictly interpreted, a letter repetition is impossible.
• Loosely interpreted, a letter repetition could be accepted sometimes, but only if the two letters are not in adjacent positions.

In the Spanish writing system, repetition of letters in adjacent positions occurs infrequently; in the Italian writing system, however, duplication of letters (particularly of consonants) occurs very frequently. These differences between the two systems prompt this comparative study of children exposed to these two different graphic realities of the alphabetic system of writing.

Graphic Letter Duplication in Spanish and Italian

Spanish

In Spanish, the repetition of letters in adjacent positions involves only a few letters. The vowels that can be doubled are *e* and *o* and only in rare cases. The *e* can double in some verbs, such as *leer* or *creer* (i.e., bisyllabic words with the tonic accent on the last syllable). The *o* can double when the morpheme *co-* is placed before words beginning with *o*, such as *cooperar* and *coordinar* and in words derived from Greek, for example, *zoologia*, *zoologico*, and *zoologo*. The consonants that can be doubled are *l*, *r*, *c*, and *n*. Doubling *l* creates a new letter, the digram *ll*, corresponding to a different phoneme. The same occurs with *r* and *rr*, but in this case there is an additional graphic constraint: The Spanish orthography does not allow the use of *rr* at the beginning of a word. Thus, words beginning with multivibrant consonants cannot be written with the digram *rr* but must use the *r* that corresponds to the simple vibrant. Double *c* appears in a few words (e.g., *accion*, *accidente*, *restriccion*), corresponding to the pronunciation of /ks/. Double *n* occurs even less frequently and only in rarely used words (e.g., *perenne*); in this case, the graphic doubling corresponds to an effective doubling of the consonants that is more similar to the way it is in Italian. Double letters can appear only in certain positions in Spanish words:

- Only the letter *l* can be doubled at the beginning of a word.
- Double consonants cannot appear at the end of a word; only the vowel *e* can be doubled at the end of a word (e.g., in some forms of the verb *leer*).
- Double letters most frequently appear not at the beginning or at the end of a word but at an internal position, except for the beginning double *l*.

More than one doubled letter is rarely found in the same word. There are a few words with two sets of double letters (e.g., *correccion* and *desarrollo*), whereas there are no words with three sets. These features are specific to the Spanish lexicon and do not account for the words coming from other languages (particularly English words in the Mexican spoken language).

Italian

In Italian, letters in adjacent positions are very frequently doubled. About one fourth of written Italian words have double letters. This holds especially true for consonants, whereas it is rare with vowels. All consonants of the Latin alphabet may be doubled except the *h*, and the *q* is doubled only in one word: *soqquadro*. A double *u* is never found, whereas double *o* and double *a* appear only in the scientific lexicon and in words coming from Greek (e.g., *zoo*, *zoologo*, *oosfera*, *Nausicaa*). The double *e* occurs more frequently, because it is needed to form the plural of female words ending with *-ea* in the singular (e.g., *idea* and *idee*). The same holds true with the *i*: Doubling is necessary in masculine words ending with -*io*, with tonic accent on the *i* (e.g., *zii, pigolii*).

Double letters can appear only in certain positions in Italian words:

- No consonants can be doubled at the beginning or at the end of a word, except in some foreign words such as *jazz* or *stress*.
- Double vowels can appear, although this is rare, at the end of a word (e.g., *idee, zii*) and still more rarely at the beginning of a word.
- Double letters most frequently appear at internal positions in words.
- Relatively frequently, more than one set of double letters is found in the same word in Italian, in contrast to Spanish.

By doubling a letter, Italian spelling represents the strength of consonants inside words, because this has a distinctive value (e.g., *pala* vs. *palla*), but it does not distinguish graphically the phonetic doubling of beginning consonants when preceded by vowels (e.g., the writing of *è notte* is pronounced /ɛ nnotte/).

The preceding example introduces the complex relationship between a phonological system and a graphic system (Camilli, 1965). In Italian, phonological doubling occurs more frequently than does graphical doubling. Although Italian can be considered a language that, comparatively speaking, has a coherent and regular written representation, some incoherencies still remain. De Mauro (1977) distinguished two types of incoherencies. The first type comes from the persistence of Latin graphic transcriptions: The doubled *affricate* dental /tts/ should be written as *zz* (e.g., in *bozza, destrezza, razziali*), whereas in words ending with a vowel +*zione* (e.g., *azione, nazione, torrefazione*), it must be written as *z*; the same occurs in *ozio, vizio*, and *negozio*, where *z* always has the same phonological value. The second type of incoherencies comes from the lack of correspondence between the orthographic system, which is built on the High Italian pronunciation, and the varied pronunciations actually used in Italian, which can be classified as Northern, Roman, and Southern. Although coherently differentiated in graphic transcription, in spoken Italian the doubled /b/ and /g/ are distinguished from the simple /b/ and /g/ only in the High Italian spoken in Tuscany (e.g., the *b* in *tubi* from the *bb* of *dubbi*). Elsewhere in Italy, there is no correspondence between pronunciation and graphic transcription. In many dialects of the northern regions, all words are pronounced without doubling /b/, whereas in the Roman dialect, these same words are pronounced with double *b* (e.g., *tubbi* and *dubbi*).

The persistent orthographic "errors" that occur well after the period of beginning literacy cannot be explained only by the features of nonstandard spoken language used by most Italians, as was stated by Morchio, Ott, and Pesenti (1989). Rather, as we have shown, it also depends on a lack of complete correspondence between phoneme and grapheme, although Italian is considered a regular language compared with English.

Historical Trends in Writing Standardization:
The Italian Case

In the historical development of writing, some evidence can be found of both the appearance of double letters and their disappearance. As Ullman (1932) said:

> Another invention of those who used the Eastern Greek alphabet was the doubling of consonants. This began in the eighth century, apparently in Miletus. Before that time consonants were doubled in speech, but not in writing. The poet Ennius introduced his practice into Latin in the second century B.C. and from Latin it has come into the modern languages. As a result we have the curious situation that in early Greek and Latin, consonants pronounced double were written single, whereas in modern English they are written double, but pronounced single. Italian is the best example of a language which has the doubled pronunciation. (p. 30)

Given the specific situation of Italian, it may be useful to recall some aspects of Italian orthography, starting with its first stabilization in the second half of the 16th century (Migliorini, 1955). The standard language became the literary language. Tuscan variety (theorized by Bembo) also became the standard graphic rule. Print was another strong factor in conventionalization, but the notation of double versus single letters was one of the most difficult and problematic aspects of this standardization.

Double consonants that were already present in the Latin orthography were also reproduced in the Italian orthography, as in *anno* and *bello*. When the standard Italian pronunciation differs from the Latin orthography, the single graphic form has been preferred (e.g., *comodo, comune*). In the same way, some words (e.g., *facto, septe*) then introduce a written double letter (e.g., *fatto, sette*). In other cases, the double forms remain only for a first period after print diffusion (e.g., *auttorità*), and then they disappear following standard Italian pronunciation.

A trend in the history of Italian orthography is that of eliminating most graphical doubling. This is true for composite writings, in which the first element should require a phonological doubling. In these cases, after a period of the presence of both graphical forms (e.g., *diffetto* and *difetto, deffinire* and *definire, proccurare* and *procurare, diffesa* and *difesa*), the plain form prevails. Another confirmation of this trend appears in the syntactical doubling between two morphemes, a phenomenon that is present largely in Italian phonology. After a first period in which it was graphically represented (e.g., *a ccapo, le ssedie, a llui, a cciò*), the doubling was eliminated, except for cases in which it appeared inside the same word (e.g., *daccapo, appunto, giacché*). Typographic standardization probably led to the elimination of double letters at the beginning of words, because it would have introduced different graphical representations of the same word.

Print standardization resulted in the elimination or transformation of other cases of graphic doubling that are still present in the manuscripts. It is no longer acceptable to write *lasciarre, camppo,* or *bagnno,* and, in particular, the *qq* was transformed into *cq* as in *piaqquemi*, which became *piacquemi*. This also occurred in other languages. In German, the *kk* was transformed into *ck*, as in *Ecke*. In Carolingian writing, the *ii* was transformed into *ij*, and in 7th-century English, the *uu* and *vv* were transformed into a new letter, *w*, which "as for its two parents *u* and *v* retains the name of the former and the appearance of the latter" (Ullman, 1932, p. 157). Generally speaking, the typographic standardization of orthography had more double letters that were eliminated than those that have remained until now.

This historical digression is not aimed at supporting a hypothesis of parallelism between the psychogenetic and the ontogenetic development of writing, although historical data could show that an internal variety principle was also at work in the historical orthographic standardization. It is possible, however, that during the acquisition of written language the child is faced with some fundamental problems that were present in the historical development of written languages.

Problem Setting

The question underlying our work is this: To what extent does the internal variety principle take into account the peculiarities of the graphic transcription of a specific language? If the origin of this principle lies in children's exploring the written language of their environment, we would expect to find great differences between children exposed to Spanish and children exposed to Italian. In particular, Spanish-speaking children would think that letters are never doubled, whereas Italian children would be more flexible and tolerant about doubling letters.

This hypothesis appears to emerge from an ingenuous empiricism that is incompatible with the data available on children's conceptualizations of written language. Moreover, this hypothesis does not work when considered in light of the other organizational principle, minimum quantity. In both Spanish and Italian, the high-frequency words (i.e., mainly function words, such as articles, prepositions, and conjunctions) are written primarily with one or two letters, which does not prevent children from thinking that at least three letters are the "right" minimum quantity of letters of any writing that will be readable and interpretable. Contrasting the two languages could suggest more solid bases to falsify the initial hypotheses, while still allowing a more detailed account of the origin and growth of the internal variety principle.

METHOD

Experimental Technique and Sample

We designed an experimental situation that, with some variations, was used with children from 4 to 6 years of age enrolled in kindergarten or first grade. Most children of this age normally begin to explore the qualitative and quantitative features of written language and to elaborate tentative hypotheses on the relationship between written and spoken language.

In semistructured individual interviews that allowed the experimenter to test some of the hypotheses in children's answers, we used the following experimental procedure:

1. We presented each child with two cards containing identical writing, except that one had a doubled letter.
2. We prompted a comparison of the two cards.
3. We asked which card contained the written version of the word pronounced by the experimenter. In some cases, that word had the doubled letter; in other cases, it did not have the doubled letter. In any case, the uttered word was one that existed in the lexicon of the language.
4. We asked for an interpretation of the card that had not been chosen.

Data collection was organized in three phases. Interview A involved a sample of 19 Italian children: 15 kindergartners (mean age: 5;2) in an innovative school setting, and 4 first graders (mean age: 6;9). The interviews were conducted by the three authors together. Interview B1 had a sample of 14 Italian children: 9 kindergartners (mean age: 5;9), and 5 first graders (mean age: 6;8). This interview was conducted in the same school as Interview A, but 1 year after; 4 kindergarten children were interviewed twice (in both Interview A and B1). These interviews were conducted by one of the authors (C. Z.). Interview B2 had a sample of 31 Spanish-speaking children: 22 kindergartners (mean age: 5;2), and 9 first graders (mean age: 6;2). These interviews were collected during the same period as B1 and were conducted by one of the authors (E. F.). The Italian children were interviewed in Rome, whereas the Spanish-speaking children were interviewed in Mexico City.

As a result of Interview A, the B1 and B2 interviews were modified in terms of the following:

1. When the interpretation of the unchosen card was requested. In the first phase, this had been requested immediately before presenting the next card, whereas in the following interviews it seemed best first to obtain the children's first choices and then to come back to the interpretation of the unchosen card. When a child could not give an interpretation, the experimenter suggested various alternative interpretations that had been suggested by other children in the same task (this was done in Interview B2).

2. The way in which this interpretation was requested. In Interview A, we asked directly, "What does this mean?" This request, however, presupposes implicitly that something was said on the card, that is, that the written words could be read and interpreted. Thus, we modified the question to "Does this

mean something?" and eventually added a request such as, "Is this word well written?" If the child answered "Yes," we also asked "What does it mean here?"

3. The positions in which the cards were presented to the child. We noted that some children focused more on a card's position than on its content (e.g., some children always chose the upper card or the right). During B1 and B2, we systematically varied the position in which the correct cards were presented.

In addition, in the three interviews, we also used cards other than those present in the sample set. We included other requests for interpretations of words or production to obtain more information to help us understand specific children's answers. The utility of this procedure will be appreciated when we present the individual cases.

Procedure and Data Analysis

For the interviews, we used 10 to 12 pairs of cards (6 cm × 3 cm) on which words (with or without double letters) were written in upper-case format; the pairs presented in each interview were the following:

Interview A.[1] *CANE*–CANNE; GATO*–*GATTO*; *ROSA*–ROSSA; PALA–*PALLA*; SABIA*–*SABBIA*; CARO–*CARRO*; PIZA*–*PIZZA*; PACO*–*PACCO*; FREDO*–*FREDDO*; CAFE*–*CAFFE*; GOMA*–*GOMMA*; *IDEA*–IDEE.

Interview B1. *CANE*–CANNE; GOMA*–*GOMMA*; *ROSA*–ROSSA; FREDO*–*FREDDO*; PALA–*PALLA*; CAFE*–*CAFFE*; CARO–*CARRO*; SABIA*–*SABBIA*; *IDEA*–IDEE; GATO*–*GATTO*.

Interview B2. *GATO*–GATTO*, CARO–*CARRO*; LAVE–*LLAVE*; *TACO*–TACCO*; *GOMA*–GOMMA*; GALO–*GALLO*; POLO–*POLLO*; *TREN*–TREEN*; *CAFE*–CAFEE*; *RIO*–RRIO*; PIZA*–*PIZZA*.

The complete interviews were audiotaped and transcribed. For Interview A, each experimenter separately analyzed the transcriptions to identify the specific ways in which children were solving the double letter problem. Each analysis was discussed and compared with the others to reach a more systematic definition of the different ways that children used and a common identification of levels in which the children's answers were organized. The answers in Interviews B1 and B2 were then grouped in these categories. Sometimes we added new, jointly agreed-on categories corresponding to new answers given by children;

---

[1]In the card presentations, the italic words were uttered by the experimenter (e.g., "Where does it say *gatto* (cat)?"). The words with an asterisk (GOMA*) have no meaning in either of the two languages.

cases that were not easily categorizable were discussed until we reached a consensus.

Description of the Main Levels

In this section, we describe the main levels in which the children's answers were organized. A first result of this work was the unique classification constructed for both Italian and Spanish children's answers.

Group I. The difference between the two cards was not sufficient to create a difference in their interpretation. The problem we posed was not yet a problem for these children. When they compared the two cards, they "saw" them as the same. When the experimenter suggested that they differed, the children seemed not to take that into account. When they chose a card (which they were compelled to do), they acted for episodic reasons (i.e., because of the position of cards on the table or to make some alternative choice, i.e., to accept one and reject the next). The card not chosen always "said the same" as the chosen one or could say anything, also with no relation to the word uttered by the experimenter.

Examples

Francesca (A) Italian-Speaking (4;4). She always chose the lower card, that is, the card closer to her. The similarities between the two written words overrode the differences. Francesca says it clearly: "In the two the same thing is written" and "The writings are the same."

Eric (B2) Spanish-Speaking (5;0). He thought that the cards were the same, because both were composed of the same letters. When the experimenter pointed to the difference, Eric continued to think that the cards were equal. He always chose by the card's position: the lower card if the cards were presented vertically; the right-hand card if they were presented horizontally. For Eric, the card not chosen often meant the same as the chosen one or anything else, with no relation to the words uttered by the experimenter initially.

Alma (B2) Spanish-Speaking (5;2). She described several sets of cards as sometimes "the same" and sometimes "different." This difference did not change the main criterion of choice, which was based on the relative position of the cards. The unchosen card could have said anything, with no relation to the word uttered by the experimenter initially (e.g., she chose *TREN* for *tren* (train), and she thought that *TREEN* was pronounced *mariposa* (butterfly); she chose *POLO* for *pollo* (chicken), and she thought that *POLLO* is pronounced *balena* (whale)).

Group II. The children began to note the difference between the writings and said that they thought that the two cards could not say the same thing. However, it was very difficult for them to decide which writing corresponded to the word uttered by the experimenter. Because they lacked a stable criterion, they swung between the choices and interpretations. In the interpretations of the unchosen writing, the following types of answers were found: (a) the children proposed a word meaning that had no relation to the meaning of the word uttered by the experimenter; (b) the children proposed a word that had a se-mantic relationship to the word uttered by the experimenter; (c) the children proposed a lexical derivative of the word uttered by the experimenter (e.g., a diminutive or an augmentative). This latter alternative is the most developed, because the children tried to take into account both differences and similarities between the two writings; that is, they thought they said almost, but not exactly, the same thing.

Examples

Alessio (A) Italian-Speaking (4;7). He clearly preferred the writings that had no doubled letters. He interpreted the other comparable words, which were often diminutives or augmentatives: *palletta* (small ball) for *PALLA* (ball); *pizzetta* (small pizza) for *PIZZA; rosona* (big rose) for *ROSSA* (red); *idee piccoline* (small ideas) for *IDEA* (idea). However, being able to decode the sound of each letter, Alessio began to change his answers at the end of the interview. Reading aloud each letter of the two writings, he became aware that they were made of the same sound sequence. For this reason, he preferred to eliminate the previously observed differences between the writings, saying that both cards had the same word written on them.

Lorena (B2) Spanish-Speaking (5;0). She began the interview without a clear criterion, choosing alternatively the writing with doubled or no doubled letters. Later, when the experimenter asked for an interpretation of the unchosen cards, Lorena began to choose systematically the writing with doubled letters. This criterion enabled her to solve the interpretation problem: Lorena always inter-preted the writing without doubled letters as diminutive: *GATTO* as *gato* (cat) and *GATO* as *gato chiquito* (small cat); *GALLO* as *gallo* (cock) and *GALO* as *gallito* (small cock); *CARRO* as *carro* (car) and *CARO* as *carrito* (small car). The reverse of this same criterion was used with the word *PATO* (duck); the experimenter, after saying that the word *PATO* means *pato*, transformed the written word into *PAATO*, asking Lorena if it was possible to write this word. Lorena said that it was possible, interpreting the word as *patote* (big duck). Lorena also accepted the written word *PAATTO*, interpreting it as *patotote* (big big duck). Lorena did not accept the written words *PAAATO* or *PPAATTOO* as proper words.

Group III. In this group, a stable criterion was used to choose between the two writings: Writing containing double letters was always rejected. These same children said explicitly that the word was "not well written" or that it "doesn't say anything," and they refused to give an interpretation of it. The common feature of this group is that the use of double letters was regarded as strange.

Examples

Francesco (A) Italian-Speaking (6;8). He always chose the writing without double letters and always refused to interpret the writing with doubled letters: "It is longer but it doesn't say anything." This also happened when he phoneticized the double *s* of the word *rossa* (red), saying that it is a word without meaning. After this episode, he avoided reading aloud the writing with doubled letters and read each letter separately. This is seen explicitly in his reaction to the word *ATTAC-CAPANNI* (clothes hook): "There are too many syllables, with too many words; it doesn't work, so it doesn't mean anything." This case is particularly interesting, because he is a first grader at a full alphabetic stage. It confirms the persistence of the interpretation of this anomaly in children who know and use the alphabetic code, emphasizing how a "correct" letter doubling is more a matter of knowing and accepting the orthographic conventionality of a given language than a problem of auditory acuity.

Paulina (B2) Spanish-Speaking (5;6). She systematically chose the writing with no doubled letters. When the ninth pair of writings was presented, she spontaneously said, "Where there is only one [letter], it says *rio* (river); in the other, it doesn't mean anything." She refused the semantic alternatives that the experimenter proposed for the interpretation of the words with doubled letters, saying: "It doesn't work; it is badly written; it doesn't say anything."

Group IV. The children in this group showed a certain level of orthographic awareness and knowledge. They knew that sometimes letters are doubled, although they did not know exactly when and why. This introduced a new uncertainty in the choices. They knew that the presence of a double letter caused a phonetic difference, but they could not decide what that difference is. The difference is phonetic, but it is not the conventional one. Some children of this group always chose the writing with the doubled letter, thinking that this agreed with a general rule, whereas the writings without double letters were the exceptions.

Examples

Marco (B1) Italian-Speaking (6;9). Marco seemed to know that doubling is related to a phonetic variation, but in uttering doubled consonants, he prolonged the vowel pronunciation: *CANNE* as *caneee*; *POLLO* as *polooo*. In other cases, however, Marco tried to interpret the writing with semantically related words or expressions (as did the children in Group II): *DONNA* as *maschio; IDEE* as *idea buona.*

Mauricio (B2) Spanish-Speaking (5;10). He preferred the undoubled writings. In some cases, he hesitated because he knew that letter doubling exists and that it is related to phonology, although he did not know exactly how. For example, he read *TACCO* as *cao* and *GATTO* as *jato.*

Group V. These children knew that letter doubling is a distinctive feature of written language and that it corresponds to specific phonetic change. Their choices always corresponded to the conventional orthography, although they did not always succeed in justifying them properly. For this reason, there were some variations in interpreting the unchosen writing.

Examples

Emanuele (B1) Italian-Speaking (7;3). He chose to follow the conventional system and correctly read aloud the unchosen card. The interpretation he gave was the following: *FREDO* was read as *fredo;* "It does not mean anything . . . but if you write it down it exists . . . it could be a family name." *CAFE* was read as *café;* "It is something to eat; if you write it down, it should say something." At the end, *GATO* was read as *gato;* "It does not mean anything . . . for the others I have given a justification, but for this I can't say anything . . . if you write it, it is for playing the game."

Gabriele (A) Italian-Speaking (5;1). He chose conventionally, and he always refused to give a semantic interpretation for the unchosen label ("it does not say anything"). He accepted only one doubling per word and never more than one. For this reason, he refused *ATTACCAPANNI,* saying: "It is not well written, because they are all double letters; with some doubling it could work, but not with all doubling."

Salomon (B2) Spanish-Speaking (5;10). His choices were conventional, and he knew of the digrams *RR* and *LL.* He read correctly *CARRO/CARO* and *LLAVE/LAVE.* In the other cases, he tried to "lengthen" consonants or vowels that were doubled. At the end of the interview, he gave a very interesting interpretation of the doubling, by treating it as signal of the presence of a tonic syllable (a function that, in Spanish, is performed by the accent). So, if the graphic double vowel is placed at the same place of the tonic syllable, it is considered a good written string: *SOFIIA* = /so/fi/a/. "Yes, it works well, because it says /sofi/i/." He said that *SAUUL* "works well" but *SAAUL* "does not work" (the name has a tonic /u/), and that *SEERPIENTE* "does not work" (because the tonic /e/ is in the next syllable) but *AUTOMOOVIL* "works well" (double letter at the place of tonic vowel).

Intermediate Cases

In addition to the cases mentioned in the preceding group levels, we found some cases that we define as intermediate, because, during the interview, the children changed the criteria of choice and/or of interpretation of the writings, in ways that corresponded to different group levels. There were 11 intermediate cases (7 Spanish-speaking children and 4 Italian-speaking children). These children's answers always alternated between two contiguous group levels, which supports the validity of the sequence we are proposing.

Examples

Juan Carlos (B2) Spanish-Speaking (6;5). His answers were intermediate between Groups I and II. In the first pair of writings, he chose undoubled writings. In the other six pairs, he chose the doubled writings. Then he began to vacillate, alternating his choices. When the experimenter asked for his interpretation of the unchosen writing, he said that the two writings say the same thing. In other cases, he interpreted by semantic contiguity: Because *CARRO* means "car" in Spanish, *CARO* is read as *motor*. At the end of the interview, he interpreted *PATO* as *pato chiquito* (little duck) and *PPATO* as *pato grande* (big duck). He explained his reasoning: "When you must write *pato grande*, you must write it with two *p*s. And when you must write *pato chiquito*, you must write it with one." He always refused the writings with two double letters (e.g., *PAATTO* and *PAATOO*). Because of his uncertainties and alternations of choices and interpretations, Juan Carlos' performance lies between Groups I and II.

Cristian (B1) Italian-Speaking (5;8). At first, Cristian rejected the cards with double letters, saying, for example, *GOMMA* "does not say anything because there are two /ms/." After identifying *CAFFE'* as a word that should be written with a double letter, he began to choose the doubled card regularly, and he interpreted the other card with a criterion that combined both semantic and sounding proximity: *GATO* was read as *gatti* (cats); *CARO* was read as *carezza* (caress). Cristian began with answers typical of Group III and ended with answers typical of Group IV. For this reason, we consider his performance as intermediate between these two groups.

Alice (A) Italian-Speaking (5;9). At the beginning of the interview, Alice's performance placed her in Group III, because she always refused the doubled card and also refused to interpret it. She said: "It does not say anything; it is not a word; you could not read a thing that is not true." Her system began to vacillate when the cards *MAMMA/MAMA* were presented, because she knew the conventional writing of the first word. So she chose *MAMMA*, saying, "There are some words in which there is a double *m* and also many other doubled letters." After that, she conventionally interpreted both *CARRO* and *FREDDO*. For this reason, Alice was intermediate between Groups III and IV.

The distribution of all samples, Spanish and Italian, in the main and intermediate groups is shown in Table 8.1. Note that this distribution is generally homogeneous, and the ages are distributed about the same in the two samples. This confirms that the group levels are consistent and correspond to the types found in the first phases of beginning literacy. Note also that the number of children in Group III (i.e., those children rejecting the presence of double letters) is substantially the same in the Italian and Spanish samples.

To overcome the quantitative difference between the two samples, we have analyzed the percentages of answers in the main group levels (see Table 8.2). The intermediate cases were equally distributed between the next lower group level and the next upper group level. The distribution remains the same (see Fig. 8.1): The highest frequency for both samples was in Group III, which is particularly evident for the Italian sample (39.4%).

We have included the children's ages (see Table 8.1) to show how high the age range was within each group. Our analysis was carried out without explicit reference to the children's ages, because we do not have a specific hypothesis about this. There is, however, a statistically significant correlation ($r = .460$; $p < .005$) between age and group level; the lower mean age (4;9) and the higher one (6;1 and 6;3) are found at the edges of the distribution (see Table 8.1).

Problem Evolution in Some Children

Four children in the Italian sample were interviewed twice, 1 year apart. These cases allow us to present some preliminary considerations about the evolution of children's ideas concerning letter doubling. In the second interview, these children's answers were all at a higher group level. The specific changes were as follows: Francesca from Group I to Group II, Glizia from I to III, and Marco and Valeria from II to IV.

The amount of change is directly proportional to the change that occurred in the general level of construction of written language: Francesca, who exhibited a small evolution in the double letter problem, evolved only within the prephonographic period, whereas Glizia, who developed from the phonographic phase to a syllabic one,[2] passed from considering the double letter a problem to systematically rejecting doubled writings, as shown in the following interviews.

---

[2]These periods in children's writing development are described and discussed in chapter 1 of this volume.

TABLE 8.1
Group Distribution

	Group I	Intermediate I/II	Group II	Intermediate II/III	Group III	Intermediate III/IV	Group IV	Group V	Total
Italian	3	2	6		12	2	3	5	33
Age range	4;4–5;8	5;4–5;5	4;4–6;0		4;9–7;0	5;8–5;9	6;0–6;9	5;1–7;10	
Spanish	4	4	3	1	9		2	8	31
Age range	4;0–5;2	5;0–6;5	5;0–5;7	5;0	4;0–7;2		5;9–5;10	5;0–6;6	
Total	7	6	9	1	21	2	5	13	64
Mean age	X = 4;9	X = 5;4	X = 5;3	X = 5;0	X = 5;9	X = 5;8	X = 6;1	X = 6;3	

TABLE 8.2
Percentage Distribution of the Two Samples in the Main Groups

	Group I	Group II	Group III	Group IV	Group V	Total
Italian	12.1%	21.2%	39.4%	12.1%	15.2%	100%
Spanish	19.4%	19.4%	29.0%	6.4%	25.8%	100%

Interview A: ROSA/ROSSA

Experimenter: Are these writings the same?
Glizia: Yes (she makes a qualitative correspondence between each letter)
Experimenter: Where do you think *rosa* is written?
Glizia: [she points to ROSA]
Experimenter: And here (ROSSA), what could be written?
Glizia: It is written the same thing, because [the writing] is the same.

Interview B1:

Experimenter: Are these writings the same?
Glizia: (she carefully controls each letter) No, here (ROSSA) there are two and here (ROSA) there is one. . . . We should take away this one [she points to one *S* of ROSSA].
Experimenter: Where do you think *rosa* is written?
Glizia: Here (ROSA) . . . not here (ROSSA).

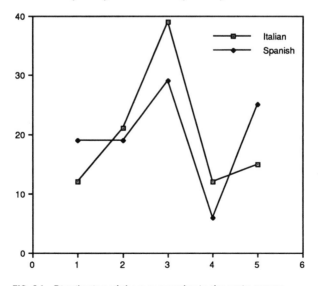

FIG. 8.1. Distribution of the two samples in the main groups.

Experimenter: And here (ROSSA) what could be written?
Glizia: Nothing, because there are two of these [she points to the
                  s].

The same changes occurred in Valeria and Marco, who, in the year between
the two interviews, developed from a prephonographic level to an alphabetic one.
In fact, we found for all the children involved in this study a statistically significant
correlation between the group levels just described and the levels of construction
of written language ($r = .882$; $p < .001$). Apparently, for children to become aware
of the double letter problem, they need to be at least aware that differences in the
writings have to correspond to differences in the word meaning.

The Doubled Letter Rejection

Given our special interest in the systematic rejection of doubled letter writings,
we carried out a detailed analysis of the children's answers in Group III: those who
rejected any doubling. Not only did these children systematically prefer the
writings with single letters, but they also explicitly refused the doubled writings.
A careful analysis of the arguments children proposed for this rejection is useful:

Vanessa (B2) Spanish-Speaking (6;6): She always said: "It is not well written:
It could not say anything."

Sarahi (B2) Spanish-Speaking (6;10): "It is not well written. We can't read it."

Francesca (A) Italian-Speaking (4;9): Observing the written word GOMMA, she
said: "They made a mistake to insert this *M*." She refused to read the word,
saying: "It is an error; a single *M* is enough."

Glizia (B1) Italian-Speaking (6;2): Observing the written word GOMMA, she
said: "We must erase this *M*." She thought that the word was not well written,
precisely because "there are two *M*s."

Silvia (A) Italian-Speaking (5;0): Observing the written word ZII, she said: "I
can't understand it," whereas she accepted the written word SI "because it
is right with a single *i*."

Elisa (B1) Italian-Speaking (6;8): She said that all the written words with doubled letters are the nicknames of the words without double letters. Specifically, she said that GOMMA is the nickname of *gomma* (that is written as
GOMA) and GATTO is the nickname of *gatto* (that is written as GATO).

Alice (A) Italian-Speaking (5;9): She said that in the written words with doubled
letters "It says nothing; it is not a word"; "What you read in it is not true."

Valeria (A) Italian-Speaking (5;4): Observing the pair CANE/CANNE, she said:
"I can't read when there are two *N*s, because I read the same *cane*; it is an
error. . . . here (CANE) is *cane* well written and here (CANNE) is *cane* not well
written."

Cristian (B1) Italian-Speaking (5;8): Observing the written word GOMMA, he said: "It can't say anything because there are two *M*s."

Laura (A) Italian-Speaking (6;9): Observing the written word ATTACCAPANNI, she said: "Here it is not well written, because there are all double letters. With some double letters it can work, but not with all."

Such a clear rejection, even in the Italian sample, points toward a paradox. In our "naïve" hypothesis, we expected Italian children to be more tolerant than Spanish children when confronted by double letters. Not only was this not true, but the largest group of Italian children (39.4%) also completely refused the cards with doubled letters, calling them "not good" or "strange." Children who have had more opportunities to see doubled writings in their environment are frequently those who refuse their acceptability in the written language. Genetic epistemology has taught us that the presence of an environmental phenomenon is not sufficient to make it an observable phenomenon. Our study presents an extreme case: the explicit rejection of a phenomenon potentially observable in children having a certain degree of familiarity with written language. In fact, the children of this group should not be considered beginners in written language acquisition, because none of them was at a prephonographic level, and more than half were at an alphabetical level. Indeed, the clear rejection of doubled letters appears only at a certain level of development in writing. We suggest the following hypothetical explanations to interpret this result: These children, who had recently become literate, probably considered letter duplications as "anomalies" of the alphabetic system, and for this reason, they preferred to reject it and, thereby, not disturb their recently acquired competence in the system.

CONCLUSIONS

A comparative study shows its usefulness in specifying what should be considered general and what should be considered specific in the process of becoming literate. Through contrasting situations, this comparative study allows us to evaluate the significance of one variable in the evolution of specific aspects of the construction of written language competence.

The results of the comparison of Italian and Spanish children who had been exposed to alphabetic systems that differed from an orthographic point of view confute our first hypothesis, based on naïve empiricism. The different frequencies of doubled letters in the writing system did not change the fundamental principle of internal variety (followed by children) in which one letter cannot be used two or more times in a given word. The results allow us not only to reject our first hypothesis but also to show new data: The rejection of double letter writing is present and explicit in Italian children.

Although we do not know exactly the origin of the internal variety principle, we can confute a possible cause: It is not a direct effect of the written material present in the environment in which the child lives. This statement does not imply that the environmental information does not affect the evolution of children's competencies about the writing system. There are at least two ways of viewing this influence. In one, the environment directly affects the evolution of children's representations without any mediation; in the other, the environmental information is actively analyzed by a child's cognitive system, which transforms it by assimilating it (see Tolchinsky Landsmann, chap. 6, this volume). Our data clearly oppose the first view of environmental influence but do not exclude the second view. More research is needed to explore the possible origins of the internal variety principle.[3]

This study throws some light on a possible motivation for Italian children's most frequent "mistake" in their early writings: the lack of some doubled letters. This is partially due to an objective fact of the Italian orthography in which—apart from the regional variations of pronunciation that present different variations from the standard Italian—there is not a full correspondence between doubled phonemes and doubled graphemes (in both directions). However, this is also due to the tendency of beginning writers to avoid letter repetition in adjacent positions because of the internal variety principle. It is probable that, while becoming literate, children leave out this principle and are able to catch the information from their ambient print. At this point, they accept the use of doubled letters and assume ideographically the way of writing certain morphemes independently from their pronunciation. This happens in the case of words ending in -azione, in which the doubled affricate dental /tts/ is written with the single grapheme z, whereas in other cases (e.g., abbozzo) it is written with a double z.

Thus, even in the Italian system of writing, which is considered transparent because it has an almost regular grapheme–phoneme correspondence, there are particular problems that all beginning writers must solve when passing from an alphabetic to an orthographic way of writing. One of these problems concerns doubled letters. An interesting fact, on which more descriptive data about children's writing are needed, is that, as far as we have seen in a corpus of children's writings of the story of Little Red Riding Hood, children tend to underuse (more than to overuse) doubled letters.

Thus, the problem of the correct orthography of doubled letters should not be posed only in terms of detecting the right correspondence between sound and writing, as teachers frequently do (Zucchermaglio, 1991). Even in Italian, this correspondence is dependent on internal conventionalities of the ortho-

---

[3]One of us has hypothesized that the origin of this principle could be in the intention of organizing the graphical universe in three classes: the iconic, the ornamental, and the "other" (neither iconic nor ornamental) representing the written signs. Symmetries and repetitions are characteristic features of the ornamental class (Ferreiro, 1988).

graphic system more than on a precise relationship with a word's pronunciation, particularly when considering the regional variations of this pronunciation.

Literate adults should be aware of how different their representation of language is compared with children's representation, because it is mediated by being literate in a writing system. Once more, it is writing that creates the categories through which we represent speech (Olson, 1993).

ACKNOWLEDGMENTS

The writing of this chapter was supported by a grant from the Italian Council of Research for a comparative research on "Written language acquisition in different cultural contexts" (CNR.91. 03855.08). A previous version of this chapter was published in *Età Evolutiva*, June 1987. The authors thank the journal for granting permission to reproduce parts of it.

REFERENCES

Camilli, A. (1965). *Pronuncia e grafia dell'italiano* [Pronunciation and writing of the Italian language]. Florence: Sansoni.

De Mauro, T. (1977). *Scuola e linguaggio* [School and language]. Rome: Editori Riuniti.

Ferreiro, E. (1988). L'ecriture avant la lettre [Writing before literacy]. In H. Sinclair (Ed.), *La notation grafique chez le jeune enfant: Langage, nombre, rythmes et melodies* [Graphic notation in children: Language, number, rhythms and melodies] (pp. 17–70). Paris: Presses Universitaires de France.

Ferreiro, E., & Teberosky, A. (1982). *Literacy before schooling.* New York: Heinemann.

Migliorini, B. (1955). Note sulla grafia italiana nel Rinascimento [Notes about Italian writing in the Renaissance]. In AA.VV., *Saggi Linguistici* (pp. 197–225). Firenze: Monnier.

Morchio, B., Ott, M., & Pesenti, E. (1989). The Italian language: Developmental reading and writing problems. In P. G. Aaron & R. M. Joshi (Eds.), *Reading and writing disorders in different orthographic systems* (pp. 143–161). Amsterdam: Kluwer Academic.

Olson, D. R. (1993). How writing represents speech. *Language & Communication, 13*(1), 1–17.

Pontecorvo, C., & Zucchermaglio, C. (1988). Modes of differentiation in children's writing construction. *European Journal of Psychology of Education, 3*(4), 371–384.

Pontecorvo, C., & Zucchermaglio, C. (1990). A passage to literacy: Learning in a social context. In Y. Goodman (Ed.), *How children construct literacy* (pp. 59–98). Newark, DE: IRA.

Ullman, B. (1932). *Ancient writing and its influence.* Cambridge, MA: MIT Press.

Zucchermaglio, C. (1991). *Gli apprendisti della lingua scritta* [The apprentices of written language]. Bologna, Italy: Il Mulino.

9

REFLECTIONS ON THE COMMA

Raffaele Simone
Third University of Rome

Although punctuation developed relatively late in the evolution of writing, it represents a cornerstone in the organization and functioning of writing, for both the writer and the reader. But, despite this, learning to use it remains a difficult task, and even the most educated adults occasionally make blatant elementary errors in punctuation. Fully literate (in the narrow sense of knowing how to use the letters of the alphabet) people may well find punctuation difficult. This difficulty involves the whole punctuation system and, in a quite particular way, the comma.

This chapter aims to shed some light on one of the most puzzling and neglected features of literate competence: the comma. Although it may appear to be a curious subject for study, and despite its slender graphic "body," the comma is a highly sensitive and delicate tool in literate behavior. For example, it is a common stumbling block in the early stages of writing in children and even in the writing practice of adults. Moreover, as discussed later, many rules are involved in the proper use of it, and describing them requires adequate theoretical justification. It is rather surprising, therefore, that hitherto researchers have almost completely neglected the use of this crucial writing device.[1]

The reason for this specific difficulty in the learning of the comma is evident even at a *prima facie* scrutiny. The comma fulfills various different functions and

---

[1] The only linguistic studies on the delicate problem of punctuation and, in particular, the comma are those by Conte and Parisi (1977) and Halliday (1985b).

offers an interface between several structural levels: It simultaneously conveys syntactic, textual, pragmatic, and other information that, when put together, brings about complex phenomena of overlapping and neutralization.

The aim of this chapter is to make clear: how the comma functions, that is, what rules govern its use; what functions it performs in texts; why its use is so difficult to master; and why the use of the comma developed so late in the evolution of writing. My discussion is instantiated with some references to the punctuation system of the Italian language. In other languages (e.g., English and German), comma use may be significantly different. Despite this deliberate limitation, however, most of my comments may hold true for other languages as well.

Some Semiotic Assumptions

Before proceeding, it is useful to make explicit a set of basic semiotic assumptions on which the following analysis relies.

1. In spite of appearances to the contrary, the graphic system of a language is by no means the sheer reproduction of the sound system that it "transcribes." The graphic system consists partly of a rough approximation of the phonological system and partly of an independent semiotic system endowed with its own grammar. As a consequence, learning to speak a language is essentially different from mastering its graphic counterpart.

2. Being only a rough approximation of the primary phonological system, certain elements of the graphic system, although remaining physically stable, perform very different functions. As a consequence, they may have such a heavy functional load that it can occasionally blur the way they function. The comma is especially interesting from this point of view, because its functions are numerous and not easily superficially observable. In fact, compared with the varied functions it must perform, the material form of this element (its *graphic substance*, to use Hjelmslev's definition) is relatively inert.[2]

3. One of the most important functions of the punctuation system is to reveal structure. It adds to the written text crucial instructions, that, when interpreted, show how utterances are structured (i.e., that they are equipped with different hierarchically ordered layers). This creates a striking contrast to the linear appearance they first present. In other words, the punctuation system does not

---

[2]The inertia of the comma compared with the variety of functions it performs is also illustrated in some uncertainties in the historical tradition of reflections concerning punctuation. A system of punctuation was established in European languages only relatively recently, that is, around the 16th century, with the invention of the printing press. Chiantera (1986) gave a brief but interesting historical account of this; historical and structural considerations were also recorded by Mortara Garavelli (1986).

mark out and segment a line; it represents just the superficial trace of that flattening process that the utterance structures undergo in the linearization.

On this basis, the comma will be examined from the point of view of the structures it reveals, the relationship between units, and intonation.

A Structural Analysis

From the structural point of view, we can discern two different types of commas: the opening and/or closing comma and the serial comma, each conveying a specific type of information.

The Opening and/or Closing Comma (OCC). This type of comma graphically marks out units (e.g., words, phrases) that are syntactically embedded or nested into larger units, where it signals the beginning and the end of them. We refer to these units as *marked units*. Generally, when a marked unit opens with an OCC, it must be matched by a correlated one that closes it, as in:

John, if he wants to, can sleep in this room.

If the marked unit is at the very beginning of the utterance, only the closing OCC will appear:

If he wants to, John can sleep in this room.

Conversely, if the marked unit is placed at the end of the utterance, the latter contains only the opening OCC (the other comma being neutralized by a stronger punctuation mark, such as the semicolon or full stop):

John can sleep in this room, if he likes to.

These considerations also show, from a general semiotic point of view, that both punctuation marks are ordered in a hierarchical scale of strength, and the OCC can be neutralized by some stronger mark. The stronger punctuation marks neutralize (i.e., cancel and replace) all the weaker ones likely to occur in the same position, according to the following scale:

. > ; > ,

This notation should be interpreted as meaning that the full stop is stronger than the semicolon; and the semicolon is stronger than the comma. (The semicolon is not discussed here.) As we shall see later in more detail, a comma can also neutralize a variety of other commas. We call this special kind of comma *archicomma*, taking over the prefix *archi-* from the classic structuralist terminology.

The OCC has direction: The opening OCC signals that a closing OCC (or a stronger marker neutralizing the opening OCC) is likely to occur a little later in the text, so it is right-oriented; similarly, the closing OCC makes reference to an opening OCC on the left and is, therefore, left-oriented. Because of this, the OCCs may be compared with brackets, another direction marker having a specific exponent to open the unit and another one to close it. Unlike brackets, however, which do not neutralize each other (the strongest brackets, i.e., the staple ones, do not cancel the weaker ones such as square and round brackets), OCCs may be canceled by stronger signs.

Because these commas are direction markers and in view of their resemblance to brackets, we use square brackets to distinguish one from the other: '[' for the opening OCC, ']' for the closing OCC.

In some cases, brackets occur not in pairs but only individually. This means that they form a virtual pair, that is, there exists only an opening or a closing OCC, but not both of them.

The examples quoted earlier can be rewritten as follows:

John [, if he likes,] can sleep in this room.
If he likes,] John can sleep in this room.
John can sleep in this room | [, if he likes.

In written language, the OCCs may occur in highly complex forms. For example, different pairs of OCCs may cross, or they may embed into each other at different levels of depth. In brief, the OCCs have their own syntax, the hierarchical organization and complexity of which is comparable with those of the syntax of language proper. The next example illustrates some syntactic hierarchical phenomena of the various OCCs. The numbers indicate the different pairs of OCCs; the bracket with double number refers to an archicomma, namely, a single comma that represents the closing of two different pairs:

Le riunioni dei gruppi $_1$[, durante le quali sono state ascoltate circa duecento relazioni,]$_1$ si sono tenute in appartamenti privati $_2$[, poiché la sala grande $_3$[, che era stata affittata dagli organizzatori,]$_{2,3}$ era chiusa per restauri.
(The group meetings, during which around 200 reports were presented, were held in private flats, because the large hall, which had been rented by the organizers, was closed for restoration.)

The Serial Comma. This type of comma (known hereafter as SC) marks similar units or, to put it another way, units with the same "syntactic weight," and also signals a succession of different exponents of the same unit, such as those in the following list:

I took the coat, the hat, the umbrella, and the boots.

The SC is clearly different from the OCC; the former occurs only in isolation and not in virtual pairs. The SC will be indicated by the sign >. The SC may appear in "train" form, that is, in relatively long sequences, as seen in the following example (the sign > indicates the SC):

The people who attended the meeting included the mayors of Rome >, Chicago >, New York >, Paris >, London >, and other big cities around the world.

It is interesting to note that a text may contain various combinations of the different types of commas just discussed. For example, the next example includes different pairs of OCC and one SC, one of which is an archicomma:

The people present included Herbert von Karajan [, the famous conductor ,]> and Luchino Visconti [, the great Italian film director.

Commas and Boundaries. From the preceding comments, it is clear that the comma serves occasionally to indicate phrase boundaries, that is, it works as a boundary marker. Because the theory of unit boundaries is crucial to syntax and other linguistics fields, this point requires some more detail. Phrases are hierarchical units that can embed into each other in telescopic form. Because of this property, several different boundaries can occur exactly in the same position in the chain, the effect of which is for them to overlap.

As a consequence, an abstract utterance such as ABCDEF can be analyzed according to the usual step-by-step phrase analysis as shown in the following example.

A	B	C	D	E	F		1
A	B	C	D	E	F		2
A	B	C	D	E	F		3

(a)

The (a) indicates the point at which several boundaries meet: the one separating AB from the whole CDEF (Step 2) and the one separating AB from the smaller CD (Step 3). This analysis can be shown more clearly in a more concrete form. Imagine that the pattern just illustrated is the phrase marker of:

According to John, when we read, we always dream a little.

This situation may be represented by the following scheme, which highlights the overlapping of the boundaries (each level of * stands for a different boundary):

```
                    *

        *                   *
      (a)               (b)
```
According to John, when we read, we always dream a little.

The (a) is the point where, in theory, two commas should exist, one for each of the boundaries passing through this point. There may be even more complex examples of this. Theoretically, at least, three or more boundaries might overlap at the same point, with each requiring a specific kind of comma. This theoretical possibility, however, is filtered out by a rule of written Italian (which presumably holds true for all other languages as well) that forbids the immediate duplication of the same written element. The comma that simultaneously indicates more than one boundary and in fact neutralizes the many commas that in theory should occur at that same point is the archicomma referred to previously.

Relationships Between Units

Besides the structural point of view, the comma can also be considered for the semantic relationships between units. In the utterance, each clause (or part of it) produces a *communicative dynamism* because[3] it increases the amount of new knowledge the utterer sends to the receiver and, in a certain sense, "carries" the communication "forward." Because clauses are arranged not in random strings but in textual structures, communicative dynamism is carried out along specifiable preferential paths. In other words, between one clause and another, specifiable semantic relationships are set up.[4] Some of these relationships are signaled by special connectives, as in the following, where *that is* signals that A explicates B:

> *I formatted the text,* that is, *I laid it out graphically.*
>   A   B

Consider the next example:

> *I lent him the money for the car*; what I mean is *I gave it to him.*
>   A   B

---

[3]The idea of communicative dynamism was presented and developed by the Prague linguists Danes and Firbas as part of their "functional sentence analysis" (cf. Firbas, 1964).

[4]Semantic relationships between clauses are one of the most crucial areas in discourse analysis. See Halliday (1985a) for an introduction.

What I mean signals another type of relationship: compared with A, B supplies the "real" interpretation the utterer attributes to A.[5] Note that although some connectives can be deleted, others cannot. *That is,* for example, can be canceled: The earlier example can be reformulated to read *I formatted the text, I laid it out graphically.* Other connectives are more resistant, however, because their deletion would destroy the semantic relationship between the clauses.

In written text, punctuation (particularly the comma) can be employed together with text connectives to mark the semantic relationships between clauses or parts of clauses. Consider the next example:

Napoleon [, the French emperor,] was imprisoned on an island several times.

The two OCCs signal that what is on the left of the former is co-referent to what is on the right of it (*Napoleon = the French emperor*). Conversely, in another possible use, the OCC can also indicate an explicative relationship between clauses. Unlike the relational connectives referred to earlier, the comma is relatively inert; this is because it seems to be capable of providing a graphic expression only for a limited range of interunit relationships.

The type of the relationship indicated by the comma depends largely on that of the unit marked. If this unit is an embedded clause, the comma represents a generic dependence signal; on the other hand, if the unit is a noun phrase, the comma stands for a coreference signal (i.e., it indicates that the text on the left and that on the right are co-referent), as in the example. Another important aspect remains to be considered: If, instead of examining an utterance from the point of view of its phrase structure, we study it from that of the thematic structure, we see that the OCC isolates the theme and enables it to stand out from the *rheme:*[6]

Il libro, l'ho preso io.
(The book, I took it.)

Di mettersi a studiare, non ha alcuna intenzione.
(Getting down to studying, that's something he has no intention of doing.)

The SC is a device employed in listing, indicating sequences, or showing that the units it marks are coordinated among themselves. These various uses are set out in Table 9.1.

---

[5]The purpose of the traditional classification of connectives, which, for example, distinguished among adversatives, conclusives, and explicatives, was identical: to establish the role of each individual clause in communicative dynamism.

[6]The analysis of the utterance into theme and rheme was suggested by the Prague linguists (Firbas, 1964). See also Halliday (1985a).

TABLE 9.1
Types of Relationship Signaled by Commas

Type	Relationship Signaled
OCC	A. Encloses an embedded phrase
	B. Indicates co-reference
	C. Isolates the theme
SC	D. Indicates a list or a series
	E. Indicates coordination between elements with the same syntactic "weight"

The Intonational Aspect

The preceding considerations should now be inserted into another context, that is, the phonological structure, which will make them more complex. We know that written utterances are punctuated according to the structure of their intonation and pauses (which correspond, albeit not completely, to the phrase and thematic structure of the utterance itself);[7] on the other hand, during the phonic performance given to the utterance in reading, the reader employs punctuation as a crucial path to give it an appropriate intonational contour. Here we are dealing with the complicated subject of the phonological–structural interface, which is made even more intricate because its form here—at least in this study—is not phonological but graphic.

This issue is interesting because the various types of commas previously identified involve different types of intonation and virtual pauses. For instance, the OCC forms just a single type from the phrase point of view, but from the phonological one, it appears to be divisible into several types, classifiable according to the semantic relationship they mark. A discussion of one outstanding example of this follows.

1. The first type of OCC, in which it encloses an embedded phrase and is employed to indicate a general syntactic dependence only, activates an intonational contour made of "terraces": The pitch used to pronounce the material enclosed between two of these OCCs is lower than that used for the material outside:

[The child, |went out for a while.]
          after finishing her homework,

The intonational contour of this utterance may be represented in the following way:

---

[7]The concept of intonation as something independent of syntax has been reiterated on several occasions by Bolinger (1984), among others.

If a pair of OCCs includes a second, a third, or more commas, the intonational level is lowered to indicate each level of embedding, as in the following:

[The child,   went out for a while.]
        after finishing her homework,
                which she had a lot of today,

The intonational contour of this utterance is shown in the following representation:

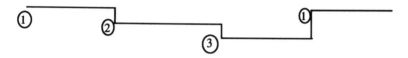

On the other hand, in another type of relationship discussed in Table 9.1—the co-reference—the comma activates a slightly rising contour in the left-hand unit, and a falling–rising contour on the right. We represent this phenomenon in the form of notation on a stave, as shown in the following representation:

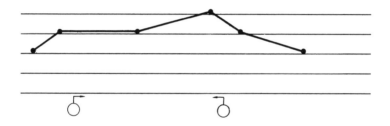

2. The SC marks a succession of feet, each of which supports a level tone; the series of level tones ends with a rising one as in the following example and representation:

I bambini, i genitori, le zie e gli zii passano insieme le feste.
(The children, their parents, their uncles and aunts spend the holiday period together.)

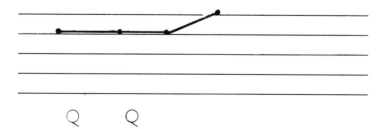

These observations are obviously oversimplified. Each of the patterns identified includes a variety of subtypes; however, it is unlikely that these subtypes seriously affect the phenomena presented there.

The User's Point of View

This chapter shows, albeit in a simplified way, that the comma is a complex phenomenon due to the interaction of various levels of organization (e.g., phrase structure, semantic relationship interface, intonation) and to a large variety of types, all of which emerge from a totally inert graphic element. It is not surprising, then, that children use the different types of commas according to an evolutionary sequence when learning to read and write. In linguistic terms, the various commas respect an accessibility hierarchy.

Even a *prima facie* examination shows that children encounter the following typical set of difficulties when writing and reading:

1. Practically the only forms of the comma that children use when they write—starting from a relatively late age (around 8 years old)—are Type A OCC (marking dependence) and Type C OCC (isolating the theme).

2. When the OCC should be used in virtual pairs, children almost always use the opening OCC but not the closing one. For some reason, they believe that the opening OCC is somehow "stronger" than the closing one. Moreover, the second comma is even weaker, because it happens to be an archicomma.

3. The Type B OCC (see Table 9.1) is often used to separate the subject from the predicate (as in *La mamma di Luigi, mi ha detto di andare a pranzo da lei*, or, Luigi's mother, she told me to have lunch with her), especially when the subject is superficially long. This "rule" is unlike the written one governing adult punctuation behavior, which does not require this kind of comma. The Type B OCC is often found in children's writing, however, probably because children perceive the thematic function of certain subjects better than adults do. In addition, children appear to perceive thematic structure (a phenomenon also seen in their writing) better than phrase structure.

4. The only comma adopted correctly almost immediately is the Type D SC marking out lists and sequences.

5. In both reading and writing, the Type B OCC comma (which represents co-reference) is virtually unknown: Children are unable to use it or to understand its meaning when they read until relatively late (around 10 years of age).

These considerations may be interpreted in a host of different ways. From our point of view, the most interesting one is that the commas form, as already mentioned, a hierarchy of accessibility or naturalness, which can be set out as follows (in descending order of accessibility):

SC   D
OCC   C
OCC   A
SC   E
OCC   B

The validity of this scale should be investigated by an extensive empirical study. If it is valid, we may assume that the order of acquisition may be explained according to a structural principle: The first commas that children acquire are those indicating a smaller quantity of structure and those requiring less cognitive processing.

REFERENCES

Bolinger, D. L. (1984). Intonation signals of subordination. *Bulletin of the Berkeley Linguistic Society, 10*, 401–413.

Chiantera, A. (1986). Alle origini della punteggiatura [The origins of punctuation]. *Italiano e Oltre, 1*, 149–152.

Conte, R., & Parisi, D. (1977). Per un'analisi dei segni di punteggiatura, con particolare riferimento alla virgola [An analysis of punctuation marks with emphasis on the comma]. In D. Parisi (Ed.), *Per un'educazione linguistica razionale* (pp. 363–385). Bologna, Italy: Il Mulino.

Firbas, F. (1964). A three-level approach to syntax. *Travaux Linguistiques de Prague, 1*, 225–240.

Halliday, M. A. K. (1985a). *Introduction to functional grammar*. London: Arnold.

Halliday, M. A. K. (1985b). *Spoken and written language*. Deakin, Australia: Deakin University Press.

Mortara Garavelli, B. (1986). La punteggiatura tra scritto e parlato [Punctuation in writing and reading]. *Italiano e Oltre, 1*, 154–158.

10

CHILDREN'S USE OF PUNCTUATION MARKS: THE CASE OF QUOTED SPEECH

Emilia Ferreiro
Die-Cinvestav, Mexico D.F.

Cristina Zucchermaglio
University of Rome "La Sapienza"

Our knowledge of young children's ideas about punctuation marks is very limited. We know (Ferreiro & Teberosky, 1982) that children's first conceptual distinction is expressed in terms such as "It's not a letter; it's something else"; they are "sticks" or "dots" that "go with the letters." The first step is probably the graphic differentiation between punctuation marks and closely related graphic forms (e.g., letters or numbers), followed by the use of generic terms (e.g., marks) and/or particular names, but the terms used give little hint about the function. In fact, whereas letters are there "to say something," punctuation marks are silent marks.[1]

Catach (1980) observed that, from a linguistic point of view, punctuation seems to be "a new subject," but, in fact, it is "a forgotten subject," because Greek grammarians—as well as medieval and Renaissance authors—showed considerable interest in punctuation. Simone (chap. 9, this volume) showed us the great interest of studying a single punctuation mark: the comma. Chafe (1987) and Nunberg (1990) explored the functions of punctuation marks in textual frameworks. Halliday (1990) investigated how punctuation relates to grammar and phonology.

From a historical point of view, we clearly have, in European writing systems, a double division line related to uses and functions of punctuation marks: before

---

[1] Marina, 5 years old, called the question mark "the head's letter," and, from then on, she expressed the function of other punctuation marks as "little dots, for the head" because "you think them, but you don't say them" (Ferreiro & Teberosky, 1982, p. 47).

and after the beginning of silent reading, and before and after the advent of printing.

Establishing a list of accepted punctuation marks is far from a straightforward task. For instance, including the apostrophe in the list (as Halliday does) obliges us to differentiate this mark, which concerns two adjacent words, from others located at the suprasegmental level (e.g., question marks). Should the list of punctuation marks include upper-case letters and even blank spaces (as Catach's does)? There are at least two good reasons to include the space and upper-case letters: The stop is obligatory when followed by an upper-case letter; the blank space defines one variety of the stop that has a particular name in many languages (e.g., *point à la ligne* in French, *punto y aparte* in Spanish, and *punto a capo* in Italian). Objections to including upper-case letters and blank spaces in the list of punctuation marks are also obvious: The upper-case letter *is* a letter, not one of the marks that "go with the letters" (as children say); the blank space is not a mark but the absence of a mark (i.e., "a negative sign," in Catach's words).[2]

Historically speaking, the relation between punctuation marks and breathing is very clear. For a reader from our century, however, the syntactic, semantic, emphatic, and organizational functions of punctuation marks may be more evident than their original function of indicating "the time to breathe" or intonation contours. Of course, this fact depends on the kinds of text the reader is reading. The functions of punctuation marks are so varied that it is necessary to specify the type of text involved.[3]

Note, however, that today the normativity of the spelling of words is not found in the use of punctuation marks. Except for a rather limited list of compulsory conventions (e.g., initial capital letter; full stop at the end of a paragraph, followed by a capital letter; comma in a list of nouns), the rest is a matter of choice.

This absence of normativity (or, from another point of view, this flexibility that makes the choice a matter of preference or style) is heavy with pedagogical consequences. In fact, teaching punctuation is one of those gray areas where almost everything is left to the intuition of teachers and pupils. The various methodologies for teaching written language say little about punctuation. In addition, instructions given by teachers to use punctuation marks in a reading task differ from those given by the same teachers in a composition task.[4]

---

[2]"*Et d'abord, que veut dire élément graphique? En l'absence d'un signe de ponctuation, que reste-t-il? Un blanc, lequel est déjà un signe, le plus primitif et essentiel de tous, un signe en négatif*" [First, what does *graphic element* mean? Without a punctuation mark, what remains? A blank space, that is, already a mark, is the most primitive and essential a negative symbol] (Catach, 1980, p. 18).

[3]Punctuation use provides one of the key elements in identifying a writer's style. For example, Racine made scarce use of punctuation, whereas Proust's use of parentheses was so unique that studies have focused on it.

[4]For instance, we have observed teachers speaking about "complete ideas" to justify a full stop, saying that the comma "separates, but less than the period" and that the semicolon is halfway between the two. These same teachers translate the punctuation signs into breathing pauses of "three, two, and one" when they give instructions to read a text aloud.

Very few children use punctuation marks in their pre-alphabetic period. Most children start using them only after they begin to understand the alphabetic nature of the writing system and when they begin to face spelling problems. Punctuation marks introduce graphic elements that are alien to the main principles of an alphabetic writing system. Children must deal with them as an autonomous subsystem that does not affect the letters themselves (except in the distribution of lower and capital forms of the letters). Do they immediately grasp the main functions of some punctuation marks, and which ones? Do they attribute to some punctuation marks a function that is alien to an adult's use? Do they tentatively classify the punctuation marks and, in the case of a positive answer, on what basis? These questions help frame our inquiry, which provides no definitive answers. What follows is a preliminary mapping of some relevant aspects that we have started to identify. Many specific studies will be required to clarify the complexities of children's acquisition of punctuation marks.

STUDY I: AN EXPLORATORY STUDY OF SPANISH CHILDREN'S USE OF PUNCTUATION MARKS[5]

To obtain a preliminary mapping of the frequency of use and distribution of punctuation marks in children, we asked 7- and 8-year-olds (in second and third grades) to write a traditional story well known to all of them. We chose the story of *Little Red Riding Hood* (LRRH) for various reasons. First, the majority of children know it so well that there was no need to review it orally before having them write it down; therefore, there was no need to choose one among the many written versions of that story in print as the real one (which is particularly important in cross-cultural and cross-language studies). Second, this story presents many occasions for the use of quoted speech. Specifically, at the end of the story, the dialogue between LRRH and the wolf disguised as her grandmother is an essential part of the story in which the exact wording is carefully preserved in all the published versions. We refer to this dialogue as *canonical dialogue*.

The LRRH story provides an interesting textual space, making it almost imperative to distinguish between the narrative discourse (constructed by an indefinite third person who is not necessarily the child as actual narrator but can be assumed to be a generic narrator retelling a well-known story) and the quoted speech (particularly a dialogic form of quoted speech in which the speakers alternate).

This study began on the basis of the assumption that punctuation marks would tend to appear more frequently in quoted speech than in the narrative. However, we also had a more qualitative assumption that some children would

---

[5]Study 1 is an abridged version of a chapter previously published in Italian (Ferreiro, 1991). The responsibility for Study 1 belongs to the first author of this chapter.

show a discriminative use of punctuation marks, keeping some of them for quoted speech and some for the narrative discourse. Of course, the latter assumption would be of no particular interest if a child used, for instance, exclamation or question marks for quoted speech and commas or full stops in narrative parts. It would be extremely interesting, however, if children made a discriminative use of marks that could appear, in the conventional use, in either textual space (e.g., full stops and commas). This possibility is discussed in the analysis of our results.

Procedure and Sample

The children were asked to write the story, as they remembered it, in the best possible way, because their productions would be compared with others written by children of various countries. The task was carried out collectively in the classroom (variable number of children between 10 and 20). The children were given approximately 1 hour of school time to complete the task. When they had completed their writing assignment, they were permitted to draw. They wrote on a blank paper using a pen (to avoid invisible corrections) and were encouraged to make as many corrections as they wished.

Children from two Spanish-speaking countries, Mexico and Argentina, participated in the preliminary research. In all, 222 texts were collected, 120 from Mexico and 102 from Argentina. School script differs between the countries: Cursive script is used in Argentina, and separate characters (simplified print) are used in Mexico. Socioeconomic origin of the children also differed: The Argentinian children were from five public schools in the suburbs of the capital city of Buenos Aires and nearby (medium-low social sectors); the Mexican children were from three private schools of the capital city (middle or upper-middle social sectors).

Methodology of Data Analysis and Results

These texts were intended for analysis in various studies, although the present analysis focuses only on punctuation marks. In accordance with our assumptions, texts that did not use any form of quoted speech (as well as the few that told a completely different story) were eliminated from the sample, leaving 159 texts: 77 from second grade and 82 from third grade.

Not all of the children used punctuation marks in their texts. Some texts (19 in all, or 12%) did not have punctuation at all. Another group (43 texts, or 27%) used extremely limited punctuation, consisting of only an initial capital letter and/or a final full stop, to indicate the outer boundaries of the text. The difference between the latter group and the former group is not irrelevant, but the two groups are similar in terms of our fundamental inquiry: None of these children made a distinction inside the text using punctuation marks (although some did so using lexical, syntactical, or other graphic means such as the layout, which are not our concern here). This shows that a large number of 7- and 8-year-olds did not think it was necessary to introduce any punctuation mark, although all of them wrote at least one episode of the story in quoted speech.

As a result, after setting aside the texts with no internal punctuation, we had a sample of only 97 texts. These texts were distributed evenly across the countries (52 from Mexico and 45 from Argentina) and across the school grades (46 from second grade and 51 from third grade).

We performed three kinds of analysis: (a) a quantitative analysis of the frequency of use of each punctuation mark, (b) an analysis of the distribution of these marks in the main textual spaces (e.g., narrative, quoted speech, and boundaries between the two), and (c) an analysis of some microtextual spaces where we observed particular concentrations of punctuation marks: onomatopoeia, exclamations or interjections, and lists (e.g., lists of nouns concerning the content of LRRH's basket, such as "I am bringing bread, milk, eggs, and butter," as well as the repetition of two or more identical sequences, such as the onomatopoeia of "*tan-tan*," "*¡pum! ¡pum!*," and "*la, la, la, la*").

As expected, the quantitative analysis showed a concentration of punctuation marks inserted in pieces of quoted speech. There were 356 punctuation marks in the quoted speech but only 180 in the narrative, out of a total of 736 punctuation marks. The other punctuation marks were distributed as follows: boundaries (i.e., when there is a change of discourse genre) = 102; lists = 64; interjections + onomatopoeia + exclamations = 34. The important thing is that the children's punctuation marks appeared in quoted speech not only with greater frequency but also with greater variety. In fact, all the different punctuation marks, except the semicolon (14 in all),[6] appeared in passages of quoted speech.

Considering each graphic mark by itself, we observe that the most polyfunctional ones (comma and full stop) were also the most frequently used (the 282 commas used represent 38% of the 736 marks, whereas the 212 full stops represent 29%). These frequencies did not occur among only a few children.[7] However, the great variety of punctuation marks used is also worthy of note. Indeed, all existing signs appeared at least once.

The punctuation used by these children is, in general, highly coherent: Although they did not use all the punctuation required, when examined globally what they used was appropriate for the textual space in which it was located. For instance, to separate elements of a list, they used the comma a great deal,

---

[6]Note that Spanish has two different marks that do not exist in the English system: an admiration mark that opens and an interrogative mark that opens (in addition to the ones used at the end of a given statement to close it).

[7]For instance, the 65 full stops that appeared in quoted speech were produced by 29 children, the 97 commas by 32 children, and the 35 colons by 14 children. There were, however, a few exceptions: The hyphen appeared 61 times in passages of quoted speech; only eight children produced these hyphens, one of whom used it 22 times.

TABLE 10.1
Distribution of Texts as a Function of the Number of
Different Punctuation Marks Utilized (in %)

Number of Different Punctuation Marks	Second Grade	Third Grade
1	54%	37%
2	17%	25%
3 or 4	22%	29%
5 or 6	6.5%	8%

the hyphen or suspensive dots rarely, and nothing else; for interjections or onomatopoeia, they preferred to use exclamation marks and, to a lesser extent, inverted commas; at the boundary between narrative and quoted speech, they used only full stops and commas, except for two semicolons (the only two semicolons produced in the entire sample). This "coherence," however, includes particular uses of punctuation marks that are far from being conventional. We now turn to the analyses of individual texts, the only place where this aspect could be meaningfully considered.

Categorization of Individual Cases

In categorizing individual cases, we tried to account for both the variety and the frequency of punctuation marks used by each child. The minimum use of punctuation is represented by those texts that presented a single mark only once. This did not happen infrequently: 20 texts belong to this category. The next group, consisting of 23 texts, also used a single punctuation mark, but it was used more than once. Another group with little punctuation consisted of five texts with two different marks, each used once.

On the other hand, some texts presented between two and six different punctuation marks, using them with variable frequencies but always more than twice (e.g., those texts that presented three different punctuation marks had a mean occurrence of 11).[8]

Table 10.1 shows the distribution of children in the sample as a function of the number of different punctuation marks used (without considering the frequency of use of each one, which, in fact, shows great variability). Table 10.2 also shows the number of different punctuation marks used by children, but with the focus on another variable: the exclusive, discriminative, or preferential use of the marks in a particular textual space. The total number of texts included

---

[8]In this preliminary research, the marks that constitute a graphic pair [¿? ¡! " " ( )] were counted as only one occurrence. In Study 2, we modified the procedure for counting because of the exigencies of the comparative study with Italian orthography. Thus, the numbers of punctuation marks in both studies are not immediately comparable.

TABLE 10.2
Distribution of the Exclusive, Discriminative, or Preferential
Use of Punctuation Marks in a Particular Textual Space

	Number of Different Punctuation Marks							
	1	*2*	*3*	*4*	*5*	*6*	*Total*	
Nondiscriminative	11	1		1			13	(17%)
Exclusive	13						13	(17%)
Discriminative		10	9	6	3	1	29	(38%)
Preferential		4	1				5	
Preferential 1		6					6	
Preferential 2			2	5	1	1	9	} (28%)
Preferential 3				1			1	
Preferential 4						1	1	
Total	24	21	12	13	4	3	77	(100%)

in Table 10.2 is 77, not 97, because we excluded the 20 texts that used only one mark only one time. We speak of *discriminative* use in the case of a mark concentrated in a particular textual space, allowing for exceptions of up to 10% of total frequency. When the exceptions amount to between 11% and 20%, we speak of *preferential* use. Table 10.2 shows that discriminative use of all the punctuation marks used characterizes the 38% of the texts produced (29 out of 77) and that it happens across all the variations in the number of different punctuation marks used (from two to six).

The preferential type of use could apply to all the marks used or to only some of them. Thus, we distinguish in Table 10.2 a row labeled *Preferential* and four rows with an associated number, to mean, respectively: preferential use of one of the marks utilized (Preferential 1), being the total of different marks > 1; preferential use of two of the marks utilized (Preferential 2), being the total of different marks > 2; and similar criteria for Preferential 3 and Preferential 4.

To illustrate, we analyze here one column and one row of Table 10.2. There are 21 texts in Column 2 using two different punctuation marks; 10 of them make a discriminative use of both marks, whereas 4 of them make a preferential use of both marks. Another group of six makes a preferential use of only one of the marks, placing the other mark in various textual spaces. Finally, only one child made a nondiscriminative use of the two marks used. In row Preferential 2, there are nine texts (or children): two with children using three different marks, five with children using four different marks, one instance of a child using five different marks, and another of a child using six different marks. All nine children make a preferential use of two of the punctuation marks they use.

Many interesting observations could be drawn from this table. First, only a minority of the children (17%) made a nondiscriminative use of the punctuation marks; that is, they put any punctuation mark in any of the textual spaces already defined (main spaces: quoted speech, narrative, boundaries between two speech genres; microspaces: lists of nouns, interjections, or onomatopoeia). An equal number of children, using only one mark two or more times (group exclusive), placed the marks exclusively in a particular textual space (any one of the main or micro spaces already listed).

One of the most interesting examples of discriminative use was provided by Vanessa (second grade, Argentina). She used the comma 15 times and the full stop 6 times. She did not use any other punctuation mark. The full stop appears only in passages of quoted speech (particularly between turn taking); the comma appears in narrative passages or at a border between narrative and quoted speech or quoted speech and narrative. The following two examples are from Vanessa's text:[9]

> *se fue cantando a la casa de su abuelita, se encontró unas flores, había un lobo que era malo, él le dijo para dónde vas*
> (she went away singing to her grandmother's house, found some flowers, there was a wolf who was wicked, he said to her where are you going)
>
> *para escucharte mejor. que nariz tan grande*
> (to hear you better. what a big nose)

If we were to consider the allocation of each mark in isolation, we would observe that the full stops are not followed by capital letters, but we would not grasp the contrastive character of the distribution. Vanessa's case is particularly interesting because her punctuation marks (comma and full stop) are not normally used in the restrictive way in which she used them. However, most examples of discriminative use correspond to a more conventional distribution (e.g., question marks in quoted speech; commas and full stops in narrative parts).

Table 10.2 suggests that, in their attempts to understand the complexities of the location of punctuation marks, some children made an attempt to link specific marks to specific textual spaces. This does not necessarily mean conventional use. The following examples[10] from passages by Juan, Carlos, and Gabriela illustrate some nonconventional uses of punctuation marks.

Juan (second grade) used question marks instead of exclamation points:

> *¿y ten mucho cuidado?*
> (be careful)

---

[9]All examples present the text with normal spelling and word segmentation to allow a focus on the punctuation marks. We preserve upper-/lower-case letters as they were in the original, however, because they are closely related to punctuation marks.

[10]We present examples from the Argentinian sample, because those from Mexico will be used in the comparative study, and some of them are discussed in Study 2.

Three times Carlos (second grade) used a very infrequent punctuation mark: the row of dots called *suspension points*. He used them first after the ritual beginning and followed them with a line change:

Había una vez . . .
(Once upon a time . . .)

He used them on two other occasions in a very particular way, with the onomatopoeia of knocking at the grandmother's door:

to . . . n   to . . . n

Gabriela (third grade) used question marks twice, as if they were inverted commas, at the beginning and at the end of passages of quoted speech:

le dijo ¿caperucita roja anda a la casa de tu abuelita llévale esta canasta con comida cuidado que en el campo está el lobo? caperucita roja se fué
(she told her ¿little riding hood go to grandmother's house take her this lunch basket be careful of the wolf in the field? little red riding hood went away)

In this study, many children used special graphic procedures to enhance exclamations or onomatopoeia. These procedures are very close to those that appear in comics: repetition of letters, repetition of exclamation marks, bigger shape of letters, and so on. Some examples are:

¡¡¡AUXILIO!!!   aaaaay!   ¡¡Bang!!

It is possible that comics, with their overuse of punctuation marks, have an impact equivalent to (or perhaps bigger than) that of school teaching on this particular subject.

It should be noted that there is no correlation between the number of different punctuation marks used and/or their frequency of use, on the one hand, and knowledge of their function, on the other. In the subset of 20 texts that used a single punctuation mark just once is the story written by the only child in the entire sample who used parentheses in a very fine way:

entonces tocó el lobo y dijo la abuelita quien es soy yo caperucita roja (con una voz muy dulce) y la abuelita dijo entra y entro
(so the wolf knocked and the grandmother said who is it it is little red riding hood (in a very sweet voice) and the grandmother said come in and he came in)

It is hard to believe that this is the only punctuation in a text of 35 lines!

There were also cases of spurious punctuation, that is, points, hyphens, or commas between words, as well as numbered lines (at the left) or full stops (at the right). These are the result of traditional school teaching. They appear only in the texts of the youngest children of the low socioeconomic group.

Many of the signs used in an appropriate way by these children are those that appear, in Spanish orthography, in pairs (question and exclamation marks, inverted commas, and, to a lesser extent, hyphens). We do not know whether their function is easier to understand because they "open and close" a given statement or because they are more frequent in comics or, perhaps, because they are less plurifunctional than others (e.g., the comma; cf. Simone, chap. 9, this volume). The results of this preliminary study indicate the need for a comparative study. As shown, Spanish provides the learner with a clear indication mark at the beginning and at the end of each exclamatory or interrogative expression or sentence. This is not the case in most alphabetic writing.

STUDY 2: A COMPARATIVE ANALYSIS OF PUNCTUATION MARKS IN ITALIAN AND SPANISH NARRATIVE TEXTS

Aims of the Study

This study was conducted as part of a larger research project.[11] Here we present a comparative analysis of the distribution and frequency of punctuation marks in texts written by Italian- and Spanish-speaking children of the same age, the same primary school grade, and from similar socioeconomic backgrounds. These children were asked to write the same traditional story about Little Red Riding Hood. This task was carried out in the conditions as indicated in Study 1. For the dimensions and distribution of this sample, see Table 10.3.

Data Analysis

All written texts were entered into a computerized system (TEXTUS) for which software was developed by Garcia Hidalgo (1992). The research group designed a complex coding system, including: division of the text into clauses, transcription peculiarities (e.g., segmentation, spelling, repairs), morphological features, and structural and discursive categories.

The punctuation marks, which were produced by the 507 children in their written stories, were categorized following an ad hoc coding system, allowing a description of the data in terms of frequency of utilization, variety of marks utilized, and exact place of the marks.

---

[11]The system was developed within a bilateral research project coordinated by Clotilde Pontecorvo and Emilia Ferreiro.

TABLE 10.3
Distribution of the Sample of the Comparative Study

	Spanish	Italian
Second grade	92	149
Third grade	160	106
Total	252	255

The data are organized both by types and by variety of punctuation marks and, only for the point, for types and variety of categories linked to it. Although the full stop is indicated by only one graphic mark, we have distinguished at least three main types of points: the graphic point that is followed by written words in the same graphic line, the graphic point that leaves an empty space at its right because the following written word is on another line, and the graphic point at the very end of the story.

Our coding system respects the peculiarity of the Spanish and Italian punctuation systems. The most significant difference between the two is the presence, in the Spanish system, of question marks and exclamation points at both the beginning and the end of a word, a group of words, or a sentence. This difference between Spanish (with these paired marks) and Italian (which is like English in this respect) is particularly significant in the case of quoted speech, and it is one of the major reasons for our interest in a comparative study. The complete coding system used in this study is presented in Table 10.4.

TABLE 10.4
Punctuation Mark Coding System

,	vi	comma
;	pco	semicolon
:	dpu	colon
.	pus	point
.	pua	full stop
.	puf	full stop (end of story)
...	psus	suspensive dots
-	gio	dash
-	gia	dash (opening)
-	gic	dash (closing)
"	cma	double quotation (opening)
"	cmc	double quotation (closing)
¿	ica	question mark (opening)
?	ici	question mark (closing)
¡	ada	exclamation mark (opening)
!	adc	exclamation mark (closing)
(	para	parenthesis (opening)
)	pare	parenthesis (closing)

TABLE 10.5
Categorization of the Main Episodes of the Story

Episodes of the Story	
Episode 0	Title
Episode 1	Presentation of the main character
Episode 2	Little Red Riding Hood is asked to go to her grandmother's house
Episode 3	Little Red Riding Hood goes into the woods
Episode 4	Little Red Riding Hood meets the wolf
Episode 5	The wolf goes to the grandmother's house
Episode 6	Little Red Riding Hood is in the grandmother's house (canonical dialogue)
Episode 7	Arrival of the hunter (or similar) and solution
Episode 8	Conclusion

Another aim of this study is to analyze the relationship between punctuation marks and textual organization. For that purpose, we have categorized both the structural aspects of the text, through an identification of the main episodes of the story, and the type of discourse of each clause of the text (see Table 10.5).

With regard to the relationship between punctuation marks and type of discourse, which are presented in Table 10.6, we have analyzed in detail only the text portions related to quoted speech: specifically, the introduction of the speaker to whom the following words are attributed, the postponed introduction of the speaker (which is located afterwards), and the quoted speech itself.

RESULTS

Distribution of Punctuation: Occurrence and Variety

The number of children who used no punctuation marks in their written stories differed between the two samples. We added to this distribution of nonpunctuated texts those texts having the full stop at the end of the story only once. The complete distribution is shown in Table 10.7. Only 8 children in the Italian group (of 255) used no punctuation, whereas in the Spanish group, 82 children (of 252) did not. Most of the nonpunctuating children in the Italian sample were enrolled in second grade, whereas in the Spanish sample, most of these children were in third grade.

To obtain an overview of the general evolutionary pattern of punctuation,[12] we analyzed both the occurrence of punctuation and the variety of punctuation.

---

[12]The nonpunctuated texts were not considered in the general analysis of development of punctuation. Without them, the Spanish sample consisted of 147 children, whereas the Italian sample consisted of 229 children.

TABLE 10.6
The Coding System of Types of Discourse

Type of discourse	
T	Title
P	Presentation of the main character
E	Introduction to quoted and reported speech
EB	Postponed introduction
D	Quoted speech
I	Reported speech
N	Narrative (third person)
Z	Onomatopoeia
F	Conclusion (only Episode 8)

An overview of the distribution of different punctuation marks is presented in Table 10.8.

The ranks of the more frequently used punctuation marks is similar in the two samples. The marks used most by Italian children are in the following order of frequency: the point (taking together the three types of point that we identified), the double quotation marks, and the comma, followed by the colon, question mark, exclamation point, dash, semicolon, parenthesis, and suspension points. The order is the same for Spanish children, except that they used double quotation marks less than the Italian children did. Italian children appeared to prefer to use the double quotation marks to signal quoted speech, whereas Spanish children used double quotation marks more to emphasize a word or a clause. This difference is probably present because of both the cultural setting and the educational practices through which children learn punctuation.

Distribution of Punctuation in Story Episodes

The distribution of punctuation marks across the different episodes that frame the story is analyzed here in order to begin to explore, early in the mastery of written language, in which part of a text most punctuation occurs (see Table 10.9). Although there are large differences in frequencies, the rank of episodes in terms of presence of punctuation marks is similar in the two samples (see

TABLE 10.7
Distribution of Nonpunctuated Texts

	Second Grade		Third Grade		
	Spanish	Italian	Spanish	Italian	Total
No marks	29	7	53	1	90
1 mark (only puf)	9	18	14	0	41

TABLE 10.8
Variety of Punctuation Marks

	pus	pua	puf	vi	pco	dpu	psus	cma	cmc	gio	gia	gic	ica	ici	ada	adc	para
	.	.	.	·	;	:	...	"	"	-	-	-	¿	?	¡	!	(
Second-grade Spanish	58	74	43	51	0	18	0	13	13	0	1	0	5	4	13	12	1
Third-grade Spanish	116	103	75	255	2	67	0	19	18	23	18	17	54	55	40	39	0
Total	174	177	118	306	2	85	0	32	31	23	19	17	59	59	53	51	1
Second-grade Italian	196	252	71	280	2	102	2	74	56	7	24	13	/	55	/	48	3
Third-grade Italian	410	342	78	407	19	422	5	475	454	6	63	66	/	111	/	108	2
Total	606	594	142	687	21	524	7	549	520	13	87	79	/	166	/	156	5

TABLE 10.9
Distribution of Punctuation in Story Episodes

	Episode 0	Episode 1	Episode 2	Episode 3	Episode 4	Episode 5	Episode 6	Episode 7	Episode 8	Total
Spanish	48	65	225	54	280	117	330	62	38	1,222
Italian	38	191	710	184	1,146	448	1,113	236	100	4,168
Total	86	256	936	238	1,427	566	1,444	304	146	5,390

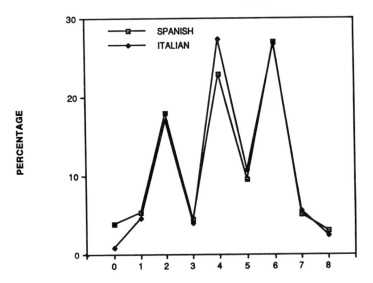

FIG. 10.1. Graph of the distribution of punctuation in story episodes.

Fig. 10.1). The episodes containing the higher number of punctuation marks are the second, the fourth, and the sixth, which are precisely those episodes that should contain the dialogues between the main LRRH characters. This confirms the hypothesis that most punctuation marks are used around the quoted speech portions of text, at least in the very early phases of acquiring written competence. In these textual spaces, there is a great need to insert marks to separate different discourse genres and to signal the change of speaker. It means that punctuation marks are inserted with a precise textual function, as we shall see later.

Distribution of Punctuation in the Different Types of Discourse

Most punctuation marks were found in quoted speech in both types of samples (see Table 10.10 and Fig. 10.2). To better understand the use of punctuation marks in quoted speech, however, we also need to consider two other types of

TABLE 10.10
Distribution of Punctuation in the Different Types of Discourse

	D	N	E	P	F	I	Z	T	EB	Total
Spanish	545	296	151	64	38	24	55	48	1	1,222
	(44.6)	(24.2)	(12.3)	(5.2)	(3.1)	(2.0)	(4.5)	(3.9)	(0.08)	
Italian	2146	986	501	191	101	85	51	38	70	4,168
	(51.5)	(23.6)	(12.0)	(4.6)	(2.4)	(2.0)	(1.2)	(0.9)	(1.7)	
Total	2,691	1,282	652	255	139	109	106	86	71	5,390

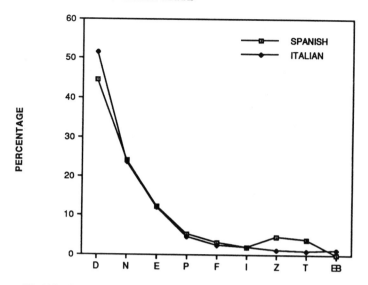

FIG. 10.2. Graph of the distribution of punctuation in types of discourse.

discourse that are adjacent to reported speech (E = introduction and EB = postponed introduction), and identify the speaker to whom the quoted speech is attributed. For this reason, we did a more detailed, qualitative analysis from inside the written story, considering the *type* of punctuation with which children manage the complexity of the written form of quoted speech.

Punctuation Marks in Relation to Quoted Speech

Blanche-Benveniste (1991) suggested that reported speech acts are better understood through the metaphor of theater play. A person who uses quoted statements in his or her speech is at the same time an author, an actor, and a *metteur en scène*. The use of the textual space makes a clear contribution to the creation of the scenario for the *mise en scène*, where the various actors will come in and come out, their entrances and exits being indicated by particular choices among the set of punctuation marks.

In fact, the main functions of punctuation marks inside and around quoted speech are clearly identifiable. They indicate the boundaries between narrative clauses and the beginning or the end of quoted speech; the main speaker; and changes in turn taking. Today, exclamation points and question marks have an accepted place in dialogic pieces of quoted speech, as do double quotations, dashes, and colons. In this domain, however, there is no normative model to follow. Books of children's stories vary in their methods of indicating quoted speech, introducing the main speaker, and so on. What happens with the use of punctuation marks in general also happens with quoted speech: In the newspapers, magazines, and propaganda of both Italy and Mexico, there is a great typographic variety.

For the purpose of this study, we selected a sample of 48 written texts containing the greatest number of punctuation marks: 15 Mexican texts with 20 or more punctuation marks, and 33 Italian texts with 40 or more punctuation marks. These texts all present passages of dialogue in quoted speech. The numerical difference between the two languages is not our concern here; instead, we focus on the various solutions adopted by children to manage the previously mentioned functions of punctuation, utilizing the different features and peculiarities of the two punctuation systems (Spanish and Italian).

Children's Solutions: A Comparative Analysis

We have analyzed the various solutions that children proposed to solve the multiple problems around the use of punctuation marks in quoted speech. These children found solutions that are specific to Spanish and Italian, as well as some problems that are common to both languages.

The Stability (or Lack of Stability) of Punctuation Marks Throughout the Text. In general, children had difficulty using punctuation marks consistently throughout the quoted speech portions in their texts. This was particularly true in those texts containing long portions of dialogue. Some children, both Spanish and Italian, began to use a stable system of punctuation (e.g., in the first dialogue between LRRH and her mother) but abandoned punctuation marks in the following dialogues. These instances seem to be dependent on the length of the text and of the dialogues. Text composition for children 7 and 8 years old implies some cognitive request other than that of inserting punctuation marks. Lack of attention to punctuation marks does not necessarily imply lack of attention to other important textual aspects.

This is illustrated in the following examples. In the passages by Martha (Spanish second grade, 6/26),[13] all the occurrences of these marks are concentrated in the quoted speech of Episodes 2, 4, and 5. Arriving at the canonical dialogue, however, she omitted all punctuation marks, including capital letters:[14]

Yo abuelita adelante y entró
(It is me grammy and she came in)

---

[13] The first number (in this case, 6) represents the number of different marks used by the child, and the second one (in this case, 26) represents the occurrences of the different marks.

[14] In these examples, we have used a clause-by-clause presentation to facilitate comparison between the different marks used by children to signal turn taking. We also have included the symbol | to indicate the end of the graphic lines as they appeared in the original texts of the children.

abuelita que | nariz tan más grande tienes
(grammy what kind of big nose you have)

para olerte | mejor
(to smell you better)

que boca tan más grande tienes
(what kind of big mouth)

para | comerte mejor
(to eat you better)

Claudia (Italian third grade, 6/46) began her text (Episode 2) with a systematic use of the colon after each portion of quoted speech. Then, in Episode 4, she added double quotation marks:

e la nonna disse
(and grandmother said)

"chi è?",
("who is?",)

Starting at the very beginning of canonical dialogue, however, Claudia used only periods and capital letters to indicate each pair of LRRH requests and grand-mother's answers:

Nonna che naso grande hai
(Grammy what kind of long nose you have)

per odorarti meglio bambina mia. |
(to smell you better my baby.)

Nonna che gambe lunghe che hai
(Grammy what kind of long legs you have)

per prenderti meglio bambina mia. |
(to take you better my baby.)

The Spanish sample contained two clear examples of punctuation marks that were used at the beginning and then disappeared. Did the punctuation marks disappear because of the heavy load on the writer, who became tired at the end of the story? That did not always seem to be the case. Ana (Spanish third grade, 11/40) used double quotation marks in the title as well as in her presentation of the main character:

por eso le pusieron "Caperucita Roja"
(for this reason they called her "Little Red Riding Hood")

Very soon, however, this particular mark disappeared. She opened the quotation of the mother's speech in Episode 2 with this sign but did not close the quote. However, the short reply of LRRH was opened and closed with double quotations, leaving the declarative verb inside:

"Si mamá dijo"
("Yes mamma she said")

After Episode 3, there were no double quotations. In Ana's case, the disappearance of this punctuation mark could be considered, at least tentatively, as uncertainty about its function.

A different case is that of Gabriella (Italian second grade, 7/42), who used a colon at the beginning of her text to serve two different functions: to distinguish the words of a list (a very widespread use among all children) and to indicate a difference between two portions of quoted speech in Episode 2:

la mamma le aveva dato un cestino con dentro: | *ciambelle, e tanti altri dolci,*
(the mother gives her a basket with: ring-shaped cakes, and much other cakes)

Non passare nel bosco |
(Don't go through the wood)

perché c'é il lupo,
(because there is the wolf,)

capito?
(do you understand me?)

Sì!
(Yes!)

risponde Cappucetto Rosso. |
(answers LRRH.)

Even if this text suggests that Gabriella had a good knowledge of and familiarity with this plurifunctional punctuation mark, it was absent in the rest of the text.

The Turn-Taking Problem

The solutions to the problems posed by using punctuation marks to indicate turn taking can be grouped around two extreme points: overuse of marks (two or three consecutive marks) or no punctuation at all. Between these two extreme points, we observed lexical solutions, contrastive use of punctuation marks, or mixed solutions.

Lexical Solutions. A clever use of declarative verbs can help the reader understand who is the main speaker in turn taking, despite the absence of punctuation marks. Consider the following example.

Guadalupe (Spanish third grade, 8/26) illustrated oscillation in the use of punctuation marks. She concentrated her use of punctuation in Episodes 4 and 6; the dialogues at the beginning (Episode 2) and the end of the story (Episode 7) had almost no punctuation, because the declarative verbs took charge of indicating turn taking, as in this excerpt:

ye le dijeron qué te pasa niña
(and they said what's happened to you little girl)

y resp- | ondió un lobo está en la casa de mi | abuelita
(and she answered a wolf is in my grandmother's house)

Overuse of Punctuation Marks. Both the Spanish and the Italian samples contained examples of overused punctuation marks, together with some peculiarities. The Italian sample had more double quotations (" ") and colons (:) than the Spanish one did. The following passage by Paolo (Italian third grade, 8/48) illustrates that overuse:

"Buon | giorno bella bambina, dove stai andando?",
("Good morning beautiful child where are you going?",)

"Sto andando dalla nonna"
("I am going to my grandmother")

disse Cappuccetto Rosso.
(answers LRRH.)

"Vai in quella direzione, |
("If you take this way)

farai prima.".
(you will arrive soon.".)

Lorenzo (Italian second grade, 8/48), used double quotation marks and a dash at both the beginning and the end of each piece of quoted speech, but he omitted the conventional upper-case letters:

"–vado a casa di mia nonna-",
("–I am going to my grandmother's house-",)

"–posso venire anch'io-"
("–Can I come with you?-")

Alessandra (Italian third grade, 8/54), used the colon as a symmetrical sign placed at the beginning and at the end of each quoted speech:

Cappuccetto Rosso incontra un | lupo
(LRRH meets a wolf)

che gli dice:
(that says to her:)

"bambina mia dove devi andare?": |
("where are you going baby?":)

Cappucetto Rosso risponde:
(LRRH answers:)

"io vado dalla nonna
("I am going to my grandmother)

a | portare le focacce fresche":
(to take her fresh cakes":)

A passage by Georgina (third grade, 6/39) provides one of the few cases of frequent use of the colon, together with upper-case letters, in the Spanish sample:

y de repente se apareció | el lobo
(suddenly the wolf appeared)

y le dijo: Hola ¿cómo te llamas? |
(and said: Hello what's your name?)

y Caperucita le dijo: Me llamo Caperucita Roja. |
(and LRRH said: My name is LRRH.)

El lobo le dijo: Qué bonito nombre.
(The wolf said: That's a beautiful name.)

Quieres | jugar conmigo a quién llega primero a aquella | casa.
(Do you want to race with me to see who will reach that house first.)

Contrastive Solutions. One possible solution that was well documented in our sample was the use of punctuation marks to indicate the beginning and the end of a given piece of quoted speech together and the absence of punctuation for the reply. In this case, the alternate use of punctuation/no punctuation helped the reader to identify the main speaker.

Ana (Spanish third grade, 11/40) used the double Spanish interrogative marks for each LRRH question in the canonical dialogue and no marks at all (or upper-case letters) for the wolf's replies:

cuando llegó le preguntó:
(when she arrived she asked:)

¿Abuelita, por qué tienes esos ojos tan grandes?
(Grammy, why do you have such big eyes?)

para | verte mejor mi amor
(to see you better my darling)

¿Abuelita, por qué tienes esa nariz tan grande?
(Grammy, why do you have such big nose?)

para | olerte mejor mi amor
(to smell you better my darling)

¿Abuelita, por qué tienes esas orejas tan grandes?
(Grammy, why do you have such big ears?)

para | oirte mejor mi amor
(to hear you better my darling)

¿Abuelita, por qué tienes esa boca tan grande?
(Grammy, why do you have such big mouth?)

¡para | comerte mejor!
(to eat you better!)

As this shows, the double interrogative marks and the double exclamation points of the Spanish punctuation system are very helpful in implementing this type of solution. Italian children, however, also made abundant use of the double quotation marks, and they also achieved the same solutions, as in the case of Ilaria (Italian third grade, 8/43):

dentro il bosco Cappucetto | Rosso incontra il lupo
(in the wood LRRH meets the wolf)

che gli dice:
(that says to her:)

"Vuoi fare una | gara"
("Do you want to race")

Sì
(Yes)

allora il lupo dice:
(then the wolf says:)

"Io prendo la | strada più lunga".
("I will take the longer way".)

Va bene
(Well)

disse Cappucetto Rosso.
(answers LRRH.)

This presents an interesting problem: How should we define the unit of a dialogic quoted speech? This problem is particularly apparent in the way that the canonical dialogue is rendered. Does the speech unit consist of each turn taken by one of the main speakers? Or is it each coupling of one question and the answer to it?

In the next example, Claudia (Italian third grade, 6/49) chose the second alternative, with clear consequences in the choice of punctuation marks: She used a capital letter only at the beginning of LRRH's quoted speech, whereas the wolf's answers are unmarked and are characterized only by using a stereotyped expression, *bambina mia* (my baby), with a period at its end:

> *Nonna che naso grande che hai*
> (Grammy what kind of nose you have)
>
> *per odorarti meglio bambina mia.* |
> (to smell you better my baby.)
>
> *Nonna che gambe lunghe hai*
> (Grammy what kind of long legs you have)
>
> *per prenderti meglio bambina mia.* |
> (to take you better my baby.)
>
> *Nonna che bocca grande che hai*
> (Grammy what kind of great mouth you have)
>
> *per mangiarti meglio bam* | *bina mia.*
> (to eat you better my baby.)

Lucia (Italian third grade, 9/78), used the double quotations but only at the beginning and the end of the entire dialogue. Inside this canonical dialogue, turn taking is indicated both by an exclamation point at the end and by a capital letter at the beginning:

> *"Oh nonna!* | *che mani grandi hai!*
> ("Oh grammy! what kind of big hands you have!)
>
> *Per toccarti meglio bambina* | *mia!*
> (To touch you better my baby!)
>
> *Che naso grande hai!*
> (What kind of big nose you have!)
>
> *Per sentire il tuo buon* | *profumo!*
> (To smell your good perfume!)
>
> *Che orecchie grandi che hai!*
> (What kind of big ears you have!)
>
> *Per sentirti meglio* | *bambina mia!*
> (To hear you better my baby!)

Che bocca grande che hai!
(What kind of big mouth you have!)
Per mangiar | ti meglio!". |
(To eat you better!".)

Mixed Solution for Turn Taking (Lexical + Punctuation). The next examples (as well as the preceding ones) illustrate that it is not useful to separately analyze each quoted speech turn, because the marking is given by the contrastive use of both lexical and punctuation solutions. The first example shows an interesting transformation of a conventional single sign (colon) into a symmetrical one. Sebastiano (Italian third grade, 7/49) had trouble with overusing signs and also with the postponed introduction of the speaker in relation to punctuation marks:

:—Va bene risponde Cappuccetto:—
(:—Well answers LRRH:—)

The same procedure reappears in the following lines:

:—Va bene:—
(:—Well:—)

rispose impaurita Cappucetto.
(answers frightened LRRH.)

Norma (Spanish third grade, 12/53) used an overabundance of punctuation and lexical procedures in Episode 4 to indicate the postponed introduction of the speakers:

Iba en el camino muy feliz,
(She was going very happy,)

y se encontró | a un lobo
(and she met a wolf)

¡Ah!!—exclamó Caperucita— |
(Ah!!—exclaimed LRRH—)

No tengas miedo—le dijo el lobo—.
(Don't be afraid—said the wolf—.)

Qué | traes ahí? preguntó el lobo—
(What do you bring there? asked the wolf—)

unas galletas | para mi abuelita—repondió— |
(some cookies for my grandmother—she answered—)

¿Por qué no hacemos unas carreras?–preguntó el | lobo–
(Do you want to race?–asked the wolf–)

bueno–contestó Caperucita.
(well–answered LRRH.)

Overpunctuation is extremely difficult to control in young children. A similar difficulty arises that is related to a kind of overexplicitness involved in indicating the main speaker through turn taking in dialogues. Norma's passage is a case in point. She managed to use four different declarative verbs (*dijo/preguntó/respondió/contestó*) and to control a systematic postposition of the speaker presentation, but the result is an overloaded text. The same happened with Alessandra (Italian third grade, 8/54) in the canonical dialogue:

Cappuccetto | Rosso entra
(LRRH enters)

e chiede al lupo:
(and asks the wolf:)

"che occhi grandi | che hai":
("what kind of eyes":)

il lupo risponde:
(the wolf answers:)

"per vederti meglio": |
("to see you better":)

ancora Cappuccetto Rosso dice:
(still LRRH says:)

"che orecchie grandi che | hai":
("what kind of ears":)

il lupo dice:
(the wolf says:)

"per sentirti meglio":
("to hear you better":)

Some texts provided another interesting variation: that of making a double introduction of the main speaker once before and once after the quoted speech. This happened, for instance, in a passage by Ilaria (Italian third grade, 10/70):

Avviandosi
(By the way)

incontrò il lupo
(she meets the wolf)

che le disse: |
(that says to her:)

"Dove vai?"
("Where are you going?")

chiese il lupo:
(asks the wolf:)

"Dalla nonna!".
("To my grandmother!".)

Rispose Cappuccetto Ros | *so.*
(Answers LRRH.)

Does such a double presentation of the main speaker result from lack of attention or from lack of revision of the text? Perhaps, but in view of the many examples of symmetrical use of punctuation marks (even in the absence of any conventional model of reference), other hypotheses are also possible. For instance, perhaps children look for homogeneous ways to open and close each portion of quoted speech. The search could address graphic means but should also consider lexical choices.

FINAL REMARKS

The conclusions of this comparative study can be grouped around three main points:

1. Despite the great differences in the total quantity of punctuation, most punctuation was found around quoted speech in both samples. This confirms our quantitative assumption, but provides only hints for the qualitative and functional assumption that is to be the core of our ongoing work.

2. Both samples revealed the same hierarchy of use of punctuation marks, except for the double quotation marks in the Italian sample. The mark most used by Italian children is the period, followed by the double quotation, the comma, the colon, the question mark, the exclamation mark, the dash, the parenthesis, and the suspension points. This is also true for the Mexican sample, except that the double quotation marks come in the sixth place. Is this difference due to a difference in the cultural and linguistic uses of punctuation, or is it mainly due to differences in the educational practices by which children "learn" the punctuation marks? With regard to this question, we are currently investigating both the teachers' representations of the punctuation system (and the teaching practices used in the classroom) and the qualitative and quantitative distribution of punctuation in some children's books.

3. To compose nonambiguous and comprehensible texts for readers, children must learn to coordinate the multifunctional uses of punctuation around quoted speech. Given the quantity of marks needed to write a conventional dialogue, a child may fall into a cognitive and graphical overload. In trying to overcome this overload, children may discover some clever and elaborated solutions utilizing the different features and peculiarities of the Spanish and Italian systems of punctuation. These solutions show the need to study punctuation more through comparison and contrast with other textual and syntactical means used by children than in terms of simple quantity. This is particularly clear in the solutions proposed for the turn taking problem: Some children, using at the best the contrastive function of written marks, solve that problem in very efficient and economic, although nonconventional, ways. In this sense, we could also observe that children are very sensitive to the textual function of punctuation marks (which is not always the case in adults' representation of punctuation functions; see Rametti, 1993), sometimes using punctuation as an alternative means to other lexical and textual solutions. Our comparative analysis points to the need for a more detailed and exhaustive study. It seems particularly necessary to search for general and common solutions (as opposed to the idiosyncratic ones) to the problems posed by the written version of dialogue.

ACKNOWLEDGMENTS

The study presented here and the writing of this chapter were supported by a Bilateral Research Project of the Italian CNR (National Research Council) and the Mexican CONACYT (Consejo Nacional de Ciencia y Tecnología) for 1990–1993 and aimed at developing an international database for early literacy.

REFERENCES

Blanche-Benveniste, C. (1991). Le citazioni nell'orale e nello scritto [Reported speech in oral and written language]. In M. Orsolini & C. Pontecorvo (Eds.), *La costruzione del testo scritto* (pp. 259–273). Firenze: La Nuova Italia.

Catach, N. (1980). La ponctuation [The punctuation]. *Langue Francaise, 45*, 55–68.

Chafe, W. (1987). *What good is punctuation?* (Occasional Paper No. 2). Pittsburgh, PA: Carnegie Mellon University, Center for the Study of Writing.

Ferreiro, E. (1991). L'uso della punteggiatura nella scrittura di storie di bambini di seconda e terza elementare [Use of punctuation in written stories of second and third grade children]. In M. Orsolini & C. Pontecorvo (Eds.), *La costruzione del testo scritto* (pp. 233–258). Firenze: La Nuova Italia.

Ferreiro, E., & Teberosky, A. (1982). *Literacy before schooling*. New York: Heinemann.

Garcia Hidalgo, I. (1992). *TEXTUS system*. Unpublished manuscript, DIE-CINVESTAV, Mexico City.

Halliday, M. A. K. (1990). *Spoken and written language*. Cambridge, England: Cambridge University Press.

Nunberg, G. (1990). *The linguistics of punctuation.* Stanford, CA: Center for the Study of Language and Information.

Rametti, F. (1993). *Punto per punto: Evoluzione dell'uso della punteggiatura nei bambini di scuola elementare* [Point to point: Evolution in the use of punctuation of primary school children]. Dissertation work, Università degli Studi "La Sapienza," Faculty of Psychology, Rome.

LEARNING DIFFERENT USES OF WRITTEN LANGUAGE

11

THE USE OF INFORMATION IN EXPOSITORY TEXT WRITING

Pietro Boscolo
University of Padua

In recent years, several studies have focused on children's expository writing (e.g., Bereiter & Scardamalia, 1987; Boscolo, 1990, 1991; Cox, Shanahan, & Tinzmann, 1991; Hidi & McLaren, 1991; Newkirk, 1987; Raphael, Englert, & Kirschner, 1989). Unlike some research that refers to exposition as a broad, nonnarrative genre, this study deals with the type of text whose primary objective is to express information and/or ideas and is well exemplified in school textbooks. This study is particularly concerned with scientific text, that is, text that provides information on a topic and usually presents a definition of the main object or event (e.g., a plant, an animal, or an atmospheric event), information on its origin or geographic location, a description of its features and/or effects, and classification of subcategories. The comprehension of expository text is by no means a new research field, but the production of this type of text represents a relatively little-explored field, at least from a developmental and educational point of view, although expository writing is a frequent activity in schools.

Some recent studies on expository text (e.g., Boscolo, 1990; Englert & Raphael, 1988) have shown that elementary school children have to deal with two main difficulties in expository writing. The first concerns text organization. Young children's expository texts (until fourth grade) usually consist of sentences that appear to be connected to each other, in that they refer to the same topic, but show no overall organization. Text organization features, such as rhetorical predicates and metaexpository devices, are generally missing in elementary school pupils' written productions, and only at the end of middle school do pupils seem to be able to use an expository structure. The second difficulty concerns the sequence of information in the text. Expository text does not have a structure as strong as, for instance, narrative. In a narrative, episodes are usually organized in a sequence; in expositions, information sequence is less compelling. In fact, it can proceed either from general concepts to more specific ones or, inversely, from the description of specific cases to a general definition. However, expository writing requires information ordering. This is a demanding task for young writers, who only in the late elementary school grades are able to make their expository texts conform to the sequence generally followed in textbooks and in teachers' explanations (e.g., definition and description of the object/event → explanation of its origin → list of types or categories → description of an example).

A major problem in research on expository writing concerns the effect of the writer's knowledge of the topic on text construction. Although the influence of topic knowledge is a crucial problem in all writing research, it seems to be particularly relevant in expository writing where one usually writes only on well-known topics. This makes it difficult to investigate the writer's expository competence (i.e., his or her ability to sequence and organize information) independent of specific topic knowledge.

The difficulty of keeping these aspects relatively distinct is due to the characteristics of the writing tasks usually employed to assess competence in expository writing. There is a direct method, which consists of giving the subject a written production task on a topic, and some indirect methods, such as the arrangement of the sentences of a text or the individuation of the relevant parts of a text. Both types of procedure present some limitations. A written production task allows free organization of a text, but only on a well-known topic. Therefore, it is difficult to distinguish writers' knowledge of the text structure from their knowledge of the specific topic on which they write. On the other hand, the sentence arrangement task can be carried out on texts of any topic, but that is very different from a true writing task. The study reported here used a third procedure, which consisted of supplying the subjects with information items concerning a topic and asking them to write a text using these items. This procedure allowed the subjects to handle information items referring to well-known and unknown topics, and allowed us to compare their expository writing strategies across different text topics. Our method, a type of procedural facilitation (Bereiter & Scardamalia, 1987), can facilitate subjects' processes of idea disposition in the text. In fact, they do not have to generate ideas but only to select and write them.

The aim of this study was to investigate the ways in which elementary and middle school subjects construct an expository text by means of information items supplied ad hoc. By *text construction* I mean the organization of supplied information and its transcription in a written text. This study was mainly concerned with three aspects of organization and transcription: the selection of sentences to be used, the positioning of sentences in the written texts, and the use of cohesion devices in order to make the text more cohesive and complete.

Based on the results of several studies on expository writing (e.g., Bereiter & Scardamalia, 1987; Boscolo, 1990, 1991; Raphael, Englert, & Kirschner, 1989; Scinto, 1986), a general developmental trend in text construction was expected. Sentence sequencing conforming more and more to adult writing and an increasingly competent use of cohesion devices were expected in older subjects. To analyze the development of sentence sequencing, three expository passages were composed according to a "canonical" structure, that is, the sequence usually followed in school textbooks. The validity of this sequence across the three passages was checked in a preliminary study conducted with adult subjects. As for the use of different passages, we were interested in analyzing children's expository writing across different text topics. Our hypothesis was that supplying different groups of subjects with sentences referring to different topics would make both the similarities in the expected developmental trend and the differences related to the contents of each passage emerge by comparison/contrast.

SUBJECTS

The subjects of the preliminary study were 75 psychology students at the University of Padua. In our principal study, the subjects were 180 pupils from Grades 2, 4, 6, and 8 of an elementary and middle school in Padua.[1] The children had previously taken a reading comprehension ability test (Cornoldi, Colpo, & Gruppo M. T., 1981). Only the subjects who scored sufficiently high participated in the writing task.

MATERIAL

Three passages were used as experimental material. The first concerned the wind. It was composed both on the basis of a schema of expository functions suggested by Kintsch (1982; see also Weaver & Kintsch, 1991) and on texts on the same topic written by elementary and middle school pupils. The second passage described the *manuk*, a social custom of a fictitious people. The third described the *balmo*, a fictitious tropical fruit. The second and third passages were modeled on the wind passage. In choosing the passage topics, we followed two criteria. The first was to differentiate the passage on a well-known topic (the wind) from two passages on unknown objects or events. Obviously, all the passages contained old and new information. The wind is often the subject of classroom conversations in elementary school, and, therefore, this topic can be considered well known, although the children might not know some information (e.g., what trade winds are or features of the anemometer). On the other hand,

---

[1] In Italy, elementary school goes from Grade 1 to Grade 5 and middle school from Grade 6 to Grade 8.

the information in the two invented passages was necessarily new to the children, although they might already have seen some tropical fruit or heard or read a description of people from a different culture.

The second criterion was to choose three different types of passages. The wind and the balmo passages described physical objects and were similar to a scientific text, such as those presented in geography or science textbooks. However, the manuk passage described a social event and contained such elements as aggressive behavior, trade exchange, social interaction, and religion, which are common in social science literature and in narratives.

Two basic criteria were followed in text matching:

Length: Each passage consisted of 16 sentences.

Expository functions: The sentences were grouped into three blocks:

1. Four sentences represented a definition of the object or event, an evaluative comment on its importance, an explanation of its origin, and the main features of the object or event.

2. Three sentences concerned the positive and negative effects of the object or event.

3. Six sentences provided a classification of the main types of object or event, ranging from a general introductory sentence ("There are two types of . . .") to the description of a specific subtype.

4. There were three "free" sentences. One concerned the measurement device appropriate to the object or event, another concerned the presence of the object or event in poetry and legend, and the third referred to the use of the object or event in ancient times.

Thus, the three passages had different contents but were similar in length, structure, and variety of expository functions (e.g., definition, description, and exemplification).

Following are the three passages used in this study.

The Wind

1. The wind is the displacement of an air mass.
2. The wind is a very important atmospheric factor.
3. The wind is formed by a difference in air pressure.
4. The main characteristics of wind are intensity, that is, the strength it blows, and direction.
5. The wind moves the seeds of many plant species from zone to zone.
6. Wind strength is used for producing electric energy.
7. When it blows too strongly, the wind may uproot trees and destroy buildings.
8. There are constant and irregular winds.

9. Constant winds always blow in the same direction.
10. Among constant winds are the trades and the polar winds.
11. Irregular winds depend on air temperature.
12. The Bora, Mistral, and Sirocco are irregular winds.
13. The Bora is a cold and strong wind.
14. Wind velocity is measured by an instrument called the anemometer.
15. In ancient times, sea transport was made possible by the wind.
16. Ancient Greeks believed winds were ruled by a god called Aeolus.

The Manuk

1. The manuk is a characteristic feast of the Maiori Islands people.
2. The manuk is a very important public meeting.
3. The people of the Maiori Islands often have the manuk because they are sociable and like working together.
4. The main features of manuk are the number of people who take part and its duration.
5. The manuk allows people from faraway islands to meet.
6. During a manuk, the islanders exchange agricultural products and handicrafts.
7. During the manuk feasts, people often get drunk, fight, and hurt each other.
8. There are fixed and special manuk feasts during the year.
9. Fixed manuks are held at the beginning of every season.
10. Among fixed manuks are the sarak (summer feast) and the sidar (fall feast).
11. The sarak goes on for several days, with songs, dances, and races.
12. Special manuk feasts are held when some important event occurs.
13. The sagri (wedding feast) and the posir (feast for the birth of a tribal chief's son) are special manuks.
14. The people of the Maiori Islands use a special calendar to count each year's manuks.
15. In ancient times, the manuk gave all the islanders the opportunity to hear the king's decisions.
16. The ancient people of the Maiori Islands believed that the gods should be invited to every manuk; otherwise, they would get angry.

The Balmo

1. The balmo is a roundish fruit, with smooth and shiny skin, that is plentiful in tropical countries.
2. The balmo is a very important fruit in tropical countries.
3. The balmo tree grows in the tropics because it needs a hot and humid climate and does not like cold temperatures.
4. The main features of the balmo are its red color and strong scent.

5. The skin of the balmo is rich in vitamins.

6. The balmo pulp is nourishing and is also preserved.

7. Overripe balmos cause nausea and giddiness.

8. There are giant balmos and sweet balmos.

9. Giant balmos are very big but don't have much sugar.

10. The balmos that grow on river banks in Thailand are giant.

11. Sweet balmos have a high content of sugar.

12. Among sweet balmos are the tamio, which grows in Brazil, and the rengo, which grows in Africa.

13. The rengo is much used in cake production.

14. To measure the amount of sugar in balmos, a special device is used that extracts their juice.

15. Since ancient times, the balmo has been used as basic nourishment by people of the tropics.

16. The ancient people of the tropics believed that the balmo pulp could heal most serious diseases.

PROCEDURE

To check the hypothesized structure of the passages with adult subjects, the scrambled sentences of each passage were first submitted to the 75 psychology students (25 for each passage). The students were requested to read and order the sentences according to the sequence they considered the most suitable. They were warned that there was no "right" sequence. The results of this preliminary study (discussed later in the chapter) showed the structural homogeneity of the three passages, which were then submitted to the elementary and middle school subjects.

The elementary and middle school subjects were given a warm-up task represented by the sequencing of 10 sentences about the equatorial jungle. The aim of the warm-up task was twofold: to make the children familiar with the experimental task and to screen out the subjects with language problems. The children were given the following instructions:

A sentence concerning the equatorial forest (jungle) is written on each of these cards. You are asked to write a text on this topic by means of these sentences. You have to write a text like those in schoolbooks, not a story or a tale, but a text that makes this topic understandable to people who know nothing about it. Ten sentences are available to you. Please read all of them carefully, then pick out those you consider more important, and arrange them to write a text. You may use all the sentences or only some of them. Afterward write on the enclosed sheet the text that you constructed and add words and punctuation marks in order to connect the sentences better and make the text clearer and well written. If you want, you may add other sentences.

As a result of this warm-up task, four elementary school subjects with language problems were screened out.

Three days after the warm-up task, the subjects participated in the arrangement task. The instructions given in the previous phase were repeated. The children carried out the task individually. The younger ones worked in groups of five or six, under the guidance of an adult who repeated the instructions. The older ones carried out the task in their classrooms. No difficulty emerged during the arrangement and writing tasks, for which no time limit was set. For each school grade level, 15 subjects were allocated to each of the three passages.

RESULTS

Preliminary Study

In the analysis of the adult subjects' sentence ordering, two main aspects were considered. The first aspect concerned the constrained sentences (i.e., the sentences of the definition, classification, and effect blocks), for which a position or a sequence had been hypothesized. The second aspect concerned the "free" sentences, for which no constrained position was expected.

As for constrained sentences, both the sequence of the blocks (definition, classification, effects) and the position of sentences within each block were considered. Although the definition or description of the main object or event is usually at the beginning of the text, the position of the other two blocks is more flexible, because classification can either precede or follow the description of functions or effects. As for the positioning within a block, classification implies a sequence that begins with a general statement ("There are two types of . . .") and ends with a description of a specific subtype. Sentence position in the other blocks is less constrained. Definition is usually at the beginning but may be preceded by a general evaluative comment. Also, the description of positive and negative effects has no set sequence. Therefore, each subject's text was analyzed to compare the sentence position of the three blocks with the expected sequence. The following criteria were used:

- The position of the definition block was considered correct when Sentence 1 (definition) and at least one sentence of the block were placed at the beginning of the sentence arrangement.
- The classification block was considered correctly organized if the six sentences were ordered from the general statement (Sentence 8) to the specific description of types, regardless of the order of the type description (e.g., one

type preceding or following the other) and the position of the block in the arrangement.

• The effect block was considered correctly organized if at least two sentences of the block were contiguously positioned, regardless of the position of the block in the arrangement (see Table 11.1).

As for the free sentences, the following criteria were followed:

• Sentences 15 and 16, both referring to ancient times, were often coupled in the three passages. Sentence 16, also coupled with 15, often had an introductory function and preceded the definition block or was inserted in it. When Sentences 15 and 16 preceded the definition block or were inserted in it, the definition block was considered altogether at the top (see the first criterion). Sentence 15 was sometimes positioned contiguously to the effect block sentences.

• Sentence 14 (measurement tool) had different positions in the three passages. It was grouped with Sentence 6 (effect of wind strength) in the wind passage, with Sentence 11 (features of sweet balmos) in the balmo passage, and used as an introduction to the classification block in the manuk passage.

The results of this preliminary study showed that the adult subjects basically agreed on the position of the definition block and on the structure of the classification and effects blocks, and that the agreement covered all three passages. Because the aim of this study was to check the structure of the passages before submitting them to the children, the results are not commented on in the discussion section.

Principal Study

The children's texts were analyzed in terms of the number of sentences used by the subjects, the position of the sentences in the texts, and the text organization.

Number of Sentences. A 4 × 3 ANOVA was carried out on the number of sentences used by the subjects. This analysis concerned only the supplied sentences, not those added by the subjects. The analysis showed a significant main

TABLE 11.1
Adults' Sentence Ordering

	Wind (N = 25)	Manuk (N = 25)	Balmo (N = 25)
Definition	20	21	23
Classification	23	21	20
Effects	24	21	23
Sentences 15 & 16 as an introduction	13	11	10

effect of the school grade factor ($F = 127.68$, $df = 3,168$, $p < .001$), no effect of the type of passage, and no interaction. As expected, the use of sentences increased with school grade, particularly between second and fourth grades (Fig. 11.1).

In Grade 2, the choice of sentences seemed to be random and/or influenced by salience. For instance, Sentence 7, describing negative effects, was most chosen in the manuk and balmo passages, as was Sentence 12 (high quantity of sugar in sweet balmos) in the balmo passage. It is worth noting that the same average number (about seven) was found for sentences written by second graders in a free expository writing task (Boscolo, 1990). The problem here is whether this limitation was due to a developmental factor (e.g., children's difficulty in coordinating a larger number of sentences due to memory or fatigue factors) or to the specific task instruction. In fact, the instruction to select the most important sentences might be understood by the younger subjects as a limitation of sentence use. At the higher grade levels, the subjects used almost all the supplied sentences. Therefore, we focused not on those most used but on those least used for each passage. Sentence 14 (measurement tool) was the least used by the fourth graders in the three passages and by sixth and eighth graders in the balmo text. In the wind text Sentence 5 was the least used, whereas in the manuk text Sentence 15 was the least used by the sixth graders and Sentence 12 was least used by the eighth graders.

Sentence Position. The criteria followed in analyzing the adults' sentence positioning were also adopted for the children's text analysis, with two differences. The first difference concerned definition. Unlike adults, several children

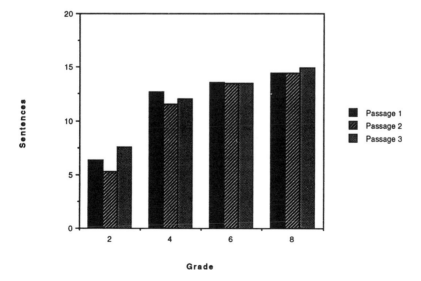

FIG. 11.1. Average number of sentences used.

positioned only Sentence 1 at the beginning, not followed by other sentences of the block. This use of Sentence 1 was considered an index of correct use of definition, although distinct from the use of Sentence 1 plus at least one sentence of the block. The second difference concerned classification. The use of this block was considered correct when the subjects correctly ordered the sentences although omitting one or two of the type descriptions.

Definition. Three main uses of the definition block were distinguished in the written texts (see Table 11.2):

d_0 = Sentence 1 not positioned at the beginning

d_1 = Sentence 1 positioned at the beginning

d_2 = two or more sentences of the definition block (including Sentence 1) positioned at the beginning

A three-way log-linear analysis (Grade × Passage × Use of definition) was performed on the frequencies of the three uses of definition. Two significant first-order interactions emerged: Grade × Definition use ($\chi = 59.24$, $df = 6$, $p <$ .001) and Definition use × Passage ($\chi = 13.15$, $df = 4$, $p < .01$). The post hoc analyses for interaction Grade × Definition showed the expected trend in definition use. The most interesting result of this analysis was the positive interaction estimate, d_1 × Grade 2 ($z = 2.709$, $p < .05$), which shows a significant use of definition at the beginning of the second graders' texts. As for the interaction Definition use × Passage, there was a positive interaction estimate for Wind × d_2, which showed that the definition block sentences were used more in the wind passage. There were also a positive interaction estimate Manuk × d_1 and a negative interaction estimate Manuk × d_2. These results showed that, in the

TABLE 11.2
Use of the Definition Block

		Wind	Manuk	Balmo
Grade 2	d_0	10	9	10
	d_1	5	5	5
	d_2	0	2	0
Grade 4	d_0	3	5	8
	d_1	2	7	3
	d_2	10	3	4
Grade 6	d_0	2	3	4
	d_1	0	5	0
	d_2	13	7	11
Grade 8	d_0	1	4	2
	d_1	1	3	2
	d_2	13	8	11

manuk texts, Sentence 1 was used more and the global definition block was underused.

Classification. The second graders constructed a faulty classification sequence in which not only half of the sentences of the block were usually missing, but also those used had no order (e.g., the exemplification preceded the listing of subtypes, and both preceded introductory Sentence 8). Although in the manuk and balmo texts Sentence 8 was not infrequent (7 out of 15), it was used as autonomous information at the end of the text or after the description of the subtypes it should have introduced.

The classification was more clearly reproduced in the fourth graders' texts. Also at this grade level, the wind texts showed a more correct reconstruction of classification than the other two texts. In the balmo passage, one fourth grader put Sentence 8 after the other classification sentences but justified this position in the following way: "Therefore there are two types of balmos!" However, what differentiated the fourth from the second graders was not only the increasing frequency of correct classifications but also the block organization. This aspect will be analyzed in the text organization paragraph. At sixth grade a large number of subjects correctly reproduced the classification block, whereas at eighth grade the classification block was reproduced by almost all the subjects (see Table 11.3).

In order to perform a log-linear analysis, two uses of classification were individuated:

$$c_0 = \text{no or incorrect sequence}$$

$$c_1 = \text{correct sequence}$$

From the analysis, two first-order interactions emerged: Grade × Use of classification ($\chi = 95.39$, $df = 3$, $p < .001$) and Use of classification × Passage ($\chi = 8.41$, $df = 2$, $p < .05$). As for the first interaction, the post hoc analyses showed, unsurprisingly,

TABLE 11.3
Use of the Classification Block

		Wind	Manuk	Balmo
Grade 2	c_0	12	15	15
	c_1	3	0	0
Grade 4	c_0	5	7	9
	c_1	10	8	6
Grade 6	c_0	0	2	4
	c_1	15	13	11
Grade 8	c_0	1	0	2
	c_1	14	15	13

the positive interaction estimates for $c_0 \times$ Grade 2 ($z = 5.560, p < .001$), for $c_1 \times$ Grade 6 ($z = 3.170, p < .01$) and $c_1 \times$ Grade 8 ($z = 3.891$); and negative interaction estimates for $c_1 \times$ Grade 2 ($z = -5.560$), $c_0 \times$ Grade 6 ($z = -3.170$), and $c_0 \times$ Grade 8 ($z = -3.891$). These results showed that the older subjects reproduced correct classification more frequently and incorrect classification less frequently and that the younger subjects did the reverse. Regarding the interaction Use of classification $\times$ Passage, from the post hoc analysis two significant positive interaction estimates emerged for $c_1 \times$ Wind ($z = 2.044, p < .05$) and $c_0 \times$ Balmo ($z = 2.035, p < .05$), along with two negative interaction estimates for $c_0 \times$ Wind ($z = -2.044$) and $c_1 \times$ Balmo ($z = -2.035$). Thus, the trend was quite opposite for the wind and balmo texts. The more frequent incorrect use of classification in the balmo texts could be ascribed to the salience of the "sweet" sentences. In fact, several writers inserted sentences concerning the sweet balmos (e.g., Sentences 5 and 14) without completing the classification sequence.

Effects. The effect block was never entirely reproduced by the second graders, although some sentences of the block were used. In a few texts (four for the wind and manuk, six for the balmo passages), two sentences referring to the block were contiguous, but this appeared to be fortuitous for the first two passages. Instead, in the balmo passage the connection between the two sentences, although not explicit, seemed to be stronger, which may have been due to the salience of the semantic relationship underlying the effect sentences (i.e., the balmo as a sweet food). This tendency was more apparent in the fourth graders' texts. It is worth noting that, as in the adults' sentence arrangement, Sentence 15, concerning the use of the fruit in ancient times, was often coupled with some sentence of the block, whereas this rarely occurred in the other passages. The use of the block increased with school grade, although not with the same frequencies as definition and classification.

As for classification, in order to perform a log-linear analysis two uses of the block effect sentences were distinguished (see Table 11.4):

$$e_0 = \text{no correct sequence}$$

$$e_1 = \text{correct sequence}$$

A three-way log-linear analysis (Grade $\times$ Passage $\times$ Use of classification) was performed, from which a significant interaction of Grade $\times$ Use of effect emerged ($\chi = 19.16, df = 3, p < .001$). The post hoc analysis showed the expected trend, that is, the correct sequence significantly less used in second grade and more used in eighth grade, and the opposite for the incorrect sequence.

Text Organization. By *text organization* we mean the strategies that writers use in connecting sentences and highlighting information in a text. The following aspects of text organization were analyzed in this study: the development of

TABLE 11.4
Use of the Effect Block

		Wind	Manuk	Balmo
Grade 2	e_0	11	11	9
	e_1	4	4	6
Grade 4	e_0	6	6	4
	e_1	9	9	11
Grade 6	e_0	8	5	5
	e_1	7	10	10
Grade 8	e_0	5	4	2
	e_1	10	11	13

cohesion links, sentence connection in the classification and effect blocks, and introductory phrases.

In order to analyze the effects of school grade and type of passage on the use of cohesion devices introduced by the subjects in writing, the ratio of cohesion devices to the number of used sentences was computed for each subject (see Fig. 11.2). The ratios were submitted to an ANOVA, from which a significant effect of school grade ($F = 60.175$, $df = 3,168$, $p < .001$) and of passage ($F = 3.062$, $df = 2,168$, $p < .05$) emerged. In regard to the increasing use of cohesion links with school grade, a remarkable difference between elementary (second and fourth grades) and middle school children (sixth and eighth grades) emerged. The second graders almost never used cohesion devices and punctuation marks except full stop. They merely rewrote sentences, with a new line after each sentence. The older children used conjunctions and pronouns. Some-

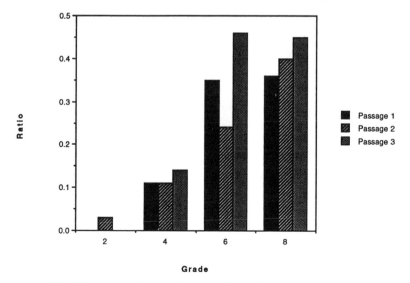

FIG. 11.2.   Ratio of cohesion devices to the number of sentences used.

times, in the case of contiguous sentences referring to a same block or subtopic, full stop was replaced by a comma. In fourth grade, the writers began to connect sentences, and the single sentence was often replaced by a set of two sentences connected by a comma or a semicolon. Cohesion was used much more by sixth and eighth graders, with reference and conjunctions being the most frequent links.

As for the passages, the use of cohesion devices was more frequent in the wind texts. The use of pronouns was less frequent in the manuk passage, which might have been due to the younger subjects' difficulty in replacing *manuk* with a pronoun. In fact, this word was new to them, and its meaning was less definite for them than the wind (a well-known phenomenon) and the balmo (for which a physical description was given in the passage). The use of ellipses appeared, although less frequently, in eighth grade, particularly in the manuk and balmo passages.

In analyzing the increasing use of sentence connection devices across the grade levels, two types of connection frequently appeared in the classification block. One was vertical connection, which consisted of keeping the two types separate and introducing cohesion links between the sentences referring to each type, as in this example:

> There are. . . . Irregular winds depend on air temperature and are. . . . Constant winds always blow in the same direction and are. . . .

The second type of connection was horizontal, in that the sentences referring to the two main types or the subtypes were connected by an adversative conjunction, as they are in the following two examples:

> Constant and irregular winds exist. Constant winds always blow in the same direction and we find the Trades and the Polar ones, *while* irregular winds depend on air temperature. . . .

> In a year there are fixed and special manuks: among the fixed manuks we mention the sarak and the sidar, *in contrast* the special manuks are the sagri and the posir.

The first type of connection was more frequent in the wind and manuk passages, whereas the second was mainly used in the balmo passage.

In Grade 4, children began integrating two sentences of the effect block by means of cohesion devices such as *while, but,* and *however.* This increased in the older subjects' texts. Although the occurrence of contiguous sentences concerning effects was the same in all the passages, what clearly differentiated the wind and balmo passages from the manuk passage was the frequency of integrated sentences. In fact, in the sixth and eighth grades the effect block sentences were usually integrated with cohesion devices, as they are in the following examples:

> The wind strength is nowadays exploited for the production of electric energy. Moreover the wind moves the seeds of several plant species from. . . . However, a tornado can be dangerous: it can uproot. . . (sixth grader).

> The skin of the balmo is rich with vitamins and its pulp is also preserved, but should we try to eat too ripe a fruit, we would feel at once sickness and giddiness (eighth grader).

Only one sixth grader and no eighth graders integrated the effect sentences in the manuk passage. This difference seems to be due to the specific nature of the manuk passage, in which the effects are not physical transformations (as for the wind) and cannot be grouped under the category of food (as for the balmo). Although the frequency of contiguous sentences was the same in the three passages, the aspects related to a social event seem to be less easily grouped under the same category.

The use of horizontal connection seems to represent a crucial step in the development of paragraph structure. By *paragraph* we mean a set of sentences that are tightly connected by thematic unity (i.e., refer to a same subtopic), are anticipated by an introducing sentence, and are signaled by new line and/or indentation (Longacre, 1979). In the eighth graders' texts, the classification and definition blocks were in paragraph structure, whereas the effects were paragraphed less frequently, often being inserted into the definition block or connected to Sentences 15 and 16.

When introduced to the writing task, the subjects were told they could add sentences in order to improve their texts. In the second and fourth grades, the added sentences were of the following types:

- In the wind passage, information on the wind.
- In the manuk passage, elaborations on some sentences (e.g., the effect of drinking too much). These elaborations were present only in second graders' texts.
- In the balmo passage, analogies or differences with known tropical fruits.

In the sixth and eighth grades, the added phrases or sentences had an introductory function, as in the following examples:

> There are several ways to use the wind strength (eighth grader).

> What is a manuk? The manuk is. . . (eighth grader).

> Another characteristic of the manuk is the following (eighth grader).

Sentences 15 and 16 were often coupled due to their common reference to ancient times. They were sometimes used as an introduction, particularly in the manuk texts.

DISCUSSION

The study reported here had two objectives. The first was to investigate the strategies children use in expository writing at different school grade levels. The second was to compare the use of these strategies across different text topics.

As for the first objective, a clear developmental trend emerged in the subjects' texts. Although this trend was expected, some aspects, in our opinion, should be stressed. Expository writing does not seem to develop according to a homogeneous trend. In fact, although the increase in number of selected sentences was remarkable between the second and fourth grades, for text organization the crucial increase was between the fourth and sixth grades.

Regarding sentence positioning, the results are not clear cut. Definition turned out to be the expository function most used by younger subjects, but as school grade level increased, classification was the most correctly used function. This different trend is most probably related to the connection among the sentences in each block. The definition block consisted of four sentences with a definitory function, that is, telling what the wind (or the balmo, or the manuk) is, what its main features are, and its origin, although the true definition was given in Sentence 1. The four sentences are relatively autonomous, and the first suffices to define the topic. Instead, no single sentence of the classification block is sufficient to express the classification. At least three sentences are needed in a specific sequence. Moreover, the sentences of this block appear to be connected referentially. Therefore, whereas definition seems to ask the subject to select one or more "representative" sentences, classification implies not only the selection of a minimum number of sentences (at least three) but also their arrangement: in other words, a complex operation that the subjects were able to perform adequately starting in the sixth grade. Hence, the use of definition, although limited to one sentence, begins relatively early, and this seems to reflect the children's early awareness of the importance of definition in an instructional text. The use of classification occurs later, probably due to the subjects' increasing ability to coordinate—and not just select—information. It is worth noting that expository text processing—either comprehension or production—seems to represent different areas of difficulty for young readers/writers, in that its parts may imply different levels of cognitive complexity. In the effect block, there was no compelling sequence, and the subjects were free to organize it as they wished. This block appeared to be the least regular, probably due to the differences among the three passages.

The horizontal connection between the sentences of the classification blocks brings to mind Bereiter and Scardamalia's (1987; see also De Bernardi & Levorato,

1991) concept of idea coordination constrained by the writer's memory capacity. These authors examined how children cope with the problem of coordinating content idea in expository and argumentative writing and distinguished several levels of integration. For instance, a Level 1 integration occurs when a child writes only one information unit at a time. The classification task is more complex, because the correct reproduction of classification requires sequencing of the information units. In fact the integration of sentences in the block requires the following steps: (a) distinguishing the correct sequence, (b) connecting the sentences referring to one main type by inserting cohesion links and replacing sharp boundaries between sentences (full stop) with a comma, and (c) connecting two symmetrical sentences (i.e., both referring to the main types or two subtypes) by an adversative conjunction.

As for the second objective of this study, although some aspects of the development of expository competence seemed to be independent of the specific topics, other aspects, such as cohesion devices, use of definition, and sentence integration, appeared to be related to the specific passage topics. The wind and balmo passages, dealing with physical entities, turned out to be more easily handled with regard to cohesion devices and integration. The wind text also showed a more extensive use of the definition block. Moreover, some elements of the specific content in the balmo texts made the use of classification difficult. The differences in text organization can only be tentatively ascribed to some features of the three passages. Although we aimed at structural similarity in composing the passages, some expository functions assumed a different salience and, consequently, different possibilities of position and integration in the subjects' texts. Although this seemed to result from difficulty in matching text structure across different text topics, the variability in text organization was probably due to the very nature of expository text, in which some functions or blocks have a privileged position (e.g., definition at the beginning), whereas others do not. The relevance of information units in an expository text is a question not only of sequence but also of the adequate use of text organization devices. Although they positioned definition at the top and correctly reproduced the classification and effect blocks, the older subjects used a large variety of information sequences in text construction. However, in the sixth and mainly the eighth grades, several texts turned out to be coherent and well organized, due not only to the use of introductory phrases, cohesion links, and adequate punctuation marks, but also to the exclusion of unrelated sentences, such as Sentence 14.

The development of expository writing competence has been explained in terms of the transition from a knowledge-telling strategy to a knowledge-transforming strategy (Bereiter & Scardamalia, 1987). We think that these strategies represent the poles of a complex developmental process through which the novice writer learns to integrate the constrained and free elements in a coherent and cohesive expository text. In our opinion, the phases of this process deserve to be thoroughly investigated.

Finally, the writing task used in this study calls for a methodological comment. The task required the subjects not only to arrange the sentences but also to modify them in order to produce a well-written text. Although each sentence was autonomous to avoid any cohesion cue influencing the subjects' choice, constructing a text with supplied sentences implies not only combining them but also decomposing and restructuring the sentences. Although several eighth graders were able to use the sentences freely, the younger subjects (particularly the second and fourth graders) seemed unable to use the information independent of its linguistic structure. Bracewell (1980) showed that elementary school children find it difficult to code information items in a complex sentence when information is supplied in sentence format. However, we think that this type of task is fruitful, because it allows the researcher to compare writing strategies across different text topics. Obviously, it can be modified and improved in both sentence and block construction. A relevant aspect to be considered is the dimension of familiarity for selection of the passages. The subjects' degree of familiarity with the topics was not assessed for this study. Such a prior check would have allowed us to analyze the relationship between text topics and the development of expository competence in a more precise and convincing way.

ACKNOWLEDGMENTS

The preparation of this chapter was supported by a grant from the National Council of Research (CT 89 02071.08). The author wishes to thank Camilla Gobbo for her helpful comments on an earlier version of this chapter.

REFERENCES

Bereiter, C., & Scardamalia, M. (1987). *The psychology of written composition*. Hillsdale, NJ: Lawrence Erlbaum Associates.

Boscolo, P. (1990). The construction of expository text. *First Language, 10*, 217–230.

Boscolo, P. (1991, April). *How children construct an expository text: Effect of teacher's presentation of a topic on the organization of pupils' written productions*. Paper presented at the Annual Meeting of the American Educational Research Association, Chicago.

Bracewell, R. J. (1980). Writing as a cognitive activity. *Visible Language, 14*, 400–422.

Cornoldi, C., Colpo, G., & Gruppo M. T. (1981). *La verifica dell'apprendimento della lettura* [The assessment of reading learning]. Firenze, Italy: Organizzazioni Speciali.

Cox, B. E., Shanahan, T., & Tinzmann, M. B. (1991). Children's knowledge of organization, cohesion, and voice in written exposition. *Research in the Teaching of English, 25*, 179–218.

De Bernardi, B., & Levorato, M. C. (1991). How writers integrate information in written text production: A developmental study. *European Journal of Psychology of Education, 6*, 141–153.

Englert, C. S., & Raphael, T. E. (1988). Constructing well-formed prose: Process, structure, and metacognitive knowledge. *Exceptional Children, 54*, 513–520.

Hidi, S., & McLaren, J. A. (1991). Motivational factors and writing: The role of topic interest-ingness. *European Journal of Psychology of Education, 6*, 187–197.

Kintsch, W. (1982). Text representations. In W. Otto & S. White (Eds.), *Reading expository material* (pp. 87–102). New York: Academic Press.

Longacre, R. E. (1979). The paragraph as a grammatical unit. In T. Givon (Ed.), *Syntax and semantics* (Vol. 12, pp. 115–134). New York: Academic Press.

Newkirk, T. (1987). The non-narrative writing of young children. *Research in the Teaching of English, 21*, 121–144.

Raphael, T. E., Englert, C. S., & Kirschner, B. W. (1989). Acquisition of expository writing skills. In J. M. Mason (Ed.), *Reading and writing connections* (pp. 261–290). Boston, MA: Allyn & Bacon.

Scinto, L. F. M. (1986). *Written language and psychological development.* Orlando, FL: Academic Press.

Weaver, C. A., & Kintsch, W. (1991). Expository text. In R. Barr, M. L. Kamil, P. B. Mosenthal, & P. D. Pearson (Eds.), *Handbook of reading research* (Vol. 2, pp. 230–245). New York: Longman.

12

LOOKING FOR STYLISTIC FEATURES IN CHILDREN COMPOSING STORIES: PRODUCTS AND PROCESSES

Clotilde Pontecorvo
Raimonda Maria Morani
University of Rome "La Sapienza"

IS A LITERARY ANALYSIS OF CHILDREN'S WRITING STYLE POSSIBLE?

The main aim of this chapter is to explore whether and how it may be possible to use new methods for studying children's style in producing narratives that can be considered good, not only from a structural point of view, but also from an expressive and literary point of view. We present data collected in a pilot experiment that is part of a research project (Morani, 1991) aimed at finding, testing, and analyzing ways in which children who are becoming literate (during the first years of school) can actively participate in different types of writing experiences in order to become more aware of and expert in using different stylistic devices.

The larger research project assumed that certain educational practices can affect children's stylistic development. These practices include the use of different reading conditions, such as expressive reading by an adult to help develop "pleasure in the text," and playful reading, involving interruptions at specific points in the text to help children understand that a narrative text can have different possible alternatives (Orsolini & Pontecorvo, 1989). However, the main focus has been on types of composing conditions: using pair interaction, using dictation to an adult, varying verbal or figurative inputs as a starting point for the writing request, and varying the features of the inputs (more or less unusual).

One aim of the research was to try out methods that could analyze both products and processes. The text analysis had to be sensitive to the differences in linguistic and stylistic features of children's narratives, whereas the process analysis was aimed at investigating the cognitive, social, and linguistic factors that guide and support a child's production.

Psychological research has devoted much attention to story structure and more recently to the role of narrative in development. Studies on story grammar, carried out by cognitive scientists, have emphasized the general and invariant structure in order to support hypotheses about the role of schemes in comprehension and memory: Stories were compared with schemes and scripts in different types of cognitive tasks (Mandler, 1979). Developmental psychologists have given attention to identifying categories of general story structure (Stein & Glenn, 1979), emphasizing the importance of causal links between different episodes and ways to create cohesion (Trabasso, Secco, & van den Broek, 1984; Trabasso, Stein, & Johnson, 1981).

The latter studies have focused mainly on the general and invariant aspects of the story structure that are central to comprehension, memorization, and probably also to oral production. Until now, not much attention has been given to the stylistic features that differentiate children's invented stories and contribute to a better understanding of their invention process. This exploratory study examines ways of analyzing the process of text composition in peer interaction in order to detect cognitive, social, and linguistic factors that guide children's production activity.

The research issue explored in this chapter is whether and how early literate children begin to master some of the formal mechanisms and stylistic devices that characterize "literariness" (or *literaturnost*, from Jakobson, 1980). Our first problem was choosing a type of product analysis that is most sensitive to differences and microgenetic developments in formal and stylistic developments of children's narratives.

Suggestions came from the semiotic and linguistic analyses of literary works, which have been interested in the role of parallelism, repetition, rhythm, verbal jokes, rhymes (Jakobson, 1980, 1985; Lotman, 1972; Segre, 1985), and, more recently, iconicity (Givon, 1990). Looking at the phenomenon of parallelism—defined as the correspondence, in sense or in construction, of successive elements—Jakobson (1980) reported that Tolstoy, fascinated by the narratives invented by peasant children, tried to come closer to "children's wisdom." In such attempts, "The linearity of proceeding by parallels had the elementary precision of folklore" (Jakobson, 1980, p. 105).

A convergent point of view was offered by the insightful suggestions of Italo Calvino (1988), who analyzed aspects of folk narratives and different ways in which they are told and transcribed. Narrative in popular tradition avoids pointless detail and favors repetition. Children's pleasure in storytelling rests on the expectation of what is repeated (e.g., situations, phrases, formulae). In songs and poetry, rhymes scan the rhythm, whereas in narratives, events "rhyme" one with the other. Calvino also liked the narrative effectiveness and the poetic suggestion of folk tales (that he transcribed and "re-wrote" in his "Fiabe italiane") for their economy, internal rhythm, and the essential logic with which they are constructed and told.

Is it possible to find such qualities in children's narratives? How much are children guided by rhythms and symmetries, and how sensitive are they to the synthetic qualities of a text structure? Do they try to reproduce these elements in their own retold or invented stories?

Because our narratives were produced by very young children and were closer to some typical features of oral production than to refined literary narratives, we used a syntactic analysis, which was developed by Blanche-Benveniste (1990) for spoken French and applied by Teberosky (1988) and by other scholars (Tolchinsky, 1990) to narrative, descriptive, and informative texts produced by children in order to identify configurations and patterns of children's written texts. It can be reasonably assumed that children use at least some of the production devices that also guide oral production: repetitions, reformulations, enumerations, symmetries, internal rhythms and rhymes, as well as formulaic (frozen) elements, use of quoted and reported speech, and particular verbal forms for narrating stories.

This type of syntactical analysis is based on a particular type of grid (*grille*) in which texts are displayed "comme des strophes, avec des unités qui ressemblent à des sortes de mètres d'une prosodie très particulière" ("as *strophes*, with elements that are like the 'meter' of a particular prosody"; Blanche-Benveniste, 1979, p. 164). Teberosky (1988) applied this same procedure to children's narratives to examine discursive configuration (e.g., symmetry, rhythm, and repetition) and syntactical organization in children's stories produced in an interactive setting.

This chapter focuses on data collected with a small group of first-grade children (some of whom were also interviewed during their second-grade year) and our attempts to carry out a parallel analysis of products and processes that can begin to map and clarify some of the research problems mentioned earlier.

SUBJECTS

Eight children were observed at least twice (some three and four times) on different tasks. They were enrolled in the same classroom in a school following a Montessori tradition, where no particular attention was given to developing children's written composition. Children were mainly of middle-class social background. Our first observations occurred at the end of the first grade, when the children (mean age: 6 years, 9 months) were writing conventionally but had large differences in their mastery of independent writing, in both form and content. The children were asked to compose two different narratives, one in dyadic peer interaction and another in an adult–child setting. Four of these children were also observed in a second and third round when they were enrolled (with the same teacher) in second grade (mean age: 7 years, 8 months).

PROCEDURE

Different types of tasks that were given to the children in different sessions are described in the following paragraphs.

Task A. Children were grouped in pairs that were not too heterogeneous. They were asked to work together, alternating the role of writing and dictating, in order to write down a story that both of them already knew well. One of us (Morani) attended and audiorecorded, avoiding any intervention and answering only children's procedural questions. In some instances, Morani left the room for a certain period during the task, leaving the tape recorder running. Both children wrote their common story on the same piece of paper, but the different contributions could be distinguished because they were given different colored pens. In the transcribed protocols, we also noted the actions that children applied to their texts while writing, such as erasing part of it or changing characters or words.

Task B. In a second task, each child was asked to dictate a story to the experimenter, so that she could write it down, starting from a figurative input. This situation was similar to that used in previous studies by Pontecorvo (Pontecorvo & Zuccchermaglio, 1989). Children were given an image, divergent and unusual, and purposefully strange, as suggested by Rodari (1973). The figurative stimulus was a drawing of a table with a broken leg and with tears coming out from a sketched face (see Fig. 12.1). This second task appealed to the children's imagination, producing a possible conflict between the features of an inanimate and everyday object and the induced attribution of animacy.

Task C. Four of the eight children were observed and videotaped in second grade and were asked to compose a story in dyads, starting from drawings representing figures in motion: a child jumping many times, and two children

FIG. 12.1. Adaptation of an image from Bruno Munari.

FIG. 12.2.   Adaptation of a drawing from Maurice Sendak (Cochet & Vassalli, 1988).

running in the rain (see Figs. 12.2 and 12.3). One dyad produced a story based on a verbal input: a witch whose magic was always wrong.

CORPUS OF DATA

The corpus of data consists of (a) four known tales written in pairs, (b) six stories invented by individual children and *dictated* to the scribe, (c) two stories invented by a dyad starting from figurative inputs and dictated to the scribe,

FIG. 12.3.   Adaptation of a drawing from Peter Spier (1983).

and (d) three stories invented and written by two second-grade dyads starting from figurative and verbal inputs.

All the interactions with their verbal and nonverbal aspects were fully transcribed from audio- and videotapes. In this study, our analysis of the processes concentrates on the protocols of the nine peer interactions.

PROCEDURE FOR PUTTING THE STORIES IN GRIDS

Aiming at analyzing the children's stories from the point of view of variations in the possible stylistic devices used by children, we found no satisfactory suggestions in the existing psychological literature on children's stories or in the traditional linguistic approaches to written texts. Rather, we thought that the procedure of the *grilles* (grids) developed by C. Blanche-Benveniste (1990) could be very useful because: it assumes that even nonliterate composers look for conventional and even formal ways of writing; it does not analyze the text into molecular pieces but retains larger textual units; and the resulting visual presentation of children's products permits us to emphasize literary phenomena such as repetition, parallelism, and rhythm. We put all our narrative texts in grids, which served as useful devices for visual presentation and for analysis.

The starting point of our analysis is not the sentence but the syntactic constructions that in most cases coincide with the verb phrase. In the latter situation, the verb is the governing element (*élément recteur*) from which other elements depend, such as subject and complements that can also be replaced by pronouns or null forms (clitic pronouns and person/number suffixes in the verb). Before or after the verb, it is possible to find many associated elements (certain types of adverbs, connectives, or prepositional phrases) that cannot be replaced by pronouns.

The elements that are organized by the verb receive from it the modality (e.g., assertive, negative, or interrogative). Sentences can also have contrastive features, as in the following example:

Tutti i bambini sapevano saltare e lui no
(All the children could jump, and he couldn't)

The elements can also be topicalized and dislocated at the beginning of the sentence (this is frequent in Romance languages), as in the next example:

Era il lupo che stava a letto al posto della nonna
(It was the wolf who was in the bed at the place of the grandmother)

The associated elements can be in different places; some can also have a parenthetical role, such as *for example*. We found phrases of this type in children's rewritten stories, when they introduced a narrator's comment such as

come si era già previsto
(as it was already foreseen)

The elements that depend on the verb are completely determined by the argument structure of the verb itself. For example, a verb such as *put* has two obligatory elements: the thing that is put and its location. In the grid, however, verbs are always put in the same column, even if they have very different features and number of complements.

Verbs of "saying" are those that introduce the characters' talk and/or thinking. They are distinguished from the others and put in another column because they introduce particular types of complements. From the point of view of children's narrative development, it is particularly interesting to see whether and how much narratives are constructed through quoted or reported speech.

Eugenia's invented story (see Table 12.1) illustrates the procedure. The elements that play the same syntactic role (the subjects, the complements) are located in the same column, following the order they have in the sentence. Thus, the text can be read on two levels: the horizontal level of the *rows* (the syntagmatic axis) that corresponds to the natural sequence of the text and the vertical level of the *columns* (the paradigmatic axis) that emphasizes the ways in which different syntactical roles are filled. Each syntactical element has a place, as is the case for the postponed subjects (which are located in column E of Table 12.1). In some rows there can be many blank spaces; some columns correspond to a syntactical structure that is present only in some portions of the text. This is the case of the quoted speech going from columns H through K and following the mental verb of column G.

The grid is an instrument for discovering configurations and looking at expressive aspects. The graphic display of the texts permits us to discover and present the configurations (patterns) of the rewritten and dictated texts. Teberosky (1988) said that the visual configuration shows how children's stories develop between the narrative of events and the quotation of reported speech, and how the text (in its original etymological meaning) progresses both by repeating the same syntactical schema represented by the horizontal axis and by varying the paradigmatic elements represented on the vertical axis.

STRUCTURAL LEVELS OF CHILDREN'S STORIES

To develop a synthetical comparison of all 15 stories, we used a simplified analysis of goal structure drawn from studies on story grammar (Stein & Glenn, 1979; Stein & Policastro, 1984), which permitted us to distinguish between different levels in story structure. This was a useful basis for comparing the stories

TABLE 12.1.
Eugenia, Level 8, Story 8

	A	B	C	D	E	F	G	H	I	J	K
1.				C'era una volta	un tavolo che era stato buttato via						
2.			tutti	passavano		da quella strada					
3.	e			gli davano		calci					
4.		un giorno		gli si ruppe	una gamba						
5.				passano	i mesi						
6.				passò di lì	un operaio						
7.	e						pensò				
8.				lo aggiustò				se aggiusto	questo tavolo	lo potrò portare	a casa
9.	e			se lo portò		a casa		perché uno, due, tre, quattro, cinque, sei			

produced in the different tasks by pairs of children and by single children, respectively. Table 12.2 shows the results of this analysis. The attribution of a structural level to the stories written by the children does not show big differences due to the conditions (inventing versus rewriting), and also because children's stories are, for the most part, at high levels of structural articulation, particularly when they are produced in dyads. Rather, the type of input given to children should be well analyzed. In the example of the table with the broken leg that is crying, the children were faced with the problem of deciding whether the table was still an inanimate object or a possible animate protagonist. There were different solutions to this problem, including good solutions given by Eugenia (Table 12.1) and by Laura (Table 12.3). In Eugenia's story, the table is the object of bad and good actions from humans, whereas in Laura's story, the table becomes a protagonist and can also think and speak.

PARALLELISM AND REPETITION AS STYLISTIC DEVICES

The arrangement of the stories in the grid sheds some light on mechanisms guiding children's production of stylistic features such as parallelisms and repetitions. Lotman (1972) considered *repetition* an important organizing principle of poetic text: He said that different types of repetition constitute a texture of

TABLE 12.2
Story Structures

Task 1: Invented story from figurative input (First grade)

1.	Patrizio	Level 3 (action sequence)
2.	Federica	Level 4 (reactive sequence)
3.	Giordano & Tommaso	Level 4 (reactive sequence)
4.	Neri	Level 6 (goal without obstacle but with ending)
5.	Caterina	Level 8 (goal with obstacle and ending)
6.	Laura	Level 8 (goal with obstacle and ending)
7.	Tommaso & Giordano	Level 8 (goal with obstacle and ending)
8.	Eugenia	Level 8 (goal with obstacle and ending)

Task 2: Rewriting a well-known story in interaction (First grade)

9.	Neri & Simona	Level 6 (goal without obstacle and ending)
10.	Patrizio & Federica	Level 6 (goal without obstacle and ending)
11.	Eugenia & Giordano	Level 8 (goal with obstacle and ending)
12.	Laura & Caterina	Level 8 (goal with obstacle and ending)

Task 3: Invented story from figurative and verbal input (Second grade)

13.	Eugenia & Giordano II	Level 8 (goal with obstacle and ending)
14.	Laura & Caterina IIa	Level 8 (goal with obstacle and ending)
15.	Laura & Caterina IIb	Level 8 (goal with obstacle and ending)

TABLE 12.3
Laura, Level 8, Story 6

	A	B	C	D	E	F	G	H	I	J	K	L	M
1.								C'era una volta un tavolo che aveva troppe cose sopra					
2.	e	allora			si rompe	una gamba							
3.	e				incominciò a far	tantissime lagrime							
4.	e	poi					disse		povero me		chi mi aggiusterà	questa gamba?	
5.									povero me	se se ne accorge il padrone	mi tirerà	insieme alla spazzatura	
6.									io invece non voglio essere rotto				
7.	e								non è colpa mia	ma è colpa del bambino			
8.								quindi	voglio subito far rompere			questi vasi	
9.								così almeno		se la prende		col bambino	che mi ha messo queste cose
10.				il padrone	se ne accorse								
11.			come aveva pregato	il tavolo	sgridarono	il bambino							

238

complex meanings that lie on common linguistic structure. Jakobson (1980) considered *parallelism* an important mechanism, a system of correspondence that operates at different levels: in the composition and ordering of syntactical constructions, of morphological forms, of lexical synonyms, even of prosodical schemes. Parallelism is expressed through links of similarity, contiguity, and contrast between units. It is present particularly in traditional and folk narratives, which children's stories closely resemble.

By describing the different types of repetition that produce parallelism, Lotman underlined some principles regarding metrics of words and verses: Isometrism of two words is a necessary condition for their replaceability. The children's texts collected in this research contain both parallelisms and different types of repetition. In Patrizio's story (see Table 12.4), which is a sequence of actions (Level 3 from the point of view of story structure), the style is strongly paratactical (clauses are simply put in succession) and the rhythm is given by the isometry of the verbs. The text is organized around verbs that are bisyllabic and unaccented. A rhythmic principle seems to be the organizing mechanism of the text.

Lotman (1972) distinguished between two main types of repetition: the repetition of elements that are semantically different and the repetition of elements that are semantically homogeneous, such as synonyms or even the repetition of the same word. Eugenia's story (see Table 12.1) contains a repetition of the first type. The Italian verb *passare* has two different meanings indicating: first, the passage of time (row 5), and second, the physical action of walking (row 6).

In Caterina's story (see Table 12.5), we found a more complex use of repetition that assumes different forms of parallelism. At the beginning of each new line (and sentence) in the grid, there is regular alternation for seven times of the two characters (the table and the lady). This alternative presentation produces a parallelism around which the whole text is organized.

In this same text, at a local level, another use of repetition produces a peculiar stylistic effect (see lines 8 to 12). From the metrical point of view, the expressions in Column *E* are isometric segments (all of senary meter); semantically, whereas the adjective is always the same (*piccolo* = small), the nouns listed are all part of the same category (cooking and eating tools).

TABLE 12.4
Patrizio, Level 3, Story 1

	A	B	C	D	E	F
1.			*Un tavolo*	*si apre*	*il cassetto*	
2.	*poi*			*si rompe*		
3.	*poi*			*piange*		
4.	*poi*			*ride*		
5.	*poi*	*dopo dopo succede che*		*si rompe*	*tutto il tavolo*	
6.	*poi*			*si rompe*	*tutta la casa*	
7.	*poi*					*finita*

TABLE 12.5
Caterina, Level 8, Story 5

A	B	C	D	E	F	G
1.		*C'era una volta una signora che aveva comprato una pentola*				
2.			*la mise*	*sul tavolo*		
3. *e*		*il tavolo*	*si spezzò*	*una gamba*		
4.		*la signora*	*chiamò*	*un falegname*	*che aggiustò*	*la gamba del tavolo*
5.		*il tavolo*	*era contento*			
6. *e*		*la signora*	*non comprò più*	*pentole pesanti*		
7. *e*		*il tavolo*	*non si spezza più*	*le gambe*		
8.		*la signora*	*ci appoggia solo*	*pentole piccole*		
9. *e*				*piatti piccoli*		
10. *e*				*bicchieri piccoli*		
11. *e*				*stoviglie piccole*		
12. *e*				*padelle piccole*		
13. *e*	*così*	*il tavolo*	*non si spezza più*	*le gambe*		
14. *e*			*non piange più*	*per tutta la vita*		

These segments are "rhythmical equivalents" (Lotman, 1970). Their order can be reversed without changing the meaning, as happens with poetical verses. The segments are ruled also by the principle of secondary synonymy, according to which two words are perceived as being equivalent because they are isometric. Caterina's text is organized on this basis, and repetitions are used in a rather sophisticated way that is similar to that of a poetic text.

A similar repetition strategy is in operation, at a higher level of invention, in another story that was produced by interaction between Laura and Caterina when they were in second grade, on the basis of a verbal input (i.e., a young witch whose magic was always wrong). The story's plot (see story 15 in Table 12.6) is built around the young witch's repeated and continuously failing attempts to transform one thing or person into something else. Transformation, as Propp (1927/1988) said, is a typical mechanism of fairy tales. The two girls use this mechanism and develop the plot both by repeating the same syntactical structure and by varying the lexical elements. The story is structured in a symmetrical way that generates a comic effect. Each "magic" attempt by the witch to transform herself into something beautiful and attractive results in an unattractive and even repellent animal. The repetition of these transformation errors creates the comic mood of the story.

TEXTUAL ASPECTS: FORMULAIC ELEMENTS, VERBAL SYSTEM, AND QUOTED SPEECH

In children's stories, particularly in rewritten ones, it is possible to find elements of formulaic origin that could be taken directly from the original story. It is easier to find such "frozen" elements among the "associated" ones (as they were defined earlier) because they appear in two rewritten stories (e.g., "Little Red

Riding Hood" by Eugenia and Giordano and by Laura and Caterina: *strada facendo* (on the way), *in verità* (indeed), and *nei paraggi* (in the surroundings). These associated elements are used as cohesion (and coherence) devices; often they are locutions that are not part of the basic spoken vocabulary and are rather rare. As has been found in oral narratives (see Orsolini & Di Giacinto, chap. 4, this volume), the more frequent use of these expressions in well-known stories reveals the role played by memorization of "frozen" pieces, which is also the case in early written production. However, because these formulaic elements are more present in the rewriting of well-known stories in sentences characterized by a syntactical complexity (e.g., the presence of a hypotactical style with refined forms of subordination), it can be hypothesized that written forms are more easily internalized by remembering those narrative modes that are built on repeated experiences of storytelling and story reading done by adults.

The procedure of putting stories in grids revealed a large prevalence of verbal constructions compared with other constructions. Even the more simple stories are composed mainly of action sequences and quoted and/or reported speech. Two other aspects of children's stories need further analysis: the verbal system and the use of quoted speech.

As concerns the verbal system, previous research on preschool children's narrative skills (Pontecorvo, 1994) suggested looking at children's use of different past tenses in story construction. Surprisingly, even very young children tried to use the past perfect form (*passato remoto* in Italian) when telling a story, although this verbal form has almost completely disappeared in Italian everyday spoken language (with the exception of the language spoken in a few regions of southern Italy) and has been replaced by the composed forms of the past.

This trend was confirmed in our corpus. Out of a total of 238 definite verbal forms (that have a directing role in the clause), 100 (42% of the total) are past perfect forms. Contrasting highly structured stories (nine stories of level 8; see Table 12.2) with poorly structured ones (six stories of levels 3 to 6; see Table 12.2), the mean number of past perfect forms is 10.2 versus 1.3. There is a very strong link between story organization and use of past perfect. This is also true of the verbs of "saying" that, in most cases, introduce quoted speech (where past tense is never used). This is additional evidence that the past perfect is the form of the (traditional) narrator's "voice" (Bakhtin, 1975).

Quoted speech (more than reported speech) is another characteristic element that is present in a distinct way in syntactically complex stories and that is revealed through the grids, because a special space on the right of each grid is reserved for it. This permits us to note at least two modes of using the quoted speech in children's stories. One mode inserts quoted speech *within the narration*, alternating narrative and quoted speech in a rather balanced way. The other mode separates the narrative from the sequences of quoted speech in a rather clear-cut way. The two modes are exemplified by two different stories of the same dyad (Laura and Caterina, IIa and IIb); their different uses of quoted speech

TABLE 12.6
Laura and Caterina IIb, Level 8, Story 15

	A	*B*	*C*	*D*	*E*	*F*	*G*	*H*	*I*	*J*	*K*	*L*	*M*	*N*	*O*	*P*	*Q*	*R*
1.			*C'era una volta una strega che ne combinava di tutti i colori*															
2.			*una volta*				*doveva trasformarsi*	*in una farfalla*										
3.		*invece*					*si trasformò*	*in un ragno*										
4.					*lei*		*non se ne accorse*		*in città*	*vestita da ragno*								
5.		*e*					*andò*											
6.					*il suo fidanzato*		*si spaventò*											
7.		*e*									*disse*		*aiuto un ragno*					
8.		*e*									*disse*		*è vero se lo sente*	*la mia fidanzata*	*mi lascerà*			
9.		*allora*			*la strega*		*tornò*		*nel suo laboratorio*									
10.		*e*					*si trasformò*	*in una principessa*										

11.					si trasformò	in un rospo	disse	così	non va	dovrei essere		un pò più precisa
12.	e				andò							
13.	e				se ne accorse							
14.	e				la vide	in città						
15.			il suo fidanzato	quando			disse		mamma mia che paura			
16.	e						disse	adesso		non torno		più a casa
17.								ma		resto così		
18.		dopo un pò eccolo	il suo fidanzato									
19.	e						disse	ora		ti piaccio		
20.	e						disse			sei		molto più bella
21.										credevo	che fossi scappato	
22.								quando		mi hai visto così		
23.									o noi	era	solo per finta	
24.								allora		hai fatto	solo per finta	che non ti piacevo

are evident from the two grids. Table 12.6 offers an example of the first mode, and Table 12.7 gives an example of the second mode. This shows that when a certain level of articulation is reached, a certain use of quoted speech appears.

This is particularly evident in the rewriting of "Little Red Riding Hood," in which there is a canonical dialogue between the protagonist and the disguised wolf (as exemplified in Ferreiro & Zuccdermaglio, chap. 10, this volume). In this, as in other cases, the use of quoted speech is a device for coherently developing and connecting the text, as observed by Orsolini, Devescovi, and Fabbretti (1991) in storytelling of younger children.

THE INTERRELATION BETWEEN WAYS
OF INTERACTING AND WAYS OF INVENTING

In order to reach the second aim of this chapter, we will complement the preceding analysis of the products with an exploratory analysis of children's interactions. We focus on five interactions produced by two dyads (Laura & Cate and Eugenia & Giordano) in first and second grade under different conditions, which are specified in Table 12.8.

The five interactions appear to be rather different. They differ strikingly in the number of turns used by the dyads to produce the story together. Both dyads used the highest number of turns in rewriting "Little Red Riding Hood" when they were in first grade, whereas the lowest number of turns was used in inventing a story from a figurative stimulus when they were in second grade. There was an effect of familiarity and mastery of the task, because all second-grade interactions were shorter and had many fewer digressions. However, there could also be an effect of the visual stimulus (versus the verbal one), because the images of one child jumping or of two children running in the rain could be a more effective stimulus for the dyadic interactions; the collective invention might be facilitated by the images representing characters who are moving, as if they support the anchoring of sentences as a third party in the interaction. This effect is particularly strong for story 14 by Laura and Caterina in Table 12.7.

In comparing the type of interaction carried out by Laura and Caterina in three different tasks, we can see how the two girls differ in their ways of writing and reading. In first grade, Laura is faster in producing expressions and in writing them; Caterina asks for a rereading of the already written text (and she does it better than Laura); she is annoyed by nonconventional writing and often says to her partner, "You made a big mistake." Although she is aware of spelling errors in a piece of writing, often she cannot tell which word is misspelled. In the first line of excerpt 1, Laura finds a mistake in Caterina's writing of the word *cacciatore* (she has written *cacatore*) by reading aloud, and she jokes about it because the writing resembles a naughty word; Caterina, on the other hand, is really worried about this type of error.

TABLE 12.7
Laura and Caterina IIa, Level 8, Story 14

	A	B	C	D	E	F	G	H	I	J	K	L	M
1.			C'era una volta un bambino che voleva imparare a saltare										
2.	e				non sapeva								
3.			tutti i bambini		sapevano saltare								
4.	e		lui		no								
5.		un giorno	un bambino		si prese gioco	di lui							
6.	e				si mise a piangere								
7.			il bambino	dalla rabbia	fece	un salto molto alto							
8.	e		il bambino		rimase sbalordito								
9.	e				scappò via								
10.			il bambino		si mise a ridere								
11.	e		il bambino		tornò	a casa	saltellando						
12.	e		la mamma					disse		dove		hai imparato a saltare	
13.										perchè	un mio amico	mi aveva fatto arrabbiare	
14.										e così		ho saltato	così in alto
15.	e		la mamma					gli disse	bravo			ti vorrei mandare	
16.	e		la mamma					pensò	no			io non ci voglio andare	al circo
17.			il bambino					rispose				non ti mando	
18.									vabbene				
19.									però			dovrai saltare	per tutta la vita

TABLE 12.8
Type of Request, Number of Turns and Words, and Ratio of Turns to Words

	Stories	Number of Turns	Number of Words	Turns/ Words
11. Eugenia & Giordano I	"Little Red Riding Hood"	1,036	166	6.241
12. Laura & Cate I	"Little Red Riding Hood"	418	155	2.697
13. Eugenia & Giordano II	"Children Who Are Running" (visual stimulus)	249	77	3.234
14. Laura & Cate IIa	"Boy Who Is Jumping" (visual stimulus)	71	124	0.573
15. Laura & Cate IIb	"Young Witch" (verbal stimulus)	134	164	0.817

Excerpt 1: Task 1, First Grade (turns 378–386)

L: *Cacatore*, what does it mean? [she comments on what Caterina has written]

C: *Cacciatore* (Hunter)! *Ca ccia* ... [she reads by emphasizing the double letter]

L: She has written *cacatore* [Laura addresses the observer]

C: But I wanted to write *cacciatore* (hunter)!

L: *Cacatore* ... ehm ehm! [Laura teases Caterina]

C: *Caccia* ... [she whispers, and then she erases the previous writing]

L: With two Cs and one I ... *cacciatore* [she carefully pronounces all the letters]

L: *Cacatore* [she makes a song]

C: But don't use it! It is also a naughty word!

They finally correct it, but Caterina is much more worried than Laura about this spelling problem. Laura cares more about composing, and Caterina cares more about transcribing. Their interaction is full of conflicts and negotiations and, consequently, is rather long. Typically, the conflicts concern ways of spelling and, just a few times, ideas or word choices. In general, the ideating aspects are secondary: There is only one attempt at macro-ideation, done by Caterina (at the half of their interaction), which is related to the wolf's trickery about the longer or the shorter way to reach the grandmother's house. As was seen in the previous data, the lack of interaction about ideation seems to be attributable more to the representation of the writing task in children just becoming literate (*writing* means *transcribing*) than to the fact that they have to write a known story.

The second graders' interactions are completely different. First, they are much shorter and much more focused on the invention dimension. In particular, when the two girls invent the story starting from the visual stimulus (which shows a boy jumping many times), the ideation challenge is perfectly shared by them. They alternately assume the role of ideating and that of writing each piece of the text (which is never less than one clause) in a regular way, without any discussion of graphic and spelling questions as they did the year before. This is apparent in excerpt 2.

Excerpt 2: Task IIa, Second Grade

L. says and C. writes:	Once upon a time there was a boy who wanted to learn to jump.
C. says and L. writes:	And he didn't know how to do it.
L. says and C. writes:	All the children could jump and he couldn't.
C. says and L. writes:	One day a child teased him because he couldn't jump and he began crying.
L. says and C. writes:	The boy was so enraged that he made a very high jump.

This type of interaction goes on until the end of the story. The dyad composes a story of 26 clauses and of 124 words through a limited number of turns (71), as compared to the other interactions with very few repetitions and only one negotiation sequence (about replacing *okay* with *very well*). As shown in Table 12.8, it is one of the smallest ratios between turns and text length. It seems as if the image plays the role of a common ground that defines the production framework as an anchoring device (Resnick, 1991) to which they refer implicitly.

Moreover, in their second-grade interactions, the two girls are much more competent in composing, as illustrated by the second story based on the verbal stimulus. The interaction here is of still another type: The person who is creating a piece is also writing it down directly (different from what was exemplified in excerpt 2), and the written sequences are much longer than in the previous case. The two girls produce much longer and more complex narrative sequences, because the story has a multi-episode structure. The different episodes are offered by the successive mistakes of the young witch who does not succeed in performing the desired magic transformations, as shown in excerpt 3.

Excerpt 3: Task IIb, Second Grade

Caterina:	Once she had to transform herself into a butterfly and instead she transformed herself into a spider.
Laura:	She didn't realize it and went to town dressed as a spider; her boyfriend was frightened and said help a spider and said . . .

PLAYING WITH WORDS: THE SEARCH FOR STYLE THROUGH LEXICAL AND MORPHOLOGICAL CHOICES

Even when the dyad members have the same level of competence, the two children can still be very different, both in the type of competence and in their attitude toward the task. This is the case for Eugenia and Giordano, who have different attitudes and different competences in text composition. Their first-grade interaction is full of conflicts and negotiations (it lasts 1,036 turns), mainly about spelling and graphic questions but also concerning lexical and syntactical choices. Giordano is faster in reading and in producing adequate expressions for the story. Eugenia is taken with the difficulties of decoding single words; she is worried mainly about the graphemic aspects of writing, and she dictates dividing in syllables. They succeed, however, in adapting themselves to each other's needs during the interaction.

These children differ in the way in which they figure out how the story of "Little Red Riding Hood" should be rewritten. Giordano wants to introduce amusing variations, such as giving a name to the wolf ("A wolf whose name was Giovanni"; see excerpt 4a), but Eugenia strongly rejects this. Both of them laugh about rhymes that came out accidentally (*nonnina–malatina*; see excerpt 4b) and about linguistic games that emerge from mistakes in writing (*Lupo–pupo*; see excerpt 4c), but Eugenia is really worried about the risk of introducing any variation in the known and ritualized story and does not accept any change in the story, not even by introducing some elements of a linguistic joke (4d).

Excerpt 4: Task 1, First Grade

a. (turns 314–318)
G: *Strada facendo* (going on her way)
G: *Incontrò un lupo* (She met a wolf)
E: **Ma stai zitto tu!**[1] (But don't tell anything!)
G: *che si chiamava Giovanni* (whose name was John) [Both smile]
G: **Ma io la so così la storia!** (But I know the story in this way!)

b. (turns 492–499)
E. *Dalla mia nonnina* (to my grammy)
G: *che* (who)
E: **Ehi! Hai scritto soltanto con una n! Nonina hai scritto!** (Ehm! You have written with only one N! You have written *nonina*.)
G: **No ... no ... ah è vero!** (No ... no ... it is true!)
G: *che è molto malatina* (who is very ill) [he is joking about the rhyme created by the two diminutives, but E. does not accept it]
E: *che è molto malata* (who is very ill).

c. (turns 517–525)
G: *dove sto andando ... dalla mia nonnina che è molto malatina* (where I am going ... to visit my grammy who is very ill)
E: **No! C'è scritto: nonnina che è molto molatina!** (No! Here it is written *nonnina* who is very *molatina*)
G: **Come molatina?** [they smile about the change of letter]

---

[1]The text to be written is in italics; the comments are in boldface.

G: [now seriously] *malatina*

E: **No! Non mi piace così!** (No! I don't like it so!)

d. (turns 528–532)

E: *che è molto malata . . . e il lupo gli disse . . .* (who is very ill and the wolf told her)

G: *Il . . . il . . . l/l/lup . . .* [He articulates the letters while writing]

E: *il pupo* [teasing him for the mistake: both are amused by the joke, because *pupo* means *baby*]

G: *Il pupo gli disse* (The baby said) [smiling]

E: [becoming serious] *il lupo . . . il lupo . . . gli disse* (the wolf . . . the wolf . . . told her)

It could be that their different attitudes correspond to possible different phases in reproducing a well-known story. Giordano seems to master both the story structure and tropes. He invents larger pieces of text, and he is more familiar with appropriate verb tenses, such as the past perfect in Italian (see excerpt 5a). Both are aware of the need to use appropriate narrative locutions (see excerpt 5b and 5c).

Excerpt 5: Task 1, First Grade

a. (turns 211–224)

E: *E la mamma gli dice di andare* (And the mother tells her to go)

G: *gli disse* (told her)

E: *gli dice* (tells her)

G: *gli disse* (told her)

E: *gli dice* (tells her)

G: *gli disse* (told her)

E: *Dov'è?* (Where is it?)

G: *Qui . . . gli disse* (Here . . . she told her)

E: *Ma va bene "gli dice!"* (But tells her it is very good)

G: *Sì, ma è meglio "disse!"* (Yes, but told her it is better)

b. (turns 248–264)

G: *Strada facendo* [a typical narrative locution meaning *going on her way*]

G: *Incontrò il lupo* (She met the wolf)

c. (turns 899–905)

E: *in quel momento . . .* (at this point)

E. and G. [together]: *In quel momento* (at this point)

E: *Nei paraggi . . .* (in the surroundings) [a rather unusual locution]

G: *Che succede?* (What happens?)

E: *Vai avanti . . . scrivi nei paraggi* (Go on . . . write in the surroundings)

G: *nei par . . .* [whispering]

E: *Nelle vicinanze vorrebbe dire . . . invece che vicinanze . . . paraggi con due*
      g: paraggi . . . c'era . . . c'era (It should mean nearby . . . instead that
      nearby . . . *paraggi* with a double g . . . there was . . . there was) [E. ex-
      plains the meaning of this unusual locution by offering a synonym.]

Traditional stories provide important linguistic knowledge for situations and
expressions that children can use both in rewriting and inventing; perhaps only
after that is a certain threshold of familiarity reached. Then, in a successive
phase, it is possible to use parts and pieces of this knowledge to build new
stories, beginning with introducing variations in the story's *suzjet* and keeping
the *fabula* (according to the distinction made by Jakobson, 1985).

When the same two children interact in second grade in order to invent a
new story, their interaction is much shorter (249 turns) and easier. The topics
of the negotiation activity have changed completely. There are only two spelling
observations versus nine sequences devoted to punctuation and nine devoted
to aloud reading what has already been written. The children are engaged in a
cooperative ideation that is very rich and complex; therefore, reading the text
that has been written after producing so many variants is a necessary strategy
for remembering and distinguishing what has been invented from what has also
been transcribed. Laura and Caterina in task IIa (exemplified in excerpt 2)
transcribe all that they invented, whereas Eugenia and Giordano leave out many
alternatives. There are many sequences concerning narrative and stylistic
choices (that mainly concern the choice of more suitable expressions).

All these interactive sequences can be usefully analyzed with the grids that
we used for the products. This transposition requires us to isolate those parts
of the interaction that are proposals of the text that has to be written, by
eliminating all the conversational parts (this method has been applied systematically to another study; see Pontecorvo & Morani, 1993). The transposition,
which keeps the turns' order, permits us to see that most of the invention style
of this dyad is done along the paradigmatic axis; that is, through repetition and
variation of items that occupy the same column in the grid because they play
the same syntactical role. Three sequences are reproduced here.

In the first one, which concerns the very beginning of the story and needs
30 turns, the two children formulate different choices for the beginning of the
story, trying out both traditional and unusual ways. The final result is rather
mixed (see Table 12.9 for the interaction in grids).

In the second example, the object is the emotional response of the two
protagonists. The dyad tries out the expressive force of three locutions (frightened, nervous, fearful) and checks their relative stylistic effectiveness in order
to express appropriately the emotional response of the two protagonists (see
Table 12.10).

In the third example, the negotiation about the central part of the plot (i.e.,
about a part of the "initiating event") requires 15 turns, and the children utter

and then leave aside three main alternatives concerning the behavior of the two protagonists and of their parents: "eventually the parents found them," "the children were hidden," "the children were hidden in a bench of another house." The final solution chosen is "the children got lost" (see Table 12.11).

It is important to emphasize how the grid is adapted to represent the very composition process in the dyadic interaction, because it shows the types of proposal and transformation, the length of the text on which common elaboration takes place, and the syntactic elements that are taken into consideration.

CONCLUSIONS

The different types of analysis that we have carried out on stories produced by children and on the interactive processes through which invention and transcription were realized by them led us to conclude that even early literate children use peculiar stylistic devices and look for better "literary" solutions when composing stories.

In particular, data analysis shows that:

1. Mechanisms of parallelism and repetition are followed by children in their individual composition, together with rhythmical patterns and isometrism.
2. Stylistic questions concern lexical choices (e.g., the use of peculiar locutions operating as connectives), syntactical constructions (e.g., ways of using quoted speech), and morphological choices (e.g., concerning the verbal system).
3. The stylistic aspects of children composing stories came into evidence when we analyzed the different ways two dyads interacted on different tasks in which at least two dimensions had to be taken into account:
   a. The peculiar ways of functioning of the dyads when faced with the need of negotiating text ideation and transcription, thus the "form" of their interaction.
   b. The "content" of these interactions, that is the choice of the objects of their discourse.

Concerning this last point, we found that dyads have rather different ways of interacting that could depend on age, familiarity with the task and with the partner, the type of elicitation, and their text production style. This aspect, which needs further research work, was more systematically explored in another study (Pontecorvo & Morani, 1993) in which 13 dyads (of two age groups) were observed twice on two different tasks, using three types of composing behaviors as dependent variables (what is proposed or repeated and written, what is only proposed, and what is only written).

TABLE 12.9

Eugenia and Giordano, Second Grade: Interaction Sequence for the Beginning of the Story

E:		*c'era* (there was)	*una volta* (once upon a time)	
G:		*c'è* (there is)	*oggi* (today)	
G:	*e* (and)	*ci sarà* (there will be)	*domani* (tomorrow)	
E:			*una volta* (once upon a time)	
E:			*una volta* (once upon a time)	
G:			*una volta* (once upon a time)	*due signorine* (two young ladies)
E:			*una volta* (once upon a time)	
G:			*una volta* (once upon a time)	

	c'era	una volta			a casa	
E:				di notte (at night)		
G:	c'era (there was)	una volta (once upon a time)		di un giorno (at one day)		
E:		una volta (once upon a time)		una notte (one night)		
E:		una volta (once upon a time)		di notte (at night)		
E:			un diluvio universale (a universal deluge)		a casa (at home)	mia (of me)
G:		una volta (once upon a time)			a casa (at the house)	di due bambini (of two children)
E:		una volta (once upon a time)	due bambini (two children)		a casa (at the house)	di due bambini (of two children)
E:			due bambini (two children)			
G:		una volta (once upon a time)				

253

TABLE 12.10

Eugenia and Giordano, Second Grade: Interaction Sequence for the Emotional Response of the Two Protagonists

G:	i due bambini (the two children)				che (who)	non sapevano che fare (didn't know what to do)
E:					che (who)	non sapevano che fare (didn't know what to do)
E:			impauriti (frightened)			
G:			impauriti (frightened)			
E:			nervosi (nervous)			
E:			nervosi (nervous)			
E:		e (and)	nervosi (nervous)			
G:				dalla paura (by the fear)		
E:		e (and)	nervosi (nervous)	dalla paura (by the fear)		
G:			impauriti (frightened)	dalla paura (by the fear)		non sapevano che fare (didn't know what to do)
E:	I due bambini (The two children)		impauriti (frightened)	dalla paura (by the fear)	che (who)	non sapevano che fare (didn't know what to do)

TABLE 12.11

Eugenia and Giordano, Second Grade: Interaction Sequence for the Initiating Event

G:	finalmente dopo un po' (eventually then)	i genitori (the parents)	li trovarono (found them)	di un'altra casa (of another house)
G:		i bambini (the children)		
E:		i bambini (the children)	si erano nascosti (were hidden)	
G:		bambini (children)		
E:		i bambini (the children)	si eran nascosti (were hidden)	nella credenza (in the bench)
E:		i bambini (the children)	si erano persi (got lost) / persi (lost)	
G:		i bambini (the children)	si erano persi (got lost)	

Generally speaking, the results from the collaborative settings used in this research push us to reconsider any clear-cut dichotomy between oral and written language (Olson, 1977). The texts we analyzed—before they were written down—were uttered, repeated, varied, and negotiated. They were oral texts, they were the object of an oral discourse, and they were affected by oral narratives that children experience long before becoming literate.

Although written language is "a complex cultural product" (Vygotsky, 1978) both in its macrostructure and microstructure, we must not consider the distinction between orality and literacy in a simplified way, in particular when the aim is to understand children's development in written language from both a stylistic and an expressive point of view. There are overlapping situations in which there is an intertwining between orality and literacy that should be assumed. It is also necessary to take full account of the genre that is produced. The narrative is present earlier and more often than the essay and appears in both the everyday and the school experience of young children. According to Pontecorvo and Zucchermaglio (1989), when writing narratives is considered as a textual composing process (putting aside the transcribing aspects and the acquisition of a writing system), it emerges from oral practices that are present in the culture and in the child's experience, such as knowledge of story genre and experience with different types of narratives. That happens not only through storytelling and story reading but also through pretend play and in family and school communication—basically, anytime children are asked to recount actions and events. For this reason, looking for stylistic devices and mechanisms we have to consider this important interaction between orality and literacy, considering that orality cannot be reduced to dialogue and that certain forms of oral discourse, largely used in the narrative genre, can directly affect the related written forms.

ACKNOWLEDGMENT

The research work reported here was carried out with an Italian Ministry of University and of Scientific and Technological Research grant assigned to C. Pontecorvo for the years 1990–1991.

REFERENCES

Bakhtin, M. M. (1975). *Voprosy literatury i estetiki* [Fiction and aesthetics]. Moscow: Izdatel'stvo Chudozestvennaja literatura.

Blanche-Benveniste, C. (1979). Des grilles pour le Français parlé [Grids for spoken French]. *Recherches sur le francais parlé, 2*, 163–208.

Blanche-Benveniste, C. (1990). Un modèle d'analyse syntaxique «en grilles» pour les productions orales [Syntactical analysis in grids for oral production]. *Anuario de Psicología, 47*, 11–28.

Calvino, I. (1988). *American Lectures.* New York: Basic Books.

Cochet, M., & Vassalli, P. (Eds.). (1988). *Maurice Sendak. Raccontare le immagini tra fantasia e sogno* [Maurice Sendak. Telling about images between phantasy and dream]. Rome: Edizioni Romane.

Givon, T. (1990). *Isomorphism in the grammatical code: Cognitive and biological considerations* (Report No. 7/90). Eugene: University of Oregon, Institute of Cognitive & Decision Sciences.

Jakobson, R. (1980). *Magie de la parole* [Word magic]. Paris: Flammarion.

Jakobson, R. (1985). *Poetica e poesia: Questioni di teoria e analisi testuali* [Poetics and poetry: Questions of textual theory and analysis]. Turin, Italy: Einaudi.

Lotman, J. M. (1972). *La struttura del testo poetico* [The structure of poetic text]. Milan: Mursia.

Mandler, I. M. (1979). Categorical and schematic organization in memory. In C. R. Puff (Ed.), *Memory organization and structure* (pp. 259–299). New York: Academic Press.

Morani, R. (1991). *Scrivere storie e filastrocche: narrazioni e versificazioni in bambini di scuola elementare* [Writing stories and nursery rhymes]. Unpublished doctoral dissertation, University of Rome "La Sapienza."

Olson, D. R. (1977). From utterance to text. The bias of language in speech and writing. *Harvard Educational Review, 47,* 13–26.

Orsolini, M., Devescovi, A., & Fabbretti, D. (1991). Dettare una storia: Che cosa cambia tra i 5 e gli 8 anni [Dictating a story: What changes between ages five and eight]. In M. Orsolini & C. Pontecorvo (Eds.), *La costruzione del testo scritto* (pp. 99–117). Firenze, Italy: La Nuova Italia.

Orsolini, M., & Pontecorvo, C. (1989). La genesi della spiegazione nella discussione in classe [The genesis of explanation in classroom discussions]. In M. S. Barbieri (Ed.), *La spiegazione nell'interazione sociale* (pp. 161–187). Turin, Italy: Loescher.

Pontecorvo, C. (1994). Narrative in early childhood. In D. Stern & M. Ammaniti (Eds.), *Narrative and representation* (pp. 231–242). New York: Academic Press.

Pontecorvo, C., & Morani, R. (1993). *Invention and transcription of stories in children's dyads.* Paper presented at the Vth EARLI Conference, Aix-en-Provence, France, August 31–September 5.

Pontecorvo, C., & Zucchermaglio, C. (1989). From oral to written text: How to analyze children dictating stories. *Journal of Reading Behavior, 21*(2), 109–126.

Propp, V. I. (1988). *Morfologia della fiaba* [Morphology of the fairy tale]. Torino, Italy: Einaudi. (Original work published 1927)

Resnick, L. B. (1991). Shared cognition: Thinking as social practice. In L. B. Resnick, J. M. Levine, & S. D. Teasley (Eds.), *Perspectives on socially shared cognition.* Washington, DC: American Psychological Association.

Rodari, G. (1973). *Grammatica della fantasia* [The grammar of phantasy]. Turin, Italy: Einaudi.

Segre, C. (1985). *Avviamento all'analisi del testo letterario* [Introduction to the analysis of the literary text]. Turin, Italy: Einaudi.

Spier, P. (1983). *Piove!* [It rains!] Milan: Mondadori.

Stein, N. L., & Glenn, G. (1979). An analysis of story comprehension in elementary school children. In R. Freedle (Ed.), *New directions in discourse processing* (Vol. 2, pp. 53–120). Norwood, NJ: Ablex.

Stein, N. L., & Policastro, M. (1984). The concept of a story: A comparison between children's and teacher's perspectives. In H. Mandl, N. L. Stein, & T. Trabasso (Eds.), *Learning and comprehension of text* (pp. 113–155). Hillsdale, NJ: Lawrence Erlbaum Associates.

Teberosky, A. (1988). La dictée et la rédaction de contes entre enfants du même âge [Reciprocal dictation and composing of tales by children of the same age]. *European Journal of Psychology of Education, 3*(4), 399–414.

Tolchinsky, L. (1990). La reproducción de relatos en niños entre cinco y siete años: Organización sintáctica y funciones narrativas [Informative text in five- to seven-year-old children: Syntactical organization and narrative function]. *Anuario de Psicología, 47,* 65–88.

Trabasso, T., Secco, T., & van den Broek, P. (1984). Causal cohesion and story coherence. In H. Mandl, N. L. Stein, & T. Trabasso (Eds.), *Learning and comprehension of text* (pp. 83–111). Hillsdale, NJ: Lawrence Erlbaum Associates.

Trabasso, T., Stein, N. L., & Johnson, L. R. (1981). Children's knowledge of events: A causal analysis of story structure. In G. H. Bower (Ed.), *The psychology of learning and motivation* (Vol. 15, pp. 237–282). New York: Academic Press.

Vygotsky, L. S. (1978). *Mind in society.* Cambridge, MA: Harvard University Press.

13

INFORMATIVE TEXTS OF YOUNG SCHOOLCHILDREN

Ana Teberosky
University of Barcelona

The study reported here is based on 300 written texts in the Catalan language by children 6 to 9 years of age who were in first, second, and third grade in a state school in Barcelona. Our research concerns a particular type of text: the newspaper article written by the press. In analyzing our data, we have tried to answer the following questions:

- Are there linguistic forms and lines of organization specific to news texts?
- What intrinsic linguistic restrictions and obligatory features are learned by children when dealing with this type of material?
- What new phenomena are revealed when small children write in this genre, given that this is a rare occurrence?

INTRODUCTION

Newspapers report public events that we experience only indirectly through someone else's report. Larsen (1988) referred to these as *reported events*, those public events we know by listening to a friend, reading a newspaper, or watching television. The most important characteristic of such reported events from the mass media is that the information is presented to the perceiver by another human being in an act of communication. That is, it is linguistically coded and socially communicated. Reported events have a double structure: event and narrative. According to Larsen (1988), the *event structure* refers to the chronological, causal, and hierarchical relationships among parts of the event. The *narrative structure* refers to the second structure when the events are narrated. In news, the narrative structure is imposed on events by the reporting, particularly by the press. We do not know the events and the narrative report of them separately. When we receive the news, it is in a narrative form. In summary, the information about a public event is linguistically coded, socially communicated, and narratively structured.

The press is responsible for communicating reported events to the general public in written form. The press includes several subclasses of newspaper articles, all of which are similar with respect to their communicative purpose: They represent a genre of public information that is addressed to a general audience and is produced by specific social institutions, such as newspapers, radio, and television. This informative genre uses specific media (newspapers, news broadcasts) and specific technical channels (printed material, audiovisual means). These subclasses of texts are subject to regulations concerning their content and form, which are enforced by the very same institutions in order to control the practice of public communication (Bautier, 1984; Diari de Barcelona, 1987; El País, 1990; Imbert, 1989).

In general, informative texts have conventional forms that are extremely precise, but the subclasses of texts (e.g., politics, sports, society, spot news) can differ by subject matter, purpose, rhetorical structure, or style (Biber, 1988), and each of them can have its own lexicon, expressions, and syntax. We cannot classify the newspaper news article as an individual genre, because it is included in the narrative nonfiction genre; it has its own textual characteristics, however, that have made it an object of pragmatics and linguistics studies (Biber, 1988). These textual characteristics can be examined at three levels: words and expressions, the sentence, and the plan of the text (Bautier, 1984). As used here, *type of text* refers to groupings of texts that are similar with respect to their linguistic forms. Similar to *dimensions* in Biber's writing, here *linguistic forms* can be defined as "linguistic features that co-occur in texts because they work together to mark some common underlying function" (1988, p. 55).

Informative texts have enormous social diffusion but little school use. One of the few pedagogical experiments using the press in school was undertaken in France by Freinet (1957). Children were asked to compose texts by freely choosing both topic and form; these texts were then to be printed on the school typographical set. However, because the school had always used writing to establish communication in a narrative form, particularly in the story format, and had emphasized children's personal experiences, the topic, rhetorical structure, and style of these "free" texts turned out to be stories, mostly real life or fictional. The tendency to understand reported events in terms of personal events does not mesh with the double structure of reported events. Without a precise structure with which to communicate personal events, freedom becomes a moot point. Free texts are not the only possible discursive activity in a classroom. Research has indicated how very young children acquire the canonic organization of traditional stories from untutored contexts outside the school setting (Pontecorvo & Morani, chap. 12, this volume).

The work reported here had a twofold objective. On the one hand, I wanted to show how to stimulate children to produce other types of text by influencing the conditions under which they produce the material. On the other hand, I wanted to undertake a linguistic analysis of that material. I began with the following basic hypothesis: If children are receiving options in the form of diverse models, even at a young age, they may use texts other than narrative fictional or personal reports, that is, informative texts. According to Wagner (1968, cited by Blanche-Benveniste & Jeanjean, 1986), the distinction between discursive modalities relates to the level of the commentator's commitment to his or her sentence. One topic can be the vehicle for either a report or a narrative. However, some topics are conventionally related to narratives, and others are conventionally related to journalism.

By influencing the conditions under which the children produced their material, I aimed to influence the choice of topics, supports, and channels consulted in class for information by creating an attitude to explain and write something in a journalistic way. Although there is no simple correspondence between situation and linguistic features, it is possible to obtain informative texts by influencing the conditions of text production.

BACKGROUND OF INFORMATIVE TEXTS

Several observations should be made. First, when nonprofessional people have to give a public accounting of an event (e.g., when being interviewed), they adapt their language to certain normative guidelines. In this way, they select expressions, vocabulary, and pronunciation according to the image they have of the suitable level of language for a given situation. If the situation is important for determining normative attitudes, people should also respond fittingly to the normative guidelines when the social conditions (we could say *rituals*) exist in which they can participate.

My second observation refers to the relationship between this type of conduct and frequency of interaction with the world of writing. The further removed the commentator is from books, the more marked is his or her attitude toward the differentiation between public speech and everyday speech (Blanche-Benveniste, 1982). If frequent interaction with writing is important, children in the process of learning to read and write should also show this tendency to differentiate between public speech and everyday speech.

My third observation refers to the distinction between oral and written language. My point of view is that if we concentrate on the circumstances and attitude of the speaker, two types of language are produced after age 6, corresponding to what we have until now called *oral* and *written* or *conversational* and *formal* language. One of these types of language could be accompanied by the act of writing (Blanche-Benveniste & Jeanjean, 1986). Whether the material production of the writing is carried out by the children themselves or by an adult must be related to the level of training in the graphic notation and its rules and not to the production of the language itself. Although all language theoretically can be reproduced in writing, Blanche-Benveniste (1982) pointed out that only professional writers can write with rules of everyday language. Illiterate children and adults think, however, that writing reproduces the formal language of prestige.

My fourth observation refers to the reflections of Loris Malaguzzi (1987) on the conflict of the idealistic image of infancy that the school has (that of a child who does not grow up, who is not mature enough to receive certain information) and the adult image of the technological society in which a child is not different from grown-ups. In effect, in our consumer society, messages are directed overwhelmingly at consumers, be they children or adults. One consequence of this diffusion is the early access of children to topics previously reserved for adults. However, this is not necessarily catastrophic, because another consequence of the technological impact of TV on children is its role as a teacher of reading and writing through its audiovisual, journalistic, and advertising language. If this influence is important, it is plausible to hypothesize that, although there are few occasions nowadays to use the language of prestige, there are more opportunities to hear a public language of social prestige. Consequently, exposure to hearing such language no longer depends on family experiences.

Finally, research of Ferreiro and Teberosky (1979) indicated that children, beginning at 5 years of age, differentiate among types of written material. In an experimental situation using a simulated reading based on another text (e.g., reading children a fictional story in a newspaper and a news item in a story book), Ferreiro and Teberosky (1979) observed that many 5-year-olds can predict the contents of some material support. In storybooks they expect to hear "things that don't happen," whereas in newspapers they expect to hear "true information" or "things that happen." They have apparently developed interpretative skills and expectations about the relationship between the type of text and the material support.

In an interesting work on the spontaneous writing of his son, Bissex (1980) described how Paul produced a newspaper, from the age of 6, using "large pages with various sections of jokes, leisure, news, and advertisements, separated from each other by lines or being boxed in" (p. 45). Paul continued writing newspapers until the age of 9, motivated, according to Bissex, by his desire to partake in the adult world.

With this information and these observations as orientation, I gave children 6 to 9 years of age the opportunity to write news items, despite their initial graphic difficulties, which did not inhibit the extensive and abundant production of texts. We did not think of children as a self-contained age community from a linguistic point of view, but as a group connected to the adult in continuous communication (Pratt, 1987).

THE RULES OF JOURNALISTIC WRITING

According to Bautier, to be well written an article must meet criteria at three levels. At a vocabulary level, the article should avoid uncommon words but, if they are essential, define them when used; use short words rather than long ones; and eliminate lazy or useless adjectives. That is to say, the words used in a well-written article should have four properties: a high frequency of use in everyday speech, consistency, a specific meaning, and a precise denotation. It is important to locate the "key words" (those words that will especially attract attention to the topic) in the headlines and subtitles (1984, p. 81).

At the sentence level, a well-written article should consist of short sentences of no more than 30 words, and should be divided, if possible, into sequences of fewer than 12 words. The headlines should have a simple structure (subject, verb, object) and should be in the present tense, the active voice, and the affirmative (Bautier, 1984). The active voice is preferred in sentences, although three means are recommended to emphasize some elements: the use of the passive voice, topicalization, or reflexive passive verbs, which are frequent in Catalan (Diari de Barcelona, 1987). As a rule of style, journalistic language avoids the first person singular or plural and substitutes formulae, such as "according to latest reports, the [name of newspapers]" or "in a statement made to [name of newspaper]" (Diari de Barcelona, 1987; El País, 1990).

The level of language in a well-written article refers either implicitly or explicitly to the spoken language. The level of language in the Anglo-Saxon press seems to be closer to the spoken language than in the Spanish press.

The purposes of public information and the constraints of modern news mass media communication have produced a different type of narrative structure (Larsen, 1983). The news text should also be short. The journalistic structure is the opposite of the dissertation: The journalistic structure attempts to catch attention immediately. In news, the text starts with a short summary of the main event in the title and in the introduction (the *front-piece* or *lead*, in journalistic terms), which contains the essence of the information and should answer six questions: Who? What? When? Where? Why? How? This should be followed by information in order of decreasing importance, with an eventual short, sharp ending. Brown and Yule (1986) used the term *public narrative* to refer to writing in this structure.

In addition, journalistic writing must adapt itself to two factors: the type of support available (the newspaper itself) and the audience. Bautier (1984) affirms that, in France, 50% of the readers have a primary level of education and 60%

have a job that does not demand reading. (In Catalonia, one in six adults is illiterate; "Uno de Cada," 1990.) A third factor, competition with TV, obliges the press to be more precise and concise.

Two final points should be highlighted. The first is the "rhetoric of fact" (e.g., concrete data, precise numbers, proven facts, short interviews, specific details), which gives the news an air of live, real documentation (van Dijk, 1977). The second is the "discourse of the facts," which must be objective without personal opinions: 95% fact and 5% opinion, according to Todd-Guénot (cited by Bautier, 1984).

THE EDUCATIONAL CONTEXT

In the context of a pedagogical experiment with children who are learning to write Catalan in a state school in a working-class area of Barcelona, I have influenced the teachers' curricular decisions in two ways. On the one hand, I have tried to modify traditional schooling practice with an aim of improving the general learning conditions. On the other hand, I have tried out some activities concerning the reproduction of nonconventional texts in the traditional scholastic way. My focus has been on teacher training within a framework of a theory broad enough to incorporate all the new teaching techniques at a more global level: the theory of constructive learning of the written language (Ferreiro, 1987; Teberosky, 1992). Using this approach, it was necessary to attend as much to the notational and conventional aspects of the written texts as to the content of the written language. That is, it was necessary to pay as much attention to how the children learned to write as to what the children wrote and under what conditions. Starting from the general hypothesis that it is impossible to isolate, on the one hand, the activity of language (producer of language) and, on the other, the result of this activity (the utterances) either at an oral level (Blanche-Benveniste, 1982) or a written level (Biber, 1988), I believe that both aspects should exert a mutual influence in order to learn to write and to express or communicate through writing.

I outline here only the methodology of classwork; later in the chapter I focus on the linguistic analysis of the texts. The methodology used to stimulate the writing of news articles consisted of three phases: (a) collective oral elaboration of the pre-text before writing; (b) consultation and reading of written documents—the various newspapers that the teacher put at the children's disposal; and (c) individual or dyadic writing of the news item, with the teacher or a more advanced child as scribe (the teacher or the child carefully writes down only the utterances dictated, without revision).

We used the concept of pre-text in the sense of *avant-texte*, like the draft from a professional writer (Bellemin-Nöel, 1972): all documents produced in creating the text. Phases /a/ and /b/ correspond to the elaboration of the pre-text. On the one hand, information is given to the child on the thematic content in Phase /a/. On the other hand, information is given on the graphic notational aspects in Phase /b/. We confer the greatest importance to these two phases of the pedagogical work. The contents were worked on in class in a conscious way before being written. Consulting graphic material also functions as a source of confirmation of information received orally (via TV, radio, or adult speech of parents and teachers) and as a source of new information.

To summarize, two ideas guided the methodology of the classwork. On the one hand, we made use of the differentiation between content and written expression: We took advantage of the information of the adult world to which children have access by previously organizing their work on the cognitive contents of the messages. On the other hand, we also made use of the presence of conventional models of written expression and the adult world that are at the disposal of the children and can be consulted.

The children could consult newspapers during the writing session. We used the concept of consultation in the sense of an intertextual activity and of a real presence of the conventional model and not in the sense of passive copying. Several authors have demonstrated children's difficulty in expressing new meanings in their own words (Collerson, 1986; Jenkins, 1986).

Not all newspaper news is converted into newsworthy items for small children. We have observed that children prefer police events, sports news, news related to well-known national and international figures, and atmospheric phenomena that may have affected the community.

DATABASE AND ANALYSIS

Our written corpus is made up of 300 news texts collected during 1985–1986 and 1986–1987 from first- to third-grade classes. We call the news items *informative texts* to differentiate them from narrative fiction texts, although we know that they share many characteristics with the narrative genre.

In analyzing the texts, I used two points of reference: the distributional analysis of spoken and written French, developed by the Groupe Aixois de Recherche en Syntaxe (GARS, 1983), and the rules of journalistic writing mentioned earlier (Bautier, 1984; Diari de Barcelona, 1987; El País, 1990). I used the syntactic analysis to find the particular forms and lines of organization of this type of text and then compared them with the normative restrictions characteristic of this material.

The syntactic analysis was undertaken with reference to the grammar of the language. The starting point of our analysis is not the sentence but the syntactic constructions with a kernel element, in general, the main verb, endowed with everything necessary, such as complements and adjunct elements (Blanche-Benveniste, 1990; Pontecorvo & Morani, chap. 12, this volume). For example, each main verb has the power to construct types of elements that can be described in relation to it and that make up its areas (when, where, why, how), including the subject or the complements. Other types of elements can be associated with the verb but are not constructed by the verb. These are elements adjuncted to the verb. This type of analysis allows us to move quickly to verbal and nonverbal constructions that are distributed in units of construction. In effect, not all elements interrelate through grammatical rules. For this reason, we can find, for example (and, indeed, we have found) nonverbal constructions: lexical relationships of discursive linking that escape a grammatical analysis based on the categories. Because our interest lies in the analysis of the discourse, I have retained the three types of constructions:

1. A direct verbal construction made up of a main verb and adjunct elements governed by or associated with the verb, among which we can find the subject and complement of the verb and associated elements with different semantic values.
2. A noncanonic verbal construction made up of a verb and its adjunct elements, without subject, verb, and object grammatical relationship (e.g., found in sayings, proverbs, or idiomatic expressions).
3. Nonverbal constructions that are based either on grammatical categories (e.g., nominal constructions) or on symmetrical constructions.

The GARS (1983) suggested that a format representation in grids provides a visual representation of the text that is somewhat difficult to achieve by using a conventional linear arrangement. Syntactic constructions are represented on each horizontal line, as the analysis is undertaken on the original text, without modifying their order in the discourse. The blank spaces do not indicate pauses in the discourse, which is read line by line. Each different type of construction is located in another line of the grid, and the same syntactic categories can be seen "in lists" shown in the vertical columns. A visual representation of this type allows us a quick viewing of the discursive phenomena: types of constructions and the way in which the units link up by repetition, coordination, or apposition.

When there is a direct verbal construction, the main verb is located first, with the direct and/or indirect complements in the closest areas (see line 2 in Table 13.1). Only one verb is represented per line (i.e., the main verb and its governed elements), but two verbs may appear in each line, one being the main verb and the other being the construed verb (as in the case of a two-verb construction, where one is the main verb and the other is of a subordinate clause). Table 13.1 provides the first of two examples of children's informative texts in a visual representation, shown first in the original Catalan version and then in translation. Table 13.2 presents the second example.

Our analysis centered on:

• The form, that is, the syntactic units that we found in this type of discourse; characteristics of the subject, the verb (especially tense and voice), and the elements governed by and associated with the verb.

TABLE 13.1
Joan (8 years old)

1.		*Un canvi en el Barcelona* (Only one change in the Barcelona team)
2.	*Terry Vanables* (Terry Venables)	*farà* (will make)	*un canvi pel parti del R . . . .* (only one change for the match against Real Madrid.)
3.		*serà* (The change)	*aquest* (will be this.)
4.			
5.		*van lesionar* (Calderé was injured in the match against Mallorca.)	*Carrasco per Calderé ja que Calderé estava a lesionat* (Carrasco for Calderé because Calderé has been injured.)
6.		*es va veure obligat a fer aquest canvi*	
7.		(and the trainer found himself obliged to make this change.)	

TABLE 13.2

Oscar (9 years old)

#				
1.	*Un transtornat es suïcida d'un 6è pis* (An unbalanced person commits suicide from a sixth floor.)			
2.	*un home amb problemes mentals* (A man with mental problems)	*es va tirar* (threw himself)	*d'un 6è pis* (from a sixth floor)	*devant de les càmeres …* (in front of TV cameras.)
3.	*fotògrafs* (photographers)	*van acudir*		
4.	*i moltes persones* (and many people gathered to watch the scene.)			
5.	*el suïcidat* (The deceased)	*era* (was)	*mecànic* (a mechanic)	
6.		*i es deia* (by the name of)	*M. N.* (M. N.)	
7.		*tenia* (He was)	*55 anys* (55 years old.)	
8.		*i era* (and he)	*solter* (was single)	
9.	*abans que es suïcidès* (Before he committed suicide) *una persona* (a person)	*el va veure* (saw him)		
10.		*i va cridar* (and called)	*als bombers* (the fire brigade)	
11.			*a la policia* (and the municipal police)	
12.			*i una psicòloga municipal* (and a local government psychologist)	
13.	*la conversacio entre la psicòloga* (the conversation between the psychologist)			
14.	*i M. N.* (and M. N.)	*va durar* (lasted)	*mitja hora* (half an hour)	
15.	*pero finalment* (but he finally)			
16.		*es va suïcidar* (committed suicide.)		

- The type of discursive constructions, that is, the way in which the units are linked.
- The type of lexical relationships.

I describe the informative texts in terms of opposition to both the oral preliminary part and the written narrative fiction texts. Both types of texts (oral conversation and narrative) have been well documented in children 5 years of age and above. For that reason, I refer as much to the general characteristics of the informative texts as to the peculiarities that differentiate them from other types of texts. In studies on spoken and written language, differences were found between the oral production and written production that affect the subject forms, the use of specific verb tense, a certain type of discursive construction, and lexical use (Bilger, 1988; Blanche-Benveniste & Jeanjean, 1980; Halliday, 1987). As Halliday showed, writing creates other forms of language: the forms of discourse that arise as a result of the change of medium and as a result of a complex historical process based on its functions in society. The discourse of written language is a nominalized discourse with a high lexical density and packed grammatical metaphors (Halliday, 1987). These features enable discourse to become more informative and technical.

FEATURES OF CHILDREN'S INFORMATIVE TEXTS

The Verbal Constructions

The Subject Forms.   The informative texts analyzed in this study have grammatical subjects always expressed by lexical forms, except when there was no explicit subject (grammatically acceptable in Catalan). Pronominal forms in the text appeared principally in situations involving direct speech in interviews with witnesses. Nouns were the most frequent lexical form and were accompanied by either definite or indefinite articles. We also found determinative relative clauses, as well as appositions, which were much more frequent in this type of text than in other genres, such as fictional narratives. With regard to position, we observed some examples of grammatical subjects in postverbal position, which is acceptable in Catalan.

Forms Governed by or Associated With the Verb

Two points should be made about constructions with elements governed by the main verb. First, with regard to the position of the governing elements, the majority were to the right of the main verb. Their position is important because, in oral conversation, most forms with governing elements have been found to the left of the main verb (Blanche-Benveniste & Jeanjean, 1980). Second, the frequency of utterances introduced by *why, when, for, because of, due to,* and *if* was greater than in narrative or conversation texts.

Concerning constructions with elements associated with the verb (but not constructed by it), one has to point out the semantic value of precision. In general, these constructions contain adverbial phrases that are specific, accurate, time–space values that relate to the speaker of the discourse (e.g., *yesterday, at 6:45, in the north of France*). Accurate semantic values are important, because they mark a difference with respect to fictitious narrative: The informative texts are established by reference to the speaker (e.g., *yesterday, last year*), whereas fictitious narrative is established with reference to the discourse itself (e.g., *one day, then*).

Analysis of the Verb

Informative texts are characterized by the use of verbs in the indicative mood, alternating between affirmative and negative forms (exclusively the interrogative if there is an interview), and the verbs are conjugated in the present and past tenses. The most frequent forms of the past tense used are the equivalent of the past simple and present perfect in Catalan. Of the tenses, perhaps the simple present and the present perfect are symptomatic of the informative text, because these indicate simultaneity and proximity in time and also precision of a fact in relation to the speaker.

The passive voice is used frequently in conventional forms with inversion of subject and object and the prepositional complement with *by*. The use of the passive voice is interesting as a discursive resort to focus on the topic in question (discourse topic entity), but it is also interesting to see its almost total absence in other types of texts (Bilger, 1988). Passives have been associated with decontextualization, and some have claimed it to be more characteristic of writing mode than speech (Chafe, 1986). On the other hand, use of the passive voice has usually been seen as a way of evaluating the dominance of the syntax. In this sense, the children interviewed did not seem to have any great difficulties.

We have also noted constructions with *se*, which is a grammatical form in Catalan (e.g., reflexive verbs that are expressed by using the passive in English). The set of forms is summarized in Table 13.3.

TABLE 13.3
Utterances in Informative Texts

Verbs			
Indicative Mood: present, present perfect, past simple, past continuous			
Affirmative and Negative forms			
Voice: Active and passive			
With subject	Indefinite article + Noun + Apposition	or Definite article + Noun + Pronoun	Name
With complements	Valence	Governed by verb	
Associated with the verb	Temporal	Spacial	Quantitatives

In summary, there is a co-presence of the following features: the mood, form, and tenses of the verb; the types of subjects; the determiners and appositions in the subjects; the governing complements introduced by prepositions and conjunctions, such as *why*, *when*, and *due to* elements associated with values of precision and localization. Based on these factors, I interpreted the texts in our study as informative texts containing reports of events and localizers, with justifications that suggest a specification of the conditions (Jeanjean, 1986).

Nonverbal Constructions

The nonverbal constructions registered in our basic material are nominal and appear in the headlines.

The Assigning of the Lexis

The text advances at the same time as a syntagmatic development (represented on the vertical axis). This placing allows a clear view of a particular discursive recourse: the assignment of lexicon. We have been able to highlight three phenomena in the procedure of lexical assignment: enumeration, repetition (resources that journalism approves and school rejects), and the search for lexical precision. In the vertical columns, which represent the execution of events of verbal value, we can see the recourse to repeating the same lexical execution or even repeating the same syntactic unit. In the first place, there is repetition and, in the second, enumeration or listing. These executions can occur in the same or different positions in the syntagmatic units. Evidently the variations in the texts depend on the type and position of the repetition or listing.

Construction Types Found. Construction with a repetition of the same verb of the same type of verbal construction:

1. R.M. *took* the money out of Catalonia
   he *took* it to America

2. Barcelona *has won* 107 to 102
   it *has been* an exciting game
   but the Wanderers *have lost* 99 to 100
   it too *has been* exciting.

Constructions with a repetition of the same type of nominal elements:

3. Chernobyl has affected a part of Catalonia
   England
   Moscow
   Italy
   the South of France
   Greece.

4. A long time ago *a man*
           Charles Darwin
           a scientist . . .

Constructions by repetition of nominal/pronominal or verbal elements:

5. *He took them* at 9 o'clock
   He took them to the station place.
6. ETA planted a *bomb*
           the *bomb exploded* at 5 o'clock
           it   *exploded* between *the sixth*
                           and *the seventh* floor.

Constructions with a repetition of a part of syntactic unit:

7. he learned to hunt *with* stones
           and *with* sticks . . .

Constructions with a repetition of elements in different positions in the syntagmatic units:

8. the *street* all the *street* was very wet[1]
9. yesterday *the Challenger* exploded
   when   *the Challenger* exploded the people . . .

Thus, there are various types of discursive recourses for the assigning of the lexicon: apposition, enumeration, coordination, and symmetrical constructions, to which we can also add repetition. This concerns a process of lexical "filling out" (Blanche-Benveniste, 1982, 1990) of the assignation of lexicon to the same syntactic positions or to different positions, as in the case of symmetry.

I am concerned with these recourses for at least two reasons: the presence of lexical elements in relation to co-reference is a factor that ensures textual cohesion (Halliday & Hasan, 1976); and lexical precision, cohesion, and density have been seen as traits of written discourse in contrast to the imprecision and cohesion through prosodic elements of oral discourse (Halliday, 1987).

Having looked at recourse to repetition and enumeration, we now turn to some examples of lexical precision.

Oscar (9 years old)

    A mentally unbalanced person commits suicide from a 6th floor

A man with mental problems threw himself from a sixth floor in front of TV cameras photographers and many people gathered to watch the scene *the*

---

[1]Acceptable in Catalan; children tend not to use regular and conventional punctuation.

deceased was a mechanic by the name of *M. N.* he was 55 years old and he was single before he committed suicide a person saw him and called the fire brigade and the municipal police and a local government psychologist the conversation between the psychologist and *M. N.* lasted half an hour but he finally committed suicide.

Here we have: a mentally unbalanced person = a man with mental problems = the deceased = M. N., which form a way in which to construct the reference by inclusion.

Joan and Miguel (9 years old)

A millionairess gets married to a massai

Silvia Jenkins a rich German heiress renounced civilization for her love of a massai whom she met on a beach in Mombassa thousands of kilometers from her home ...

Here we have: A millionairess gets married to a massai = Silvia Jenkins = a rich German heiress. The reference is constructed by both bracketing and apposition, but the effect is the same: Each new element adds information that constructs the representation of the character.

Two observations complete the aspect of assignation of lexicon. We have seen children in class showing interest in finding the "right word" appropriate for each topic, and that word then substitutes for the previous versions and is quickly socialized. This socialization is so quick that sometimes it seems to happen even before its meaning is understood. This type of phenomenon is difficult to observe in small children if they are only dealing with sentences or more fixed texts. In the news, however, the words are more closely linked to the content of the social experience of the community, and in constructing the content, the forms of designation are simultaneously constructed.

The Characteristics of News Structure

One outstanding characteristic of news language is the concentration of information in the headline and the introduction. The reader must receive the maximum amount of information from the first lines, according to Giraud (cited by Bautier, 1984). As van Dijk (1977) affirmed, all journalistic discourses have a summary that is expressed at least through its titles or, more extensively, in the headline. Then, in descending order, come pieces of information, with those of lesser importance toward the end of the text. Let us look at two of the children's texts in terms of structure. The scheme of the news in Oscar's example can be represented in the following way:

Line 1:   Title (headline).
Line 2:   Introduction where the subject is taken up again and with some
          lexicon and some syntactic turns of the title.
Lines 3 to 8:   Zooming in with detailed information, figures, lists, dates, and
          other facts of precision.
Lines 9 to 14:   The ending.

Joan and Miguel's example can be represented as follows:

Line 1:   Title (headline).
Line 2:   Introduction where the subject and lexicon of the headline are taken
          up again.
Lines 3 to 5:   Explanatory development.
Line 6:   The ending.

Many of the texts in our study, written by children between the ages of 6 and
9, show a professional use of journalistic style.

CONCLUSION

After brief instruction, many children around the age of 6 can write news; that
is to say, they can use the adult model. How can such an early understanding
of journalistic rules be explained? The simultaneous influence of various factors
should be examined, including the legitimacy of a pre-text exercise as a form of
appropriating the rules of the different types of discourses, and the differentiation between the contents and the expression of the language, together with the
presence of the printed models of the commercial press. Of course, the intention
of journalism is to reach the reader quickly, and from this objective comes the
type of structuring of the message that facilitates its comprehension (Larsen,
1988). A good example of this is the news in children's texts, as illustrated here.
    Nevertheless, critics have occasionally said that this exercise is good for
rewritten material but unsuitable for developing children's free expression. I
think, however, that, instead of demanding that children "express themselves,"
the proposal of models can be very effective, especially when children have
nothing interesting to write. Moreover, we regard it not only as a way of initiating
children into new subject matter, but also as a way of respecting their theories
on the type of language that must be written: the formal, adult, public language.
And, for the child, this type of language has well-defined linguistic features.
    I have tried to demonstrate that, under the pedagogical conditions described
here, children can produce texts that respect journalistic rules when judged by
the type of syntactic unit, the way in which these units are linked together, the
type of lexicon and its relationships, and the structure. I have also pointed out

that even some syntactic turns are more frequent in informative texts and less so in other types of written and oral texts, including appositions, use of the passive voice, use of specific verb tenses, the precise assignation of the lexicon, and nominal constructions in the headlines. All of these are similar to the recommendations on how to write a good news story.

If we take into account the makeup and the typographic and punctuation resources with the structure, the syntactic construction, and the lexicon, we can conclude that children 6 to 9 years of age, under the pedagogical conditions herein described, can approach the writing of journalistic news in a comprehensive and specific way.

REFERENCES

Bautier, R. (1984). Sur le journalisme: Des règles d'écriture aux représentations de la communication journalistique [On journalism: From writing rules to representations of journalistic communication]. *Etudes de Linguistique Appliquée, 53*, 79–91.

Bellemin-Nöel, J. (1972). *Le texte et l'avant-texte* [Text and pre-text]. Paris: Larousse.

Biber, D. (1988). *Variation across speech and writing*. Cambridge, England: Cambridge University Press.

Bilger, M. (1988, April). *Pour un apprentissage de la rédaction* [For composition learning]. Paper presented at the XIIè Journées Pédagogiques sur le Français, Barcelona.

Bissex, G. (1980). *GNYS AT WRK. A Child learns to write and read*. Cambridge, MA: Harvard University Press.

Blanche-Benveniste, C. (1982). La escritura del lenguaje dominguero [The writing of the Sunday language]. In E. Ferreiro & M. Gómez-Palacio (Eds.), *Nuevas perspectivas sobre los procesos de lectura y escritura* [New perspectives on the reading and writing process] (pp. 247–270). México City: Siglo XXI.

Blanche-Benveniste, C. (1990). Un modèle d'analyse syntaxique "en grilles" pour les productions orales [A model of syntactic analysis "in grids" for oral production]. *Anuario de Psicología* (Universidad de Barcelona), *47*, 11–28.

Blanche-Benveniste, C., & Jeanjean, C. (1980). *Evaluation comparée des moyens d'expression linguistique d'enfants* [Compared evaluations of children's linguistic means] (Recherche nº 2,14,01). Groupe Aixois de Recherche Syntactique, Département de Linguistique Française, Aix-en-Provence, France.

Blanche-Benveniste, C., & Jeanjean, C. (1986). *Le français parlé* [Spoken French]. Paris: Didier Eruditions.

Brown, G., & Yule, G. (1986). *Discourse analysis*. Cambridge, England: Cambridge University Press.

Chafe, W. (1986). Differences between speaking and writing. In D. Olson, N. Torrance, & A. Hildyard (Eds.), *Literacy, Language and Learning* (pp. 105–123). Cambridge, England: Cambridge University Press.

Collerson, J. (1986). Copying and composition: Text and context in children's informational writing. *Educational Review, 38*, 139–150.

Diari de Barcelona. (1987). Un model de llengua pels mitjans de comunicació [A language model for the journalist]. Barcelona: Editorial Empuries.

El Pais. (1990). *Libro de estilo* [Book of style]. Madrid: Editorial El País.

Ferreiro, E. (1987). L'écriture avant la lettre [Writing before letters]. In H. Sinclair (Ed.), *La notation graphique chez l'enfant* [Graphic notation in children] (pp. 17–70). Paris: PUF.

Ferreiro, E., & Teberosky, A. (1979). *Los sistemas de escritura en el desarrollo del niño* [Literacy before schooling]. México City: Siglo XXI.

Freinet, C. (1957). *Le journal scolaire* [The school journal]. Vienna: Rossignol.

Groupe Aixois de Recherche Syntactique. (1983). *Fascicule de travail pour l'étude du français parlé* [Handbook for studying spoken French]. Aix-en-Provence, France: Author.

Halliday, M. A. K. (1987). Language and the order of nature. In N. Fabb, D. Attridge, A. Durant, & C. MacCabe (Eds.), *The linguistics of writing: Arguments between language and literature* (pp. 135–154). Manchester, England: Manchester University Press.

Halliday, M. A. K., & Hasan, R. (1976). *Cohesion in English.* London: Longman.

Imbert, G. (1989). *Le discours du journal El País* [The discourse of El Pais]. Paris: Editions du Conseille National de Recherche Scientifique.

Jeanjean, C. (1986). La distribution syntaxique de "un N" sujet en français parlé [The syntactic distribution of 'un N' subject in spoken French]. *Recherches sur le Français parlé, 7,* 89–115.

Jenkins, E. (1986). How original is it? The models on which children base their writing. *Educational Review, 38,* 151–160.

Larsen, S. F. (1983). Text processing and knowledge updating in memory of radio news. *Discourse Processes, 6,* 21–38.

Larsen, S. F. (1988). Remembering without experiencing: Memory for reported events. In U. Neisser & T. Winograd (Eds.), *Remembering reconsidered* (pp. 87–103). Cambridge, England: Cambridge University Press.

Malaguzzi, L. (1987). Opinioni sull'altalena: Alla ricerca di uno status dell'infanzia [Opinions on the seesaw: Searching a status for infancy]. *Bambini, 6,* 4–5.

Pratt, M. L. (1987). Linguistic Utopias. In N. Fabb, D. Attridge, A. Durant, & C. MacCabe (Eds.), *The linguistics of writing: Arguments between language and literature* (pp. 48–66). Manchester, England: Manchester University Press.

Teberosky, A. (1992). *Aprendiendo a escribir* [Learning to write]. Barcelona: Ice/Horsori.

Uno de cada seis catalanes es analfabeto funcional [One out of six Catalans is functionally illiterate]. (1990, January 11). *El Periódico de Barcelona,* p. 10.

van Dijk, T. A. (1977). *Text and context.* London: Longman.

14

USES OF WRITTEN LANGUAGE IN PRIMARY SCHOOL: CODIFYING, RECORDING, AND INTERPRETING

Lydia Tornatore*
University of Florence

LEARNING TO SPEAK; LEARNING TO WRITE

There are many reasons behind the recent interest in written language learning processes. On the one hand, this interest can be regarded as an expansion in a psychopedagogical direction of the interest in written language shown in many fields, particularly anthropological and historical research. On the other hand, there is a socioeducational motive related to the periodic bouts of alarm regarding the state of literacy among schoolchildren of all levels.

The specific nature of written language highlights problems regarding the relationship between oral and written production and didactic proposals for those problems. In any case, speaking is of far greater relevance than writing for both the child and the adult. With regard to the problem of orality, Havelock (1986) observed that, before learning to read and write, all children live in a world of oral culture. Access to writing is influenced by many factors. In contrast to what happens when learning to speak, learning to write is affected by cultural diversity to a far greater extent. In Vygotsky's work, which originated a research trend on the psychopedagogy of written language, interest in written language and the cultural conditions of cognitive development were strictly linked. Children learn to speak in ways that are sufficient for their needs in various environments, and they learn to write to the extent that they live in an environment that is characterized by the presence of writing. Children learn to write by using a few instruments that are more or less manageable. In our culture, they learn to write from left to right and to use an alphabetic system. Children learn to speak in contexts in which speaking is functional; they learn to write by writing,

*Lydia Tornatore died while this book was in preparation. The editors want to recall here her original contribution to educational research.

which is done primarily with the aim of learning to write. Writing learning may be considered spontaneous inasmuch as it is being motivated by the environment or can be seen as a school activity at the direct request of an adult.

The history of teaching is full of clues regarding the process of learning to write. Global or whole language methods stress the writing–meaning connection, but this connection is much more complex and demanding in writing than in speaking. Bruner (1971) emphasized the passage from modes of reference of spoken language to modes of reference of written language: Situation-based contextualization is replaced by a different kind of contextualization that is expressed in particular linguistic forms.

The potential of an instrument is linked to the capacity to use it. Using an instrument that has not been mastered is one way of learning to use it, but limitations derived from a lack of mastery may also be experienced. A less adequate but more easily mastered instrument might turn out to be more suitable.

Critics of education have repeatedly and from various perspectives pointed out the damage caused by scholastic exercises that, in the name of instruction, require children to do something they cannot do. The problem is particularly delicate in the case of language, because it is very difficult to distinguish between cases in which there is clearly a clumsy attempt to adapt to models imposed by the adult and cases in which the writer is able to use the language instrument by gradually mastering new aspects of it and continually improving his or her skills.

In reviewing the relationship between writing and cognitive development, Applebee (1984) criticized the lack of clarity surrounding this problem, because it is widely accepted that good writing and careful thinking go hand in hand; however, research on writing has been remarkably slow to examine the ways in which writing may be related to reasoning. According to Applebee:

> Two different traditions contribute to this reluctance: The first treats the process of writing as the rhetorical problem of relating a predetermined message to an audience that must be persuaded to accept the author's point of view. The second tradition assumes that the process of writing will in some inevitable way lead to a better understanding of the topic under consideration, although how this comes about tends to be treated superficially and anecdotally. (p. 577)

In the first place, it is not clear what *writing* means and what modes or levels of knowing how to write should be examined within the sphere of cognitive development. The process of acquiring skills relative to the written language is a long one, and the more relevant cognitive skills come into play only at advanced levels. The question should therefore be examined at specific levels.

WRITING FOR A PURPOSE

Assessing the effective role of practice exercises in the linguistic field is a difficult task. If writing is regarded as a cognitive process, learning to write falls within the bounds of the development of cognitive activity; the pathway to acquiring skills relative to the writing of texts cannot, then, be exclusively placed within the ambit of writing practice. It might be more appropriate to look to uses of oral language that bring into play skills of the same type as those required by written language. According to Orsolini (1988):

> The idea that writing means transcribing oral language is perhaps an inevitable step in the initial phase of the learning of writing. . . . However, what can be meaningfully transcribed is oral discourse that has the characteristic of text and uses modes of organizing information that are not tied to the here and now of communication. Fairy tales and stories are especially suitable oral genres for transfer into writing. (p. 372)

In a similar perspective, other researchers have identified other activities, for example, symbolic play:

> By engaging in dramatic play, preschool children are using language in a symbolic manner. For example, they may be defining roles for the players or the objects used in role-playing. The symbolic play may in turn contribute to an increased ability to write isolated words, an ability that requires ability to write isolated words, an ability that requires the use of decontextualized language. (Beach & Bridwell, 1984, p. 229)

Generally speaking, the problem of indirectly strengthening writing skills should be faced by keeping reasons for writing to the fore. Thus, the exercise of cognitive activities within which writing acts might turn out to be more functional than are oral linguistic acts deserves special attention.

When the focus is on communication, writing can substitute for oral discourse production in particular situations when direct communication is not possible. In contrast, during an activity that requires examination of observations, a form of written recording is obviously an important instrument, not sufficient in itself, but one for which oral discourse cannot substitute. These activities may be deliberately cognitive or may involve daily life contexts that require some form of data recording.

Scientific research and organizational activities linked to daily life assist the development of written language; this is confirmed by the history of writing (Ong, 1982). It should be emphasized, however, that the use of written forms of recording in research and practical activity does not require the production of self-sufficient texts, inasmuch as a text can be self-sufficient. Note taking, for example, is an activity in which oral discourse plays a major part and whose form is suited to its aim (i.e., rapid consultation in the context of the activities in question).

Historical research on the transformation of modes of thought linked to writing has stressed the importance of forms of recording that are different from text writing. Goody (1977), who studied the use of lists in historical periods when writing first started to be widespread, said:

> A characteristic of the presentation of information in the form of lists is that it must be processed in a different way not only from a normal speech, but from other ways of writing, ways that we may consider at once more typical and closer to speech. The list relies on discontinuity rather than continuity; it depends on physical placement, on location; it can be read in different directions, both sideways and downwards, up and down, as well as left and right. Most importantly it encourages the ordering of the items, by number, by initial sound, by category, etc. (p. 81)

In his study of the development and diffusion of the logic of Ramo, Ong (1979) highlighted how the new possibilities of visual presentation provided by the press could explain logic's development.

From the point of view of the process of acquisition of language skills that are not just ends in themselves, the early learning of writing should be extended to include forms of writing that are not text writing. These include forms of writing that can precede not only the acquisition of text organization skills but also the mastery of alphabetic writing; they may be single words with annotational value or invented and agreed-on graphic signs.

Thus, the nursery school child who learns to trace marks expressing a cognitive operation is writing; the child who makes recordings at any level in the form of a table is writing. A form of data labeling or recording by means of conventional signs can be used if alphabetic writing has not yet been mastered. Sometimes verbal discourse is not the most suitable instrument because of the level of skill or because of the limits of natural languages.

A written text can be reread, reexamined, discussed, and reworked. That is why writing is regarded as having a positive effect on cognitive development. This also applies to data recording, for example, in a double entry table: It needs to be set out, filled in, read, reexamined, discussed, and reworked. The examples that follow were taken from data collected in nursery and elementary schools in the Saint Croce school district of Florence and in Bagno a Ripoli by Gisella Paoletti.

Reading a table is both similar to and different from reading a text. The individual signs used (invented signs or words) are read in forms that depend partly on their position in the recording context and partly on the cognitive operation involved in the reading. For example, if a sign means *rain* and another sign means *sun*, the reading might be "Today it is raining" or "Today it is sunny" when recording observations carried out on one day; however, the reading might be "On Tuesday it was sunny" if establishing what the weather was like on Tuesday, or "It was sunny on Tuesday and Thursday" establishing on what days of the week it was sunny when recording daily life. Compared with a text, a table requires less effort to decipher and greater effort to interpret. Reading a table may be described as translating from a recorded language to verbal discourse under the guidance of a cognitive plan.

Children learn to carry out such operations during the same period that they encounter the long process of acquiring the principles governing alphabetic writing and those governing the writing of texts. At this point, a wide field for research has opened up, because most normal school subjects (e.g., mathematics, science, environmental studies) and classroom activities are involved. Each of these activities should be examined in the context in which it occurs and in its relation to the development of verbal language skills, paying particular attention to the relations between oral and written language at all stages.

Learning to write ought to mean learning to use forms of graphic recording appropriate to intention. As intention varies, the skills involved also vary. For example, writing in order to remind and reexamine may not require text composition skills but rather skills in organizing information to make it available.

AN ALTERNATIVE USE OF WRITTEN LANGUAGE: RECORDING

The use of forms of recording that differ from the writing of linguistic utterances is widespread in the early stages of schooling when children have not yet started or only recently started learning to write. At a later stage, such activities are found in domains varying from mathematics to environmental studies.

If one thinks in terms of children engaged in the alphabetic writing comprehension process, the use of different forms of symbolization could be regarded as disturbing or something to be abandoned quickly. However, if the problem of the acquisition of writing technology is posed as an initiation into the various aspects and functions of written language, a different conclusion might be reached.

The simplest form of recording other than written language, which is of great interest from the point of view of linguistic–cognitive skill development, consists of using conventional signs or linguistic expressions directly referring to a single object (e.g., the title of a drawing) or a class of objects or actions (e.g., a mark refers to all the objects of a certain type, or a linguistic expression codifies any practical suggestion).

Forms of recording that are aimed at enabling elaboration are much less simple, although they are accessible at many levels. They are usually charts, tables, or integrated systems in which a chart shows data related to a single element and a table includes all the data and invites different interpretations. The following types can be distinguished: (a) recordings of classroom life pertaining to attendance, attendance at school lunch, food eaten or refused, or turns taken in activities and games; (b) recordings of daily weather observations; (c) recordings of the world of nature; or (d) recordings of family, houses, and neighborhood. Generally speaking, these activities can rapidly reach high levels of complexity, ranging from a first stage in which data recording is immediately related to direct experience to forms of reading data that involve classifications, comparison, choosing criteria, and organizing information.

Type (a) recordings usually involve rethinking an experience, with or without a practical objective. For example, one might determine the most liked or disliked food in classroom, check alternation of turns, or distinguish open-air from indoor games. The reading involved in this kind of table can be guided by a precise criterion because it seeks the answer to a question, or it can be supplemented by free verbalization and thereby motivate conversation.

Type (b) recordings represent one of the most widespread uses. Weather observation recording can be done at many levels, and it provides many opportunities for tackling various problems: choosing a symbol, criteria to adopt in categorizing observations, or the environmental conditions to be considered. Summarizing and comparing activities can be much richer and more complex here than elsewhere.

Type (c) recordings about the natural world, particularly about plants and animals, produce different kinds of records. The table can be used in various ways, for example, in comparing predictions and observations (see Table 14.1) about what will happen (part A) and what has happened to objects in the water (part B). Consequently, they refer to two different moments of the activity, but the objects involved are the same.

TABLE 14.1
Model of the Sheets Given to the Children

A. Predictions		
Which Objects Will Sink or Float in the Water?		
	Will Sink	Will Float
Stone		
Small stones		
Page		
Sponge		
Chalk		
Plasticine wood		
B. Observations		
Which Objects Sank or Floated in the Water?		
	Sank	Floated
Stone		
Small stones		
Page		
Sponge		
Chalk		
Plasticine wood		

There are equally varied and complex opportunities for recordings in the social field. In Type (d) recordings, the personal involvement of children is very strong, and the shift from news or observations supplied by each child to recordable data involves a considerable amount of oral discourse. The problem of categorization is more complex and explicit in Type (d) recordings than in other types: For example, if parents' work activities have to be examined, one must first understand what constitutes a work activity and then determine acceptable categories and names for these activities. It should be noted, however, that when this categorizing and recording activity is done in a class that regularly exchanges letters with a comparable class in another town, the communication of the different recordings (done in the two classes) can produce a shift from rethinking and organizing the results of the direct experience of classmates to reading and organizing the results of the other class. In this case, real understanding can be greatly supported by aspects of social interests and coparticipation.

A school is generally restricted by the instruments available to it. From the first year of school, the computer may open up new possibilities and contribute to an expansion of practices that today are often omitted. Computer use brings with it a general perspective on language that is not restricted to natural language. Cognitive aspects and conventions come to the fore. Although the benefit that linguistic development receives from writing texts with word processing programs is undoubtedly significant, equal attention should be paid to using the computer to broaden written language experience. The computer provides alternatives to tables and charts and has a richer, more efficient consultation potential, providing a strong stimulus for processing data.

CONCLUSION

The use of writing for nontextual purposes is extremely important in literate societies and in adults' everyday life. It can be considered one of the most important practical uses of writing. The results of this writing can also be read as a propositional string and can be analyzed from both a logical and an informative point of view.

Schools should not neglect this type of writing activity, because it is particularly appropriate for the aims of ordering, organizing, and interpreting information that can concern different types of phenomena (social, scientific, everyday ones). In other words, this writing has a clear cognitive import: It can facilitate the cognitive activities of understanding and inferring, and it requires the children to categorize, codify, and—in particular social settings—negotiate the meanings of the categories and the records. From this point of view, it is clearly linked to scientific procedures that can begin to be introduced even in preschool settings.

Moreover, it is simple and motivating for children to practice different types of recording from the beginning of their writing development. They can use tables, partially prepared by their teachers, and they can begin by using invented symbols to represent persons or situations. For young children (as well as for all people), using marks as symbols is a main step toward symbolic development, which includes writing acquisition. They can "play" with the different ways in which a table can be "read." Last but not least, these alternative ways of using writing can be introduced even when children are still beginners in alphabetic writing and can support their motivation to understand the writing system. It is rather typical that, in classes in which records are kept (e.g., of children's attendance, weather observations, turns in using equipment), children also use their first names that are written as sources of introduction to letters and words.

ACKNOWLEDGMENT

The author thanks Gisella Paoletti for her cooperation in collecting data on which this paper is based.

REFERENCES

Applebee, A. N. (1984). Writing and reasoning. *Review of Educational Research, 4,* 577–596.

Beach, R., & Bridwell, L. S. (1984). *New directions in composition research.* New York: Guilford.

Bruner, J. S. (1971). *The relevance of education.* New York: Norton.

Goody, J. (1977). *The domestication of the savage mind.* Cambridge, England: Cambridge University Press.

Havelock, E. A. (1986). *The muse learns to write.* New Haven and London: Yale University Press.

Ong, W. J. (Ed.). (1979). *Ramus, method, and the decay of dialogue.* New York: Octagon Books.

Ong, W. J. (1982). *Orality and literacy. The technologizing of the word.* London and New York: Methuen.

Orsolini, M. (1988). Parlare e scrivere [Speaking and writing]. *Scuola e città, 34,* 369–373.

WRITTEN LANGUAGE IN EDUCATIONAL CONTEXTS

15

LITERACY IN FIRST GRADE: TRADITIONAL AND EXPERIMENTAL SITUATIONS

Marina Pascucci Formisano
University of Rome "La Sapienza"

This chapter examines how the first stages of literacy education are put into practice in some first-year elementary classes in central and southern Italy. The situations presented first can be called *normal* situations, because they can be found daily in Italian schools, often characterized by a pedagogic tradition and common methodological and didactic practices that are not always explicit to teachers themselves. The content and the form of the educational process in such situations are then compared briefly with the form, content, and informative criteria of an experimental situation (Pontecorvo, 1989; Pontecorvo, Tassinari, & Camaioni, 1990).

OBSERVING TEACHERS' WRITING AND READING ACTIVITIES

To collect information about the way teachers introduce their 6-year-old pupils to written language, we observed teaching methodologies and class activities focused on "content." Procedures and content can enlighten both teachers' psychological theories and their pedagogical beliefs about what writing and reading are and how they can be taught and learned. In gathering data on teachers' methodological and didactic practices in teaching our children, and in order to investigate differences in children's learning, I have followed a three-part research design.

First, keeping in mind the discrepancy between what is normally said about methods used in the class and what is actually practiced (Chall, 1967), we interviewed 10 teachers individually. The content of these interviews, which took place before the beginning of the academic year, covered the methods that they would follow, the teaching aids they would use, what they would ask their children to do, and the modality of work (e.g., small groups, individual work, or the whole class as a group) that they would favor. According to recent studies, the modality of work most widely and frequently used by elementary school teachers in Italy is still that of the class as a whole engaged in parallel work. This differs from the practice of teachers in nursery school, who have children work in small groups for expressive activities or socialization games. A previous study has shown that the ideal modality of teaching favored by the majority of teachers interviewed from both types of schools is tutorial work, that is, a one-to-one relationship between teachers and students (Formisano, 1991).

The second method used in this study was an ecological observation of children and teachers in actual situations of learning/teaching the written language. An observer attended each class three or four times a week, recording the activities and verbal interactions produced in the whole time dedicated to linguistic activity, which generally varied from 90 to 180 minutes every time. Paper-and-pencil observations always accompanied the tape recording. These observations were carried out daily from the beginning of the school year until January and then once or twice each week from February until June.

It should be emphasized that the main interest was not the teaching method used (in the sense of adherence to a certain consolidated practice) but rather the meaning the teachers gave to reading and writing as objects of knowledge and tools for knowing. We wanted to know what, in fact, is being offered to the children: what the teachers considered important, useful, and effective to introduce children to literacy in a broader way. We also wanted to know in which sociocommunicative situations those literacy activities occurred.

Third, we carried out three different assessments (at the beginning of the school year, in December, and in May) of each child's level of conceptualization of the written language, according to a scale proposed by Ferreiro and Teberosky (1979) and used in other research in Italy (see Pontecorvo, 1985). In this way, we hoped to gather and measure the effects of different types of methodological and didactic practices on real levels of written language conceptualization for each child.

The sample group that we observed was composed of classes from 10 state elementary schools in central and southern Italy: four from Rome (high socioeconomic level), three from Bari (middle socioeconomic level), and three from Salerno (low socioeconomic level). The teachers were between 35 and 45 years of age, and all had several years of experience in the first year of elementary school (except Teacher C from Salerno).

SOME CONSTANTS: WHAT HAPPENS

Despite the geographic and socioeconomic differences, the 10 situations that we analyzed revealed some common features, both in what was used and in what was absent. The common root to didactic and methodological options we describe is the consolidated idea that written language can only be directly taught through a one-way transmission from the teacher, as a "professionally competent" subject, to the pupils. The same model considers the pupil to be incapable of any autonomous conceptual elaboration.

One of the constant elements in the 10 situations is that reading and writing were treated for the first five months as only one subject. More attention and time were dedicated to writing, whereas reading had only a secondary function, as a simple and implicit means of checking what was learned. Generally, the children were engaged in a series of activities that reductively focused on the acquisition of the alphabetic code, with work drastically reduced to the code itself. A brief examination of factors that the different situations had in common reveals the following:

- "Language" is "done" every day, at the least for the first two hours but very often for the entire morning (although this includes a considerable amount of time when little or nothing is being done due to lack of time organization).
- Work directly on the alphabetic code begins with no previous activities on the nature of symbols or the prediction of meaning.
- In some cases, the children receive prewriting exercises related to the class texts in the first two weeks of September; they are also given pages of little circles and squares that have to be completed either in class or at home.
- In most cases the classroom is a bare environment, where it is not possible to find any type of written material.

In 9 cases out of 10, the only examples of written language were wall charts of the alphabet. The one exception was in the classroom of the youngest teacher, who had never taught in the first grade before. In her classroom, strips of paper containing sentences from stories in the textbook had been hung on the walls.

The didactic and methodological procedures recorded here are based on the traditional notion that all children are equally ignorant with regard to the written language. Therefore, they are offered the same things in the same way, according to the same sequence and the same timing, by the teacher who possesses, manages, administers, and gives out knowledge.

To that end, and for that reason, it is always the teacher who speaks. In this context, then, we can understand the following comments made by Teacher B and Teacher A, respectively: "The first year is always a suicide," "Every time that I've done it, I've got inflammation of my vocal cords" (Teacher B was from Rome, and Teacher A was from Bari). Table 15.1 shows how the daily reality of "doing language every day" takes shape.

WHAT DOES NOT HAPPEN

Clearly, the process of early literacy requires a considerable time with the alphabet in the spotlight, but such attention cannot be the only way of approaching the written language. An approach centered on the code overturns the function of the code from being a means to being an end in itself and results in slowing down or wiping out motivation for learning and for an articulated use of the skills of reading and writing. This limitation is extremely negative, because it does not consider that work on the code, according to Ferreiro and Teberosky, should be undertaken as an end point of conceptualization processes and of complex and articulated activities, rather than as a common starting point for all children (Ferreiro & Teberosky, 1979). Furthermore, it professes to complete the alphabetization process with the simple possession of the code, excluding

TABLE 15.1
Raw Frequencies of Different Types of Activity
on the Alphabetic Code (September–December)*

	Bari			Rome				Salerno		
	Ia	Ib	Ic	Ia	Ib	Ic	Id	Ia	Ib	Ic
Total number of observations	33	31	31	39	39	36	34	29	28	31
Presentation of isolated words for analysis of single letters		daily			daily				0	
Looking for words that begin with the same letters	10	15	10	19	11	18		10	12	15
Juxtaposition of syllables	11	13	14	10	20	25		25	13	16
Phonemic/graphemic association using alphabet charts		daily			daily				daily	
Copying from the board, reading		daily			daily				daily	
Group dictation of isolated words, syllables		0		18	14	15			0	

*Numbers indicate how often the activity occurred.

any conception and any form of enlarged literacy from among the various meanings associated with this term.

This explains how, in the 10 situations that we observed, activities dealing with certain areas were systematically absent (see Table 15.1), including the following:

- Symbolization, meaning recognition and use of conventional symbols given to or produced by the children themselves.
- Spoken language, that is, conversations and discussions on particular topics in small or large groups.
- Children's narrations of known or invented stories and of real events that they participated in as either individuals or part of a group.
- Stories narrated by the teacher.
- Meaningful texts read by the teacher.
- Individual or group production by the children of captions or titles for drawings, or of different real texts dictated to the teacher.

With regard to the list of exclusions, a brief comment should be made about the real significance of not providing or planning for activities of spoken interaction. In other words, no type of conversation/discussion occurs, except spontaneously, during pauses, between periods, during routine activities, or while doing classwork. Teacher B in Rome, for example, considered it appropriate to announce on the first day of school: "Boys and girls, we aren't in kindergarten any more! At school you *mustn't* talk; you should work in silence!"

The reading by the teacher of meaningful texts is also among those activities not carried out in the first year of elementary school. Just as in nursery school, where the teacher narrates fairy tales or stories, the child here is never engaged in proper reading activities, in which the reading of different texts is aimed at trying to understand the meaning of what has been read. In class, teachers do not read for their students or for themselves.

WHAT IS READ AND WHAT IS WRITTEN

This section provides a detailed description of the contents of the material provided to the children as written language, which was the same in 8 out of 10 situations. To give prominence to the initial vowel, *ape* (Italian for *bee*) is the first word presented. For seasonal reasons, however, *uva* (grape) provides hot competition. This leads necessarily to an enlargement of the semantic sphere to include *acini* (a rarely used scholastic, technical word for *berries*)! These words are presented without meaningful context and are chosen merely because they are short and they begin with a vowel that has been singled out for presentation.

September 24: Bari Teacher B

T: [writes on the board in printed capital letters: /U/ and /A/]
       "What's missing?"
Only one child: "The one like this." [making the sign of a /V/ with his fingers]

November 17: Bari Teacher A

T: [writes the date on the board and says] "Copy."
       "Now draw *uva* (grape)."
T: [when they all have finished] "Now on the narrow line you should write
       /U/, /V/, /A/. The /U/ as in *uccello* (bird), the /V/ as in *vaso* (vase), *UVA*
       and the /A/ with the little leg."

When words are no longer presented in isolation, we get strings of words
juxtaposed but not connected with a verb to which a meaning or description
can be attached, as for the materials from textbooks as illustrated by Teacher
C in Bari who assigned the following task on November 13:

T: "Open your books to page 19. Mark the place. (reads)
       *SUL MARE VOLANO I GABBIANI. SPIAGGIA. ONDA. NAVE. SCOGLIO. I
       PESCATORI RITIRANO LE RETI. PESCATORE. RETE. FARO. PORTO.*
       (Seagulls fly over the sea. Beach. Wave. Ship. Cliff. The fishermen pull
       in their nets. Fisherman. Net. Lighthouse. Port.) You have to copy these
       sentences in longhand in your notebooks for homework."

There is no need to dwell on such examples, but it is evident that they result
in reading with the mouth and lips or, even more likely, reading with the ears,
inasmuch as this form of chorus repetition practiced at school leads to memorization. In this way, reading as a search for meaning is replaced by repetition
of what one has heard.
     Our analysis of the practices of the 10 teachers in our study showed that their
only linguistic objective was to teach children to read and write. Such an objective
was translated as and reduced to teaching/learning the alphabetic code. In
particular, *reading* is defined and seen as "identifying graphemes in a correct
spatio-temporal sequence" and *writing* as "composing letters" (Deva, 1982).
     In the preceding section, we mentioned that copying from the board was a
daily practice. The following examples show how this was carried out and what
the children were asked to do:

November 17: Bari Teacher B

T: "Now that you've finished copying *UVA*, do a *PERA* (pear) [draws a pear
       on the board]. Now on the narrow lines *PERA* [raises voice] individually!
       Now, the /P/ as in *pane* (bread), the /E/ as in *erba* (grass), the /R/ as in
       radio, the /A/ as in *ape* (bee).

January 24, 1988: Rome Teacher B

T: "Will you pay attention, without getting distracted!" The teacher writes /Thursday/ January 24th/ on the board and you copy it neatly. "You'll need to use two squares!" [Leaves the room, then comes back] "Below the date make a drawing; draw a picture of your school friends, and then we'll write: 'At school we are friends.' Isn't that right? Friends." [While the children are drawing, the teacher writes on the board] /At school we are friends/ (in longhand) /AT SCHOOL WE ARE FRIENDS/ (in printed capital letters)

T: "When you finish you can have a snack. Copy without making mistakes! At home do a page of /Friends/ in longhand together with your mothers."

From these didactic procedures, it is easy to trace the teacher's idea of the child on the one hand, and the model of teaching and learning on the other, as well as her or his concept of writing and its use and functions.

Text Composition

Starting in January, the percentage of time spent daily on spelling decreased and attention was directed instead to exercises on specific spelling difficulties, with time allotted to the composition of short sentences on a given theme. For this writing activity, the teacher proposed both subject and number of sentences (from three to five): "Write three sentences about your mother." Hence, autonomous composition was only possible at home, because at school the sentences were usually suggested or dictated, as in the following examples:

Oranges are sweet.

Oranges are orange.

Oranges are good for you.

This illustrates how the dictation of words is replaced by the dictation of ideas or sentences. Even when the teacher's topic is connected to an actual fact that interests the entire class, the collaborative construction of a text is prevented by the teacher's dictation of more or less logically connected sentences. This is shown in the following example in which the first three sentences are connected, but sentences 4 and 5 follow without any continuity solution.

Teacher A in Rome

1. The teacher has brought the calendar.
2. There are twelve months.
3. Today is Francesca's birthday.
4. God created the world.

5. The radiator keeps us warm.

The procedures followed by the teachers in our study during first grade reveal that the teachers consider children as passive, cognitively impoverished, and incapable of thinking anything by themselves or of articulating a thought in a verbal form (in fact, no oral language activities are proposed). These children could not write, even after they had learned the alphabet, because they were not taught to write in the sense of composing real texts with different aims and different audiences in mind.

Our study showed that, in the second year of elementary school, neither the exercises nor the teaching methods changed. Many examples from the following year demonstrate this, including the following from Teacher B in Rome, who, as usual, gives her own ideas and a dictation before moving the children along to a composition:

Rome, January 23, 1989—10:45 AM

"Take out a big lined notebook, because we're going to write about winter fruits and how they are made." Holding up an orange and a tangerine, she reads the dictation, showing the children, from behind her desk, the parts that she names (e.g., the peel, the shape).

"Oranges, tangerines, and lemons belong to the citrus family, just as cats belong to the feline family, rats to the rodent family, just as Simone belongs to the Lorini family. Is that clear? Right, everyone ready to write, and make sure that you keep up with me." (The children do the dictation.)

"Now, after the dictation, draw a nice big orange, and near that, draw a nice section of orange, and then an orange sliced in half. Get to work and work quickly because we've got to do something else, and I don't want to see anything messy. I want to see nice drawings." (She goes out.)

"Now there's going to be trouble for anyone who moves about; find a clean page and write with a red pen. Look at the orange and the lemon, and write how they're similar and how they're different. You should begin like, you can say that the teacher showed you a lemon and an orange ... that the orange is orange and the lemon is yellow; that the orange is round and the lemon is oval; that the orange has a thick, rough, porous peel and the lemon's got one that's thinner, smoother, and less porous, and what can you make with an orange and with a lemon?" (Children respond, in chorus: "Juice.")

"So, start like this: The teacher showed us a lemon and an orange, full stop, because the sentence is finished so don't forget when you finish a sentence to put a full stop."

Obviously, the 10 situations represented in this study are not completely representative of the Italian pedagogic and didactic approach. Teachers who have had training connected with CEMEA (Centers for Training in the Methods of Action Education) or with MCE (The Movement for Educational Cooperation), for example, pay close attention to aspects of individual and group expression. They are also aware of the aesthetic and expressive dimensions of teaching, even when working on the alphabet, which is never reduced to a singular linguistic activity.

A DIFFERENT WAY

Children can be taught in a different way. The following paragraphs illustrate this by describing activities run in an experimental context. In contrast to the previous observations, the situations that follow are drawn from an experimental program of educational continuity (Pontecorvo, 1989) involving children from 4 to 8 years of age (thus, officially attending nursery school and elementary school) in Rome and Florence. In this program, a curriculum for the linguistic area was worked out (Formisano, 1990a; Formisano & Zucc99 hermaglio, 1989), drawing on the theoretical model of Ferreiro and Teberosky (1979) concerning the processes of spontaneous development of the written language.

The curriculum developed for this experiment resulted from specific contributions from the researchers and the teachers from the University of Rome and the University of Florence, as well as from interpersonal and group interactions among these people.

From the beginning, five areas of work were identified:

- Symbolization.
- Spoken language.
- Spontaneous construction of written language.
- Written language.
- Reflections on language.

Both the researchers and the teachers shared two assumptions about the learning mechanism underlying children's acquisition of literacy. The first is that the structure of the written code has to be partly "discovered" by children through an active process of hypothesis testing. This process of discovery requires a literate "environment" in which the materials and means of a literate culture are present, including various writing aids, books, newspapers, periodicals, paper and pencils, typewriters, and Freinet printers. These materials were made easily accessible to the children. The second assumption is that the acquisition of literacy is a sociocognitive process, focused on discovering the "meanings" of written texts, not only on mastering the structure of the written forms. This process requires educational practices that predominantly use peer interactions, discussions, and collective production of texts (Damon, 1984; Pontecorvo, 1986) as meaningful and effective ways of developing knowledge in a Vygotskian perspective (Formisano & Zucchermaglio, 1987; Pontecorvo, Ajello, & Zuccher-maglio, 1991).

A summary of how time was spent in the classroom in Rome during the periods dedicated to linguistic activities (Formisano, 1990b) shows that these children also "did language" every day, but time was organized and distributed in a different manner, and activities and "contents" were finalized to different aims.

Among the 5- and 6-year-olds, the largest amount of time was dedicated to the spoken language (e.g., storytelling, discussion, and planning), followed by written language development activities. In this category, we do not consider pre-graphism activities or copying or writing the same letter or the same word several times (Formisano, Pontecorvo, & Zucchermaglio, 1986); instead we refer here to all the activities of a first approach to written language, aiming to promote analysis and reflection on what is written, what can be written, and how. Practice in written language, that is, listening to and understanding texts read by the teacher, and production of texts to be dictated occupied the least amount of time.

In the following year, when the children were 6 and 7 years old, the time spent on speaking and language development was reduced because children had the benefit of the experiences and activities of the preceding year. On the other hand, the amount of time dedicated to written language increased. These activities included production of texts, individual reading, and listening to read-ings by the teacher or some of the more able classmates.

The last part of this section summarizes our observations of the classroom environment and activities of 5- and 6-year-old children at the school in Rome. A great deal of special attention was given to a widened and comprehensive approach to the search for and organization of knowledge and the use of reading and writing. With these principles as a foundation, the importance of direct work on the alphabet and, consequently, the amount of time dedicated to it were greatly reduced. The children, who were immersed daily in a literate environ-ment, participated regularly in small groups or as a whole class in varied expe-riences of reading different texts for different reasons. They also directly pro-duced oral and written texts, which the less able members of the class did in the form of dictations to the teacher or a competent peer. In this way, the difference between the aims and forms of written and spoken language was quite clear at the level of immediate use.

The written language curriculum provides one way of conceiving of and dealing with the problem of the first stages of literacy. To develop the children's written language ability, small groups were engaged in two activities for 90 minutes daily: production and comparison of spontaneous writings and guessing the meaning of written words from different sources (e.g., on labels and food packets; see Table 15.2).

These activities were aimed at building in children both a basic expectation that written texts have a meaning and their skill in using context to interpret the text's meaning. An example of this is Franco's (5.3) attempt at guessing what

TABLE 15.2
Language Curriculum
(from Formisano, 1990b)

Area	Frequency	Age/Type of Group
1. Processes of symbolization		
• Development and use of symbols for the class register and the weather	Daily	5 and 6 years of age, class as a whole
• Games of codifying and decodifying symbols	Occasionally	Class as a whole
2. Spoken language		
• Conversations and discussions	60 minutes daily	5 and 6 years of age, class as a whole
• Storytelling (for children 5 and 6 years of age)	Occasionally	
• Communication games	Occasionally	5 and 6 years of age, class as a whole and medium-sized groups
3. Development of the written language		
• Prediction of meaning of written texts using various aids, including illustrated texts	90 minutes daily	Small heterogeneous group with prevalence of 5-year-olds in the second part of the year
• Spontaneous production	" "	" "
• Interpretation of pictures and illustrated sequences	" "	" "
• Personal reelaboration of written forms (presyllabic, syllabic, syllabic–alphabetic, alphabetic)	" "	" "
4. Written language		
• Listening and understanding different types of texts (captions under pictures, signs, recipes, labels, and personal writing)	Daily or twice per week, about 60 minutes, plus individual "space"	Small and medium groups; individual; pairs; according to time
• Production of various texts according to individual ability	Daily, 90 minutes	Small groups; pairs
• A child's day book	Once a week	Alternating small groups
• Texts written together (reports, news)	Once a week	6 years of age, small groups
• Elaboration of stories, invitations, and recipes	Once a week and according to circumstances	5 years of age, small groups
• Composition and dictation of stories to a more competent scribe		
5. Reflections on language		
• Nursery rhymes, rhymes (also written by the children), and stories	During games	Small or big, homogeneous or mixed groups
• Reflections on the stylistic features of written material	Occasionally	6 years of age, small groups

was written on a medical certificate for readmission to school: "He no longer has a temperature: He can go back to school." Another example is the children's view of a memorandum from the school's principal. When the children were asked if the principal had written them a fairy tale, they said that the text probably was about school regulations or provided the school's meal schedule.

Guessing the meaning of written texts encouraged children not only to link the meaning to the context but also to compare different interpretations of the more formal aspects of the written form. For that reason, we tried to get children to treat written language as a system that needs to be discovered, not just "learned." Thus, interaction among children was the means of encouraging an attitude that searches and investigates and forms and checks hypotheses. More specific details of these activities can be found elsewhere (Formisano, 1990c).

SOME COMPARISONS

In this section, I briefly provide some evidence of the impact that traditional or innovative situations can have on children's reading and writing. That evidence is provided in Zucchermaglio's (1990) study, which compares children's performances on reading–writing tests in the experimental program described earlier and in a traditional program. In her study, the traditional situation consisted of classes using didactic techniques and curricular orientations quite similar to those described in the first part of this chapter. Children in these traditional classes were matched to children in the experimental group in terms of age, gender, socioeconomic status, and order of birth in the family. Children of both the traditional and the experimental groups were tested for their reading and writing skills when they were 5 to 6 and 7 years old.

The children in the experimental group obtained significantly higher results in most of the tests administered in the three years of the study. In particular, the 5-year-olds in the experimental group (officially in the last year of nursery school) demonstrated a clear advantage over their classmates in the control group. In fact, at this stage the children in the experimental group usually gave answers at the syllabic level, according to the model of Ferreiro and Teberosky (1979), and knew how to use a piece of writing by relating it to themselves. At the same time, the children of the control group still did not understand that our written language is based on a transcription of the spoken language. Furthermore, the competence of the experimental group increased constantly and continuously throughout the three years, whereas the competence of most children in the control group did not develop consistently and, after the first year of elementary school, it dramatically declined. The children of the experimental group developed the capacity to use knowledge about books in a functional way (e.g., to identify a title, author, or publishing house; to use the index to find a certain story quickly), whereas those educated with a traditional approach to literacy did not. This ability to use a book does not automatically accompany or emerge from learning the alphabet.

It is worth giving some examples of the different cognitive activities and attitudes underlying children's reading in the experimental and the traditional groups. The following is a description of two tests administered individually to 5- and 6-year-olds. In the first test, children were shown a picture of a police officer directing traffic at a street crossing with two children riding their bicycles. This picture was shown to the children twice, each time with one of two different captions below the picture:

1. The children are riding their bicycles.
2. The policeman is directing the traffic.

The children were then asked, "What do you think is written here?"

This test explored children's reasoning about the relationship between context and text. In particular, it addressed the question of whether children realized that differences in the texts written below the same picture involved a difference in the meaning of these texts. If a child gave the same interpretation of both captions, he or she was asked "Is the same thing written under both pictures, or are they different?" The test also assessed children's level of reading.

Several examples of answers from children in the traditional classes follow:

P: "There's the same thing written because the picture's the same: 'bicycle and car.' "
F: "City ... houses ..."
G: [in caption 1 reads] /policeman/, /bicycle/, /car/, /bicycle/.
    [in caption 2] "I've already read it. It's the same."
A: [indicating all of caption 1] /bicycle/
    [indicating all of caption 2] /car/

Most of the children in the experimental group noticed the difference in the captions. Consequently, being aware that different written forms carry different meanings, they tried different hypotheses.

C: "What's written is different; but the picture's the same!"
V: [in caption 1] "Don't go too fast!" [referring to what the policeman is saying]
    [in caption 2] "Don't go too f ... no! They're different! Don't go slow!"
E: [in caption 1] "The boy and the girl are *going to* school" [then] "The pictures are exactly the same!"
    [in caption 2] "The boy and the girl are *coming from* school"
S: [in caption 1] "You go and you stop"
    [in caption 2] "You stop and you go." "The picture's the same but what's written is the opposite ... but I don't know how to read!"

In another reading comprehension test, the children were asked to "Draw the door that is missing on the house" (in Italian, *Fai la porta che manca alla casetta*). The house was shown on the page with that instruction, and the children were given a pencil to use.

Most of the control-group children from the first year of elementary school read without difficulty, although without intonation. They did not, however, perform the requested task, thus showing a lack of comprehension. The experimental-group children of the same age were less fluent in their reading, but most of them, after some rereading and self-corrections, managed to fulfill the request. Note the different reactions of two children from the two groups who made the same "mistake":

L: [control group, reads] *Fai la porta che mangia* [instead of: *manca*] *la casetta* [literally: "Draw the door that's *eating the house*" [instead of "that is missing on the house"].

L: "I've read it."
[He doesn't realize the mistake or the incongruency and does not do the task.]

E: [experimental group, reads] *Fai la porta che mangia la casetta.* [literally: "Draw the door that is eating the house"].

E: "That's not possible!" "What does it mean?"

E. carefully reads the sentence a few more times, always mumbling that it cannot be possible, because "It makes no sense," monitors his reading, finally corrects himself, and performs the task of "drawing the door that is lacking."

SOME CONCLUSIONS

In closing, let me summarize the major differences that emerged from our observations of traditional and experimental classes. In a traditional class, writing and reading seem to be implicitly regarded by the teacher as a more perceptual than cognitive–linguistic type of learning. The main focus is on teaching children the rules underlying an orthographic system: namely, the sounds to be pronounced in correspondence with certain letters. Teachers do not seem to assume that something should also be taught about "texts," and they are confident that children can learn about texts by copying words from the blackboard or writing what the teacher dictates. Teachers also seem to assume that children do not need to be motivated in using reading and writing for communicating.

In contrast, in the experimental classes, teachers were conscious that reading and writing require a complex system of categorizations and a multifaceted process of conceptualization. For that reason, children were encouraged to test their "theory" of the written code and to discover the basic properties of an alphabetic written system through active processes of guessing, analyzing, and comparing. Children were offered not only specific activities on reading and writing but also an environment in which they could interact with books, newspapers, magazines, and writing instruments, long before their reading or writing competence was developed. They were also encouraged to discuss their interpretation of written text meanings and to produce texts by using all the resources available, including the competence of other children.

REFERENCES

Chall, J. (1967). *Learning to read: The great debate.* New York: McGraw-Hill.

Damon, W. (1984). Peer education. *The Journal of Applied Developmental Psychology, 5,* 46–54.

Deva, F. (1982). *I processi di apprendimento della lettura e della scrittura* [Reading and writing learning processes]. Firenze, Italy: La Nuova Italia.

Ferreiro, E., & Teberosky, A. (1979). *Los sistemas de escritura en el desarrollo del nino* [Literacy before schooling]. México City: Siglo XXI Editores.

Formisano, M. (1990a). Evoluzione del lavoro dei bambini e degli insegnanti a Roma [Evolution of children's and teachers' work]. In C. Pontecorvo, G. Tassinari, & L. Camaioni (Eds.), *Continuità educativa dai quattro agli otto anni. Condizioni, metodi e strumenti di una ricerca sperimentale nella scuola* [Educational continuity from 4 to 8 years of age] (pp. 129–139). Firenze, Italy: La Nuova Italia.

Formisano, M. (1990b). Il curricolo reale dell'area linguistica [The real language curriculum]. In C. Pontecorvo, G. Tassinari, & L. Camaioni (Eds.), *Continuità educativa dai quattro agli otto anni. Condizioni, metodi e strumenti di una ricerca sperimentale nella scuola* [Educational continuity from 4 to 8 years of age] (pp. 153–165). Firenze, Italy: La Nuova Italia.

Formisano, M. (1990c). Il primo contatto con la lingua scritta [The first approach to written language]. In C. Pontecorvo (Ed.), *Una scuola per i bambini* [A school for all the children] (pp. 145–161). Firenze, Italy: La Nuova Italia.

Formisano, M. (1991). Imparare da soli, imparare insieme: rappresentazioni e comportamenti degli insegnanti [Learning on your own, learning together: Teacher's representations and behaviors]. In C. Pontecorvo, A. M. Ajello, & C. Zucchermaglio (Eds.), *Discutendo si impara* [Learning by discussing] (pp. 149–165). Rome: La Nuova Italia Scientifica.

Formisano, M., Pontecorvo, C., & Zucchermaglio, C. (1986). *Guida alla lingua scritta* [Guide to the written language]. Rome: Editori Riuniti.

Formisano, M., & Zucchermaglio, C. (1987). Costruzione sociale della lingua scritta [Written language social construction]. *Scuola e Città, 4,* 155–164.

Formisano, M., & Zucchermaglio, C. (1989). Parlare, leggere e scrivere tra i quattro e gli otto anni [Talking, reading and writing from four to eight years]. In C. Pontecorvo (Ed.), *Un curricolo per la continuità educativa tra i quattro e gli otto anni* [A curriculum for educational continuity from four to eight years] (pp. 163–179). Firenze, Italy: La Nuova Italia.

Pontecorvo, C. (1985). Figure, parole, numeri: Un problema di simbolizzazione [Drawings, words, numbers: A symbolization issue]. *Età Evolutiva, 22,* 5–33.

Pontecorvo, C. (1986). Interazione di gruppo e conoscenza. Processi e ruoli [Peer interactions and knowledge. Processes and roles]. *Età Evolutiva, 24,* 85–95.

Pontecorvo, C. (Ed.). (1989). *Un curricolo per la continuità educativa dai quattro agli otto anni* [A curriculum for educational continuity from four to eight years of age]. Firenze, Italy: La Nuova Italia.

Pontecorvo, C., Ajello, A. M., & Zucchermaglio, C. (Eds.). (1991). *Discutendo si impara* [Learning, through discussing]. Rome: La Nuova Italia Scientifica.

Pontecorvo, C., Tassinari, G., & Camaioni, L. (Eds.). (1990). *Continuità educativa dai quattro agli otto anni. Condizioni, metodi e strumenti di una ricerca sperimentale nella scuola* [Educational continuity from 4 to 8 years of age]. Firenze, Italy: La Nuova Italia.

Zucchermaglio, C. (1990). L'apprendimento della lingua scritta [Learning the written language]. In C. Pontecorvo, G. Tassinari, & L. Camaioni (Eds.), *Continuità educativa dai quattro agli otto anni. Condizioni, metodi e strumenti di una ricerca sperimentale nella scuola* [Educational continuity from 4 to 8 years of age] (pp. 297–312). Firenze, Italy: La Nuova Italia.

16

DEAF CHILDREN AND THE CONSTRUCTION OF WRITTEN TEXTS

Maria Pia Conte
Laura Pagliari Rampelli
Virginia Volterra
Institute of Psychology, Consiglio Nazionale delle Ricerche

LANGUAGE AND THE DEAF CHILD

People born deaf or who lose their hearing in the first two years of life cannot learn spoken language and, thus, commonly become known as *deaf-mutes*. This term causes considerable confusion, because, with rare exceptions, children born deaf have perfectly sound vocal organs and unimpaired language faculty that simply cannot "get working" as they normally do in hearing children. This apparently simple fact is in reality fraught with implications.

The language faculty enables babies and, thus, children to learn the language to which they are exposed. Being exposed to a vocal language implies hearing and communicating with the social environment in a particular language. Hearing, therefore, is essential in order to talk. But deafness, which is often not immediately apparent, is a more or less hidden deficiency. The families of deaf children start to become concerned only when their children fail to produce their first words after the age of 1 year; until then, the babies often seem normal and capable of understanding everything that is said to them. The families do not realize that their babies are attending not to their words but rather to the nonverbal concomitants (i.e., the gestures, actions, and facial expressions accompanying their verbal utterances).

The fully functioning faculty of sight serves as a vicarious channel for all the visually transmittable components of communication. When family communication concentrates primarily on vocal–aural channels, however, deaf children receive only a small portion of the messages, thus remaining largely isolated from the surrounding linguistic communication. The children have no opportunity to use their vocal organs or, consequently, to use their language faculty. The crucial question, then, is whether children born deaf can develop the language faculty in other ways.

From the earliest times, deaf people have chosen—or, rather, have been obliged to choose—the visual means they have at their command to substitute for vocal sounds, thus discovering the potential of gestures or signs to communicate. The visual–gestural channel takes over the aural–vocal channel. This manual form of communication has always been essential for deaf people, as demonstrated by the way it has been preserved; it has been handed down from generation to generation, even in countries where attempts have been made to suppress or fight it.

A key issue has been whether this visual form of communication can be defined as a language. As long ago as the 18th century, the scientific community took great interest in the gestures of the deaf (Lane, 1976); it was not until very recently, however, that researchers discovered and demonstrated that this form of communication not only satisfies all the cognitive, communicative, and expressive needs of a human community but also possesses all the fundamental properties of a language. In the past 30 years, a significant number of research projects have explored various aspects of sign language (e.g., Klima & Bellugi, 1979; Stokoe, 1960, 1978; Stokoe & Volterra, 1985; Volterra, 1987).

Research has shown how the various vocal languages, with their different phonetic, lexical, and grammatical–syntactical features, have come into existence and developed. Research has also shown how the various sign languages, with their own precise lexical and grammatical–syntactical structures, have grown up within the communities of the deaf. In short, the language faculty of the deaf has found spontaneous expression through its own channels.

A great deal of research in various countries has shown that deaf children exposed to sign language from birth can master it in the same period of time required for hearing children to learn vocal language and similar learning processes (Newport & Meier, 1985; Volterra & Erting, 1990). Clearly, therefore, a child born deaf can achieve competence in sign language naturally and spontaneously, whereas the same child needs systematic, explicit training to learn to understand and produce the spoken language. On the other hand, a hearing child spontaneously learns to understand and produce the language he or she is exposed to, without any specific instruction. However, can a child born deaf achieve the competence of a hearing child in the spoken and written language with specific training (Caselli, 1987; Caselli & Massoni, 1986)?

The oral method for educating the deaf that was officially adopted after the 1880 Congress of Milan was conceived with this implicit (but never fully explicit) aim. Whether and to what extent the aim has been achieved remains to be verified. That a deaf child is able to take part in a short conversation, read aloud, and write a composition does not necessarily prove that these goals have been achieved.

A rigorous evaluation of children's language skills indicates much more, including whether lexical knowledge extends from the literal to the metaphorical; the capacity to master grammar and morphological rules (which can be very complex in languages such as Italian); the ability to produce sentences, including the more complex syntactical structures; the ability to use all these skills in both written and oral forms and in expression and comprehension; and the capacity to formulate judgments of linguistic acceptability. True comprehension implies not only understanding all the nuances of a word but also the ability to identify the essential information in a text, drawing inferences, recognizing causal links, and deciding whether a sentence is linguistically acceptable.

Research projects with deaf subjects in English-speaking countries (Bishop, 1982, 1983; Quigley & King, 1980; Quigley & Paul, 1984; Swisher, 1976), have examined various language skills: lexicon, syntax, production, comprehension, and acceptability judgments. All agree that deaf children and adults rarely reach the level achieved by a native speaker in written or spoken English. Based on these results, we conclude that, compared with their hearing peers, deaf pupils generally:

- Produce shorter sentences, tending to avoid the more complex syntactical structures.
- Show poorer vocabulary in both comprehension and production.
- Reveal markedly rigid lexical concepts that prevent their mastering the various shades of meaning of individual words.
- Commit errors in the comprehension of texts containing reversible passive clauses, pronouns, prepositions, and plural nouns.
- Encounter problems in judging the acceptability of relative, subordinate, and pronominal clauses.
- Commit errors of omission, substitution, and addition with various aspects of morphology, and, in particular, with prepositions, articles, and pronouns.

Until a few years ago, no systematic research had been carried out on the language skills of the deaf in written and spoken Italian, although the educators and teachers of deaf Italians all agreed informally that their students had difficulties very similar to those encountered by the English-language researchers. There are several reasons such research was not carried out. One reason may have been the excessive stress placed on the oral approach to education, which concentrated attention on achievement rather than on the analysis of shortcomings. Another reason may have been that the teachers and educators of the deaf had no means of ascertaining regular patterns in the errors and difficulties they observed. Finally, the idea had never taken root that deaf children could achieve full linguistic competence in a form of communication that was, to all intents and purposes, a proper language; many were convinced that the deaf simply could not learn beyond a certain level.

Now, however, we need precise, reliable data to identify the real problems and to account for all the variables. Over the past five years, we have carried out systematic research on these problems (see, in particular, Beronesi & Volterra, 1986; Caselli & Pagliari Rampelli, 1989; Pagliari Rampelli, 1986; Taeschner, Devescovi, & Volterra, 1988; Volterra & Bates, 1989). On the whole, these studies bear out the findings of English-language researchers, showing that deaf Italian children and adults clearly have evident difficulty mastering certain morphological–syntactical rules.

Identification of these difficulties naturally points out the need for new educational approaches, revision of clearly inadequate didactic methods, and experimentation with new pedagogic strategies. At school, because most knowledge is transmitted vocally, deaf children waste a great deal of time before they can begin to learn what is transmitted and, even then, learn in a fragmentary, distorted manner. A severe limitation of the traditional pedagogic approach was the conviction that deaf children should be taught mainly via oral language (the teacher speaking to the whole class) or written language (textbooks; Caselli, Maragna, Pagliari Rampelli, & Volterra, 1994).

One possible strategy for preventing retarded development may be the visual–gestural approach, employing sign language for linguistic and thus cognitive education. Few teachers have a working knowledge of sign language, however, and introducing it on a large scale in the family and at school would present formidable problems. Information technology may be an invaluable tool for the deaf, substituting traditional teaching with the visual–manual channels and thus speeding up and simplifying the learning process with its unprecedented educational potential. For the first time, the deaf can have full command of the input and output of the tools they use, regulating their own learning processes with individualized rates and programming (Caselli, Pagliari Rampelli, Volterra, & Zingarini, 1988; Conte & De Mola, 1988). To realize this in pedagogic and, above all, scholastic terms, however, the didactic software must be used in controlled experimental situations, facilitating systematic evaluation of validity and practicality.

Our experience with Silvia, a 13-year-old girl severely deaf from birth, raises some issues about the effects of sign in communicative relations and, more generally, about the possibilities offered by new didactic methods and technologies in the education of deaf children. This study, conducted during the 1986–1987 academic year, is neither the only nor the most dramatic case encountered in our professional experience; indeed, we believe that it is precisely the undramatic normality of the story that makes it extremely relevant. Moreover, Silvia received the best possible care at both home and school, representing a model case of a person born deaf who grew up in contact only with hearing people communicating orally. We describe Silvia's background and personality at the time we met her, the didactic criteria adopted, our activities with Silvia, and the results obtained in terms of knowledge imparted and the learning process.

SILVIA'S BACKGROUND

Silvia's deafness was diagnosed as "severe bilateral perceptive hypacusia" at the age of 2. No information was available about the possible causes. The child was born with a hearing twin, and there were no precedents in the family history.

Silvia was equipped with a hearing aid at the age of 3 but began using it continuously only on entering elementary school. Language therapy started when she was 2½ years old and, for a short period, she was assisted by a neuropsychiatric child care center. Subsequently, she received help from a speech therapy center, which she still attends twice a week. Audiometry is regularly applied to ascertain the effect of the hearing aid on her hearing deficiency.

Beginning in nursery school, she was always among hearing peers. She completed elementary school in an institute run by nuns and went on to a state secondary school. Silvia received constant attention from her family, who concentrated all their energy and interest on the girl, organizing their life around her to the extent of planning holidays and recreation in the best way possible to benefit her education.

OUR EXPERIENCE WITH SILVIA

School

We met Silvia during the 1985–1986 academic year in the course of research carried out in secondary schools in Rome admitting deaf children. The focus of our research was on the organizational aspects of integrating deaf children in normal schools and on their language skills (Pagliari Rampelli, 1986). At the time, Silvia was in her first year of secondary school on the outskirts of Rome.

Her class consisted of 20 pupils, some of whom had also been with her in elementary school. The school has an efficient psychopedagogic team of assistants and follows legal provisions in including children with particular handicaps.

We embarked on the didactic experiment described here almost by chance the following year, when Silvia's mother consulted us about the possibility of her learning to use a computer. Silvia was 13 at the time. She liked school, got along well with her schoolmates (although she rarely saw them out of school), and communicated with the teachers reasonably well. There had been just two cases of strained relations arising when she felt she was judged with excessive severity or rejected. In her two years of secondary school, Silvia had three specialized assistant teachers, for 9 hours per week in the first year and 18 hours per week in the second.

Language Skills

During research in the school, we used a set of diagnostic material created by the "Early diagnosis and linguistic education for deaf children" Operating Unit (CNR Targeted Project PMM in Preventive Medicine) to evaluate Silvia's language skills. This material, designed to ascertain the skills of children who have experienced various types of language education, focuses on the morphological–syntactical aspects that seem to create the greatest difficulties for deaf pupils. The tests cover the use of articles, the plurals of nouns, the use of clitic pronouns (agreement in gender and number choice of case, position in sentence), the use of prepositions in comprehension and production (*sopra, dentro, di, a, da*), and comprehension of a written passage.

Silvia's answers revealed many uncertainties in a number of linguistic areas; in other areas, her knowledge was insufficient for command and application of the rules. Table 16.1 shows the percentages of errors made by Silvia compared with those made by a group of 16 deaf children attending secondary school and a group of 16 hearing children in the fifth year of elementary school (for further details, see Pagliari Rampelli, 1986). Although Silvia came close to the hearing children in a pronoun test (choice of case) and a preposition test (multiple choice), her overall performance was very similar to that of other deaf children of her age. For example, Silvia was not familiar with the articles *lo* and *gli* and tended to make the article agree with the final vowel of the noun (*le notte*), which is fairly common among the deaf. She did not use the prepositions correctly in production, encountering particular difficulty with *da*, especially in passive constructions. Although she used it fairly well in spontaneous commu-

TABLE 16.1
Error Percentages in the Linguistic Tests

	Silvia	Deaf Subjects, Secondary School	Hearing Children, Elementary School
Articles	.31	.32	.07
Plural nouns	.08	.11	.06
Clitic pronouns (subject and number agreement)	.54	.50	.04
Clitic pronouns (case agreement)	0	.39	.15
Clitic pronouns (pre- and postverbal position)	.26	.35	.06
Prepositions (to be inserted in sentences with gaps)	.33	.28	.03
Prepositions (multiple choice)	.06	.19	.03
Text comprehension			
Lexicon	.50	.36	.15
Answers to questions	.33	.25	.10
Ordering of pictures	.02	.07	.07

nication, she experienced great difficulty in the tests on the clitic pronoun, especially agreement and number, demonstrating that she was not in the habit of observing or reflecting on the tools of communication. Such difficulties are experienced by most deaf children and became particularly acute in the final test on comprehension of a written passage, where morphological–syntactical obstacles hamper the capacity to draw inferences and recognize causal relationships.

Procedure

Our work with Silvia and the computer extended over 14 meetings between November 1986 and May 1987, with an average of two per month; the meetings had to be spaced out, because we could work with her only in the mornings, which caused her to miss school.

The meetings averaged 2½ hours in length, and Silvia spent all this time at the computer. The setting was not ideal for this type of activity, because other people carried out their own activities in the same room. At times this gave Silvia the opportunity to escape from situations she found particularly difficult and prevented us from touching on some deeper aspects of the problem of deafness. The material used included a Commodore 64 computer with the Easy-script program and four tales of graduated difficulty prepared especially for deaf children.

Initial Communication

At the first meeting, Silvia was neatly dressed with a childlike expression on her smiling face; she looked up to her interlocutor from a position of excessive dependence for a child of her age and stature. She expressed herself in fairly clear Italian on everyday matters such as school and her family, although she tended to speak too hurriedly, swallowing the ends of words, which made it difficult for us to understand her. As soon as her interlocutor began talking, Silvia interrupted with some unnecessary comment that delayed the problem of understanding the message. When her interlocutor returned to the subject, Silvia watched the lip movements for a few seconds before turning her gaze away and beginning to respond to what she thought had been said, apparently unable to wait until she was sure she had understood. In fact, she behaved like a hearing person who has no need to lip-read in order to fill out what she understood with her hearing aid. Communication was, therefore, a lengthy business involving much misunderstanding.

When work progressed to analysis of the texts Silvia produced, it became necessary to point out certain errors, although care was taken to focus on one type at a time (e.g., lack of punctuation, capital letters). Silvia's reaction was to yawn, apparently preferring to avoid unpleasant realities rather than learning from them, as if every little error led back to the whole mass of her ignorance and she wished to cut off the connection.

Silvia showed severely limited cultural skills and a notable lack of lexical flexibility, being unused to using the same words in different contexts. Faced with a subject she found too difficult or uncongenial, she tried to bring up a different topic of her own choosing and, when called back to the task in question, made it clear that she wanted to abandon it as too difficult.

For every correction of her work, she looked to an adult for confirmation and, on being questioned about a well-written sentence, nevertheless hastened to correct it. Silvia thus gave the general impression of being very insecure, with extremely limited capacity to tackle difficulties and arrive at a positive solution. As a result, she took on a totally passive attitude, as if always expecting scorn when approaching a new piece of work or deciding on the various steps to carry it out.

Modes of Communication

Our recommendation that Silvia use sign language as a support for the spoken language was based on the following: She was too deaf to take in spoken language spontaneously; the language tests showed that although her previous speech therapy had been helpful, it had not equipped her to get her bearings among the morphological and syntactical components of the Italian language; and in her relations with others, she was unable to use stratagems that might have helped her, and, even if she had been able to do so, her cultural knowledge was insufficient for her to grasp the contents of a conversation suitable for children of her age by lip-reading alone.

Therefore, with her parents' permission and in the most natural, unforced way possible, we began using the signs of the language customary in our work with deaf people when speaking to Silvia. Although respecting the correct use of Italian, we structured our sentences with direct forms and simple phrases, repeating the subjects to avoid confusion and establishing spatial relations to locate subjects and tenses. At first Silvia seemed to notice nothing in particular, but, after a number of meetings, she asked us why we moved our hands. This gave us the opportunity to talk about her deafness. At first Silvia seemed to make light of the problem but eventually began to show more interest in it. The following episode was decisive in opening her eyes and inducing her to accept the use of sign. Silvia had some difficulty in distinguishing number and gender of nouns; she had some vague recollections but seemed to bundle the two aspects together, covering them with an ambiguous word that sounded like *morale* but could have been *maschile*, *plurale*, or something of the sort.

Organizing the concepts spatially, we placed the feminine and masculine alternatives to the left, articulating the words clearly while using signs we had already used for masculine and feminine examples that were well known to her.

On the right, we set out the singular and plural alternatives following the same procedure. We then gave the four possible combinations, pronouncing them clearly while signing in the allocated spaces. Silvia's face lit up, and she showed us that she understood and could distinguish among the various possibilities. We told her that her confusion of terms had been perfectly natural, because she could not distinguish the noun endings and, moreover, the words "were not in common use." Silvia seemed relieved and no longer asked why we signed but how to do it.

Using the Word Processor

We decided to give Silvia access to a word processor because we already had some experience using it with deaf children (Conte & De Mola, 1988). Because the computer offers deaf children command over the input and output processes, it encourages an autonomous approach. In particular, when exploited creatively, the word processor yields fuller, more lasting results than excessively structured exercises while stimulating the user to enter into the mental processes involved in writing.

THE STORIES

We presented four stories to Silvia in the following order: *The Three Little Pigs*, *Sleeping Beauty*, *The Sweet Pudding*, and *The Ugly Duckling*. The stories, part of a corpus designed to take deaf children from elementary comprehension levels to relatively complex levels, are presented in two forms according to the child's comprehension capacities: one richly illustrated and one with plain written text. We presented Silvia with the illustrated version, because the language comprehension test with a written text had revealed considerable difficulties.

Sleeping Beauty

Because the first story was used to familiarize Silvia with our procedure, the real work with the computer began with *Sleeping Beauty*. Our aim was to give Silvia the opportunity to set out her written work in comprehensible and, thus, effective order as she gradually became conscious of her own mental processes. We asked Silvia to read aloud the story in the illustrated version; we then exchanged a few comments on the story to verify her comprehension level; finally, we asked her to write her own version of the text on the word processor.

First draft of *Sleeping Beauty*

il re e la regina voleva una figlia
il re e la regina aveva una bambina

il re e la regina voleva la festa per
la figlia
E' venuta la fata buona domanda a il re
e dice che viene la fata cattiva
E il re risponde no!
la fata buona si regala bene
E la fata cattiva si regala male
E la fata cattiva domanda:
A il re che la sua figlia punge
E il re e la regina dice: no!
E la fata cattiva domanda: che figlia deve morire
E il re e la regina dice: no!
E la fata buona domanda: sci penso io . . .

(the king and the queen wanted a daughter/the king and the queen had a baby/the king and the queen wanted party for/the daughter/The good fairy came and asks to the king/and says that the bad fairy comes/And the king answers no!/the good fairy gives herself well/And the bad fairy gives herself badly/And the bad fairy asks:/To the king that his daughter pricks herself/And the king and the queen says: no!/And the bad fairy asks: that daughter must die/And the king and the queen says: no!/And the good fairy asks: I think herself. . . .)

Silvia's first draft reveals a certain slowness, for various reasons including because she was learning to use the word processor, absence of punctuation, inconsistent use of capital letters, use of the verb only in the third person singular, and difficulty in using direct speech and the reflexive. However, Silvia was already showing greater ability in setting out the text and ordering her thoughts in a time sequence corresponding to the actual progression of the story. Silvia herself printed out her first version of the story.

Our examination of her errors focused mainly on subject–verb agreement. In fact, Silvia wrote: *Il re e la regina voleva una figlia* (using *voleva* mistakenly for the plural *volevano*). By using the verb in the third person singular, Silvia merely indicated that the action was performed by persons other than herself or her immediate interlocutor but did not go on to consider the number of persons performing the action, an essential step in Italian grammar.

In the second meeting, we submitted the same story to Silvia without illustrations but arranged on the sheet in such a way that connection between subject and verb emerged perfectly clearly (see Fig. 16.1).

After this reading, Silvia went back to drafting her text, which now showed agreement between subjects and verbs:

E il re e la regina vedono la principessa
Il re e la regina sono dormentati

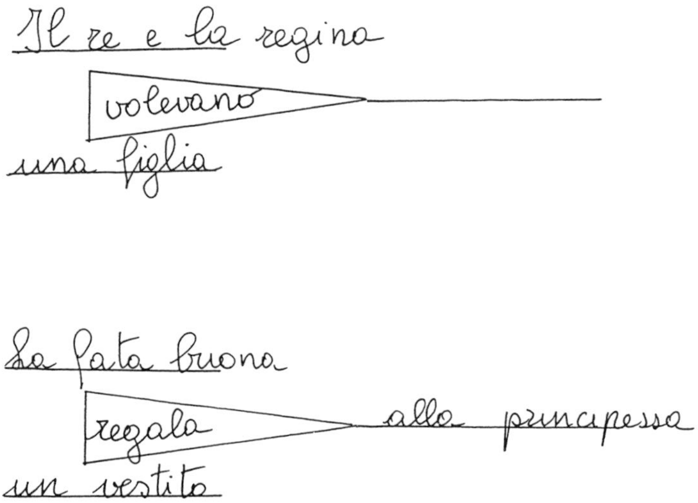

Il re e la regina
volevano
una figlia

La Fata buona
regala   alla principessa
un vestito

FIG. 16.1. Silvia's first example.

E le persone dormono nel palazzi
E un principe è coraggioso per passare

(The king and queen see the princess/The king and queen are (a)sleep/And the people sleep in the palaces/And a prince is courageous to pass)

The Sweet Pudding

For the third meeting, using the same approach, we chose a story offering comparable linguistic difficulties but greater logical difficulties than *Sleeping Beauty*. Silvia read the story and wrote her version with the computer. Her comprehension seemed unaffected by the greater logical complexity of the text, and she had assimilated the rules for capital letters and subject–verb agreement.

First draft of *The Sweet Pudding*

La mamma e la bambina non hanno da mangiare erano povere
La bambina piange perchè ha tanta fame
La vecchina dice: perchè piange?
La bambina dice: perchè ho tanta fame!
La vecchina ti da il pentolino magico la pappa dolce
La vecchina dice: cuoce pentolino cuoce la pappa dolce. . . .

(The mother and little girl have nothing to eat they were poor/The little girl is crying because she is so hungry/The little old lady says: why is she crying?/The little girl says: because I am so hungry! The little old lady gives you the magic saucepan it's the sweet pudding/The little old lady says: cooks saucepan cooks the sweet pudding . . .)

Interestingly enough, subject/verb agreement failed in the direct speech; in fact, Silvia could not establish the right roles in the dialogue. For example, in *La vecchina dice: perchè piange?*, the little old lady is addressing Silvia, and the verb should, therefore, be in the second-person singular form. However, although Silvia had placed the phrase graphically within the direct speech punctuation, she was in fact thinking of the question: "Why is the little girl crying?" This means that she had not yet learned to transfer the first person from herself in accordance with the roles in the story. Thus, for the third story, we focused on exercises involving identification of characters and their relationships.

The Ugly Duckling

We presented a version of *The Ugly Duckling* to Silvia on the word processor, placing each phrase in isolation from the next, with the consequent need to make clear both the subject and the relations between the various themes in each case:

> *In campagna fa caldo.*
> *La stagione è estate.*
> *Gli uccelli e i conigli giocano.*
> *Nel nido c'è un'anatra.*
> *L'anatra ha delle uova nel nido.*
> *Le uova dell'anatra si aprono. . . .*

(In the country it is hot./The season is summer./The birds and rabbits are playing./In the nest there is a duck./The duck has some eggs in the nest./The duck's eggs hatch. . . .)

We asked Silvia to eliminate what was not necessary, substituting such parts of speech as pronouns and conjunctions where appropriate, and making the verbs agree, thus establishing the essential links between the various characters, actions, and events. Silvia recognized her particular difficulties in this area when attempting the task and asked us to collaborate. Our assistance involved helping her identify the characters in the story and relate them within each sentence and within the sequence of sentences (see Fig. 16.2). This proved a particularly useful exercise, because it helped Silvia understand and become accustomed to the way the same characters could appear in the story in the first, second, or third persons, singular or plural, in conformity with the consequent structures displayed by the periods.

Mary Poppins

The next exercise involved a written summary of the film *Mary Poppins*, which Silvia had seen in a captioned version. The text she produced after seeing the film contained longer, more complex sentences with a greater quantity of coordinates, and embedded clauses with conjugated verbal complements and rela-

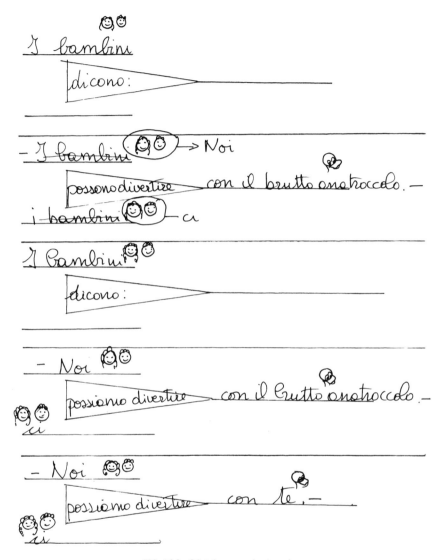

FIG. 16.2. Silvia's second example.

tive clauses made their first appearances; the syntactic structures were appropriate, and most of the errors were with verb tenses.

A summary of *Mary Poppins* follows (Silvia wrote the text by hand, filling the sheet of paper she had been given):

[. . .] C'è un uomo che si chiama Chert che lavora spazzacamino disegna per terra e balla. Chert sente un vento strano e pensava che arriva Mary Poppins e

disse che questa casa è di Ammiraglio e disse che questa casa è di una famiglia.
E c'e le due cameriere puliscono e cantano però c'è una tata era molto arrabiata
e vuole andare via perchè i bambini sono scappati dalla casa con aquilone. . . .

(There's a man whose name's Chert who works chimney sweep draws on the
ground and dances. Chert feels a strange wind and thought that Mary Poppins
arrives and said that this house is of Admiral and said that this house is of
a family. And there's the two maids clean and sing but there's a nanny she
was very angry and wants to go away because the children have run away
from home with kite.)

Free Composition

Silvia's series of exercises concluded with a composition describing her thoughts
on meeting a group of deaf children from a residential school for the deaf and
on the work she had done with us during the year. Here, with no specific input
from us, Silvia repeated almost all the errors seen earlier: omission of articles
and verbs, and incongruities of subject–verb agreement and tense. At the same
time, however, subordinate clauses of time and cause appeared side by side in
the same sentence, which was the most complex in all Silvia's written work to
date.

> *"Pensieri sul collegio e sul computer"*
>   *La scuola collegio un po' carino, perché c'è una stanza é enorme dove si*
> *giocano e ginnastica i bambini e le bambine. . . .*
>   *Io ho conosciuto le ragazze che si chiamano Barbara e Cinzia sono simpatiche,*
> *però non parlano molto bene parlano ha getti. . . .*
>   *Io ho visto film di Mary Poppins per raccontare a tutti così capisci meglio, c'era*
> *anche Manuela che spiega a Barbara, anch'io spiega a Barbara perché Barbara*
> *non ha capito bene e non sta scrivere bene. . . .*

("Thoughts on the institute and the computer")
    The institute school is a bit nice, because there's a room it's huge where
they play and gymnastics the boys and girls. . . .
    I met the girls they're called Barbara and Cinzia they're nice, but they don't
speak well they speak in gestures. . . .
    I saw the film Mary Poppins to tell everyone so you understand better,
there was also Manuela who explains to Barbara, I too explains to Barbara
because Barbara hasn't understood it properly and can't write well. . . .)

Silvia's composition consisted of a series of consecutive thoughts on events
that had made a particular impression on her because they involved her directly.
Her meeting with deaf girls who signed and spoke little reminded her of our
first meetings and the sense of strangeness and diffidence our approach had

aroused in her—feelings she had faced and to some extent worked out, thanks also to her progress in learning.

We felt that mere error analysis would not do justice to the progress Silvia had made in this period and that the structure of ideas expressed in this account was more complex than any employed in previous written work. In her early work with us, Silvia attempted no more than a description of events set out in temporal sequence, whereas, in this composition, the ideas showed powers of association, comparison, various types of evaluation, and target identification, which all suggested a real advance in maturity.

HOW SILVIA HAS CHANGED

Based on this series of meetings with Silvia, we assessed the changes in her attitude, in the forms of interaction she had with us, and in her developing language skills. Silvia has abandoned the defensive mechanisms we noted in the early stages: She looks straight at the eyes of the person with whom she is speaking, waits for her turn to talk, no longer yawns when faced with small difficulties, appreciates the help of the word processor when learning the spelling of new words, has learned the meanings of a series of signs, and occasionally uses them together with the corresponding words.

She takes an interest in her deafness and, above all, in other deaf children and has struck up a real friendship with a deaf girl a little younger than herself. Thus, she appears to have made progress in coming to terms with herself, although she still cuts off the words she utters, occasionally omitting endings or whole syllables. She believes this brings her closer to the speech of hearing people, which she considers extraordinarily rapid. In our opinion, this implies that she still has a very long way to go before she can size up reality and thus fully exploit her own potential.

Silvia now displays a lively interest in learning and, because her increased self-confidence provides support when confronted with her errors, can sustain concentration without yielding to a sense of frustration. On the whole, however, Silvia remains a child younger than her years, despite the progress she has made in behavior; she still tries to win over adults with her "good little girl" attitude.

In terms of organization of ideas, Silvia has modified her passive attitude through the use of her mind. She has "opened her eyes" and now projects an attitude of heedful attention toward people and reality in general. She sees more clearly that she can acquire elements essential for her personal enrichment from these people and this reality, and that she can conserve these elements in her inner world when the physical reality is absent. However, she has not yet acquired the capacity to forge links between the various elements on her own, and her intellectual processes thus remain at a somewhat primitive level. This is reflected in the way she relates with other people and thus in the more strictly linguistic aspects of her utterances. For example, she has difficulty attributing the use of *you* to persons other than her own first person ("The little old lady says 'Why is she crying?' ").

Analysis of Silvia's work following various types of stimuli shows that Silvia can write simple sentences when the linguistic input itself is sufficiently clear and simple. She did not take long to display the ability to organize a sequence of connected ideas correctly and to build up a story. At this stage she has taken in and assimilated simple rules, such as the use of capital letters and punctuation, which are now rooted in her mental processes.

We believe that these simplified text exercises are the only way Silvia can be exposed to the Italian language with the possibility of understanding all aspects and connections. Silvia has spent about 15 hours on this type of text (the remaining time was spent on tasks with different types of input), which proved sufficient for her to assimilate some of the simpler recurrent structures and to retain (on a short-term basis) a number of more complex forms (e.g., subject–verb agreement, use of embedded clauses with conjugated verb complements). However, it was not sufficient for her to master all the language problems she encountered in the more complex tasks and spontaneous written work.

Silvia's achievements in personal development and language skills bear out our initial hypotheses: Giving deaf children access to communicative tools such as sign language and computers (the computer being used creatively, not merely for training) enhances the learning process, enriching their ideas and endowing them with greater autonomy to the considerable benefit of their communicative capacities.

ACKNOWLEDGMENT

We thank the National Research Council (CNR) Targeted Project "Prevention and Control Disease Factors," Sub-project Stress, for financing the English version of this chapter.

REFERENCES

Beronesi, S., & Volterra, V. (1986). Il bambino sordo che sbaglia parlando [The deaf child who makes mistakes while speaking]. *Italiano e Oltre, 1*, 103–105.

Bishop, D. V. M. (1982). Comprehension of spoken, written and signed sentences in childhood language disorders. *Journal of Child Psychology and Psychiatry, 23*, 1–20.

Bishop, D. V. M. (1983). Comprehension of English syntax by profoundly deaf children. *Journal of Child Psychology and Psychiatry, 24*(3), 415–434.

Caselli, M. C. (1987). Language acquisition by Italian deaf children: Some recent trends. In J. Kyle (Ed.), *Sign and school: Using signs in deaf children's development* (pp. 44–53). Clevedon, England: Multilingual Matters.

Caselli, M. C., Maragna, S., Pagliari Rampelli, L., & Volterra, V. (1994). *Linguaggio e Sordita: Parole e segni per l'educazione dei sordi* [Language and deafness: Words and signs in the education of deaf people]. Florence: La Nuova Italia.

Caselli, M. C., & Massoni, P. (1986). Signed and vocal language learning by a deaf child of hearing parents. In B. T. Tervoort (Ed.), *Signs of life* (pp. 164–169). Amsterdam: Publications of the Institute.

Caselli, M. C., & Pagliari Rampelli, L. (1989). Il bambino sordo nella scuola materna: Integrazione e competenza linguistica [The deaf child in the preschool: Integration and linguistic competence]. *Età Evolutiva* [Children's Development], *34*, 51–62.

Caselli, M. C., Pagliari Rampelli, L., Volterra, V., & Zingarini, A. (1988). Il personal computer all'interno di una scuola per bambini sordi [The personal computer in a school for deaf children]. In C. Susini (Ed.), *Informatica, didattica e disabilità—Atti del Convegno Nazionale* [Information systems, teaching, and disability—Proceedings of the National Conference] (pp. 67–75). Firenze, Italy: IROE-C.N.R.

Conte, M. P., & De Mola, G. (1988). L'uso di tecnologie informatiche per favorire lo sviluppo cognitivo in bambini sordi [The use of information technology to enhance cognitive development in deaf children]. *Logopedia Contemporanea* [Contemporary Speech Therapy], *2*, 7–14.

Klima, E. S., & Bellugi, U. (1979). *The signs of language*. Cambridge, MA: Harvard University Press.

Lane, H. (1976). *The wild boy of Aveyron*. Cambridge, MA: Harvard University Press.

Newport, E., & Meier, R. (1985). The acquisition of American Sign Language. In D. I. Slobin (Ed.), *The crosslinguistic study of language acquisition* (pp. 881–938). London: Lawrence Erlbaum Associates.

Pagliari Rampelli, L. (1986). *Il bambino sordo a scuola: Integrazione e didattica* [The deaf child at school: Integration and teaching] (Tech. Rep.), Institute of Psychology C.N.R., Rome.

Quigley, S. P., & King, C. M. (1980). Syntactic performance of hearing-impaired and normal hearing individuals. *Applied Psycholinguistics, 1*, 329–356.

Quigley, S. P., & Paul, P. (1984). *Language and deafness*. San Diego, CA: College Hill Press.

Stokoe, W. (1960). Sign language structure: An outline of the visual communication system of the American deaf. *Studies in Linguistics* (Occasional Paper 8).

Stokoe, W. (1978). *Sign language structure*. Silver Spring, MD: Linstok Press.

Stokoe, W., & Volterra, V. (Eds.). (1985). *Sign language research '83*. Rome: I.P. CNR & Linstok Press.

Swisher, L. (1976). The language development of the oral deaf. In H. Whitaker & H. Whitaker, *Studies in neurolinguistics* (Vol. 2, pp. 59–93). New York: Academic Press.

Taeschner, T., Devescovi, A., & Volterra, V. (1988). Affixes and function words in the written language of deaf children. *Applied Psycholinguistics, 9*, 385–401.

Volterra, V. (Ed.). (1987). *La lingua italiana dei segni* [Italian sign language]. Bologna, Italy: Il Mulino.

Volterra, V., & Bates, E. (1989). Selective impairment of Italian grammatical morphology in the congenitally deaf: A case study. *Cognitive Neuropsychology, 6*, 273–308.

Volterra, V., & Erting, C. (Eds.). (1990). *From gesture to language in hearing and deaf children*. New York: Springer-Verlag.

.

17

READING ALOUD TO YOUNG CHILDREN: TEACHERS' READING STYLES AND KINDERGARTNERS' TEXT COMPREHENSION

William H. Teale
Miriam G. Martinez
The University of Texas at San Antonio

In this chapter, we examine storybook reading, the event in which an adult reads aloud to an individual child or a group of children. Many research studies indicate that the storybook reading experience is an important, positive force in young children's literacy development (e.g., Burroughs, 1972; Chomsky, 1972; Clark, 1976; Feitelson, Goldstein, Iraqi, & Share, 1993; Feitelson, Kita, & Goldstein, 1986; Greaney, 1986; Snow & Tabors, 1993; Tobin, 1981; Wells, 1985). In other words, storybook reading is an educational setting in which children learn from texts. But what constitutes the text of a storybook reading? Research of the past decade indicates that, in addition to the words of the author being read aloud, there is, among the participants in a storybook reading, considerable discussion and social interaction about the book (e.g., Cochran-Smith, 1984; Dickinson, De Temple, Hirschler, & Smith, 1992; Dickinson & Keebler, 1989; Dickinson & Smith, 1994; Green, Harker, & Golden, 1986; Martinez & Teale, 1993; Sulzby & Teale, 1987; Taylor, 1986; Teale & Sulzby, 1987). Moreover, these studies suggest that the presence of conversation and social interaction surrounding the words of the book itself is a primary reason storybook reading markedly affects young children's literacy development. It might be said, then, that the learning that results from storybook reading comes from participating in the construction of a complex text, one that includes both the language and ideas of the author and the comments, questions, and discussion about the book from the participants in the reading.

The focus of our research has been on classroom storybook readings in which a teacher reads a book aloud to the entire class of children. Such an activity is widely advocated in language arts, reading, and early childhood education teaching methods books as an important instructional practice for preschool and primary grade classrooms in the United States, and it was found to be an almost daily practice among kindergarten teachers in a random survey that we conducted in the San Antonio, Texas, area (Teale & Martinez, 1987). In our work with kindergarten teachers there, we have long advocated storybook time as a critically important instructional activity. As a result, the teachers we have worked with read to their children at least once per day and usually more often.

In the course of observing kindergarten classroom storybook readings, we noticed interesting variations in them. The differences were sometimes so striking that we decided to study systematically the phenomenon of teacher storybook reading style. The research project summarized in this chapter described the storybook reading styles of six kindergarten teachers, examined the consistency of their styles across readings, and studied the relationships between teacher storybook reading style and children's text comprehension.

RESEARCH ON STORYBOOK READING STYLE

Research indicates that adults vary in the style they use in reading storybooks to young children. Several studies have shown this to be true of parents: Different parents have characteristically different storybook reading styles, even when text factors are controlled and they are reading to children who are the same age and have the same degree of prior exposure to the text being read (e.g., Heath, 1982, 1983; Ninio, 1980; Teale, 1984; Teale & Sulzby, 1987).

Researchers have also described differences among teachers in the ways they conduct storybook reading in their classrooms. For example, Green and Harker (1982) found differences in the way the two teachers orchestrated their story readings to children of high versus low comprehension abilities. A follow-up study of the same two teachers (Green, Harker, & Golden, 1986) examined the data from three theoretical/methodological perspectives (sociolinguistic, semantic propositional, and literary-text). All three perspectives indicated variations in the ways that teachers, students, and text interacted in the two classrooms to construct the story readings.

Results from Dickinson and Keebler's (1989) investigation of storybook reading in day-care settings with 3- and 4-year-olds showed that each of the three teachers in the investigation exhibited distinct storybook reading styles that they employed across readings of different stories. Furthermore, Dickinson and Keebler established that the 3- and 4-year-olds in the study tailored their talk to their teachers' styles, suggesting that each teacher's style affected how the children responded to books.

Dickinson and Smith (1994) also found variation in patterns of talk about books that occurred in 25 preschool classrooms serving low-income children.

Cluster analysis showed three distinctive styles of reading books: (a) co-construction, in which teacher and children engaged in extended conversations that included cognitively challenging topics about the book being read; (b) didactic-interactional, in which the teacher encouraged the children to respond to questions about factual details and produce portions of the text in chorus; and (c) performance-oriented, in which the text was performed by the teacher with very little discussion during the reading but with a relatively extended discussion following the reading. Regression analyses revealed larger gains in vocabulary, story comprehension, and print skills by children in the performance-oriented classrooms than those in the didactic-interactional.

Our investigation built on studies such as these but approached the act of storybook reading from a perspective that offered different insights into the activity. The study attempted to describe the storybook reading interactions of teacher and students vis-à-vis the content and structure of a story. The conversational moves of the teacher and students were examined in relation to the piece of literature itself. In this way, the construction of text in the educational setting was examined as a literary event and as a pedagogical activity in relation to the content of the book being read. We employed such an approach because it took into account the role of literary content rather than merely focusing on a generic set of story-reading procedures or strategies that teachers used when reading aloud to children.

Theoretically, we operated from a Vygotskian perspective (Vygotsky, 1978), suggesting that perhaps the most significant influence on the nature of a storybook reading event is the adult participant. A storybook reading is clearly jointly constructed by the adult and the child(ren). However, the overall nature and structure of the social interactional patterns in the reading is heavily influenced by the adult who does the reading and scaffolds (Wood, Bruner, & Ross, 1976) the interaction.

The issue of teacher storybook reading style takes on its ultimate significance when one examines the strategies that young children develop for making sense out of written stories. In reading aloud to children, classroom teachers demonstrate and teach ways of taking from texts (Heath, 1983), because the text from which children learn during storybook time is not merely the book itself but also what the participants say about the book. Therefore, the discourse-processing strategies, literary responses, and ways of constructing meaning that are consistently modeled and scaffolded by the literate adult in the storybook interaction can become the reading strategies, literary responses, and ways of constructing meaning internalized by the child, especially if teachers engage in these behaviors on a consistent basis. Ultimately, then, there are pedagogical implications that flow from research on teacher storybook reading style.

An important goal of research on storybook reading styles is understanding the child's experience with text in the classroom and how that experience relates to comprehension of text. Although teacher storybook readings by no means constitute the range of textual (or even literary) experiences of the young child, they are a significant aspect of that experience. In this chapter, we attempt to elucidate the creation of text in storybook reading by describing six teachers' reading styles and examining the relations between these styles and the story comprehension of children in their classroom. This research has provided insight into how the children are learning to approach texts.

METHODOLOGY

Subjects

The subjects in the present investigation were six kindergarten teachers employed by two suburban school districts in a metropolitan area in south Texas and the children in their classes (age range: 5 years, 6 months to 6 years, 9 months). The classes were composed largely of children from middle-income families and were approximately 75% Anglo-American and 20% Mexican-American, with a few African-American children and children of other ethnic/cultural backgrounds scattered among the classrooms. In five of the classrooms there were 22 children, and in one classroom there were 20 children. At the outset of this study, the teachers had worked with the authors on implementing emergent literacy programs and practices into their classrooms for periods ranging from 2 to 4 years. Thus, the teachers were well known to the researchers and were regarded by them as very good teachers. In terms of the general recommendations found in language arts methods texts and books that discuss how to read to young children (e.g., Kimmell & Segel, 1991; Trelease, 1989), the teachers were engaging readers. The children were attentive when each of the teachers read aloud, and they seemed to enjoy each day's storybook reading.

Data Collection Procedures

Observations of Storybook Readings. Recordings were made of the teachers reading four stories to their classes: *Ira Sleeps Over* (Waber, 1972), *Harry and the Terrible Whatzit* (Gackenbach, 1977), *Alexander and the Wind-Up Mouse* (Lionni, 1969), and *Strega Nona* (de Paola, 1975). Teachers read in the manner they typically did with their classes. These books were chosen because they were high-quality children's literature, they were appealing to kindergarten children, and they had stories that could be analyzed by a story grammar structure (Stein & Glenn, 1979).

Interviews With Teachers. To complement data gathered from the readings themselves, the three teachers who participated in the first phase of the data collection were interviewed individually and asked to respond to the question, "Why do you read books to your students?" From the responses to this initial question, the interviewer attempted to obtain as much clarification and elaboration as possible. The interview was not scripted, but the interviewer did probe and follow up on the teachers' various responses.

Comprehension Measure. Following the reading of one story, *Strega Nona*, the researchers administered a comprehension measure on a one-to-one basis to nine children in each classroom: three children of high ability, three of middle ability, and three of low ability. Ability was determined based on teacher recommendation and performance on the *Peabody Picture Vocabulary Test–Revised* (Dunn & Dunn, 1981). The comprehension measure focused only on children's understanding of the information contained in the story grammar (Stein & Glenn, 1979) of *Strega Nona*. (See Appendix A for an outline of this information, or Teale, Martinez, & Glass, 1989, for a complete story grammar.) The measure used a combination of three strategies for assessing comprehension: retelling, assisted retelling, and cued recall questions. For the retelling, each child was asked individually to retell the story on audiotape so that a classmate who had missed the reading of the story might be able to listen to it later. When it appeared that all possible information had been elicited through the retelling, the investigator moved into an assisted retelling mode, using general probes such as "What else happened?" and "Then what?" When it appeared that no additional information would be forthcoming through the assisted retelling, the investigator continued the comprehension assessment using the cued recall questions. The construction of these questions was based on the story grammar. The questions were designed to systematically tap information in the setting component of the story and in each component of each story episode. Because most children gave relatively little information through the retelling or assisted retelling, information obtained through the three measures was collapsed into one score for comprehension.

Data Preparation

Each of the taped storybook readings was transcribed. In addition, visual information from videotapes or information from the researchers' observational notes served to flesh out the transcripts by providing details about the teachers' and children's gestures and facial expressions that played a role in the storybook reading and accompanying discussion of the story. All transcripts were checked against the audio- and/or videotape recordings by at least two researchers.

Analytic System

Transcripts were analyzed using a system that emerged directly from the data and was designed for describing group storybook readings in the classroom. The system was detailed in Teale, Martinez, and Glass (1989). Special efforts were made to take into account all of the participants involved in the construction of the text in the educational setting: the teacher, the students, and the story. The primary objective was to characterize the language and social interaction of the total storybook reading event.

The heart of the system involved classifying teacher and child talk about the stories at the level of topic unit (TU). A topic unit consisted of all contiguous talk contributed by the teacher and/or the children directed toward the same aspect of a story feature or story-related feature. A story feature refers to actual story information presented by the author/illustrator of the story (e.g., setting, initiating event, consequence). It was also helpful to think of any category of story information as being one of two general types: key information that advances a story line or minor details that flesh out the story. The difference between key information and minor details for the stories was determined by having four competent adults read and retell the story. If three of the four included a part of the story in their retelling, it was considered key, or important, information. Otherwise, it was considered a minor detail. A story-related feature refers to information that, although not included in the story itself, can be part of the story experience. Story-related features include genre, style, title, author, and illustrator. (See Appendix B for a complete list and discussion of story features and story-related features.) A new topic unit begins when a shift in the focus of discussion occurs (indicating that the previous topic has concluded) or when the teacher resumes reading the story following discussion.

In developing the classification system to describe TUs, we attended to three facets of teacher storybook reading style: the focus of teacher talk during storybook reading, the type of information that the teacher talked about and/or encouraged the children to talk about during storybook reading, and the instructional strategies utilized by the teacher. (See Appendix B for a complete description of all the coding categories in these three facets.)

Attention to the focus of story talk gave the researchers the opportunity to broadly conceptualize the storybook reading experience by examining the various aspects of stories discussed from both a story structure perspective and a literary perspective. In particular, to explore the potential impact of storybook reading on children's emerging sense of story structure, we examined the particular story features on which talk focused, as well as the extent to which talk concentrated on important story information that advances the story line. Attention to story-related features made it possible to identify different aspects of stories to which participants expressed responses.

By examining type of information, it was possible to discern how participants responded to text and how they interacted with text to construct meaning. Type of information categories reflected research on sources readers use to construct meaning based on textual information and their prior knowledge (e.g., textually explicit information, background information, inferential information) and on characteristic ways that readers respond to literature (e.g., personal associations, identification with characters or situations in the text).

Teachers' instructional strategies were examined in order to determine if teachers assumed differential roles that might influence their students' interactions with stories. This aspect of the analytic system emerged from preliminary data analyses. Once analyses began, it became apparent that one characteristic of the reading styles of the teachers who made up the sample was that they were in charge of the reading. The teachers initiated most of the talk about books, and they usually had the most influence over the content of the discussions. Thus, the teachers were not child-centered in the sense of letting children determine the nature or extent of the talk about the book. It was not that we intentionally sought out such teacher readers; rather, in retrospect, we realized that this "teacher-centered" way of reading was characteristic of every kindergarten teacher we worked with over a period of 5 years before this study. Therefore, the instructional strategy aspect of the analytic system reflects an aspect of storybook reading style commonly present in kindergarten classrooms.

All TUs were categorized in these three ways. Reliability figures for these codings as performed by three independent raters were as follows: focus, .70–.89; type of information, .59–.75; instructional strategy, .70–.89. Following this categorization of the data, analyses of both a quantitative and qualitative nature were performed. A qualitative analytic approach that grew directly from the transcripts of the readings was adopted to describe the teachers' styles, because such an approach gives the richest possible picture of the readings.

RESULTS

Our purpose in writing this chapter is to provide a description of each teacher's overall storybook reading style and to examine the relations between the children's story comprehension of one, *Strega Nona*, and the different texts of that book that were created in each of the six classrooms because of the teacher's reading style. We have previously reported results showing that each teacher had a consistent style across the readings of the four narratives, and the teachers varied in their storybook reading styles (Martinez & Teale, 1993). Detailed results about the previously mentioned three facets of each teacher's storybook reading style and about the consistency of reading styles across books were reported by Martinez and Teale (1993). We have not reiterated those details here, however, but instead have summarized each teacher's storybook reading style in narrative form and then examined selected features of each teacher's reading of *Strega Nona* and related them to the children's comprehension of that story.

A Description of Each Teacher's Storybook Reading Style

Herrera. The most distinctive characteristic of Herrera's storybook reading style was her treatment of stories as cohesive entities composed of interrelated elements. This treatment was evident in the way she moved her students through the story during the reading itself and in her orchestration of discussion after she and the children had finished going through the book. During the reading, she systematically discussed key elements in each story episode. Then, following the reading of three of the four stories—and specifically of *Strega Nona*—Herrera led her students through another discussion of key story information by systematically reviewing the entire story. In fact, Herrera was the only teacher to rely extensively on the reviewing strategy. As a result, her readings emphasized textually and pictorially explicit information more than did other teachers' readings. Moreover, it is significant to note that the explicit information Herrera highlighted was typically important information that advanced the basic story line. The following excerpt, taken from the reading of *Strega Nona*, shows Herrera beginning to review the story immediately after finishing the reading of the book:

Herrera:	Now who was Strega Nona? Do you remember her?
Student:	She was that lady.
Student:	A witch.
Student:	The good witch.
Herrera:	She was a witch. They called her Grandma Witch. Now was she a nice witch or was she a mean witch?
Students:	[in unison] Nice.
Herrera:	And Strega Nona was getting old, remember?
Student:	Yes.
Herrera:	So she needed someone to help her. And who came to help her?
Student:	Anthony.
Herrera:	Big Anthony. And when Big Anthony first came to her house, what was the first thing she told him not to do?
Students:	[in unison] Don't touch the pasta pot.
Herrera:	Did Big Anthony listen?
Students:	[in unison] No.
Herrera:	Oh no, and he. . . .
Student:	The first time he did, but the second time he didn't.
Herrera:	That's right. He listened for a while but then he didn't. What made him really not listen?
Student:	He saw Strega Nona making the pasta.

Herrera's systematic review of *Strega Nona* reflects her consistent emphasis on important but textually explicit story information.

Baxter. The distinguishing feature of Baxter's style was her emphasis on inferential reasoning. Baxter consistently engaged her students in discussions that highlighted reader-based inferences, text-based inferences, and predictive inferences. Furthermore, she typically organized these discussions in one of two ways: using a questioning procedure to guide the students through the reasoning process necessary to come up with the inference; or, if the inference was one that students arrived at on their own, guiding students through a reverse process in which they were expected to explain the basis for the inference. Baxter usually focused on important story information in discussions with her students, but she did not move students systematically through the basic events of a story. The following excerpt from *Strega Nona* is representative of Baxter's style:

Baxter:	Look at this man who went to see her up here in the corner (pointing to picture).
	Look what he's doing.
	Do that with your hand.
Students:	[imitate picture]
Baxter:	What's he doing? Why do you think he's doing that? [2 second pause] What's he doing? Why is he doing that? What do you think his trouble is?
Student:	Maybe he's a sergeant and he's. . . .
Baxter:	You think he's saluting? Any other ideas?
Students:	[no response from students]
Baxter:	He has a problem. What's his problem, Jason?
Student:	Maybe he has headaches, and he had a headache.
Baxter:	O.K. that's right. That's exactly what's wrong with him. He had a headache. If you had a headache, what would you do?
Student:	Go to the doctor.
Baxter:	You'd go to the doctor. What would you do, Alex?
Student:	Take aspirin.
Baxter:	You'd take aspirin. But what's he going to do about his headache?
Students:	[in unison] Go to the witch.
Baxter:	Would you go to a witch?
Students:	[in unison] Nooo!

Murchison. Story time in Murchison's classroom was marked by comparatively little story talk that occurred before, during, or after the reading. Not only were there relatively few topic units initiated in each storybook reading, but also those that occurred tended to be comparatively short, owing to the ways Murchison orchestrated discussion. First, she frequently used an informing strategy rather than a questioning strategy, which is more likely to open up discussion. Also, when Murchison did use a questioning strategy (eliciting or inviting), she typically worded her questions in such a way as to signal the class to respond as a group rather than individually. Finally, when Murchison asked a question and failed to obtain the desired response, she often reworded the question, turning it into a yes/no format that signaled the appropriate answer rather than guiding the students toward formulating an answer from various pieces of information.

There was one noteworthy exception to Murchison's tendency to minimize discussion. She was the only teacher to help her students understand story theme in each storybook reading, and these discussions were by far the most extensive ones that occurred during her storybook readings. In effect, this emphasis on story theme became the distinctive feature of Murchison's storybook reading style. In the following exchange, which occurred after the reading of *Strega Nona*, Murchison returns to discuss the theme of the story for the second time during the storybook reading session:

Murchison:	What would you have done to Big Anthony?
Student:	Put him in jail.
Murchison:	You would have?
Student:	Spanked him.
Murchison:	You would have spanked him?
Student:	Made him eat it all up.
Student:	I would make him . . . send him to another town.
Murchison:	Yeah, I think that was a pretty good idea, though. Since he made the mess, he had to clean it up, right?

Krauss. Rather than highlighting story information in her discussions with students, Krauss tended to focus on "word," one of the story-related features. When reading each of the four stories, Krauss repeatedly halted her reading of the story in midsentence to give her students the opportunity to predict upcoming words in text. When the discussion focused on the story, Krauss highlighted important story information; however, the relatively few times that she stopped to discuss story events were very clearly overshadowed by the numerous times that she stopped the storybook readings to focus her students' attention at the word level. This pattern is evident in the following excerpt taken from Krauss' reading of *Strega Nona*:

Story:	"Boil me enough pasta to fill me. . . ."
Student:	Up.
Krauss:	Up.
Story:	"And the pasta pot bubbled and boiled and was suddenly filled with steaming. . . ."
Student:	Oil.
Krauss:	Hot. . . .
Krauss & Students:	Pasta.
Story:	Then Strega Nona said, "Enough, enough pasta pot. I have my pasta nice and. . . ."
Student:	Hot.
Story:	"So simmer down my pot of clay until I'm hungry another. . . ."
Student:	Day.

LeBlanc. LeBlanc, like Herrera, generally highlighted important story information in each episode of a story. However, in contrast to Herrera, who concentrated on textually explicit information, LeBlanc focused on inferential information more extensively. Hence, the basic story line received somewhat less attention in LeBlanc's classroom than in Herrera's. In terms of the instructional strategies, LeBlanc relied extensively on the informing and eliciting strategies, and she used the eliciting strategy in somewhat varied ways in different storybook readings. In some storybook readings, questions were used to raise points with no subsequent attempt to discuss those points.

There were also ample instances in which LeBlanc chose to use a line of questions to guide story discussion. When she did, it appeared that she had a somewhat variable style when only the actual storybook reading was examined. However, her style was very consistent when viewed within a broader context, for LeBlanc clearly integrated story time into a broader curricular plan. For example, prior to reading *Alexander and the Wind-Up Mouse*, she shared a poem about a mouse. After discussing the poem, she directed her students' attention to the cover illustration that showed two mice—a wind-up mouse and a real one—and told the students to listen to the story and think about which mouse they would like to be. Then, after reading and discussing the story, LeBlanc asked the students to draw and write about the mouse they would choose to be. These drawings then became a springboard into a math activity that involved the creation of a bar graph showing which mouse the various students had chosen to be. Thus, in effect, storybook reading in LeBlanc's classroom tended to be part of a more global plan.

Conroy. In Conroy's classroom, a greater proportion of talk focused on unimportant information than in any of the other teachers' classrooms. Conroy emphasized explicit information, both textually and pictorially explicit, to a greater extent than did the other teachers; however, unlike Herrera, who also highlighted textually explicit information, Conroy did not move her students systematically through story episodes discussing important textually explicit information and did not review as Herrera did. For example, the next excerpt is the entire text of the discussion following her reading of *Strega Nona*:

Conroy:	And he's stringing up more pasta. Look at his stomach.
Students:	[laugh]
Student:	He's fat.
Conroy:	He *is* fat.
Student:	And he's going to get fatter.
Conroy:	And by the end of the night, he'd eaten all the pasta except that one part right there. [points to picture]
Conroy:	And that's it. Do you think he wants to have pasta for breakfast?
Student:	No!
Conroy:	[laughs] No.
Student:	Mrs. Conroy.... [interrupted]
Conroy:	Do you think he was smart or kind a, a little bit dumb?

Student:	Dumb.
Conroy:	A little bit dumb. Uh, huh (yes). Do you think he was curious?
Student:	Uh, huh (yes).
Conroy:	Little bit.

The instructional strategies on which Conroy relied were eliciting and inform-ing; however, she was generally unsuccessful in using the eliciting strategy to guide discussion. Her questions were often vague and had a skip/jump focus.

Teacher Responses in Interviews

As an extension of the analysis of the discussion surrounding storybook reading, three teachers from the first year of data collection—Murchison, Baxter, and Herrera—were interviewed individually and asked why they read storybooks to their students. The primary reason each teacher gave for reading to children was to foster enjoyment of reading. Beyond this reason, their responses di-verged. The following are key remarks from the three teachers in terms of their priorities for reading:

Murchison:

"A storybook is like a piece of art. You don't take it apart. That would take it out of the realm I want it in: the enjoyable, the entertaining. I want the children to have fun with the story."

"Plus [if the reading is interrupted too many times], they [the children] lose the story. I don't want them to lose the story."

"Storybooks also help children to get in touch with their feelings."

"I want them to be able to put themselves in place of someone else."

"In preparing to read a story, I want to know what the author is trying to tell us, if he has a meaning [that] can be applied to [the children's] situations."

Herrera:

"I want them to be interested in, engrossed in, and react to a story."

"I want them to know what's going on [in the story]."

"I want them to understand what a story has to say to them. If there are points to be made I use my voice and body language to dramatize those points."

Baxter:

"To teach them to learn how to think."

"To teach comprehension skills: to predict and to evaluate."

"To answer higher level thought questions."

"I try to ask several types of questions: predictive questions, evaluative questions, why questions."

"I use storybook reading to help kids enjoy reading and to learn to comprehend."

From her own perspective, Herrera's chief aim in reading storybooks to her students was to foster a positive attitude toward reading. She sought to accomplish this by using her voice and body language to hold the students' attention as she dramatized a story's main points. Baxter, too, expressed the desire to help her students learn to enjoy reading. However, Baxter indicated that she employed storybook reading to teach a variety of thinking skills. Murchison also wanted her students to learn to enjoy reading, but she wished her students to appreciate the story as a whole, a work of art with its own characteristic rhythms, sentence patterns, and vocabulary. In addition, Murchison wanted her students to be able to extract a *theme* from the story as a whole, a meaning that could be applied to their own experiences. Thus, the teachers' own words reinforced the patterns shown by the topic unit analyses.

Teachers' Storybook Reading Styles in Relation to the *Strega Nona* Reading

Tables 17.1, 17.2, and 17.3 report selected data on each teacher's reading of *Strega Nona*. These data were used in conjunction with results from the readings of the other three books to build the overall reading style profiles presented

TABLE 17.1

Percentage of Topic Units from Reading of *Strega Nona* Focusing on Story Information and Selected Story-Related Information

	Herrera	Baxter	Murchison	Krauss	LeBlanc	Conroy
Story						
Setting	16.1%	30.4%	15.9%	17.9%	6.9%	30.3%
Initiating event	8.1%	10.7%	12.5%	5.4%	17.2%	6.1%
Internal response	6.5%	–	–	7.1%	3.5%	–
Attempt	14.5%	14.2%	18.7%	12.5%	17.2%	12.1%
Consequence	16.1%	17.9%	18.7%	8.9%	6.9%	15.1%
Reaction	4.8%	5.3%	6.2%	1.7%	–	6.1%
Character	4.8%	3.6%	3.1%	3.6%	6.9%	3.0%
Story map	1.6%	7.1%	–	3.6%	10.3%	–
Story-Related						
Theme	1.6%	–	6.2%	–	–	–
Story	1.6%	–	3.1%	–	10.3%	–
Title	1.6%	1.8%	3.1%	5.4%	3.5%	3.0%
Author	1.6%	–	–	3.6%	3.5%	–
Word	17.7%	3.6%	9.4%	28.5%	10.3%	9.1%

TABLE 17.2
Percentage of Topic Units Focusing on Various Types
of Information in *Strega Nona*

	Herrera	Baxter	Murchison	Krauss	LeBlanc	Conroy
Textually explicit	43.3	7.8	10.7	17.6	10.7	8.6
Pictorially explicit	13.3	5.8	–	5.9	7.1	25.7
Background	15.0	7.8	14.2	17.6	17.9	17.1
Text-based inference	13.3	25.4	7.1	14.7	10.7	14.3
Reader-based inference	–	17.6	3.5	3.0	10.7	5.7
Summary inference	–	1.9	3.5	–	–	–
Evaluative inference	1.6	1.9	21.4	–	14.3	–
Predictive inference	8.3	17.6	14.2	41.2	21.5	11.4
Personal association	–	–	3.5	–	–	8.6
Identification	5.0	13.7	17.8	–	7.1	8.6
Meta	–	–	3.5	–	–	–

earlier. We present these key quantitative data from *Strega Nona* because ultimately they can serve to illuminate how reading style is related to children's comprehension of the story. Table 17.1 shows the percentages of TUs that focused on the story information and selected story-related information in each reading of *Strega Nona*. Table 17.2 depicts the percentages of TUs that focused on various types of information. And Table 17.3 shows the percentage of TUs related to the setting or different episodes of the story. Appendix A contains an outline of the information conveyed in these different parts of the story.

These tables help elucidate reading style differences that were identified. As can be seen from Table 17.1, Murchison focused more on the theme of the story than did any other teacher. Herrera covered all aspects of the story episodes (initiating event, internal response, attempt, consequence, reaction). Krauss got her children to pay much more attention than in any other classroom to word, getting them to supply the next word or phrase when she invited them to read along by pausing at numerous points during the reading.

TABLE 17.3
Percentage of Topic Units by Episodes of *Strega Nona*

	Herrera	Baxter	Murchison	Krauss	LeBlanc	Conroy
Setting	13.5	38.6	18.1	23.3	6.7	36.7
Episode 1	8.0	4.5	4.5	10.0	26.7	5.3
Episode 2	5.0	6.8	4.5	3.3	–	–
Episode 3	21.6	20.4	36.3	16.7	13.3	10.5
Episode 4	10.8	11.3	–	13.3	13.3	–
Episode 5	5.4	2.2	4.5	10.0	6.7	5.3
Episode 6	8.0	2.2	4.5	6.7	6.7	21.1
Episode 7	27.0	13.6	27.2	16.7	26.7	21.1

Both Baxter and Conroy spent considerable time discussing setting information. However, when one examines Table 17.2, it is possible to see that the discussion in Baxter's room was much more about inference making (a total 64.4% of the TUs on the five different types of inferences, compared with a total of 31.4% for Conroy). Furthermore, Table 17.2 illustrates the much higher degree to which Herrera dealt with explicit information in the story. The high number of predictive inferences in Krauss' reading was largely due to her eliciting reading from the children.

Finally, from Table 17.3 it is possible to see that teachers concentrated differentially on the various episodes of the story. Baxter was almost as concerned with setting information as she was with the story per se. Herrera covered all episodes of the story. Conroy, on the other hand, did not engage the children in any discussion about episode 2 or episode 4.

The intent in presenting the teacher profiles and briefly discussing selected aspects of the quantitative data was to provide an overview of each teacher's style and to give a feeling for how each teacher's style manifested itself in the reading of *Strega Nona*. Additional detailed information about the analyses used to develop these profiles and more detailed results on particular aspects of each teacher's storybook reading style can be found in Martinez and Teale (1993). In the next section, we examine the relationship between the styles and students' story comprehension.

Story Comprehension

Students' responses obtained through the three comprehension measures—story retelling, assisted story retelling, and cued recall questions—were collapsed for analysis purposes. In order to compare students' comprehension across classrooms, 33 items of information obtained through the 36 questions were used to analyze story comprehension. These 33 items of information corresponded to information included by the adult expert readers in their retellings of *Strega Nona*. This information was deemed important to story comprehension. Information elicited through the remaining cued recall questions was not included in the analysis of story comprehension, because it did not appear in the retellings of the expert readers.

To compare student comprehension of information contained in the story grammar across classrooms, an analysis of variance was run; the results appear in Table 17.4. The analysis of variance revealed significant differences in comprehension scores across classrooms, $F(5) = 3.44$, $p < .009$. Two-tailed t tests indicated that the comprehension scores in Herrera's class were significantly higher than the scores in the classrooms of Conroy, Baxter, Murchison, and Krauss. There was no significant difference between the scores in Herrera's classroom and those in LeBlanc's classroom. Only one other significant difference was found: The comprehension scores of students in LeBlanc's classroom were significantly higher than the scores of students in Krauss' classroom.

TABLE 17.4
Comprehension Scores by Teacher on Important
Story Elements of *Strega Nona*

Teacher	N	M	SD
Herrera	9	23.1	7.10
Baxter	9	14.6	3.91
Murchison	9	15.8	7.68
Krauss	9	11.1	5.67
LeBlanc	9	17.4	7.41
Conroy	9	15.8	7.68

ANOVA Summary

Source of Variation	df	Sum of Squares	Mean Squares	F	p
Score by teacher	5	703.93	140.79	3.44	.0097
Error	48	1963.33	40.90		
Total	53	2667.26			

Note. Significant differences: *t* test between cell means, 2-tailed, $p < .05$.
Herrera and Conroy ($p = .0188$)
Herrera and Baxter ($p = .0066$)
Herrera and Murchison ($p = .0188$)
Herrera and Krauss ($p = .0002$)
LeBlanc and Krauss ($p = .0409$)

CONCLUSIONS

The students in Herrera's classroom performed significantly higher on the comprehension measures than did the students in the classrooms of Baxter, Murchison, Krauss, and Conroy. Several distinctive features of Herrera's storybook style were identified that appeared to have a facilitating effect on students' comprehension of the story grammar information of *Strega Nona*, and in many instances these features set Herrera apart from the other teachers in the investigation. First, Herrera and her students were very story directed, and the segments of the story they highlighted in their discussion were key ones (i.e., setting, Episode 3, and Episode 7). Although the story elements they discussed generally moved the story along (i.e., initiating events, attempts, and consequences), there was also attention to the internal aspects of stories (i.e., character goals and reactions). Herrera and her students primarily tended to discuss important story information, and Herrera very consistently moved her students through the story, discussing important information in every episode of *Strega Nona*; she was, in fact, the only teacher to discuss the story in its entirety. Furthermore, this was done during the reading of the story itself and again in the review of the story that Herrera conducted after the reading of the story, and Herrera was the only teacher to conduct such a review. Thus, in effect, Herrera's students were the only ones to benefit from three replayings of the important information in the story. One replay occurred during the actual reading of the story, the second occurred as Herrera repeatedly stopped the storybook reading to discuss important story information, and the third occurred as Herrera reviewed the story with her students after completing the storybook reading. Finally, Herrera was the only teacher to emphasize textually explicit information, which was, in large part, important to the development of the story. In effect, Herrera appeared to orchestrate the discussion of *Strega Nona* in such a way as to maximize her students' comprehension.

Many of the major features of Herrera's storybook reading style were not apparent in the styles of the other five teachers. These included an emphasis on important textually explicit information, discussion of both internal and external story elements, a consistent focus on important story information in every episode of the story, and a review of the story following reading. Not only were these features not apparent in the storybook reading styles of the other teachers, but there were also some features identified in their styles that would appear to have the potential of interfering with students' comprehension of the story grammar.

In Baxter's classroom, for example, a majority of the story talk focused on unimportant information. Although extensive discussion centered around inferences, these discussions often dealt with story details rather than with more substantive information. In addition, many of the topic units that dealt with inferential information were extremely lengthy, because Baxter repeatedly called on student after student to respond to the same question. Although this clearly maximized student participation, this feature may have, in effect, pulled the students away from the basic story line for relatively extended periods of time which, in turn, may have interfered with story comprehension.

Murchison did not always appear to use a storybook reading style that fostered story comprehension. She involved her students in minimal discussion of story, and, although she did emphasize Episode 7, the portion of the story from which the theme emerges, there was only isolated attention to the story events that led up to this key episode. Baxter orchestrated discussion to maximize student involvement, whereas Murchison may well have moved to the other extreme by addressing questions to the students as a whole and then immediately rewording difficult questions to signal appropriate answers, thereby minimizing student participation in story discussion.

The dominant feature of Krauss' storybook reading style was the way in which she repeatedly engaged her students in predicting upcoming words in text. This extensive focus at the word level may well have interfered with story comprehension. In fact, Krauss' students were the only ones whose comprehension was significantly different from the comprehension of the students in two other classes (i.e., Herrera and LeBlanc).

There were perhaps, more similarities between the styles of Herrera and LeBlanc than between Herrera and any of the other teachers. Like Herrera, LeBlanc clearly emphasized important story information in her discussion of

Strega Nona, and she did so in the setting portion of the story and in every episode except the second one. This more systematic emphasis on important story information parallels the emphasis seen during Herrera's reading of the story. Furthermore, there were no significant differences in the comprehension of students in Herrera's and LeBlanc's classes. Unlike the students in Herrera's class, however, those in LeBlanc's classes performed significantly better than the students in only one other class: that of Krauss. This may have occurred because there was, overall, relatively little talk about the story itself; LeBlanc emphasized discussion prior to the storybook reading rather than during and after reading, as Herrera did.

There was relatively little talk in Conroy's classroom, and a majority of the talk that did occur focused on unimportant story information. In addition, Conroy rarely appeared to successfully engage her students in discussion, utilizing instead an informing strategy to give students information.

Although it was found that Herrera's students performed significantly better on the comprehension measure than did the students in the other classrooms, these findings should be placed in perspective. This investigation examined the impact of storybook reading style only on children's comprehension of the story grammar. Comprehension of a story involves more, however, than merely understanding the basic story grammar; for example, the manner in which Murchison's emphasis on story theme may have facilitated her students' ability to deal with this aspect of story meaning. Moreover, literacy development itself is multifaceted. Although certain features of storybook reading style may facilitate story comprehension, still other features may foster other aspects of literacy development. Thus, Baxter's emphasis on inferencing may have facilitated the development of her students' inferencing strategies for reading. This investigation did not attempt to relate these other aspects of literacy development to variability in storybook reading style, although this would certainly seem to be one logical direction in which future research on storybook reading style might move.

ACKNOWLEDGMENTS

The research discussed in this chapter was supported by an Elva Knight Research Grant from the International Reading Association, whose support is gratefully acknowledged. Special thanks also go to the teachers and children whose storybook readings provided the data for this research.

APPENDIX A: OUTLINE OF *STREGA NONA*

Setting

Strega Nona's name means *Grandma Witch*.
She has a magic touch that is used in solving people's problems.

Strega Nona is getting old, so she advertises for someone to help around the house.

Big Anthony, who doesn't pay attention, takes the job.

Strega Nona instructs Big Anthony in his jobs and tells him to never touch the pasta pot.

Episode 1

Big Anthony peeks in the window one night and sees Strega Nona cook with her magic pasta pot by singing a song to make the pasta pot cook and stop cooking.

Big Anthony thinks the pot is wonderful.

Big Anthony does not see Strega Nona blow three kisses to stop the pot.

Big Anthony tells the townspeople about the pasta pot.

Episode 2

The townspeople laugh at Big Anthony, which makes him angry.

Big Anthony swears that he'll show the townspeople.

Episode 3

Strega Nona goes out of town and reminds Big Anthony not to touch the pasta pot.

Big Anthony sings the magic song, and the pasta pot cooks pasta.

Big Anthony invites the townspeople, they all eat their fill, and Big Anthony is a hero.

Episode 4

After everyone is served, Big Anthony sings the magic song but fails to blow the three kisses.

A sister from the convent points out to Big Anthony that the pasta pot is still cooking.

Big Anthony tries repeatedly to stop the pot, to no avail.

Episode 5

Pasta fills the house and comes out the doors and windows. The sea of pasta begins to move toward the town.

The mayor says they must build a barricade.

The people build the barricade, but the pasta overruns it and continues toward the town.

Episode 6

Strega Nona returns, realizes what has happened, sings the song, blows the three kisses, and the pasta pot stops boiling.

Episode 7

The townspeople turn on Big Anthony.

Strega Nona says the punishment must fit the crime, so she makes Big Anthony eat the pasta to pay for his crime.

APPENDIX B: CATEGORIES FOR TEACHER STORYBOOK READING STYLE ANALYTIC SYSTEM

Focus

Story Features

Setting (SET): A topic unit is categorized as focusing on setting if it seeks or conveys information about the context in which a story or story episode occurs.

Initiating event (IET): A topic unit is categorized as focusing on an initiating event if it relates to a portion of the story that is concerned with the incident or circumstance that triggers a character's (or characters') resolve to attain a goal.

Internal response (INR): A topic unit is categorized as focusing on internal response if it relates to a portion of the story that is concerned with a character's (or characters') feelings about the incident or circumstance that invokes his or her resolve to attain a goal.

Attempt (ATT): A topic unit is categorized as focusing on attempt if it relates to a portion of the story that is concerned with a character's or group of characters' efforts in reaching a particular goal.

Consequence (CSQ): A topic unit is categorized as focusing on consequence if it relates to a portion of the story that is concerned with the results of a character's (or characters') efforts to reach a goal.

Reaction (RXN): A topic unit is categorized as focusing on reaction if it relates to a portion of the story that is concerned with a character's (or characters') response to the results that are obtained from efforts to reach a goal.

Character (CHA): A topic unit is said to focus on character if its primary concern is with an actor or actors in the story. A story character may be a person, an animal, or any personified entity.

Story map (SM): A topic unit is categorized as focusing on story map if it seeks or conveys a prediction about the story that is global in nature and not constrained by previously presented textual information.

Epilogue (EPI): A topic unit is categorized as focusing on epilogue if it relates to the concluding section of the book that rounds out the story (in the case of this study, on the final section of *Harry and the Terrible Whatzit,* the only story in the corpus that had an epilogue).

Story-Related Features

Genre (GEN): The focus of a topic unit is designated as genre if that utterance is concerned with or touches on the literary class of a story or stories.

Style (STY): A topic unit is categorized as focusing on style if it deals with the author's literary technique.

Theme (THE): A topic unit that relates to the central idea of a story or to its overriding premise is categorized as focusing on theme.

Story (STO): A topic unit whose central idea is concerned with the story in its entirety is categorized as focusing on story.

Title (TIT): A topic unit that is concerned with the name of the story is categorized as focusing on title.

Author (AUT): A topic unit that refers to the person or persons who wrote the story is categorized as focusing on the author.

Illustrator (ILL): The focus of a topic unit is denoted as illustrator if it refers to the creator of the book's pictorial content.

Word (WOR): A topic unit that focuses on the meaning or definition of a particular word or phrase or on the reading aloud of a particular word or phrase is categorized as focusing on word.

Text Extension (TXT): The focus of a topic unit is categorized as text extension if it seeks to obtain or convey information that can be extrapolated from or projected beyond the story.

Text-to-text (TTT): A topic unit that links or relates information from one written source to another written source is categorized as having a text-to-text focus.

Book (BOK): A topic unit is said to focus on book if it seeks or conveys information about a book part (e.g., cover, title page).

Type of Information

Textually explicit (TXP): This category refers to information made explicit in the words of the text and does not attempt to generalize about that information.

Pictorially explicit (PXP): This category refers to explicit information contained in the illustrations of the book.

Background (BKG): This category refers to information that fills in knowledge gaps related to elements (e.g., vocabulary) in stories.

Inferential: Five types of inferential information have been identified.

Text-based inference (I-TB): A request or attempt to link pieces of textual information that are not explicitly linked by the author or illustrator.

Reader-based inference (I-RB): A request or attempt to fill in information from the reader's (or listener's) scriptal (schema) information so that an inference related to the text can be made.

Summary inference (I-SU): A request or attempt to synthesize textual information and arrive at a generalization.

Value judgment (I-VJ): A request or attempt to share an affective reaction to information in text or illustration.

Predictive inference (I-PR): A request or attempt to infer upcoming information in text or illustration.

Personal association (PAS): This category refers to a request or attempt to relate prior personal experiences to textual information.

Identification (IDN): This category refers to requests or attempts to place oneself into a situation described in the story [either in text or extract to real world; e.g., "If you came to school one day and (did X) (as was done in story), what would I do?"].

Meta (MTA): This category refers to information about the activity of story-book reading itself or the concept of story.

Instructional Strategy

Eliciting (ELI): Seeking to obtain known information from the students.

Inviting (INV): Extending an open-ended invitation to share ideas.

Informing (INF): Telling students information.

Reviewing (REV): Re-examining the story in its entirety or from its beginning up to the point at which reading was stopped.

Recapitulating (RCP): Restating textual information that was read in the segment of the text immediately prior to the point at which the teacher stopped reading.

Eliciting reading (ELR): Attempting to induce the students to read part of the text.

Reacting to text (RTT): Sharing an affective response to the story with the students.

REFERENCES

Burroughs, M. (1972). *The stimulation of verbal behavior in culturally disadvantaged three-year-olds.* Unpublished doctoral dissertation, Michigan State University, East Lansing.

Chomsky, C. (1972). Stages in language development and reading exposure. *Harvard Educational Review, 52*, 1–33.

Clark, M. M. (1976). *Young fluent readers.* London: Heinemann.

Cochran-Smith, M. (1984). *The making of a reader.* Norwood, NJ: Ablex.

de Paola, T. (1975). *Strega Nona.* Englewood Cliffs, NJ: Prentice-Hall.

Dickinson, D. K., De Temple, J. M., Hirschler, J., & Smith, M. W. (1992). Book reading with preschoolers: Co-construction of text at home and at school. *Early Childhood Research Quarterly, 7*, 323–346.

Dickinson, D. K., & Keebler, R. (1989). Variations in preschool teachers' storybook reading styles. *Discourse Processes, 12*, 353–376.

Dickinson, D. K., & Smith, M. W. (1994). Long-term effects of preschool teachers' book readings on low-income children's vocabulary, story comprehension, and print skills. *Reading Research Quarterly, 29*, 104–122.

Dunn, L. M., & Dunn, L. M. (1981). *Peabody picture vocabulary test—Revised.* Circle Pines, MN: American Guidance Service.

Feitelson, D., Goldstein, Z., Iraqi, J., & Share, D. L. (1993). Effects of listening to story reading on aspects of literacy acquisition in a diglossic situation. *Reading Research Quarterly, 28*, 70–79.

Feitelson, D., Kita, B., & Goldstein, Z. (1986). Effects of listening to series stories on first graders' comprehension and use of language. *Research in the Teaching of English, 20*, 339–356.

Gackenbach, D. (1977). *Harry and the terrible whatzit.* New York: Clarion.

Greaney, V. (1986). Parental influences on reading. *The Reading Teacher, 39*, 813–818.

Green, J., & Harker, J. O. (1982). Reading to children: A communicative process. In J. A. Langer & M. T. Smith-Burke (Eds.), *Reader meets author/Bridging the gap: A psycholinguistic and sociolinguistic perspective* (pp. 196–221). Newark, DE: International Reading Association.

Green, J., Harker, J., & Golden, J. (1986). Lesson construction: Differing views. In G. W. Noblit & W. T. Pink (Eds.), *Schooling in social context: Qualitative studies* (pp. 46–77). Norwood, NJ: Ablex.

Heath, S. B. (1982). What no bedtime story means: Narrative skills at home and school. *Language in Society, 11*, 49–76.

Heath, S. B. (1983). *Ways with words: Language, life and work in communities and classrooms.* Cambridge, England: Cambridge University Press.

Kimmell, M. M., & Segel, E. (1991). *For reading out loud! A guide to sharing books with children* (Rev. and expanded ed.). New York: Delacorte.

Lionni, L. (1969). *Alexander and the wind-up mouse.* New York: Pantheon.

Martinez, M. G., & Teale, W. H. (1993). Teacher storybook reading style: A comparison of six teachers. *Research in the Teaching of English, 27*, 175–199.

Ninio, A. (1980). Picture book-reading in mother–infant dyads belonging to two subgroups in Israel. *Child Development, 51*, 587–590.

Snow, C. E., & Tabors, P. O. (1993). Language skills that relate to literacy development. In B. Spodek & O. Saracho (Eds.), *Yearbook in early childhood education* (Vol. 4, pp. 1–20). New York: Teachers College Press.

Stein, N. L., & Glenn, C. G. (1979). An analysis of story comprehension in elementary school children. In R. O. Freedle (Ed.), *Advances in discourse processes, Vol. 2: New directions in discourse processing* (pp. 53–120). Norwood, NJ: Ablex.

Sulzby, E., & Teale, W. H. (1987). *Young children's storybook reading: Longitudinal study of parent–child interaction and children's independent functioning* (Final Report to The Spencer Foundation). Ann Arbor: The University of Michigan.

Taylor, D. (1986). Creating a family story: "Matthew! We're going to have a ride!" In W. H. Teale & E. Sulzby (Eds.), *Emergent literacy: Writing and reading* (pp. 139–155). Norwood, NJ: Ablex.

Teale, W. H. (1984). Reading to young children: Its significance for literacy development. In H. Goelman, A. Oberg, & F. Smith (Eds.), *Awakening to literacy* (pp. 110–121). Exeter, NH: Heinemann.

Teale, W. H., & Martinez, M. G. (1987). *A survey of kindergarten teachers' story-reading practices* [Unpublished raw data].

Teale, W. H., Martinez, M. G., & Glass, W. L. (1989). Describing classroom storybook reading. In D. Bloome (Ed.), *Classrooms and literacy* (pp. 158–188). Norwood, NJ: Ablex.

Teale, W. H., & Sulzby, E. (1987). Literacy acquisition in early childhood: The roles of access and mediation in storybook reading. In D. A. Wagner (Ed.), *The future of literacy in a changing world* (pp. 111–130). New York: Pergamon.

Tobin, A. W. (1981). *A multiple discriminant cross-validation of the factors associated with the development of precocious reading achievement.* Unpublished doctoral dissertation, University of Delaware, Newark.

Trelease, J. (1989). *The new read-aloud handbook.* New York: Penguin.

Vygotsky, L. S. (1978). *Mind in society.* Cambridge, MA: Harvard University Press.

Waber, B. (1972). *Ira sleeps over.* Boston: Houghton Mifflin.

Wells, G. (1985). Preschool literacy-related activities and success in school. In D. R. Olson, N. Torrance, & A. Hildyard (Eds.), *Literacy, language, and learning: The nature and consequences of reading and writing* (pp. 229–255). Cambridge, England: Cambridge University Press.

Wood, D., Bruner, J. S., & Ross, G. (1976). The role of tutoring in problem solving. *Journal of Child Psychology and Psychiatry, 17,* 89–100.

18

READERS' AND WRITERS' TALK ABOUT LANGUAGE

Yetta M. Goodman
University of Arizona

This chapter focuses on a single thesis: Children use language to talk about language when they have purposeful opportunities to do so. I explore this phenomenon through narratives and examples of children's literacy events to show that:

1. Children talk about language differently, depending on the context in which the talk about language takes place.
2. What children say about language reveals their knowledge about language, their views and attitudes toward language, and their ability to learn language.
3. What children know and say about language, which is constructed as they participate as members of a literate society, reflects both personal and cultural responses to being literate.

Researchers and teachers who work with children are well aware that children talk naturally about what they are doing, and this includes talking about the language itself when language events are significant to their activities. Yet, some researchers believe that the ability to talk explicitly about language occurs only in children from middle-class environments. In addition, some researchers recommend teaching low achievers (usually based on test score data) to be explicit about language because of their conclusions that students who perform better academically seem to talk about language in more sophisticated ways than students who are less able academically.

The current term for this ability to talk about language is *metalinguistic knowledge* or *awareness*. The literature, however, reveals a wide range of conflicting definitions for this term (Yaden & Templeton, 1986). When discussing children's metalinguistic awareness or knowledge, researchers rarely have made clear whether they are referring to intuitive or conscious processes. Some researchers have decided whether children are metalinguistically aware based on carefully controlled testing or research settings in which only explicit, single correct answers are acceptable. Others have called self-corrections a form of metalinguistic awareness, even though this activity is often intuitive. Much of the discussion concerning children's metalinguistic awareness has not taken into consideration the social context in which the phenomenon is being studied.

Halliday (1982) argued that children develop understandings about language within meaningful social contexts. He maintained that, as children use language, they are involved simultaneously in three kinds of language learning: They learn language itself, they learn about language, and they learn through language. According to Halliday, all three happen at the same time and are dependent on the social context:

> A child is not an isolated individual and learning language is not a process of acquiring some commodity that is already there. Learning language is a process of construction. . . . Mental construction is not and cannot be an individual process. A child has to construct language, but he or she does not do it alone—rather in interaction with others; and the others are not simply providing a model—they are also actively engaged in the construction process. (p. 14)

In *Classroom Discourse*, Cazden (1988) explored the significance of the social nature of the classroom:

> Context is the situation as the speaker finds it, antecedent to the moment of speaking; and it is the rules for speaking in that context to which the speaker's utterance must be appropriate. . . . But speakers not only conform to rules and fit their speech appropriately to the preexisting context; they also actively speak so as to change context and create new ones "redefining this situation itself in the process of performing it." . . . Contexts are nested, from the most immediate to the act of speaking to the more distant: classroom, school, school system, community and so on; and the classroom context is never wholly of the participants' making. . . . But those who help to shape the contexts that surround the classroom have to realize their responsibility as well. (p. 198)

In attempting to understand children's talk about language, it is, therefore, necessary to make explicit the social setting in which the research takes place and the kinds of activities used to interpret the information gathered from the children's talk.

After careful consideration, I have concluded that the term *metalinguistic awareness* or *knowledge* is not helpful to understanding language use in context. Talk about language serves a major language function whenever it is used to focus on the language events taking place. This language function allows the speaker and listener to talk about language: to reflect on it, to describe it, and to show that they understand it. Commenting on the numbers and numerals in the world is not referred to as *meta-arithmetic*; commenting on the moon or stars is not labeled *meta-astronomy*. Uses of language to talk about objects of the world in specific social contexts provide humans with the opportunity to comment on and share information with others. I have, therefore, concluded that talk used by humans to comment on or discuss language phenomena should simply be addressed as such to make it clear what aspects of language use are being considered. Talk about language reflects the ability to analyze language as the language user defines, explains, compares, contrasts, and categorizes the form and/or the function of the language.

Linguists engage in this kind of language use as a major focus of their scholarship, but all humans have many reasons to talk about language. Even very young children talk about language when the social context calls for such discussion.

CHILDREN'S TALK ABOUT LANGUAGE AS AN OBJECT OF STUDY

The examples of children's talk about language are from my studies of children's developing print awareness (Goodman, Altwerger, & Marek, 1989) and the work of others. Harste, Woodward, and Burke (1984), a team of literacy development researchers, entitled their work *Language Stories and Literacy Lessons*. This title emphasizes that teachers' and researchers' stories or narratives about children's use of written language provide literacy lessons revealing how children use talk about language. Just as narratives from various societies often teach members of those societies important moral, pragmatic, and philosophical lessons, the narratives of researchers and teachers in their encounters with students involved in literacy events also teach the teaching and research communities lessons about children's literacy knowledge. I use the concept of language stories to reveal the literacy lessons that inform the conclusions I discuss.

One language story is from a classroom with a whole-language teacher. The role of a whole-language teacher is to encourage children to engage in a good deal of functionally meaningful reading and writing in the process of answering their own questions and solving significant problems, to provide a range of opportunities for talk among the students and between the teacher and the children, and to understand that children are actively involved in their own learning.

The teacher, Carol Avery, wrote the following vignette, which she shared with me (Goodman, 1991):

During a writing workshop the first week of school (Grade 1), Marlene (age 6) drew this rainbow with a person standing under it [Fig. 18.1]. Above it she wrote [what you see in her captioned illustration]. When I first looked at Marlene's writing, I saw little indication of a correlation between sounds and letters. I asked Marlene to read her writing to me.

"I am outside, under a rainbow and beside a tree," she read as she moved her finger under the letters in a very precise, deliberate fashion.

"Tell me about those Os," I responded.

Marlene looked at me and giggled that I didn't see what was so obvious. "Those aren't Os. They're circles."

"Circles?" Now I was really puzzled. "Well, why did you decide to put circles in the middle of your writing?"

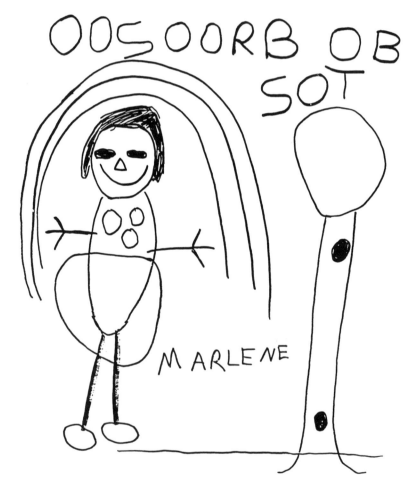

FIG. 18.1. Marlene's drawing and writing.

"Because. See, I couldn't tell what letters make those sounds so I just put circles for what goes there because something goes there only I don't know what. I can't tell what letter makes that sound, so I just put circles."

Marlene read and pointed her way through the line again. "I am—oops, I forgot to write *I.*" Her finger lands under the first circle as she says "am." She continues and I can see that Marlene has correctly written *S* for *side*, *RB* for *rainbow*, *BS* for *beside*, and *T* for *tree*. The sounds she was unable to identify are vowel sounds but Marlene was able to develop a strategy to deal with this.

When I looked again at Marlene's writing and listened to her explanation I understood that she could distinguish vowel sounds in words but could not identify them with a corresponding letter. By listening to Marlene, by allowing her to teach me what she knew, I was better prepared to provide information and direction to her. Not only am I better prepared to teach Marlene what she is ready to learn, but I can encourage her growth by celebrating her successful thinking with her. The result is an empowerment that further enhances her risk taking.

Marlene is considered to be a bright child in a middle-class community. Yet, even in such a setting, some teachers reject such thinking and explorations of language by children. Avery, on the other hand, understands enough about language, teaching, and learning to recognize her role to organize an environment in which a child is not only willing to share her developing thinking processes with her teacher but is also willing to risk questioning her teacher's conclusions (e.g., Marlene giggled as she said to her teacher, "Those aren't Os; they're circles").

Marlene is inventing a placeholder strategy by using an invented symbol to represent certain vowel sounds. Some alphabetic systems have placeholders, such as the range of vowel letters in English that represent vowel sounds in unaccented syllables. Placeholder strategies are used in other language environments as well. In English, for example, *thing* or *whatchamacallit* is used as a placeholder to represent what we have forgotten or cannot name. Miscue analysis research shows that readers often produce nonwords: word equivalents that do not exist in the language being read but often retain the phonological, graphophonic, and syntactic features of the language (Goodman, Watson, & Burke, 1987). There is an example of this in a story about a baby who was not considered to be typical. Many of the readers read the word *type-i-cal* as a nonword equivalent or placeholder for *typical*.

Placeholder strategies are important in all language processes. In a writing research study that colleagues and I conducted on the Tohono O'odham Indian Reservation, we found some children who were aware that they "wrote anything because I didn't know how to spell the word." However, such placeholder spellings often have beginning and ending consonants in common with the conventional spelling of the target word (Goodman & Wilde, 1992).

When children have the opportunity to talk about language, as Marlene did in Avery's classroom, teachers and researchers gain insights into how children construct knowledge about language as they read and write for real and functional purposes. Children's talk about language reveals their inventions or personal conceptualizations about how language works in the social contexts of the literacy events in which they are engaged. As they interact with peers and teachers, however, children eventually incorporate into their response the conventional language and views of the adult society. There is a constant tension between personal invention and social convention as children explore their "having of wonderful ideas" about how language works (Duckworth, 1987).

Young children's original responses to literacy events are personal. As reported by Ferreiro and Teberosky (1982), young children often write their names by using the number of characters representing their age or their apartment building floor. My research with preschool children, as represented in the following examples (Goodman, Altwerger, & Marek, 1989), also revealed this personal response in children's talk about language:

> Anders, age 3½, was helping his mother put away the groceries when he reacted to the supermarket bag with the word *SAFEWAY* on it, saying, as he pointed to the first A, "That's mine." He had focused on the name of the store, saw a letter from his own name, and related it to himself.

> Roberta, a 4-year-old, had a similar personal response to environmental print. In going past a pharmacy named REVCO, she said to her mother: "Look, Revco has the same face as my name."

The preschool children whom I studied used their language to talk about their literacy events, although not always in a conventional way. In English, children may say *number* when referring to letters of the alphabet, but both are within the same semantic field. In addition, all the children I have studied, who came from a range of social classes including socioeconomically poor communities, responded conventionally to various questions regarding reading and writing experiences. They responded appropriately with words such as *read*, *write*, *book*, and *letter*. For example, when I read to the children and, at the end of a page, asked what to do next, they invariably said "Turn the page."

By the age of 3, children often ask "What does this mean?" indicating an awareness that the same word can mean different things and that they are not aware of the meaning being used at that particular time. These same children point to print and ask "What does that say?" or can respond conventionally when a teacher or researcher asks them "What does that say?" Young children show their awareness of the metaphoric use of *say* during such literacy events in English, meaning "How do you read that?"

Children in third and fourth grade have accommodated to many more social conventions of literacy than preschoolers have, especially in their talk about language. Colleagues and I documented this in the research study mentioned earlier when we spent 2 years collecting writing samples from 8- to 10-year-old Tohono O'odham students (Goodman & Wilde, 1992). Seated next to selected children as they wrote in the classroom, we wrote everything they wrote and documented every behavior that accompanied the young writers' compositions. We also interviewed the children individually outside the classroom about writing, their views of themselves as writers, and what they believed made for good writing. We gathered a great deal of talk about writing and discovered that children used different kinds of talk about language in different settings.

In one classroom, for example, children sat at tables facing each other and were permitted to talk to each other and walk around the room to use resources or interact with the teacher or other peers. In another classroom, the children sat facing the front, toward the teacher, and talk among the children and movement in the classroom were discouraged. There was little talk about language among the children in the facing-front setting. Most talk about language had to do with answering the teacher's questions, which usually required a single correct answer.

In the setting where the children sat facing each other as they wrote, there was always a good deal of talk about the children's compositions. We became aware of the influences of the classroom community, including the researchers, on students' writing and on their talk about writing as well.

The following excerpt from our research notes documents a classroom situation in which five boys, seated around a table with two of the researchers, were writing in response to the teacher's request to write about anything they wanted to write:

Dana has been writing for about 5 minutes. He stops writing to inform the researcher that he has not really erased anything, although he has used his eraser. This unsolicited information lets the researcher know that Dana was conscious of what the researcher was writing and he wanted to be sure that the notes she was taking were accurate. Dana stops a number of times to observe the researchers writing quickly, trying to keep up with him. [The children we observed often observed us in turn, even to the point of correcting our notes as Dana was doing.] Dana watches two classmates at the table as they are writing. Vincent then asks Dana if he could see his writing, but Dana is so involved that he does not reply. Vincent and one of the researchers are having a discussion about how to break up a word at the end of the line by using hyphens. Dana is listening intently to this discussion. Dana looks back at his own paper and adds a hyphen to a football score (21–7) but changes his mind and erases. Dana's story up to this point is written totally in capital letters. Dana's researcher asks him why he's writing this way. He replies "I just like to write like that, it's neater." Walter then asks Dana for the spelling of a word, and Dana provides a conventional spelling. Dana rewrites his last sentence and declares "I'm finished."

From 2 years of observations, we concluded that when children were in settings in which they could talk about their writing, they did so. In our study, 80% of all talk the children participated in, when encouraged and permitted to do so, related directly to their writing (Goodman & Wilde, 1992). Their talk revealed their inventions about language when they were working out new uses of language in their compositions but most often reflected conventional knowledge about writing in school. Their talk often related to correct spellings and to neat and long papers to meet what they considered to be teacher expectations.

We documented talk about complex punctuation issues and other linguistic features. During the second year of the study, Gordon began to use hyphens at the end of a line when he ran out of space. He called this to the researcher's attention one day and said that his sister had taught him how to do it. Examining Gordon's writing, the researcher noticed that he had hyphenated one-syllable words when he ran out of room but hyphenated the two-syllable words at the appropriate syllable boundaries even when he had enough room for more letters. When asked why he hyphenated the different kinds of words differently, Gordon was unable to articulate his reasoning. A few weeks later, he was working on a sports story and asked the researcher if the word *football* goes together. The researcher asked what he thought, and he replied that it did and that he would use a small space to show that *foot* and *ball* were related. The next week, in a story he wrote the word *cup-cake* with a hyphen. When asked why he did so, he replied "Because they go together." Reminding him about the football incident in the previous week's story, the researcher asked him whether the small space option or the hyphen was most appropriate. He concluded that either option was acceptable. Gordon and his researcher were involved in sophisticated talk about language. Gordon's need to invent a form to accomplish his needs as he wrote and his opportunity to talk about it with someone else provided opportunities for him to explore the conventions of language. Careful documentation of talk about language during composing permitted us to discover many ways that children talk about language when they are in environments that permit them to do so.

ATTITUDES ABOUT LANGUAGE
IN TALK ABOUT LANGUAGE

Children's talk about language reveals not only their developing conceptual knowledge about language, but also their developing attitudes about themselves as language users and language learners. As early as 3 and 4 years of age, children reveal their attitudes in talk about language. Especially in conversation with researchers, teachers, and clinicians, children use language that reflects and is influenced by what they think adults expect to hear. This pragmatic ability provides insight into children's sensitivity to rules about language use within specific social contexts. It suggests that, although young readers and writers construct knowledge about reading and writing, they may believe at the same time that they do not have the capability to do so. If knowledgeable adults are unaware that what children say about language varies in different contexts and that what they explicitly say does not always match what they intuitively know, then children may be labeled for not knowing aspects of language that they know very well in different contexts and settings.

Some additional language stories explicate my concern about children's attitudes concerning language. The first comes from my print awareness research with children 3 to 5 years of age (Goodman, Altwerger, & Marek, 1989). Responses obtained from children in a preschool serving mostly lower socioeconomic families differed from the children's responses in middle-class communities. Although the children from both communities were equally capable of reading the common signs in their environment (e.g., stop signs; names of major supermarkets, clothing stores, and fast-food restaurants; and major brand names of toothpaste and soap products), their responses to the question of whether they could read differed considerably. The economically poorer children said that they could not read, that learning to read would be difficult, and that they would not learn to read until they entered elementary school. Children from middle-class communities were more likely to say that they were already reading or would be reading before they started elementary school. Many more children in this latter group picked up a book and read it aloud, often in response to illustrations and some aspects of the print.

On the other hand, all the children were willing to write. No children said they could not write, and all of them could talk about the functions of writing, whereas some children were less able to state functions for reading. Apparently, the poorer children had already adopted society's attitude that they are not good candidates for learning to read, whereas the more affluent children had acquired the notion that learning to read simply happens as part of their participation in a literate society.

Another story of children's attitudes toward language is from the writing study of the third- and fourth-grade Tohono O'odham students (Goodman & Wilde, 1992). When the children were writing, there was often serious talk about the meanings of what they were writing as well as about such matters as syntax, semantics, and graphics. During our interviews with the students, however, their responses reflected conventional views about language, as shown in the following dialogue:

Researcher:	Who is a good writer that you know?
Vincent:	Um . . . Frances.
Researcher:	What makes Frances a good writer?
Vincent:	'Cause she knows how to spell some words . . . that I don't know.
Researcher:	Are there other things that make her a good writer?
Vincent:	Sometimes she don't have to . . . look at things . . . and see how they're spelled. . . . She just spells them out. . . . And sometimes she gets them all right.

Researcher:	What does a good writer need to know or do in order to write well?
Vincent:	Have to ... you have to write good handwriting.
Researcher:	How can you tell when somebody's not a good writer?
Vincent:	When they write sloppy and when they misspell all their words.

During our research, we had many conversations with Vincent about the importance of writing being interesting to readers. He enjoyed writing about the events in his life that he was interested in, such as medicine men and the rodeo, and he wrote well about them. When he talked to peers or the researchers as he was writing, he enjoyed exploring the plot of his stories, the meanings of words, and the syntactic features with which he was experimenting. In formal interview settings, however, he responded with answers related to what he perceived to be conventional school wisdom. Although he wrote well and his stories were rich with language and knowledge, he never viewed himself as a proficient writer.

We need to be aware that students' responses often reflect attitudes about language that are related to the context of schooling and the values in society, without revealing the concepts, knowledge, and abilities they have developed. If students are more influenced by societal attitudes about language use, this may interfere with their ability to use language in innovative and inventive ways.

TALK ABOUT LANGUAGE AND THE CONTEXT OF SCHOOLING

Children talk about language in social situations in which there is need to talk about language, and it is important to do so. When four children sit together writing at a table, they continually interact about their compositions and discuss them using language appropriately. When young children are asked to explain their own writing and reading in situations in which their answers will be accepted as serious responses, they again reflect, as Marlene did, sophisticated knowledge about their language inventions and the language conventions of society.

In testing or clinical research settings, however, children's talk about language changes. These isolated settings often represent unfamiliar, hostile social contexts to many children, especially those from lower socioeconomic backgrounds. The researchers' or testers' verbal and nonverbal language is crucial to the kinds of responses that children give. Social contexts influence the kinds of things that children say about language. That is how language works. It is not that children do not know how to talk about language, but rather that children reflect others' views and attitudes about language and that unexamined expectations often make certain groups of children appear incapable of talking about language.

The implication of this research for teaching, then, is that we should not teach children explicit, abstract metalinguistic knowledge in settings apart from daily language use. Rather, teachers must discover what children do know about language, help the children to discover what they know, and build positive attitudes and confidence about language use.

Children who are not confident about what they know about language and can do with it are often easily convinced by teachers that they are not capable language learners. Board (1983) studied such children and identified them as *instruction dependent personalities*.

The relationship between teachers and pupils is very influential on the ways in which children use talk in the classroom. Teachers who have not thought through the power of their influence are setting students up for possible failure in the school setting. Even potentially outstanding students can opt for mediocrity or conformity in response to the ways in which the classroom is organized to support children's language learning.

The following language story, a personal communication excerpt from a journal written by a professional reading teacher who was studying her stepson's literacy development, describes how different teaching roles can impact on students' views about themselves as readers and writers:

My stepson had a great interest to read, along with a vast knowledge about print books, writing, etc. . . . He was placed in a program after kindergarten that used a phonics and rigidly leveled reading program. Well, there he stagnated! His father and I watched as his interest in learning to read for himself dwindled to zero. When encouraged to try, he declined. We continued to read regularly with him, but he was very reluctant and insecure about reading himself. He still wanted us to read all the time! His interest in invented spelling, which he had been comfortable with since he was 4 years old, also got lost during this time.

From the middle of his first grade through to second grade, his father and I finally managed to move him to D. H.'s classroom (a whole-language teacher with an exciting and inviting classroom). D. H. mentioned that Sandy was not reading independently and he was being disruptive during silent reading time. That's when I decided to let my stepson know I could maybe help if he wanted me to. He said he did. As we sat down to read, I found Sandy spending 45 to 60 seconds trying to sound out unknown words or words he believed were unknown. His reading was labored, and he sounded as if he were in pain. I noticed that, when he was in this "sounding mode," he no longer even recognized words that I knew he knew.

I said, "Sandy, just quit that! Don't try to sound them out!"

He replied, "That's the only way to read."

I said, "It's too hard that way!" I encouraged him to use the other things he knew—the pictures, the other words, what he knew about the story.

"Really?" he seemed to be asking as he looked at me with astonishment. This discussion seemed to be his breakthrough to reading. Now he is reading up a storm. I've begun to notice a difference in his listening to stories, too. His eyes are now on the words, soaking up everything!!

Teachers must understand that how they organize for instruction and their oral and verbal interactions give students all kinds of messages that significantly affect their attitudes about their abilities to become literate members of society. To inquire into and understand the talk children use in classrooms, teachers need to believe in their own professional senses and to retain an active involvement in their own professional development.

Researchers must also become more knowledgeable about the ways in which even the youngest children are sensitive to differences in social contexts, so that the examples of talk collected for analysis do reflect children's language abilities. Within classroom settings, everyone interested in children's talk and language development (e.g., teachers, researchers, teacher/researchers, teacher educators) can organize the curriculum and research designs to discover much more about the following:

1. How informal verbal and nonverbal cues affect talk and literacy learning.
2. How teachers' responses to children's language production affect talk and literacy learning.
3. How students develop their own personal constructions about language within different classroom settings.
4. How to organize a classroom environment to maintain constant talk about language.
5. What the nature of the talk children use in different classroom settings is.
6. What the talk reveals about the conceptualizations the children are developing about language.

In most societies with institutionalized educational systems, schooling has been rigid, traditional, and imposed from the outside, and has ignored the knowledge of both teachers and students. Few adults concerned with educational research and practice have experienced a life history of supportive education. Whether our professional focus is on teaching or research, we must learn to take into account what children know about language and to respect their developing knowledge and views about language. Then, we must rethink our stereotypic views of schooling. We must involve ourselves in unlearning and rejecting our dispedagogic experiences. In this way, perhaps we can participate—with children—in making the greatest use of children's talk about language in order to support the human potential for language learning.

REFERENCES

Board, P. (1983). Toward a theory of instructional influence (Doctoral dissertation, University of Toronto, 1982). *Dissertation Abstracts International, 44,* 717A.
Cazden, C. (1988). *Classroom discourse.* Portsmouth, NH: Heinemann.

Duckworth, E. (1987). *The having of wonderful ideas.* New York: Teachers College Press.

Ferreiro, E., & Teberosky, A. (1982). *Literacy before schooling.* Portsmouth, NH: Heinemann.

Goodman, Y. (1991). Informal methods of evaluation. In J. Flood, J. Lapp, & J. Squires (Eds.), *Handbook of research on teaching the English language arts* (pp. 502–509). New York: Macmillan.

Goodman, Y., Altwerger, B., & Marek, A. (1989). *A study of literacy in preschool children* (Paper No. 4). Tucson: Program in Language and Literacy, College of Education, University of Arizona.

Goodman, Y., Watson, D., & Burke, C. (1987). *The reading miscue inventory: Alternative procedures.* Katonah, NY: Richard C. Owen.

Goodman, Y., & Wilde, S. (1992). *Literacy events in a community of young writers.* New York: Teachers College Press.

Halliday, M. A. K. (1982). Three aspects of children's language development: Learning language, learning through language, learning about language. In Y. Goodman, M. Haussler, & D. Strickland (Eds.), *Oral and written language development research: Impact on the schools* (pp. 12–38). Urbana, IL: National Council Teachers of English.

Harste, J., Woodward, V., & Burke, C. (1984). *Language stories and literacy lessons.* Portsmouth, NH: Heinemann.

Yaden, D., Jr., & Templeton, S. (1986). *Metalinguistic awareness and beginning literacy.* Portsmouth, NH: Heinemann.

Author Index

Subject Index